SPLIT SCREEN KOREA

SPLIT SCREEN KOREA

Shin Sang-ok and Postwar Cinema

STEVEN CHUNG

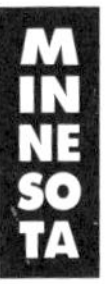

University of Minnesota Press

Minneapolis

London

The University of Minnesota Press gratefully acknowledges financial assistance provided for the publication of this book from Princeton University's University Committee on Research in the Humanities and Social Sciences.

A different version of chapter 2 was published as "Regimes within Regimes: Film and Fashion Cultures in the Korean 1950s," in *The Korean Popular Culture Reader,* ed. Young-min Choe and Kyung Hyun Kim (Durham, N.C.: Duke University Press, 2013). Different versions of chapter 4, which appeared in Korean, were published as "Melodrama, Style, and the Scene of Development: Shin Sang-ok's Rice and Evergreen" ("Mellodŭrama, sŭtail, kŭrigo kaebaljuŭi ŭi changmyŏn: Sin Sang-ok ŭi Ssal kwa Sangnoksu"), in *Korean Cinema and Democracy (Yŏnghwa wa minjujuŭi),* ed. The Korean Media Research Group (Seoul: Sonin Press, 2011), 265–303, and as "Mass Melodrama and the Spectacle of Development: Shin Sang-ok's 1960s 'Enlightenment Films' ("Taejung mellodŭrama wa kaebaljuŭi ŭi sŭpekt'akŭl: Sin Sang-ok ŭi 1960 nyŏndae kyemong yŏnghwa"), *Memory and Vision (Kiŏk kwa chŏnmang),* no. 25 (Winter 2011): 217–50. A different version of chapter 5 appeared as "Split Screen: Sin Sang-ok in North Korea," in *North Korea: Toward a Better Understanding,* ed. Sonia Ryang (Lanham, Md.: Lexington Books, 2009), 85–108.

Published by the University of Minnesota Press
111 Third Avenue South, Suite 290
Minneapolis, MN 55401-2520
http://www.upress.umn.edu

Library of Congress Cataloging-in-Publication Data

Chung, Steven.
    Split screen Korea : Shin Sang-ok and postwar cinema / Steven Chung.
    Includes bibliographical references, filmography, and index.
    ISBN 978-0-8166-9133-3 (hc : alk. paper) — ISBN 978-0-8166-9134-0 (pb : alk. paper)
    1. Sin, Sang-ok, 1926–2006—Criticism and interpretation.   2. Korea (South)—
In motion pictures.   I. Title.
    PN1998.3.S538C48 2013
    791.430233'092—dc23

                                                                            2013028408

Printed in the United States of America on acid-free paper

The University of Minnesota is an equal-opportunity educator and employer.

20   19   18   17   16   15   14   10   9   8   7   6   5   4   3   2   1

FOR MY FATHER, JU-HO CHUNG

CONTENTS

INTRODUCTION

Visible Ruptures, Invisible Borders

Focus

Amid a life saturated with the production of images and exposure within them, one photograph stands out as an exceptionally illuminating window onto Shin Sang-ok's work and its place in twentieth-century Korea (Figure 1).[1] The picture was taken in the summer of 1984 and Shin, at fifty-eight, is arguably in his prime as a maker of films. He is pictured manipulating the camera, betraying the lust for control of a director who, despite having retained the service of a small army of technicians, had always had little confidence in the skill or professionalism of his employees. His figure is highlighted in the frame, not only by the way the sun glows on his shirt and bounces off his graying hair, but because of the personal style he consciously crafts on set here, as he had since his earliest days in the film industry and as he would to his last years at work on a final epic. The half-bouffant as well as the silk scarf that is hidden here, but that he would always wear in public, bespeak the posturing of an artist and a mogul at odds not so much with the moral or political consensus of his day but with the cultural and aesthetic limitations of a society apparently not yet fully caught up with the best of the world. But it is the complex relationship between his figure and everything else in the frame that epitomizes Shin's career. He is at once aloof, isolated in the dyad between his camera and his cinematic object, but also deeply embedded in his milieu, an integral part of the mass of personnel, monitors, and spectators that gaze at the work in progress. As much as the imprint it leaves of Shin's directorial style, it is the scene that this crowd makes, arrayed against the tangle of lumber and pressed along the artificially snow-covered tracks, together with the import of their attention to the cinematic process under Shin's control, that makes this image a compelling artifact for a history of film on the Korean peninsula.

What makes it more provocative, however, is that it captures a moment on location somewhere in North Korea, six years after Shin's disappearance from the South and one year into the rebirth of Shin Films under the direct sponsorship of the Democratic People's Republic of Korea (DPRK) government. In production is an adaptation of the seminal left-wing short story "Record of an Escape," written by Ch'oe Sŏ-hae in the 1920s and largely suppressed on both poles of the postwar territorial divide for its bleak depiction of antifeudal class struggle. The filmmaking apparently occasioned what Shin describes as the highlight of his career as a producer when the DPRK authorities gave him a real train to explode for the film's climax—a story whose repeated and enthusiastic telling in interviews and publications underscores the hubris of a moviemaker long enamored of big spectacle. In an important sense, *Record* is the culmination of a cinematic project begun decades earlier in the South but impeded there by limitations of capital and shifts in social and political sensibility. The film is even now a dangerous kind of orphan, apparently banned from exhibition in the North following Shin's "escape" in 1986 and strictly controlled in the South—a planned 2002 screening of the film at the Pusan International Film Festival was halted at the last minute and a 2009 showing at Seoul's Korean Film Archive required

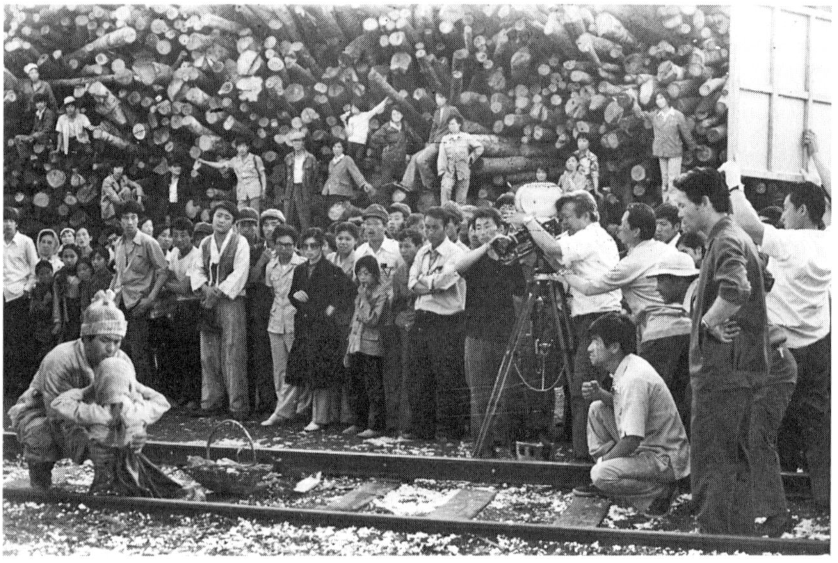

Figure 1. Shin Sang-ok on location in 1985. Photograph courtesy of Choi Eun Hee.

audiences to register their attendance with national identification numbers. But, beyond the way the photo captures a moment of remarkable geo
political fissure, which it certainly does, I am attracted more to the story it
can tell about continuity and uncanny repetition over transformations in
space and time. What the image suggests is the idea that nothing in the
purview of film—the subjects a film treats, the formal conventions used to
construct narratives, the masses captured on screens or presumed to be
watching—belongs inherently to one ideological regime or another. That is,
latent in the gap between the indeterminate time–space of the photograph
and its concrete historical referent is the insight that none of those cinematic elements are avant la lettre democratic or communist or, conversely,
purely escapist before their determinations in popular, critical, and institutional practices and discourses. The core preoccupation of this book will be
to follow the trajectories that Shin Sang-ok took, the ways in which his work
continued through ostensibly radical cultural and economic transformation. But it will also attempt to press the idea of continuity itself, interrogating its salience as a critical idea both in the study of film, a medium
synonymous with the shock of the new, and in the study of Korea, whose
very name heralds rupture and division.

But if it is by this *studium*, Roland Barthes's term for the sociocultural
significance of photographs, that I am drawn to this image, it also registers
for me a *punctum*, "that accident of which pricks me—but also bruises me,
is poignant to me."[2] Having come across this image late into my research,
I am struck by the persistent distance of the realities its strangely epic composition suggests. Shin Sang-ok is at once the central figure of postwar
Korean film, overdetermined by a palimpsest of rumor, journalistic reportage, and academic scholarship, and a subject whose identity is defined by
ideas—authorship, national cinema, Cold War ideological polarity—that
have seemingly lost their critical relevance. In attempting to suture a genealogy of Shin's filmmaking career to a picture of postwar Korean modernity,
I am confronted by the slippages, contingencies, and conflicting investments implicit in the basic act of reading images. For on the one hand lies the
basic truism that films, like any other cultural forms, are always in excess
of their medium, begging an impossible conceptual framework that could
trace their ontologies to the multivalent discourses and technologies that
condition their production and that could follow their movements through
the multiple economic and political processes that they in turn inflect. On
the other is the equally challenging fact that social and political reality is
always in excess of the means of its representation, putting to serious

question any project that would seek to leverage an analysis of film into insights about political authority or specific modalities of public discourse. In other words, so much falls outside of the frame and so much is lost within it that anything like a comprehensive history, even one confined to a single filmmaker and one, albeit divided, nation, is precluded from the outset.

But the heart of this book is precisely that divergence between what is visible and hidden, onscreen and off, which has in turn become the very engine of its critical objectives. This, of course, is for the critic the real meaning of Barthes's *punctum*, the deeply felt impact of an image that, in its blending of the strange and the familiar, elicits absorption, reflection, and theory in a way that the *studium* of an image does not. The North Korean photograph itself describes the intriguing fact of a commercial film maker's relevance in a closed socialist state, raising questions about the cultural life of a society whose very definition is hermetic concealment. Hard research unveils the perhaps surprising mechanics at play here: that Shin's work would alter the production practices of the DPRK's filmmaking industry, that his films would be sensational commercial successes in the North's city centers, that through Shin the North Korean cinema would for the first time enjoy prestige at international cultural exhibitions. But what must be inferred elsewhere are the answers to questions about how specific cultural languages can travel and translate and what cinematic performances can mean for the diverse audiences that witness them. The photograph, of course, is limited in its explicative capacity but even in its unmoving image are clues—on the faces of the onlookers, say, or the lurid pathos of the scene being captured—to how these questions can be addressed. More substantially, in this book I take up many of Shin's films, looking closely at their thematic preoccupations and formal codes in the interests of assembling a coherent cultural history of the images he produced. But just as important, I aim to theorize what is excluded from the frame, what events and discourses escape the films, what cannot be represented or can be represented only in specific ways, and what is left blank in the archives toward more expansively critical ideas about the politics of film. For if there is a good reason for taking up Shin Sang-ok and postwar Korea now, it is that the very limitations of the study of film, and in particular a subject whose time has seemingly passed, can serve as a means of exposing closures and limitations in the study of nation, culture, and politics.

Split

Shin Sang-ok was born in 1926 to a well-to-do family in the most northerly stretch of the Korean peninsula, Ch'ŏngjin city, Hamgyŏng province, an area that gave birth to a surprising number of early film practitioners such as Na Un-gyu and Yun Pong-ch'un. With the considerable resources afforded by his father, a traditional medicine practitioner, Shin attended the region's most prestigious schools, but spent much of his time and energy watching films in nearby theaters and experimenting with motion picture machinery. While the family fortunes dwindled in the later stages of Japanese colonial rule, Shin was nevertheless sent off to study in the metropole in 1944 at the Tokyo Arts University where he studied surrealist art and immersed himself in French and Japanese cinema. Shin returned home amid the chaos of the Tokyo fire bombings and, following liberation in August 1945, found work in Seoul painting propaganda posters for the newly arrived American occupation forces and for the few theaters that could restart commercial exhibition. This was his point of access to the film industry. Introduced to leading filmmaker Ch'oe In-gyu in 1946, Shin apprenticed at the elder's Koryo Films Studios (*Koryŏ Yŏnghwasa*), learning the basics of film technology and taking charge of set design for a number of productions. Shin struck out on his own in 1950, just before Ch'oe was taken north by occupying DPRK forces, and made a number of films while the civil war raged on, including the neorealist *Evil Night* (*Akya*, 1952) and the touristic *Korea* (1953), both of which starred Ch'oe Ŭn-hŭi, who would go on to be his muse and companion to the end of his life. Following the production of a number of minor literary adaptations, Shin scored big with a string of sophisticated melodramas in the late 1950s, which he then parlayed into the establishment of the sprawling, vertically integrated Shin Films in 1960. With the endorsement of the military authorities that had seized power in 1961, Shin quickly built the studio into an unrivalled entity that ground out upward of twenty-five films per year through the 1960s and employed as many as three hundred people. He also directed many of the iconic films that would become synonymous with the postwar Korean imagination, including *Romance Papa* (*Romaensŭ ppappa*, 1960), *Sŏng Ch'unhyang* (1961), *Evergreen* (*Sangnoksu*, 1961), and *The Houseguest and My Mother* (*Sarangbang sonnim kwa ŏmŏni*, 1961).

Shin's carefully managed relations with the Park Chung Hee regime could not, however, save his studios from a collision with either the erosion by the very late 1960s of the film industry as a whole or the intensified moral and political control the government would exert over all film production as it moved to advance its position in the world economy. While Shin continued to work with a wide variety of genres, which by the 1970s would include westerns, musicals, and horror films, his forte remained the treatment of popular literary material that sought, through increasingly lurid adaptation, to combat the encroachment of television on the entertainment market. The tenor of the period's films, which included the dark and idiosyncratic *Cruel Stories of Yi Dynasty Women* (*Yijo yŏin chanhoksa*, 1969) and the quasi-sexploitation picture *Female Prisoner 407* (*Yŏsu 407-ho*, 1976), would shift perceptibly to reflect impatience with social conformity and gendered violence. It was on these terms, and not explicit political dissent, that Shin came into conflict with the Park regime: in 1975, his filmmaking registration was rescinded when he screened a preview for *Wild Dog and Rose* (*Changmi wa tŭlgae*, 1975) with a kiss scene that had been censored, and his operations were closed down after nearly thirty years of consecutive production. Shin and Ch'oe Ŭn-hŭi returned to the dramatic spotlight when their disappearance was reported in Hong Kong in 1978; rumors that they had been kidnapped or had defected to North Korea were confirmed in 1984 when *The Secret Emissary* (*Toraoji anŭn milsa*) screened under their auspices at the Karlovy Vary Film Festival. The episode remains shrouded in mystery, but it is clear that Shin and Ch'oe spent eight years in the DPRK and collaborated on the production of at least twenty films, seven of which were credited to Shin's direction, before they were granted amnesty in Vienna in 1986. The couple spent the next few years giving countless interviews to American and South Korea national security agencies as well as in public, and published a handful of memoirs recounting their experiences in the North. Shin was allowed to return to filmmaking but the staid films he produced, including the disappointingly obsequious *Mayumi* (1990) and *Disappearance* (*Chŭngbal*, 1994), flopped both critically and commercially. He met with slightly better success as "Simon Sheen" and with the third incarnation of Shin Films in Hollywood (this time as "Sheen Productions") through which he would produce lightweight fare such as the *3 Ninjas* series. Planning an epic, international coproduction rendering of the Genghis Khan story, Shin passed away back in Seoul in 2006.

Following his death, a collection of Shin Sang-ok's own reflections on his tumultuous career was published under a title culled from a phrase often used to sum up his life's work, *I Was a Movie* (*Nan, yŏnghwa yŏtda*). The label, evoking the dramatic reversals and enigmatic performances of a lifetime spent making films, is characteristically overstated but nonetheless apt in its suggestion of the rich and compelling story Shin's career tells about modern Korea and the promises of filmmaking. It is, of course, that story that prompted the research for this book. Shin was active in each of the major epochs of twentieth-century Korean history, and his films palpably, if somewhat unevenly, engage the central ideological problems that conditioned everyday life over that turbulent span. The trail leading from his beginnings as a cinephile modern boy to his study at the heart of imperial power can be followed through to the worldly refinement of his early productions and into the elitist quality that was never completely shed even in his most explicitly popular films. Shin's obsessive drive to industrialize and "rationalize" the South Korean film industry, moreover, can be linked to both the vestigial forces of colonial modernity and the violently earnest developmentalist planning of the postwar authoritarian regimes. This will to modernization and national strengthening, in fact, imbues the vast range of Shin's directorial work, finding restrained expression in his portraits of sexual repression or amplified as melodramatic spectacle in his "enlightenment" films. But it is perhaps Shin's fraught relationship with political authority that is the most singular and illuminating part of his story. Standing in the 1960s and then again in the 1980s as representative filmmaker for the military dictatorships on both sides of the peninsula, Shin's work articulated the political positions that pillared domination in each half of the national division and simultaneously gave the lie to the presumed unambiguity of that ideological opposition.

Over the course of a remarkable career that spanned seven decades and yielded nearly one hundred films, Shin Sang-ok never used a split screen to divide the frame in any of his work. This fact is not surprising, given his films' basic conservatism and commitment to realism, and it is only minimally illustrative of a cinematic attitude that would not exploit a cinematic device that expands the apparatus in both conventional and avant-garde ways. Nevertheless, I invoke the split screen in the title of this book because it has, both as a metaphor and as a heuristic device, shaped the way I have thought about Shin and modern Korea. In an immediately obvious sense, the way in which the standard split screen merges two ostensibly different time-spaces into a seeming whole mirrors the manifold divisions-suspensions that imbue Shin's career: the moral, cultural, and thematic balancing of the past and present, the fraught navigation between art and entertainment, the formal and political negotiation of the national within the global, and, perhaps most notoriously, the conflicts and continuities of North–South national division. In none of these instances, however, each with their own peculiar modes of divergence, is there a resolution to some sort of sublimated unity. To build upon the split screen metaphor, the border marking temporal, aesthetic, and ideological frames never dissolves to reveal a singular artistic vision or committed political stance. In even his most blatantly propagandistic films there is always some instability in the enunciation, if not in the message itself, that resists political closure. Shin's cinema comes rather closer to embodying that split screen effect that conceals the border and stages the double presence of twins, say, or ghosts or real and imagined doppelgängers. In his films, a radically modernist vision can exist alongside banal generic convention and, in his life, the calculating impresario can also at the same time be the celebrated socialist artist. One of the most compelling dimensions of Shin Sang-ok's work, I think, is precisely this uncanny presence and how it articulates a long, schizophrenic dialogue on the contradictions of Korea and cinema in the twentieth century.

But I have invoked this minor cinematic device because it also functions as a kind of token, a reminder of the gap between the two central conceptual concerns of this book: film and nation. The heuristic implications of the split screen are themselves divided. On the one hand, in mashing together two sides of a distant phone conversation, say, or two action sequences destined for collision, the split screen embodies the voyeuristic and omniscient visuality that tends to characterize film production and spectatorship. On the other hand, its visible lines and distracting partitioning disrupt the illusion of the frame's wholeness, calling attention to the constructedness of the reality projected on screen. The great temptation in studying a subject like Shin Sang-ok, whose career was sustained over such a long period of time, is to see in it a transparent window onto the socio-political meaning and ideological depth of its formation. This illusion is ruptured in two critical ways. There are, first, serious limitations on the authority and wholeness of the archive, a condition that is true of almost any research but particularly salient in the fields of postwar history and film in Korea. The grip that grand narratives of national history—whether official or counterdiscursive—have had on the institutional and popular consciousness of modern Korea has been loosened considerably with the proliferation of minor and revisionist histories and the unleashing of long-suppressed documentation and testimony under progressive governments.[3] But the fruits of this opening beg qualification not only for their relative novelty but also because of the danger, within the reinvigorated historical materialism, of positivistically reducing the protean valences of film making to social, cultural, and political symptoms. The territory is made even more treacherous by the seemingly irrevocable gaps in the record, left both by the loss of nearly one-quarter of the films Shin directed and, paradoxically, by the substantial autobiographical materials that Shin published before his death, at least in part in the hopes of shaping his conflicted legacy.

The second rupture begins in the critical project of bringing together film and nation. At the end of his remarkably idiosyncratic study of movement and time in film, Gilles Deleuze declared in the early 1980s that "no technological determination, whether applied (psychoanalysis, linguistics) or reflexive, is sufficient to constitute the concepts of cinema itself."[4] Few who think seriously about film, of course, would now hew closely to the narrow structuralisms that throughout much of the twentieth century sought to align filmmaking forms with ideological, psychic, or gendered "determinations." Even as committed a Marxian critic as Fredric Jameson has elaborated a multivalent strategy for mapping "reification" within a process of management and incommensurate investments. But it is the force of the institution, in particular the two disciplinary formations that a study such as this one straddles, film studies and area studies, that continue to exert conceptual pressure. As Mitsuhiro Yoshimoto has shown in his studies of Japanese cinema, the discourse of cultural singularity that characterized early work on Japan and the notion of creative authorship that saturated early writings on film worked, in a mutually enforcing manner, to "establish the very questions by which Japanese cinema was constituted as an object of knowledge."[5] Clearly, the specific discourses that constitute the study of Korean cinema differ from those of Japan, but a similarly locked pattern of mutual reinforcement obtains here as well. If there has been a dominant question of the short decades of modern Korean studies, it has been about nationalism, addressing not only when it began (as "sprouts" or "resistance," etc.) and how it fueled various political and economic interests (sovereignty, "national capital," etc.) but also, more recently, how it justified state violence and repression (for "national reconstruction," "social harmony," etc.) and concealed the truth of careers built on betrayal and collusion (of "pro-Japanese" writers, "nationalist entrepreneurs," etc.).[6] Similarly, at the forefront of the study of Korean cinema, whether in the "nationalist realist" discourse that formed the foundation of film criticism in Korea, or in the idea of a regionally enthralling "Koreanness" engendered in recent speculation about the "Korean Wave," is what Rey Chow has called an "obstinate discourse of nativism" that cinches the boundaries of an already constricted research field.[7] One of the central aims of my work on Shin Sang-ok, to form a clearer picture of Korean modernity, is, ironically, badly served by this double confinement within the local and the national, for neither states nor cinemas are discrete entities but are, rather, linked in irreducibly global systems. What remains radical about film is precisely this globality, its robust and unpredictable traffic across state and disciplinary borders, and the transnationality of Shin's cinema amounts to a prompt to investigate how the national—whether cinema, culture, or identity—is formed in the global flow of images, capital, and discourse. Simultaneously, the profound complexity of his enmeshment with crucial cultural and political forces of the twentieth century opens a gap through which this work can inflect how those forces are constituted and theorized in any discipline.

Revision

Three very general and closely related questions structure the conceptual concerns of the chapters in this book and merit some preliminary consideration here. The first has to do with the bracketing of modernity within a postwar temporality. Clearly, by the time Shin Sang-ok began producing his own films in the 1950s, the extensive transformative effects of modernity in Korea had been at work for decades. Already in the latter half of the nineteenth century the grip of neo-Confucian political and cultural hegemony had loosened in the face of internal strife and popular rebellion and, with Japanese capital and military intervention at the turn of the century, radically new intellectual and experiential realities irreversibly conditioned life on the peninsula. Not surprisingly, the bulk of recent work in Korean studies has focused on these formative periods, interrogating in often massive collected works the economic, political, cultural, and indeed historiographic consequences of this colonial modernity.[8] But I want to highlight the equally dramatic transformations that characterize the postwar period and think seriously about whether it is possible to see in them the advent of a different kind of modernity. On the one hand, the post-1945 years are fraught with the survival and even active maintenance of Japanese cultural and educational practices and political-economic infrastructures that included, perhaps most notoriously, the continued authority and prestige of businessmen, public servants, and military personnel who had cooperated with imperial power. In other words, postliberation Korea, especially in the southern half of its division, was conditioned by the classic ambivalences of postcoloniality.

On the other hand, the peninsula witnessed changes that, while perhaps emblematic of what was happening contemporaneously around the world, are singular for their intensity and violence. The territory was torn by ideological conflict that would not only culminate in a war in which upward of two million would lose their lives, but which was preceded by instances of nightmarish turmoil (we might think of the still widely unknown Cheju 4.3 massacres in which as much as one-third of the island's male population was slaughtered in anticommunist crusades) and followed by decades of intense militarization, interstate aggression, and persecution carried out under the banner of ideological unity and security. The war also positioned South Korea firmly within the U.S. sphere of the international Cold War that resulted in a massive American military and diplomatic presence, continual (though uneven) cooperation with U.S. economic and political interests in the region and, of course, a robust American cultural influence that clashed uneasily with the vestiges of native Korean and Japanese cultural and linguistic forms. The dismal economic state left in the war's wake and the power of both U.S. and Japanese capital conditioned the breakneck urbanization and industrialization initiated modestly in the 1950s and intensified under the military authoritarian rule of Park Chung Hee. While the colonial period undeniably witnessed significant agricultural and industrial modernization, the sweeping effects of developmentalism—which effectively reversed the ratio of urban and rural populations, brought women in greater numbers into a highly repressive labor force, and systematized education and military service—were unprecedented. Modernity was not born in the midst of this postwar development but its experience was qualitatively new for a quantitatively significant share of the population.

What gave substantial form to this experiential novelty was the force of mass culture, which itself informs the second critical question of this volume. Again, mass culture was not invented in the 1950s, but flourished rather in the early 1920s, fostered under the limited freedoms of "cultural rule," increased economic activity in the cities, and the circulation, via Japan, of global literature and media.[9] But while the new sounds and images that were coming in from abroad and being produced domestically were undoubtedly jarring in their impact, their reach was severely limited by the extreme socioeconomic unevenness and the rudimentary industrial infrastructures that defined the cultural field through the 1950s. The mass culture of newspapers, magazines, radio, theater, and especially film was a much more robust presence following the war, strengthened by the material transformations sketched above and the flood, subsidized by the wealth and prestige of the U.S. government, of American media and celebrities that inundated Korea after 1953. I think it is important to pause here to consider how this layered ontology of foreign intervention inflects the very notion of mass culture, whose origins in the classical definition lie in the advent of democracy and technology.[10] As in so many non-Western and postcolonial societies, Korea's experience of mass culture was not as an organically developed set of cultural practices but as one that was mediated by a foreign political presence. That the U.S. form of mass culture came into contact with the Japanese (itself a hybrid form) prompted the perception that mass culture in and of itself was at least partially a mechanism of cultural suppression. For if in the classical model mass culture arose as an egalitarian alternative to the hegemonic culture of the elite, it was also, in the post colonial context, an ambivalent vehicle of both imperial domination and native resistance. Mass culture, in other words, has a crucial national-political dimension that in Korea found expression in a variety of discourses and practices, from the uncanny mimicry of singing groups like the Kim Sisters,[11] to the earnest formulation of the "enlightenment" modality of cinema.

It is precisely in this light that we need to reconsider Theodor Adorno's critical insight that modernism and the popular arts "are two halves of an integral freedom, to which, however, they do not add up." Against the assumptions of many of his interpreters, Adorno here positions high art and what he elsewhere calls the "culture industry" on the same dialectical plane, arguing "both have the stigmata of capitalism, both contain elements of change."[12] But the cultural field in postwar Korea was marked with different political inflections than those reflected in the contrast between Arnold Schoenberg and American film upon which Adorno reflected in these comments. The literary modernisms that arose in the 1920s and resurged in the 1950s constituted an active response to the new sensibilities and social order of colonial and postwar modernity. This work, rightfully or not, was ushered to the position of the avant-garde, becoming authoritative valences of social and political critique. At the same time, the autonomy and even originality of modernist artists was seriously compromised by the elite social status so many of them enjoyed and by their close connections to Japanese and American culture and education.[13] It is crucial to note, however, that mass culture did not sit at the opposite end of the cultural field. In fact, it is possible to argue that, especially apropos of culture in the colonial period, high modernism and mass culture were not "torn halves," but, rather, were integrated as modern art forms. While a gap between them formed and widened into the late 1960s, writers and filmmakers, say, or painters and poster designers often occupied interchangeable positions. Clearly, significant differences in the real or targeted audiences for both cultural forms existed, but the more important distinction by far was between work that was "pure" and "engaged"—that is, work whose artistic value was projected to be derived from transcendental aesthetic principles and work whose importance was grounded in sociopolitical relevance and realism.[14] While film's imbrication in commerce and "crass" entertainment forms placed it on a lower cultural stratum than literary modernism, both were stigmatized as derivative cultural forms. Both, conversely, were equally authorized to claim cultural legitimacy through the projection of "socially engaged" work.

These are the grounds on which I would like to approach the third question of this book, the relationship between art and politics. From his productive heyday in the 1960s through his career in the North and into the years following his death, Shin Sang-ok was marked by and large as politically conservative or otherwise apolitical, a filmmaker who privileged his craft or his success over any genuine interest in politics.[15] This assessment is built on readings of a body of work that exhibits little or no sign of implicit or explicit political criticism and confirmed in interviews in which Shin unequivocally disavows the possibility of political dissent. Shin is also compared unfavorably with other filmmakers such as Na Un-gyu or Kim Ki-yŏng, whose films were banned for political provocation or otherwise mobilized veiled attacks on repressive social and moral codes. Even recent reappraisals informed by psychoanalytic theory have encountered an impasse in Shin's work, stymied in their efforts to salvage a subversive unconscious by the troubling inconsistency of his career. Certainly, there is little evidence that Shin's work as producer or director ever put him in direct confrontation with any political regime. The scandals that precipitated the closure of his studio in 1975 can be read as an inevitable collision of market forces and misguided policy that had little to do with real dissent. In fact, the signal phenomena of Shin's career—the construction of the massive Shin Films complex and his contributions to the North Korean film industry—speak definitively of an overt willingness to cooperate with corporate and governmental authority.

But there are serious limitations in the conceptual apparatus that would consign Shin Sang-ok to political conservatism or vacuity. On one level, the basic idea that political subversion in film was possible in any given historical period, and further that such practices were matters of personal volition, both skews the historical record and misconstrues the processes of film authorship and production. The film industry was founded in Korea under the direct auspices of the Government-General, and all aspects of production and exhibition were closely monitored by censors with the authority to halt proceedings at any stage. The notion that Na's *Arirang* (1926) articulated a violently nationalist anticolonial protest, particularly if that protest was coded as allegory or, as some have argued, mediated through the improvisations of a Korean-language *pyŏnsa* (film narrator), is not entirely implausible.[16] Na's pedigree as a political prisoner of the March First Independence Movement abets the claim to a certain extent. And yet, contemporaneous criticism is at best ambivalent about the film's politics and far more invested in addressing its apparently questionable artistic merits. Further, Na continued to make films through the 1930s, none of which were notably subversive. Control over film production became nothing if not more rigorous in the postwar period, especially under the extensive policies created by the Park regime, effectively precluding the exhibition of any materials seen by the ethics committees to be remotely critical of the state's power or its programs. The historiography that argues for the existence of a "nationalist realist" tradition of nearly unbroken resistance to colonial and undemocratic repression rests precariously on insights into the private political beliefs of individual filmmakers and, more crucially, the advancement of allegory as a primary mode of dissent—neither of which could be borne out in the overexposed sphere of film culture.[17]

However, the core problem of these readings of the politics of filmmaking has little to do with questions of historical veracity or even nationalist mythology. Even the much more sophisticated scholarship that has sought to find nodes of resistance within the complex manipulations of form that characterize modernist film or that champion the verifiably politicized work of more recent documentary filmmakers succumbs to facile notions of what constitutes "political" art. What is at stake here is an undertheorized conception of political mimesis that narrowly qualifies as political only work that explicitly or through various subterfuges lays bare some political issue, which, therein, may prompt correlative political action. This is an idea, I would argue, that if taken to its logical conclusion, would consign virtually all Korean filmmaking of the postwar period to the dustbin of political conservatism or vacuity. A counterweight to this theoretical void might be taken from Jacques Rancière's recent revision of the old questions of aesthetics and politics. For Rancière, "the political" does not reside in the "message" of a work of art, whether it is addressed to some repressive state or to some ossified intellectual tradition. Criticism that would look for social practice only in acts of exposure, parody, or satire does not take account of the social and institutional iniquities that sustain and are in turn sustained by artistic production; moreover, it would rely too heavily on the evidence of measurable intentions and outcomes. In its stead, Rancière offers an idea of dissent that is attuned to the specific relationships and limitations of art:

> Art and politics each define a form of dissensus, a dissensual re-configuration of the common experience of the sensible. If there is such a thing as an "aesthetics of politics," it lies in a re-configuration of the distribution of the common through political processes of subjectivation. Correspondingly, if there is a politics of aesthetics, it lies in the practices and modes of visibility of art that re-configure the fabric of sensory experience.[18]

Art can only function qua art to introduce new subjects and heterogeneous objects into the field of perception, to give expression to those populations denied legitimacy as speaking subjects, by stating egalitarian effects within the space of performances. Part of what makes art political, in other words, is its capacity to renovate what it is possible to perceive as political. Perhaps the most important question of this book, then, is not whether or how Shin Sang-ok signified politically as a filmmaker, but, rather, how an interrogation of his work can condition a reevaluation of how politics and art are constituted in postwar Korea.

Toward an adequate address of these problematics of postwar modernity, non-Western mass culture, and political aesthetics and, further, toward care for the instabilities of film and nation as fields of analysis, I have consciously moved *Split Screen Korea* in directions beyond the deep and complex groove laid down by Shin Sang-ok and his films. So while the chapters move through a rough chronological tracing of both the major phases of Shin's career and the critical phenomena of postwar Korean culture, they each at the same time explore ideas, events, and conflicts that traverse the limits of the cinematic medium and trespass the borders of modern Korean history. The potential merits of this transdisciplinary, transnational mode of inquiry are clear: Shin Sang-ok's wildly itinerant cinema is better served by a critical vision that takes account of contemporaneous developments in global cinema and culture; and further, the effort to fully engage Shin's films itself necessitates interventions in the critical methods through which knowledge about modern culture has been produced, within and beyond Korea. My hope is that this book will demonstrate these merits and, therein, occasion different modes of reflection on postwar modernity and cinema.

Chapter 1 furnishes a history of film cultures and discourses in Korea that run parallel to Shin Sang-ok's career, making a claim for "enlightenment" as a fundamental mode of twentieth-century Korean cinema. Starting with the earliest pictures produced on the peninsula in the 1920s and looking most closely at film cultures under Japanese colonial and postwar authoritarian rule, the chapter traces a genealogy of the codes and practices that constitute the enlightenment modality. It also casts a wide net over the shaping of enlightenment discourses in literary practice and scholarship and attempts to differentiate those from the production of enlightenment rhetoric in film criticism, policy, and institutions. The core texts here are a series of roundtable discussions focused on the question of "Chosŏn cinema" published in newspapers and film journals in the late colonial period, debates about mass culture and national culture waged in print in the liberation and early division years, and the ideologically hardened positions taken up in policy and opinion statements through the 1950s and early 1960s. The chapter closes by bringing the enlightenment modality into relief in three major genres in which Shin Sang-ok worked: the war picture, the women's melodrama, and the Manchurian western. Taken together, these readings yield a view of the enlightenment modality as eminently modern, easily translatable across formal and political boundaries, and durably forceful in signifying the politics of cinema.

Chapter 2 situates Shin Sang-ok's definitive women's melodramas from the 1950s within that decade's intensified media of image production: popular magazines, the fashion industry, and cinema. Mass culture was reinvigorated following the turmoil of the peninsula's "transwar" period (1937–53), and Shin, together with a new generation of filmmakers who had cut their teeth on American intelligence productions, crafted a cinematic vision of the era's renewed sites of fantasy and consumption. Through its encounter with the ostensibly foreign and novel looks engineered by the fashion and film industries, the chapter uncovers a layered ontology in which American commodities and style were being worked through a web of vestigial Japanese and local Korean aesthetic forms. A close examination of Shin's melodramas, which were produced in markedly close connection with the fashion industry, discloses a self-conscious identification with American popular culture as well as a subtle nostalgia for the colonial period's urbanity and style that condition the films' sophisticated imagery. The chapter argues that Shin's work participated in a broader and more systematic transformation in forms of visualization that conjoined passionate attention to surfaces with fantasies of escape from postwar poverty and destruction.

Chapter 3 constitutes the narrative core of *Split Screen*, providing a comprehensive history of Shin Films from its beginnings in the late 1950s through to its shuttering in 1975. While its growth was catalyzed by the successes of the 1950s melodramas and bolstered through creative cooperation with the state throughout the 1960s, Shin Films drew its financial and cultural capital most directly from the regional investment and distribution system that structured the postwar Korean film industry. I argue that the prolific output of the studio and, more crucially, Shin Sang-ok's worldly authorial vision are best understood through the lens of this local economic and cultural base. The chapter offers a detailed description of both the regional distribution and investment system as well as successive postwar motion picture laws and shows how Shin leveraged these for the production of not only blockbuster hits such as the period piece *Sŏng Ch'unhyang* (1961) and the literary adaptation *Samnyong the Mute* (*Pŏngŏri Samnyong*, 1965), but also the many smaller, but invariably meticulously produced genre films that formed the studio's nucleus. Chapter 3 follows Shin Films through its demise in the 1970s, an era that witnessed the degradation of Korean film cultures more generally in the face of rapid urbanization, a hardening of authoritarian government, and the expanding reach of television. Shin deployed a variety of ingenious measures in an attempt to stave off failure, including counterfeit coproductions with Hong Kong studios and the production of a musical extravaganza, *I Love Mama* (*Ai rŏbŭ mama*, 1975), but the terms of the studio's invisibility were written irrevocably in the contraction of the postwar regional markets.

Chapter 4 argues that the politics of even the most explicitly ideological of Shin's films should be read against the radically unstable political discourses and practices of the early Park Chung Hee period. The chapter returns explicitly to the enlightenment modality introduced in chapter 1, building upon a very close reading of Shin's two archetypal enlightenment films, *Evergreen* (1961) and *Rice* (*Ssal*, 1963). It begins by problematizing the critical consensus that the films, and Shin's work more generally, were either complicit with authoritarian rule or, conversely, lacked any political commitment whatsoever. To this end, the chapter furnishes a synchronic historical account of how the films appropriated the dominant developmentalist discourses of the period, highlighting the divergences and convergences between state and popular rhetorics of modernization. It then moves through to a consideration of specifically cinematic pleasures, suggesting that *Evergreen* and *Rice*'s melodramatic modality as well as their mass cultural appeal inflect the explicitly didactic thrust of the enlightenment genre. The study then concludes with a reflection on the political dimension of cinematic form. Concentrating on a set of visual codes—which constitute what I call an aesthetics of development—I argue that Shin's films not only participate in the production of national discourse and the attendant transformations of South Korean postcolonial/postwar subjectivity, but also are in dialogue with a broader spectrum of global image making in a way that challenges conventional definitions of Shin Sang-ok's politics.

Chapter 5 closes *Split Screen* with a compressed rereading of key features of North Korean film theory and practice and an exploration of Shin Sang-ok's ventures in North Korea that is grounded in interpretation of the films he produced there. The chapter does not try to answer the common question of the sensational episode—that is, whether he and his wife Ch'oe Ŭn-hŭi were kidnapped or went north voluntarily—but rather attempts to account for how a filmmaking sensibility so rooted in the local markets of South Korea and the global style of Hollywood could be not only legible but, moreover, eminently successful in the ostensibly hermetically sealed North. My investigation begins with a consideration of the ideological portability of mass culture, salvaging the transformative possibilities of that portability from critical dismissal by theorists like Adorno and Max Horkheimer. I argue further that cinema as a field in North Korea had been a site for contestation and cross-pollination between Soviet and native *chuch'e* socialist realisms and was, perhaps counterintuitively, still open to creative inflection by the time Shin began making his films there in 1983. I also suggest that while the production practices and titillating words and images of Shin's North Korean productions were novel and even shocking, their basic legibility and popularity were mediated by core continuities that breached North and South Korean division. The chapter traces two of these—the primacy of family-centered affect and the enlightenment mode of filmmaking—through some of Shin's most important North Korean works, many of which had counterparts in his South Korean filmography. The chapter concludes by mapping the complex continuities and discontinuities represented by

Shin's filmmaking in North Korea against the state's geopolitical position in the 1980s, suggesting that neither "Shin Sang-ok" nor "North Korea" were as transparent as they first appeared, even to their most charitable observers.

The book concludes by returning to the historical mapping initiated in this introduction and, through a look at some films Shin made upon his return from North Korea, reflects on the local social and political conditions of his uncommonly cosmopolitan career.

1 THE CENTURY'S ILLUMINATIONS

The Enlightenment Mode in Korean Cinema

I WANT TO BEGIN with what might be called a diachronic para-history of periods of filmmaking in Korea that both describes and exceeds the bounds of Shin Sang-ok's career. I do so partly because the following chapters in this book treat Shin's work in synchronic stages, mapping it against a range of contemporaneous discourses and events. While this serves one of the book's overall aims, the assemblage of a history of postwar Korean film cultures, it also works against one of its core insights, that crucial continuities in form and thought survive otherwise radical transformations in social organization and political ideology. But I also take the long view in this chapter to argue with critical traditions that parallel the temporal duration of this study. One of these, sketched in the introduction, is the "nationalist realist" thesis that posits the primacy of an anticolonial, prodemocratic tendency in Korean cinema that is mediated via an ostensibly ethical realist modality. The other, more diffuse and in some ways more crucial, is a set of criteria for what constitutes the aesthetic value of film as well as its politics. These, I argue, depend on a limited concept of modernism and mass culture that de facto function as a set of criteria for what constitutes aesthetic value in film. I am not at all interested in salvaging the political salience or aesthetic legitimacy of what I call here the enlightenment modality; rather, I see in that knot of formal and discursive practices an important mechanism with which to rethink the meaning of ideology, form, and development in twentieth-century Korean cinema.

Enlightenment Revisited

In the history of Korean cinema, "enlightenment" (*kyemong*) has not only been cast as a future aspiration or a characterization of the present, but has just as often been figured as a remnant of the past. In virtually every period of major cultural transformation, critics and filmmakers alike have declared the obsolescence of enlightenment thought and style. Yi P'il-u, who is widely seen as Korea's first film impresario, was steadfast in the early 1920s in calling for the new "entertainment" medium to replace the "outmoded forms of the nineteenth century."[1] In a complex and troubling turn away from his commitment to socialist thought, Im Hwa, perhaps the leading cultural critic of the 1930s, pointed to the end of the age of "enlightenment idealism" and announced the dawn of "cultural industrialization" that ensued with the expansion of Japanese imperial power.[2] In the mid-1950s, following the war and in the midst of increased American cultural influence, there was nearly unanimous agreement among critics that the world had changed and that the old forms of cultural instruction were no longer relevant.[3] The same sort of rhetoric flooded newspapers and magazines in the 1980s, when the modicum of wealth and security built under the developmentalist projects of the Park Chung Hee administration and the apparent victory of the capitalist South over the socialist North seemed to negate the utility of ideological and instrumentalized cultural forms. The logic of this disavowal and assurance is twofold. It stems first from the link made between enlightenment and the premodern. Critics throughout the twentieth century continually tied the basic idea of *kyemong* to the moralistic literary culture of the defunct Chosŏn *yangban* class. Enlightenment, therein, was the antithesis of the modern subjectivities and democratic social forms that apparently lay at the core of contemporary filmmaking. It is rooted, second, in the more sophisticated idea that while enlightenment was in fact eminently modern in its utopian ideological objectives, it was now retrograde and inappropriate to the political calm that had ostensibly settled on the nation. The enlightenment film was therein an artifact of more troubling times and its overcoming signaled the arrival of a genuinely cosmopolitan Korean society.

I want to argue in this chapter, however, that no such overcoming ever occurred, and rather that these moments of rhetorical disavowal only articulated shifts in the continued predominance of enlightenment thought in the discourses and practices of Korean cinema. Certainly, periods of acute political mobilization witnessed the agitation of interests that intensified the spirit of enlightenment: the enactment of laws governing content or mandating the number of films being produced and venues for their exhibition; the preference given to or pressure placed on critics and ideologues who championed socially "engaged" and politically "healthy" filmmaking; the advent of awards, funds, and other incentives for politically accommodating filmmakers, and so on. These were especially pronounced under the mobilization movements of the late colonial period, the "national reconstruction" fervor of the immediate liberation years, and the more fluid early stages of the Park administration. But enlightenment discourse, I hope to show, was just as salient and effective in periods of apparent rapprochement and withdrawal: when state management receded from cultural production, when the explicit language of enlightenment faded from the film vernacular, and even when, as noted above, enlightenment was explicitly disavowed in critical discourse. My arguments about this seeming contradiction are built on rethinking the terms by which enlightenment has been understood in the study of Korean film, and situating it within a wider range of institutional, linguistic, critical, as well as formal practices.

The most highly visible signification of enlightenment in film, of course, is as genre, specifically, the *kyemong yŏnghwa* or "enlightenment film" genre that was formalized in the mid-1970s, when it was evoked by the newly formed Korean Film Preservation Center (now the Korean Film Archive). The designation, still used today to classify nearly two hundred films from the late 1920s through the late 1990s, identifies films with a didactic tone and a plot structure based on some variant of the *vnarod* or agrarian return narrative. The overall tenor of this genre is easily grasped by a glance at some of the titles in the range: *A New Beginning* (*Sae ch'ulbal*, Yi Kyu-hwan 1939), *Dawn for a Mountain Village* (*Sanch'on ŭi yŏ'myŏng*, San Chung-yu/ Yamanata Yutaka, 1940), *Hometown Song* (*Kohyang ŭi norae*, Yun Pong-ch'un, 1954), *Yellow Earth* (*Hwangt'o*, Kim Su-yong, 1975). The prime example is Shin Sang-ok's 1961 *Evergreen* (*Sangnoksu*), based on Sim Hun's canonical 1936 novella of the same name, which follows the ultimately tragic efforts of two students to bring modern agricultural methods and political consciousness to backward villages in colonial Chosŏn. The story, with its admixture of wholesome romance and political idealism, proved as legible and popular to readers in an increasingly repressive colony as to audiences in the comparatively liberal window between the Syngman Rhee and Park Chung Hee regimes (and again at the height of Park's "*Yusin*" system with Im Kwon-taek's 1978 remake). Like many other films that constitute the genre, *Evergreen* had an official stamp of approval, its pathos and inspiration famously said to have wrung tears from Park's eyes. Enlightenment, in this institutional form, acts as shorthand for mainstream propaganda: politically motivated and underwritten work that mobilizes stock narrative and thematic tropes in a commercial feature film format.

As in any other genre classification, the "enlightenment" name encloses an otherwise heterogeneous body of films by obscuring or eschewing critical differences in historical context and evolutions in form. But what sets it apart from, say, the family melodrama or horror categories is its foregrounding of interests outside the films themselves over the commonalities in inner/outer forms or syntactic/semantic elements that are traditionally identified as genre markers.[4] In other words, the fact of a film's attachment or service to some identifiable political goal or organization, as much if not more than its rendition of familiar stories of return and radicalization, distinguishes it generically as an enlightenment film. The instability of this naming, of course, lies in the elusive balance between political influence and formal structure, and in the heterogeneity of those political influences that are found to have worked on the films. Even the few films listed above traverse diverse political environments, with their own distinct technologies of social and cultural control. Further, enlightenment as a genre marker is often used interchangeably with other signifiers—that is, "culture" (*munhwa*), "propaganda" (*sŏnjŏn*), "purpose" (*mokjŏk*), and "policy" (*chŏngch'aek*)— that correspond to contemporaneous cultural movements or prevailing political programs that resist easy transhistorical comparison.[5] Ultimately, the limitations of a strict definition of the genre are clear: based on a broad tautology that is more inclusive and descriptive than it is analytical, the institutional classifier helps very little in understanding the films it designates. But as with all other genre categories, we need to take it seriously not only because it has been regularly deployed and to an extent naturalized in critical discourses but also because its ontology is a potent amalgam of literary, philosophical-religious, political, and commercial processes, and the formation of a broad cultural consensus.

I will attempt to trace some of the roots of that consensus below. For now, I want to propose a way around the genre conundrum toward a more precise, and at the same time more expansive, way of thinking about the maintenance of enlightenment discourse and practice in Korean cinema. In this task, I am partially guided by the intervention staged by Linda Williams in her essay, "Melodrama Revised." Writing at the tail end of the crucial debates over melodrama in the 1990s, and drawing in particular from Thomas Elsaesser's assertions about the Hollywood family melodrama, Williams boldly argued for melodrama's place as a "fundamental mode of popular

American motion pictures."[6] As a modality, melodrama for Williams cannot be equated with specific genres but should, rather, be seen as both informing and encompassing the various bodies of work—woman's films, "weepies," or family melodramas—conventionally labeled as iterations of the melodramatic genre. But more than simply suggesting that we think of melodrama as a higher unit of analysis, Williams intervenes by repositioning melodrama, alongside realism, at the core of cinematic representation. Melodrama, Williams argues, is not a "submerged, or embedded tendency within realist narrative—which it certainly can be—but . . . has more often itself been the dominant form of popular moving-image narrative."[7] Particularly germane for the present study is the way in which the scope of Williams's notion of modality enables bold and comprehensive claims about what she calls the "basic vernacular of American moving pictures."[8] Thinking about melodrama as mode allows her not only to diagnose, within film criticism, the disavowal of "feminine" pathos and spectacle in favor of "masculine" logos and narrative, but also to interrogate the syntax of innocence, victimhood, and redemption at the heart of American film experience.

It is in this spirit of speculation that I would like to propose some ideas about enlightenment in Korean cinema. The enlightenment mode is certainly most self-evident in propagandistic and socially conscious filmmaking, but its mechanisms are not confined to such narrowly defined political forms. It is as much at work in the proimperialist films of the early 1940s as in the celebrated neorealist films of the postwar years or the gaudiest genre pictures of the 1970s. At its base are radical ideas about political transformation and human possibility that function as principles for how stories should be told and as precepts linking film with nation and ideology. These not only survive but are in fact nourished by the manifold social and political upheavals that define Korea in the twentieth century. The enlightenment mode in filmmaking, however, is neither a pure remnant of premodern aesthetic discourse nor a simple product of Japanese colonial pressure. Its centrality and continuation across radically different sociopolitical milieus do not attest to some unchanging cultural essence or transhistorical political character. Rather, it is a complex effect of maintenance in critical and popular discourse. Whether it is fervently evoked in moments of acute political upheaval or renounced in times of relative calm, the enlightenment mode is both a pregnant sign and a critical effect of the nature of aesthetics and politics in Korea and the fashion in which their relationship has been rendered in contemporary scholarship.

Guiding Write

The precedents and resonances of the cinematic mode of enlightenment are multiple and sometimes contradictory. The term affixed to the genre classification—*kyemong*—was used flexibly for centuries in a variety of scientific, pedagogical, and religious treatises, usually translated from Chinese sources, and connoted a process of awakening from ignorance. The *Kyemongp'yŏn*, for instance, is an early Chosŏn text that lays out principles of childhood education. References to *kyemong* as a process of learning can also be found throughout Sŏn Buddhist scriptures (though notably its meaning is clearly differentiated from the rare Enlightenment [*ton'o*] attained through practice). *Kyemong* was also the term used, from the late nineteenth century onward, to translate the German *Aufklärung*, particularly as it pertained to developments in eighteenth-century European philosophy.

I invoke this cursory etymology not to lock enlightenment into a conceptual or cultural tradition but, rather, as a way of making sense of what can seem a relatively arbitrary institutionalization of the term in film criticism. In fact, a number of other terms were available for or put into broad use throughout the twentieth century to connote the illuminating potential of the cinematic medium: *kyohwa* (instruction), *kaehyŏk* (reform), *kyoyuk* (education), *kaehwa* (opening/enlightenment), and so on. All of these, particularly in their utilization in the early modern period, share an implication of cultural and civilizational elevation. *Kaehwa* in particular, as historian Andre Schmid has shown, saturated public discourse throughout the late nineteenth and early twentieth centuries as intellectuals and ideologues struggled to come to terms with Chosŏn's integration in the high imperialist iteration of the global capitalist system. Commonly tied to the term civilization (*munmyŏng*), *kaehwa* depended on a primitivist view of Chosŏn society and culture that projected enlightenment as a way to return Koreans to parity with neighboring and global civilizations—a conceptual ambivalence in which Schmid rightly sees a "modernist discourse par excellence."[9] That *kyemong* and not *kaehwa* was evoked in discussions of film indicates the discrete connotations of cinematic and civilizational enlightenment. *Kaehwa* as a signifier is embedded firmly in the specific pressures of the early modern period and refers exclusively to its political discourses. The stress of the *kyemong* signifier, on the other hand, was on a didactic purpose at work specifically in the field of art. For some filmmakers and commentators, as we will see in greater detail below, the enlightenment film stood at the vanguard of movements that sought advancement through the agency of compelling art. For others, as we saw above, it bore the stink of stagnant literary forms, of a tired moralizing impulse that was the antithesis of modern film culture. Conveying senses of both venerable scholarship and progressive social purpose, *kyemong* aptly served to convey the predicament of a cinema caught between an intensely politicized cultural field and the need to remain publicly visible through commercial success or state sponsorship.

These pressures of course were not unique to cinema, nor was the *kyemong* label applied only to filmmaking. The figure of enlightenment was central to modern literary practice and criticism in such a way that it is worth considering its function in those fields in addition to its relationship to the film world. A key difference is that no literary genre, let alone modality, was ever formally baptized with the enlightenment name. Rather, enlightenment exists in critical historiography as quality (*-sŏng*), tendency (*kyŏnghyang*), ideology (*chuŭi/sasang*), or discourse (*tamnon*), and read as a subjectively identified sensibility or attitude. Three major elements tie together the sort of work to which these descriptors are commonly applied: the *vnarod* or agrarian return narrative noted above, a didactic and hortatory purpose or voice, and an explicit mass political and nationalist orientation. In a variety of combinations and in the sphere of diverse literary movements, these elements can be traced in literature from the late nineteenth century through to at least the end of the military administrations in the early 1990s. In so-called new novels (*sinsosŏl*) such as Yi In-jik's *Tears of Blood* (*Hyŏl ŭi nu*, 1906), the enlightenment narrative takes the form of travel to Japan (or in some cases the United States) and return to Chosŏn, where the newly enlightened student takes up a teaching position or other form of social leadership.[10] It would take on familiar agrarian characteristics in the literature of the 1920s and 1930s (for example, in Yi Kwang-su's *Heartlessness* [*Mujŏng*, 1917]), where the modernized student would return from the Japanese metropole to spread literacy and/or improve agricultural practices; more robust nativist dimensions characterize enlightenment narratives in left-wing KAPF (*Korea Artista Proletaria Federatio*) literature (say, in Yi Ki-yŏng's *Hometown* [*Kohyang*, 1934]), wherein the student or urban intellectual, while embracing rural lifeways, would seek to inspire consciousness of social contradiction in the rural village, aiming ultimately toward the development of a properly modern subject.[11] The political stakes of the plot would shift in the *minjung* (people's) and *minjok* (national) literatures of the late 1960s and 1970s, but the core narrative arc, in which students move down from Seoul to carry out "labor praxis" in farms and factories, would remain intact. Across these modifications, the basic ideological outline of enlightenment as a genre is clear: the responsibility of the modern, radicalized intellectual elite to enlighten the poor, backward, primitive masses for a specific purpose: social, spiritual, and political awakening.

It is of course this responsibility, broadcast in essays on the meaning and function of literature and invested in a range of fictional and poetic work, that animates enlightenment literature's didactic disposition. Yi Kwang-su crystallized this sensibility in an early piece when he wrote bluntly: "writing is not a wage-earning profession, nor is it time-passing leisure. Writing is for the guidance and ministration of, minimally, the nation, and maximally, humankind."[12] While Yi's suspect political motivations have been exposed in recent critical revisions,[13] his conjoining of moral principle and mass political purpose was not far outside the mainstream of literary currents in any period of the twentieth century. The explicit politicization of literature is clearest in the colonial period, in which many of the broad-based literary camps like KAPF or the Paekjo School were founded on clearly articulated (though highly contested) ideas about literature's role in social and political transformation. Literary formations in the liberation and post-war periods, of course, were embroiled in the radical confrontations that culminated in national division, war, and intense ideological discipline on all sides of the conflict. Im Hwa, Han Sŏl-ya, and others in left-wing groups such as the Writers Guild (*Munhak'ga tongmaeng*), suppressed through the late 1930s and 1940s, published highly polemic work intended to awaken awareness of class contradiction and threats to national identity. The discursive field in the 1960s and 1970s became flatter ideologically but continued to be scored by politically motivated writing. The sensation of Nam Chŏng-hyŏn's *Land of Excrement* (*Punji*, 1965), that it could so explicitly identify South Korea as a U.S. colony, was not tempered by its often pedantic narrative voice or strained narrative organization. In fact, its indictment under the 1965 National Security Law raised precisely the question of literature's social role, with the authorities and the author at odds only over the degree to which an artist could express political dissent.[14] Though by this time the term had fallen out of use in all but literary historiography, the enlightenment impulse continued to occupy a central position in a number of important dialogues and movements, from the Marxist social-formation debate (*sahoe kusŏngch'e*) to the *minjung* literature of the 1970s and 1980s. Leading poets and fiction writers such as Kim Chi-ha and Sin Tong-hyŏp invoked folk figures and traditions such as *p'ansori* and *madanggŭk* in their vivid indictments of class privilege and authoritarian control.[15] The seemingly endless string of political crises and conflicts throughout the latter half of the century kept literary polemic and commitment to the idea of socially responsible literature in the mainstream. Though far removed from the specific pressures of the colonial predicament, the *minjung* movement literature faithfully restored the bonds of populist discourse, moral righteousness, and national consciousness that epitomized enlightenment literature under Japanese occupation.[16]

But the centrality and resilience of enlightenment discourse in literature does not amount to its hegemony, either in practice or in theory. It is crucial to note here that it was in fact highly contested with every major literary movement, and the subject of debate among writers and critics. These, clearly, are beyond the scope of this chapter, but it might be worth noting here how, in a range of contemporary criticism, the continued presence of the enlightenment modality has often been cast as a sort of parasitical vestige, in spite of its widely acknowledged foregrounding in the literary canon, core intellectual debates, and seminal manifestos. The literary historian Kwŏn Yŏng-min, for instance, characterized what he saw (particularly in lesser works of the colonial and early liberation periods) as an often dominant *kyemong-sŏng* as a sign of "the inability of the colonial literati to completely embrace the modernist approach to art and aesthetics."[17] This was a version of the "twisted" or "interrupted" modernity thesis that played a central role for decades in Korean literature studies. More recently, Ch'ŏn Chŏnghwan has noted two senses of enlightenment in colonial period literature, one the didactic force of specific texts and authors, and the other a rhetorical device in public discussions about the status of literature. Writers produced work with powerful moralizing impulses at the same time as they invoked "enlightenment quality" as a derogatory term in their criticism of what they saw as backward, premodern literature—a bifurcation that, Ch'ŏn argues, discloses the contradictions of colonial modernity.[18] Both critics read the continued presence of enlightenment thought as a symptom of Korea's beleaguered position vis-à-vis the West. For Kwŏn, it betrays immaturity on a scale of aesthetic development, and for Chŏn it speaks to the unevenness of a society handicapped in its race to catch up with Western modernity. These conclusions are worth interrogating further, if only because in broad outline they mirror the sort of disavowals I noted at the beginning of this chapter. For the moment, however, we need to consider how the critical discourse surrounding enlightenment in literary practice relates to the cinema, whose arrival in Korea roughly coincides with the advent of modernity itself and whose existence is irreducibly contingent on a new set of political, commercial, and technological forces.

Especially in its early decades, the film world had intimate links with the literary world: short fiction and novels were favorite sources of film narratives and writers often did double duty as screenwriters, film critics, directors, and even as actors. It should go without saying then that the contests over the meaning and value of enlightenment discourse in literature have broad parallels in film production and criticism. More often than not, the ideas, rhetorical strategies, and political orientations forged within literary circles were transferred wholesale to discussions about film. The force of arguments for assimiliationist literature, for instance, worked as effectively in producing the nakedly pro-Japanese filmmaking of the early 1940s as did the claims for "pure literature" in yielding the strenuously depoliticized "literary" (*munye*) films of the late 1950s. Powerful resonances in critical historiography obtain as well. The broad consensus in literary criticism that enlightenment discourse is an elite rhetorical construct, spawned within the despotism of neo-Confucian Chosŏn or the fascism of imperial Japan, and that was easily instrumentalized in the authoritarian nationalisms of both poles of postwar national division, proved highly influential in the study of film.[19] Yet these linkages between readings of literature and film are not seamless. On the one hand, one could easily argue that enlightenment projects find a more convivial home in the movie theater than in literary journals and publications: not only can filmmaking's capital-intensive production processes benefit from state sponsorship, but the central metaphors of the enlightenment mode—awakening, the opening of eyes, revelations—also match the visuality and spectacle that define the cinematic medium. On the other hand, mainstream narratives of Korean literary modernity, grounded as they have been largely on readings of literary and critical texts circulated within privileged institutions and classes, become less coherent as explanatory devices for the more populist and implicitly market-driven cinematic form. Notwithstanding the variety of movements undertaken by writers and intellectuals to bring literature and cultural criticism into closer contact with everyday or folk experience, the elitism excavated at the core of literary enlightenment discourse operates through different, often interrupted and heavily mediated channels in the mass cultural domain of the cinema. The highly regulated and commercially invested institutions through which films are produced and consumed and the more public practices through which their meanings are constructed

pose an additional set of questions about the maintenance of "enlightenment" as a cultural and political term.

The Most Modern of Arts

The earliest critics and filmmakers in Chosŏn faced the same political constraints and imperatives as the men of letters and fashioned a cinematic
enlightenment discourse that would last similarly, perhaps even more tena-
ciously, throughout most of the twentieth century. As in the literary world,
the cinema of colonial Chosŏn reflected the wide range of political positions
that ethnic Koreans were authorized to take in various historical moments.
This encompassed the socialist-nationalist filmmaking of the short-lived
"tendency school," the cultural nationalist mainstream of the late 1920s and
early 1930s, and the collaborationist policy films of the late 1930s and 1940s.
The social and political geometry of the majority of these films, further,
mirrored the didacticism and elitism of the enlightenment literary discourse
sketched above. The most celebrated films—*Arirang* (Na Un-gyu, 1926),
Rudderless Ferry (*Imja ŏmnŭn narutbae*, Yi Kyu-hwan, 1932), and *Homeless
Angels* (*Chip ŏmnŭn ch'ŏnsa*, Ch'oe In-gyu, 1941)—are almost unanimously
built on narratives of education, return, and reform. Contemporary critics
and filmmakers alike were seized with the conviction of the enlightenment
potential and therein the social responsibility of film. Mirroring the populist and didactic structures of the aforementioned writing and criticism, the
left-wing critic Pak Wan-sik wrote in the *Chosŏn Ilbo* of the importance of
film as a "popular art form" and the need for it to function as an instrument
of popular education (*kyohwa*). Crystallizing much of the discussion surrounding film at the time, Pak saw the cinema's potential for both harm and
advantage:

> In its unrivaled capacity for the crucial task of instruction, film's great impor-
> tance becomes extremely relevant and clear. It is obvious that as a popular art
> form, the cinema can also be a tool of mass education. . . . Regardless of the
> time or place, film performs the function of education for the people (*min-
> jung*). Relative to the film's content, the people can be influenced intellectu-
> ally or ideologically by the strength of emotions or the clarity of impressions.

Accordingly, Pak argued that a robust socialist movement should take
advantage of this potential and work against the "hypocrisy of bourgeois
society and its popular arts."[20] With the intensification of social and cultural

control that accompanied Japanese military mobilization, such discourse would begin to lose its nationalist coloring. Nevertheless, the core idea that film's inherently popular quality and character gave it social and even spiritual importance continued to dominate. In a 1937 article titled "Cinema and the People," Yi Un-gok argued:

> We should not fail to recognize the social power that film possesses. Thus it is necessary to examine, from the position of the people, the impact a film's contents and function can have on culture and everyday practices. It would be extremely difficult to articulate this position (of the people) with perfect clarity, but broadly speaking . . . it could be the position that is presupposed both by the people's improvement toward humanism and by the formation of the morals that spring from the people's everyday lives.[21]

Like Pak and many others, Yi saw film as a critically important political tool, one that could be badly abused if not tamed and attuned to the people's interests. This figuration of film art as an instrument through which to lead and instruct the masses on behalf of the greater (imperial/national) good is, as it was for literature of the period, a function of the class position of the artists themselves, the cultural and economic chasm that separated urban from rural populations, and the overwhelming pressures of colonial modernization. The cinema was seen as an important means through which to prepare ethnic Koreans, if not for national sovereignty, then for full civilizational realization.

Public discussion shifted drastically in the late 1930s and 1940s as Japanese war mobilization and then extreme ideological division drove the film industry to nearly total state control. Enlightenment discourse, which, despite its mass political dimension and strong associations with public policy, had remained relatively independent of official control, lost that autonomy and became absorbed in the close administration of all cultural forms in this period. The enlightenment film, as a result, became nearly synonymous with government propaganda. But this break, and the similarly dramatic transformation that followed liberation in 1945, prompts us to think carefully about the scope and specificity of enlightenment discourse in film. While the didactic voice and a populist spirit would remain features of what was termed the "new order" (*sin ch'eje*) of films, and while certainly the *kwihyang* narrative would continue to serve as the basis of a number of important works, the focus of filmmaking under the centralized Chosŏn Film Production Company (*Chosŏn yŏnghwa chejak chusik hoesa*) would change. Films like *Volunteer Soldier* (*Chiwŏn pyŏng*, 1941) and *The*

Chosŏn Straits (*Chosŏn haehyŏp*, 1943) mobilized the didactic and populist form toward inciting loyalty to and sacrifice for the Japanese empire, and critics would champion these highly affective narratives. Kim Sŏng-gyun wrote in 1941:

> Taking into consideration the very nature and effect of the cinema, as well as the current state of the Chosŏn film industry, there is no better means with which to promote Japanese–Korean cultural exchange than film. And now that film technology has developed under the reigns of political control and filmmaking has gotten its needed political training, there is no reason to suspect that films are not the best means by which to develop cultural exchange and to promote the unification of Koreans and Japanese (*naesŏn-ilch'e*).[22]

This appropriation of filmmaking via state apparatuses of centralization and censorship and the acquiescence of public intellectuals arguably mark the apex of the enlightenment mode. The films produced in this period, such as Ch'oe's *Homeless Angels*, which depicted a pastor's heroic efforts to make productive citizens out of ethnic Korean orphans, became standard bearers of the enlightenment film genre. It is worth noting, however, that the term "enlightenment" is rarely used to name this body of films in extant criticism; rather, "propaganda," "military," and "pro-Japanese" are deployed instead, effectively reserving the "enlightenment" title for ostensibly domestic and nationalistic films.

A more illuminating fact, however, is that contemporaneous criticism and rhetoric was not confined to single-minded calls for film to "educate the people" or promote "cultural exchange." In January 1939 the *Chosŏn Ilbo* published a roundtable discussion titled "The Dawn of Chosŏn Cinema" (*Yŏmyŏnggi ŭi Chosŏn yŏnghwa*) that brought together some of the leading figures in the colonial film industry.[23] While the mood of the wide-ranging conversation is genial, the overall assessment given by the filmmakers and critics is rather dark. All are agreed that Chosŏn film is second-rate: that, for instance, it lacked an actor to rival the stars of Japan or America and that, although it had been several years since the advent of sound, the industry had not yet figured out how to coordinate film with music. One of the period's leading directors, An Chong-hwa, laments the scarcity of "clean shots, backgrounds, and sets," and puts the blame on a lack of technical skill and, most especially, of a decent production studio. These failings are especially disheartening because, as Kim Yu-yŏng, another important director and screenwriter, notes, the opportunity to showcase the particular "undercurrent" (*amryu*) and "beauty" of Chosŏn film is lost because of its inability to capture that essence with any expertise. Sŏ Kwang-je, the most active and perhaps most astute participant in the group, articulates the problem as one of "sincerity," which he sees as the core of real art. Connecting the shortage in resources and technical expertise to the inability to create art, he argues that "in so many areas, everyone—directors, actors, producers—lack sincerity." The prospective venue for Chosŏn film, of course, had ostensibly expanded by this late stage of the Japanese empire to include the screens of the metropole as well as those of the old and newly acquired colonies of Taiwan and Manchuria.[24] The viewership and the proceeds promised by this fresh market were unprecedented and clearly provocative, and the conversation turns repeatedly to the question of how to "penetrate" and "pioneer" it. An Chong-hwa crystallizes the sentiments of the group when he reasons, "patriots in other countries put up huge sums of money so that their films can pioneer foreign markets; film entrepreneurs here need to be ready to make the same kind of sacrifice." He continues, energetically, that "vast improvements" in Chosŏn filmmaking could be made if only the right kind of capital was invested. Much less optimistic is Sŏ, who bleakly concludes, "there aren't any businessmen in Chosŏn."

The nature of this otherwise bland conversation becomes more interesting when we take into account the careers of its participants and the historical context of its convention. Nearly all of the group's members, with the exception of Yi Ch'ang-yong, the brash president of the Koryŏ Motion Picture Company, had all been members of the left-wing Chosŏn Film Arts League (*Chosŏn yŏnghwa yesul hyŏphoe*), the film arm of the KAPF school of the late 1920s and early 1930s. Kim Yu-yŏng had directed three of the league's five features, and An Sŏk-yŏng had written the script for one of those films (*Hwaryun*, 1931) and had worked with the likes of the writer Sim Hun on a number of enlightenment films. Perhaps more striking is Sŏ Kwang-je, who, together with Im Hwa, had been instrumental in championing Bolshevik film production and exhibition practices and who had introduced theories of Soviet montage to Chosŏn in a series of essays published in the late 1920s. All, with the exception of Kim Yu-yŏng, who died apparently of malnutrition and related kidney failure in 1940, would, by the publication of the roundtable or shortly thereafter, have their hands in the production of the promilitarist, proimperialist films that came to dominate Chosŏn cinema throughout the late 1930s and 1940s. One of the earliest iterations was Sŏ's 1938 *Military Train* (*Kun'yong yŏlch'a*), a dark and aggressively assimilationist film set in Manchuria that cast disloyalty to the imperialist mission as an unpardonable sin. An Sŏk-yŏng would direct another archetypal militarist film, *Volunteer Soldier*, but his most significant contributions to the empire lay in his leadership of important administrative bodies—for instance, the Filmmaker Competence Review Committee (*Yŏnghwa kinŭng simsa wiwŏn hoe*), which functioned to register filmmakers loyal to the empire—and in his publication of a number of writings championing cinema as an ideal tool for the promotion of the assimilationist *naesŏn-ilch'e* policy.[25]

I will not pursue the motivations or political implications of these conversions (the first of several for some such as Sŏ who, following liberation, would join and then break with the leftist Chosŏn Filmmakers League (*Chosŏn yŏnghwa tongmaeng*) to join the right-wing Film Directors' Club (*Yŏnghwa kamdok kurakbu*) and would then join the North following division in 1948) both because zealous investigations of collaboration have already been conducted elsewhere and because the question of intent lies outside the parameters of this chapter.[26] More germane to my purposes is how the language of social and political engagement is almost completely erased here and replaced with the calculation of profit and artistic merit. The historian Yi Yŏng-il characterized the output of the late 1920s and early 1930s as "Arts of Blood" and "Arts of the Soil," marking them as the heydays of nationalist agrarian revolt narratives. While there is certainly an element of overstatement here, the earnest political tendencies of films like *Arirang* and *Rudderless Ferry* and the crude socialist critique of the KAPF school are testament to that earlier period's politicization. In the 1939 roundtable, however, not a word of either anti- or proimperialist rhetoric is uttered. One of the principal aims of film production now, which will imbue Chosŏn cinema with "sincerity" and elevate it to the domain of real art, is well-executed localism—that is, the projection of the particular "undercurrent" and "beauty" of Chosŏn. It is difficult to discern in this conversation whether this aim is the means or the end itself in relation to the primary goal, the inclusion into what was widely called the "continental cinema" (*taeryuk yŏnghwa*). By 1939, two years after the formal declaration of Japanese imperial aggression and two before the implementation of wholesale imperialist assimilation policies, Chosŏn cinema's place as a peripheral region in a continuously flourishing cinematic empire was an incontestable fact. Enlightenment therein took on the form of self-ethnographic display within the films themselves, and the discourse of industrialization and continental expansion within criticism.

These arguments about art, industrialization, and ethnographic representation were made in a clearer and more sophisticated way by Im Hwa. From approximately 1936 onward, Im's writings inflect a shift toward a sustained critique of what he described as the "crudeness" and "artificiality" of the left-wing "tendency" school of theory and culture with which he was closely associated throughout the 1920s and early 1930s. In essays like "Chosŏn Cinema" ("Chosŏn munhwa ron," 1938) and the aforementioned "Treatise on Cultural Industrialization," Im signaled the obsolescence of ideologically committed movements. Im had come to accept the seeming inevitability and permanence of Japanese colonial modernity, and in particular that the task of enlightenment had been, or soon would be, completed within the new educational institutions and social development projects that were making their way even into rural areas.[27] And yet, the force and language of enlightenment had not been displaced from his arguments about culture. It had, rather, been translated from the lexicon of art and ideology to that of entertainment (*oraksŏng*) and popularity (*taejungsŏng*).[28] The task of artists and intellectuals, especially the practitioners of the cinema (which he called "the most modern of arts"), was to rise to the challenge presented by the expansion of the "continental market." And for Im this was to be accomplished through a kind of maturity, a growing out of the infancy of ideological conflict into the adulthood of self-awareness and material stability. Im's was not a facile adoption of the fascist logic of assimilation to dominant power but rather a logical working out of the problems of visibility and identity.

This translation of the terms of enlightenment discourse informs my view that enlightenment operates more diffusely and more effectively than as particular narrative forms or generic conventions, or even as pedagogic voice or sensibility. This broad distribution stems at least in part from the basic conditions of film as a medium. Lenin's early pronouncement that film was "the most important of arts" was taken seriously not only by leftists but also by the wide spectrum of practitioners, theorists, and bureaucrats who saw film's potential to inform, agitate, and guide audiences on an unprecedented scale. Further, the medium's visibility as well as its capital-intense technologies made it highly contingent on commercial and/or state investment for production, distribution, and exhibition. Finally, the easy translatability, portability, and remarkable profitability of films meant that both producers and audiences were keenly aware of developments in the style and quality of works from around the world, especially in its epicenters in the United States, Germany, and Japan. It is therefore no surprise that, although *kyemong* was rarely evoked and, as we saw above, frequently expelled from, discussions of the film industry, its codes and concerns are easily detected—most especially in anxious articulations of the desire to catch up with or match other cinemas, whether it was the centralized socialist filmmaking of the Soviet Union, or the efficiency and glamour of the Hollywood studio system. A decade before the above-cited roundtable was published, the centrist critic Pak Song focused the question of film's social responsibility and efficacy on the basic problems of finance and technology. Concerned about the relatively low quality of Chosŏn filmmaking and the fact that its products were rarely exhibited outside the major urban centers of Kyŏngsŏng, Pyongyang, and Pusan, Pak called for a wholesale "liquidation of the problems of the past." If the cinema was to be something more than "children's entertainment," he argued, the government would have to take a number of concrete measures, including the subsidization and standardization of production facilities and the formation of provincial exhibition support offices.[29] The issue was taken up in the same newspaper a year later by the socialist critic Ko Chong-ok, who claimed that the mass enlightenment potential of films was severely limited by ownership structures under Japanese control. Among a list of prescriptions (remarkably similar to Pak Song's) was Ko's call for the formation of a proletarian film production company, broad change in censorship policies, and the granting of special exhibition privileges for Chosŏn filmmaking.[30] Most observers recognized that in order for Chosŏn cinema to have significant social or political influence, it would have to overcome or at least ameliorate its absolute dependence on Japanese capital, industry, and law. In one crucial sense, the centralization of the film industry in the early 1940s destroyed these ambitions for cultural and political sovereignty. Simultaneously, it assured the film industry the capital investment and mass visibility that Pak, Ko, and the participants of the roundtable had sought.

A similar overlapping of interests arose in the early 1960s with the advent of the Park Chung Hee regime and the passing of a string of Motion Picture Laws. "Industrialization" (*kiŏp'hwa*) had become a keyword in public discussions of film in the 1950s, an era that witnessed the resurgence of commercial filmmaking following the war under a rather haphazard set of laws that focused almost exclusively on regulating content. Bemoaning the "shabby" (*ch'orahan*) look of Korean films, for instance, a December 1958 editorial in the *Kyŏnghyang Daily* suggested:

> Among the fifty or so production companies out there the only ones that show any kind of vitality are Sudo, Samsŏng, and Han'guk Yŏnye. These are the only places to find the stability and health of a real enterprise. The rest are just small-fry that make one or two films and disappear.[31]

Another editorial in the *Chosŏn Ilbo* (June 1959) noted that, "while the sheer production numbers of our film industry have shot up with astonishing speed, the preponderance of one-hit wonders [*ilsa iljak*] shows that we are still in the cradle as far as industrialization goes."[32] These feelings of inadequacy and longing tended to be expressed most forcefully on the occasions of the Asian Film Festivals, when the position of the Korean film industry could be measured more palpably against those of Hong Kong and, especially, Japan. The Motion Picture Law, passed within only four months of the coup staged in 1961 by Park's military junta and refined in 1963, aimed at a sweeping renovation of filmmaking practices. Its most obvious ideological objective was to ensure the installation of a morally and politically agreeable film culture through the creation of a stringent licensing system and the management of a film censorship committee, and further by gradually limiting the number of foreign films that had dominated the market throughout the 1950s. But the laws also dramatically, if mechanically, addressed the demand for industrialization by establishing an elaborate set of quotas for studios: for the number of films produced, the number and kind of staff employed, even the stock, grade, and quality of equipment owned and operated. The laws, in effect, mandated a studio system that, on a national scale, could rival the relative output figures of the world's leading film industries. The new regulations were met with some public outcry, especially from those (in the majority) associated with production companies that could not hope to meet the quotas. Others, such as Shin Sang-ok, who leveraged the laws to build his studio into an unrivaled power (and who was rumored to be one of the primary architects of the law itself), welcomed the legislation as a means through which to "rationalize" Korean cinema and elevate it to the "first world of filmmaking."[33] By the mid-1960s, the Korean film industry was one of the most prolific in the world, pumping out more than 140 features annually, the vast majority of which were staid genre films that presented little challenge to the status quo of economic development and industrialization.

Writing in *Film World* (*Yŏnghwa Segye*) in 1962, the director and producer Yun Pong-ch'un argued that, "we filmmakers finally have a part to play in national reconstruction. Industrialization means that we must take up our duties and make all the effort and sacrifice for the cause."[34] Popularly recognized as one of the few "patriots" that had not collaborated with the Japanese, and active throughout the 1940s and 1950s in explicitly identified enlightenment projects (under the auspices of the Enlightenment Film Association he cofounded with Pang Ŭi-sŏk in 1945), it is no surprise that the deeply conservative Yun would champion both the new film laws and the Park regime's program for "national reconstruction." Yet his linking of industrialization, nationalism, and artistic commitment is by no means idiosyncratic to the discursive field of the 1960s or any other period under consideration here. In fact, his statement efficiently captures what I see as the continuum that defines the enlightenment modality. The call for "political" filmmaking—whether for the proletarian or the imperialist cause, or framed more loosely as work that is "social" or "engaged"—has almost perpetually coexisted with the call for the improvement, expansion, and rationalization of the film industry through the support of the state. In particular moments, these interests fused, achieved a kind of hegemony, and coincided with legislation that instrumentalized cinema as a means of political and economic development. At other times, they remained autonomous and even opposed discourses, as in the mid-1950s when the "art for art's sake" principle infiltrated the film world and elevated the cultural status of "pure" cinematic works. Yet, inherent in the conceptual architecture of these discourses and in the language of their articulation are firm ideas about the role of art in political life and human subjectivity. In these otherwise diverse discussions, there is basic agreement that film has important real-world effects and that filmmakers are implicitly or explicitly accountable for the political consequences of their work. Whether the end is class-consciousness, aesthetic purity, or technical polish, film is both the active, hortatory subject of enlightenment and its passive and ethically charged object.

Enlightenment Modalized

Given that its expression tends to take the form of explicit exhortation, the enlightenment modality is relatively easy to track in critical discourse, legislative measures, and institutional forms. The manifold forces at play in film texts, however, make the task of delineating the presence and operation of that mode in filmmaking practice more challenging. Nevertheless, it is possible to glean, through even a cursory look at a broad swath of films, both the general ethos and the specific codes that structure enlightenment as a fundamental mode of Korean cinema. As we have seen, the two decades of filmmaking in the latter half of the colonial period marks the apex of the enlightenment genre, in its classical agrarian as well as in its more worldly militarist form. But on different terms and to varying degrees, the mode both predates and follows on the work of that period. The very earliest films produced in Chosŏn, in fact, were enlightenment films that were earnestly instructional and closely tied to the machinery of colonial modernization. The discussion surrounding Yun Paek-nam's *Moonlight Vow* (*Wŏlha ŭi maengsŏ*, 1923) has largely focused on the small controversy regarding its production date (and whether it, or *Border* [*Kuk'kyŏng*], another 1923 film, could be called the first natively produced Korean film), and the glamour and mystery of its lead actress, Yi Wŏl-hwa. Pushed to the fringe, thereby, is the fact that the film was funded by a grant from the Government-General's office (administered, specifically, through the postal service) and produced at least partially in the interests of promoting personal savings in the colony's newly formed banking institutions. The film concerns the prodigal Yŏng-dŭk, who is forced by his gambling debts to return from his studies in Tokyo, and the narrative turns on how the savings conscientiously invested by his fiancée's family save him from bankruptcy and enable the couple's happy marriage. Although later critics such as An Chong-hwa, who described the film as "lackluster but reasonably watchable," largely dismissed the film's quality, a contemporaneous report in the *Tonga Ilbo* noted that "the story was excellent and won great applause" and that the film's tour to advertise savings accounts would extend around Kyŏngsŏng and many of the provinces.[35] Other very early films produced by ethnic Koreans were similarly funded and produced as educational works. Some, such as *Life's Enemy: Cholera* (*Insaeng ŭi ku: hoyŏlja*, 1920), a kino-drama that compared the physical well-being of two different families, were meant to promote personal and public hygiene, while others sought to encourage the payment of taxes and promote the contracting and use of electricity. These films, of course, worked commercially through their relative novelty, by featuring fledgling stars, and through the deployment of narrative structures and genre conventions recognizable from the period's theatrical performances and dime-store novels (*sipjŏn sosŏl*). More important, they pioneered a nexus between explicit exhortation, public sponsorship, and mobile exhibition—a formula that would be exploited by left- and right-wing film organizations throughout the following decades. They also established a basic tie between modernization discourses and cinematic instruction, driving home ideological lessons through dramatic awakenings to the benefit of modern institutions and practices.

There was a resurgence of generic agrarian enlightenment films immediately following liberation in 1945. Chŏn Ch'ang-gŭn's *My Liberated Hometown* (*Haebang dŏen nae kohyang*, 1947) and Sin Kyŏng-kyun's *A New Vow* (*Saeroun maengsŏ*, 1947) followed with remarkable faithfulness the

1920s/1930s *kyemong yŏnghwa* model, only updating it with protagonists returned from labor or education in the old metropole and through more explicit declarations of the goal of national sovereignty. The different freedoms offered by liberation allowed, or perhaps mandated, the treatment of subjects and narratives theretofore barred from public expression. These were produced, moreover, by filmmakers who had spent the better part of a decade at work on various promilitarist and proassimilationist projects. Ch'oe In-gyu and his *Hurrah Freedom* (*Chayu manse*, 1947), a crude, action-filled depiction of violent anticolonial insurrection on the eve of liberation, is perhaps the most well-known case. Just as interesting, however, is the string of "national hero" films made by Chŏn Ch'ang-hwa, Ch'oe, and especially Yun Pong-ch'un. Produced under the auspices of the aforementioned Enlightenment Film Association, Yun's *The Righteous Yun Pong-gil* (*Yun Pong-gil ŭisa*, 1947), *Yu Kwan-sun* (1948), and *A Patriot's Son* (*Aegukja ŭi adŭl*, 1949) were biographies of ostensibly anti-Japanese heroes that all featured some moment of radicalization on the way toward martyrdom. Yi Yŏng-il labeled this group of postliberation films the "Cinema of Tears," calling attention to the remorse that drove the filmmakers to leverage these anticolonial narratives as testimonials to their newly (re)discovered patriotism.[36] But what is more relevant here is the continuity these films represent for the filmmakers individually and the field as a whole in this period. At the height of military mobilization, Ch'oe, Chŏn, and everyone else active in the colonial Chosŏn film industry was at work making films that almost invariably featured moments of conversion—usually a sort of ecstatic enlightenment—to the imperialist cause.[37] One may easily recall the usually sullen Ch'un-ho's reverie when he learns of the new law allowing ethnic Koreans to join the Imperial Army in *Volunteer Soldier*, or the bandits' teary vows to reform their lives in the face of Pastor Pak's generosity in *Homeless Angels.* In the more conventional agrarian films of the liberation period as well as the newly authorized heroic biographies, conversion comes as the narrative and affective high point, serving to drive home the point of personal responsibility in the midst of political transformation. Of course, it is no coincidence that, faced with the need to pledge their acquiescence to the dominant power, the filmmakers seized on conversion narratives to mirror their own transformations. But the critical point here is how the figures of conversion and instruction mediate the articulation of personal commitment in ostensibly incommensurate political environments.[38]

Here, it is now possible to submit a compressed description of the enlightenment mode in filmmaking practice: rather than being defined by a single narrative arc or stylistic trope, it informs and constitutes a range of work in a number of different genres that nonetheless come to bear on a didactic purpose, aimed at evoking some form of mass or national consciousness, leveraged through dramatic projections of awakening and conversion. A closer look at two of the dominant genres of the 1950s, the anticommunist film and the women's melodrama, will help to enliven this characterization. In the 1950s, as was hinted at in the chapter's introduction, enthusiasm for enlightenment thought faded in critical discourse. Following the brutal years between 1937 and 1953 that Yun Hae-dong has called the "trans-war period,"[39] a period that saw the maximum instrumentalization of culture on behalf of ideological conflict, the newly calm and relatively stable Republic of Korea seemed ready for a cinema, like that of Hollywood, that stressed entertainment and escape over instruction and mass appeal. Japan, imperialist aesthetics, and fascist mobilization had now been replaced as enemies by North Korea and the spread of communism, and the clear mandate of the film industry was to create pictures that could help root out the seeming vestiges of socialist sympathy. By and large the anticommunist films were generically war pictures, set either on the front lines of spectacular battle or on the home front where guerilla attack and espionage threatened to compromise security. The archetypal works of this group are Yi Kang-ch'ŏn's *P'iagol* (1955) and Han Hyŏng-mo's *Hand of Fate* (*Unmyŏng ŭi son*, 1954). The weight of propaganda in both films is placed on the depiction of the communists—the "southern partisans" of *P'iagol* and the urban spies of *Hand*—as single-mindedly ideological and brutally cold in the face of human suffering. But here again the stories turn not on external conflict but on the realizations that the protagonists come to about their allegiances and moral worth. After witnessing the horrors of partisan suspicion and violence, the once committed Lieutenant Ch'ŏl-su awakens to the emptiness and hypocrisy of the armed struggle and comes to suspect that communism is a veil for the primitive, violent impulses that are unleashed in war. Yet his realization does not drive him to the other side of the conflict. Faithful to the stark realities of the war, *P'iagol*'s only alternative space is a desert, a bleak landscape beyond the ideologically divided mountains, where Ch'ol-su collapses to close the film. Interestingly, screening of the film was halted until Yi agreed to append a final shot of the Korean flag to dispel the ambiguity apparently created by the film's unflinching realism and to verify its nationalist and anticommunist credentials. Critics have taken this as bitter proof of *P'iagol*'s transcendence of simplistic propaganda and argued for its inclusion in the small pantheon of modernist art films.[40] But whether we see the film finally as a veiled pacifist work or as a failed anticommunist film, it is clear that its affective core is conditioned by the enlightenment mechanisms sketched above. Indeed this very ambivalence is a telling sign of the salience of the enlightenment mode in both propagandistic "policy" pieces and modernist art films.

In the period's other dominant form, which Han Hyŏng-mo was to pioneer, the figure of conversion is also fundamental to the generic structure. The women's melodrama of the late 1950s was arguably one of the most important and influential of the period's mass cultural products. Following the transwar period that had expanded the workforce to include great numbers of women and within a cultural sphere that was inundated with the discourse of Western democracy and gender equality, women and women's sexuality became the most pressing social issue, covered thickly in newspapers, magazines, and all other media. Women, mostly middle-aged and urban, were also the dominant group among film audiences, and they made huge successes of films focused on women, relationships, and family in the face of postwar modernity. Many of these films, including at least four "Ch'unhyang" adaptations, as well as contemporary works like Shin Sangok's *Tongsimch'o* (1959), featured women as beleaguered keepers of neo-Confucian virtue and righteousness. But the most popular and socially significant films were the fallen women narratives like *Beautiful Femme Fatale* (*Arŭmdaun aknyŏ*, 1957), the "confession" cycle (*Confessions of a College Girl, Confessions of an Actress, Confessions of the Flesh*, etc.), and, especially, Han's sensational *Madame Freedom* (*Chayu puin*, 1956). These maudlin and intensely alluring films followed middle- or upper-class women as they discovered the pleasures of Western dress, crowded cafés, and dance halls and found independence from traditional family life. The films in a sense conspire with this "fall," taking in the fascination with foreign commodities and smooth-talking men to project a landscape of, in the vernacular of the day, the "*seryŏn*," or modern refinement. But at the same time they are moral lessons, elaborate illustrations of the pitfalls of sexual and social freedom. O Sŏn-yŏng, the liberated woman of Han's iconic film, is forced to confront both the duplicity of the elegant men she meets and the dead-end criminality of the women who offer her economic freedom. The film's final sequence follows her remorseful return to the family home, where she must beg to be allowed to return to the enclosure and servitude of domesticity. And *Madame Freedom* underscores the point that this final conversion, or perhaps reversion, is not only an individual or family issue, but one that has far-reaching national consequences. O Sŏn-yŏng's withdrawal from the English-slinging

Ch'un-ho and his Latin-esque dance halls and return to her *hanbok, hanok*, and *Han'guk hak* professor husband must be made for the sake of the child, the innocent son caught between these worlds. Whether this conversion, among the others that abruptly mark the conclusions of so many of the era's "dangerous women" pictures, is enough to displace the allure of the fall that precedes it is beside the point here (this question is taken up more directly in the next chapter). More relevant here is how these awakenings to moral righteousness and cultural tradition are anticipated as each film starts, built as they are into the structure of these particular melodramatic forms as well as the gendered script of social progress.

The first half of the 1960s witnessed a sort of renaissance of the classical enlightenment film that was directly tied to the Park administration and its appropriation of the discourse of democratic revolution. Films like Pak Chong-ho's *Lovers of the Land* (*Kŭ ttang ŭi yŏnindŭl*, 1963), Han Hong-yŏl's *Hŭksan Island* (*Hŭksando*, 1963), and Yu Hyŏn-mok's *The Sun Rises Again* (*T'aeyang ŭn tasi ttŭnda*, 1966) projected rural poverty and backwardness as a problem that could be solved through education and selfless labor. The most iconic of these were Shin Sang-ok's series of enlightenment films, the aforementioned *Evergreen, Rice* (*Ssal*, 1963), and *Mountain* (*San*, 1967), in which the agency of development and modernization is figured as the newly remasculinzed, militarist state. I will take up this body of work in detail in chapter 3. I want to close this exploration by thinking about a radically different set of films that were widely seen as being antithetical to the earnestness of the new enlightenment work. From about the mid-1960s to the early 1970s, when Korean cinema saw its productive peak and the Park administration's machinery of industrial development and social discipline was most assured, the Manchurian action picture arose as a major genre that proved to be reliably popular at the box office. Modeled loosely on the Italian "spaghetti westerns" made famous by Sergio Leone and set in the Manchurian wilderness settled by ethnic Koreans in the colonial period, films like Im Kwon-taek's *Farewell to the Tumen River* (*Tuman kang'a chal itkkŏra*, 1962), Shin Sang-ok's *The Wanderer* (*Musukja*, 1968), and Kim Yŏng-ho's *One-Armed Man of the Wilds* (*Hwangya ŭi woep'ari*, 1970) featured men with guns roaming the plains on horseback or by rail in search of riches and revenge. Crude, violent, and action-packed, the films were regularly derided as the antithesis of art, even as they proved staples for the many vertically integrated studios that produced them. *One-Armed Man*, an adaptation of Akira Kurosawa's *Yojimbo*, narrates the protagonist's attempts to leverage the blood feud between a town's ethnic Chinese gang lords to earn gold and enact justice. It is especially bombastic in its virtually nonstop gunfights, chase sequences, and countless backhanded face slaps. A number of critics have argued that, despite their apparent crudity and escapism, these films were in fact eminently political in their engagement with colonial conflict and social justice. Perhaps the most astute assessment is offered by Jinsoo An, who suggests that the genre, or cycle, embodies the "irredentist" ambitions of the historiography favored by the Park regime and, further, that in their depiction of morally ambivalent bandits who ultimately find redemption in alignment with the fight for independence—usually by turning over an object (a map, say, or money) to the independence fighters—the Manchurian action film "speaks of the romantic dream of reclamation and repossession of the land that is thoroughly engrained in the discourse of anti-Japanese nationalism . . . through perpetual recourse to generic imagination of military campaigns, espionage campaigns, and dream for the frontier."[41] The point is indisputable, I think, turning as it does on a commitment to mapping the political unconscious of even the most degraded popular cultural forms.

Yet, I want to argue that the politics of the Manchurian films do not lie solely or even primarily in the act of consciously or unconsciously articulating ostensibly political desires. Rather, it is in their invocation of the language and style of instruction and conversion that these films find their closest *analogy* with politics. *One-Armed Man* ends, as so many other Manchurian action films do, with the protagonist redeemed by his conversion to the nationalist cause. In a painfully long sequence, Jin-p'yo, a ruthless gang leader, is gunned down and with his dying breath reveals to Han, the one-armed man, that he had been, despite his reprehensibly traitorous actions, an independence sympathizer all along. Enemies to that point, the two gunfighters bluster through a tearful reconciliation over their newly discovered tie as ethnic Korean fellow travelers. The argument can very easily be made that these mostly abrupt and banal conclusions are either merely the means through which producers won the approval of state censors for otherwise politically sensitive films (we might think back to *P'iagol* here), or that they are only the guilty conscience of opportunistic filmmakers put to work on the least respected of genre pictures. I am, in fact, in agreement with the terms of these arguments, though not their tenor. Instead of assessing them in pejorative terms, it seems far more productive to think about the hackneyed and moralizing inversions in the Manchurian films, and indeed in many of the films I have examined heretofore, in the more specific context of aesthetic value. The invocation, assumption, and articulation of the enlightenment mode in films, whether frighteningly earnest or transparently opportunistic, is the very means by which films gain legitimacy as art and visibility as cultural artifacts. In each of its iterations, whether as a primitivist awakening to the political primacy of the peasant or the masculinist disciplining of "Americanized" sexuality, the figure of conversion to some form of mass consciousness corresponded to a primary aesthetic precept—that art is responsible to politics—that ensured legibility and relevance as mass cultural performances. In seemingly vacuous commercial features or their ostensible obverse, self-consciously modernist art films, the enlightenment mode was a forceful, if sometimes disingenuous, gesture of artistic seriousness and depth. Amid the wild discontinuities of twentieth-century Korean history, the enlightenment mode has been central and continuous not only, or even primarily, because it delivered political exhortation in a dramatic way, but also because of its easy translatability and the immanent capital of its signifying codes.

REGIMES WITHIN REGIMES

Film and Fashion in the Korean 1950s

Exposition

The topos of Im Ŭng-sik's iconic 1956 photograph "Early Summer, Midopa" is apparently clear: the weight of traditional Korean cultural practice is giving way to the lightness of Western lifestyle (Figure 2). The keenness of what Roland Barthes called the photo's *punctum*—that is, the deeply affective register of an image—is driven home by the seeming distress that passes on the face of the woman in the foreground: she is nearest to us, but in the burgeoning consumer culture epitomized in the scene's Western goods stores (Midopa was at the time Seoul's largest department store), she has already faded. The ascendant icon now is the almost ethereal figure of the lady of leisure, protected from the sun by her parasol, embedded in the newly scrubbed city streets (the way the patterned dresses echo the street's tiling). "Early Summer" seems to present us with an emblem of "Americanization," a compressed rendering of the classic tropes, replete with gender and class antagonisms, of cultural imperialism. But in fact the image's semantic coordinates are far from obvious. The intrusion of Western clothing, so often embodied (but rarely so artfully) in precisely this juxtaposition of women's figures, is of course a ceaselessly deployed sign of cultural loss and transformation. As such, on those terms alone the scene is difficult to date—that is, until we look with some care at the clothes themselves and see not simply the generic *yangjang–hanbok* dichotomy, but rather the bold floral prints and flared lines of the young women's dresses. To even an amateur student of fashion flows, these styles follow lines of adoption from American fashions of the 1950s, and therein to the vast apparatus of postwar occupation and Cold War containment. The image's *studium*, Barthes's complementary term for the sociocultural import of pictures, is not defined without this sense of clothing's timeliness; in this respect the clothing's historicity is itself the photo's *studium*.

But this historicity is not the photograph's critical subject. Rather, it is the woman in the foreground, in particular her clothes, that begs a closer look. For, of course, her *hanbok* is not some timeless "traditional" vestment but rather the subject of tremendous social, cultural, and political investment, regulation, and even caprice. One can think of course of the radical changes mandated in the 1894 Kabo Reforms, that frantic attempt to mark out a bulwark of Korean modernity, staked in part on a more enlightened system of dress. But more germane here is the way *hanbok* were charged with heterogeneous interest and meaning throughout the postwar era. The foregrounded woman's "early summer" dress is translucent and light, likely stitched of newly developed nylon, and the *chŏgori* short; its line is economic and its ornamentation almost nonexistent: an irreducible product of modern capital and its demand for efficiency. In the winter the outfit would appropriate another new material, velvet, to extravagant effect. The woman is therefore not as behind, and the young women not as far in the vanguard, as the photo might suggest at first blush. The image, characteristic

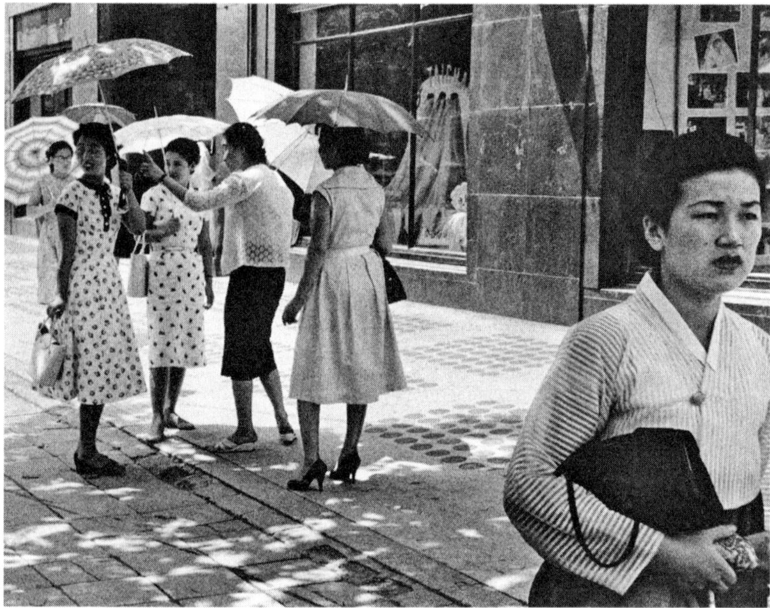

Figure 2. "Early Summer, Midopa." Photograph by Im Ŭng-sik (1956), courtesy of EuroCreon.

of a core cultural discourse of the 1950s, Americanization, is thus rather more complex and points to the multiple "systems" at play in the period. And here, it is fashion, in its traverse and ephemeral detail as much as its contingent materiality, that is the prompt for a more careful and flexible cultural history.

One of my aims in this chapter is to read Shin Sang-ok's work through the dominant codes of image production in film, fashion, and print that so acutely expressed the layered ontologies and trajectories that belie the discourse of Americanization in 1950s South Korea. I am prompted first by the period's critical though often undertheorized position in conceptualizing political transformation in modern Korea. In the overt simplifications of thinking culture in decades—in which, say, the 1930s immediately evokes urban modernism, or the 1970s calls to mind the sterility of the arts under authoritarian surveillance—the 1950s are particularly fraught with contradiction. Second, the period's meaning is also among the more ideologically staked. For the liberal political scientists writing with some despair in the latter part of the decade as well as for the ideologues rationalizing military intervention in the 1960s, the years following the war were characterized by corruption, betrayal, and retrogression. The porosity of the nation's cultural borders and the seeming ubiquity of American commodities and everyday practices were projected as emblems of the era's problems. More recently, the 1950s have come to be revised within postcolonial and feminist criticism as a period of cultural and social radicalization, throwing into even greater relief the militarized order of the periods that sandwich it. But neither this opposition nor its consequences for historiography or social analysis present any real hermeneutic obstacle. Rather, it is the intellectual habit attached to periodization, abstract teleology, that threatens a clear vision of the cultural landscape of the 1950s. For, in many politicized accounts, the 1950s marks the nadir of national independence and strength, the point from which to draw a straight line of economic and cultural development.

I am prompted here also by the fraught role of visual surfaces, embodied most overtly in fashion and film, in reading Korea's cultural discourses and diagnosing its location within global cultural circulation. As a first step, I might simply note that while the extant historiography of the period has pointed consistently to the close and revealing relationship between film and literature, film's nexus with fashion is equally illuminating. This is not only because the two forms were instrumental in shifting mass cultural sensibility palpably toward the visual, but also, as I will detail below, because the incipient state of both industries in the 1950s meant that cooperation and cross-pollination were inevitable. Filmmaking and its extensive promotional apparatus became the best way to see the latest fashions, and fashion became a crucial means through which to emulate and embody the roles and fantasies films inspired. And it is precisely this mutual productivity that highlights the centrality of film and fashion to not only cultural but also political transformation. For, as many have noted, clothing functions as a key site in contests for power in the way, on the one hand, that it can enforce discipline (i.e., school and military uniforms), mark social class, and sediment gender roles and, on the other, signal political opposition and symbolize social nonconformity. Watching films and consuming fashions in Korea, then, can be read as practices that exemplified apathy and enabled hopeless social pretension but that also facilitated modes of thinking and inhabiting social space differently. This is partly an effect of the psychic identifications central to both fashion and film: as Kaja Silverman reminds us, for Freud, "the ego is 'a mental projection of the surface of the body,' and that surface is largely defined through dress."[1] But perhaps more critically, it stems from the disavowing temporality that Barthes persuasively argued is fashion's defining feature: "As soon as the signified *Fashion* encounters a signifier (such and such a garment), the sign becomes the year's Fashion, but thereby this Fashion dogmatically rejects the Fashion which preceded it, its own past; every new Fashion is a refusal to inherit, a subversion against the oppression of the preceding Fashion; Fashion experiences itself as a Right, the natural right of the present over the past."[2] This willed amnesia and ephemerality, as I will attempt to argue below, belies the very historicity of the images of refinement and polish that dominate visual mass cultures of the 1950s.

Beginnings

Shin Sang-ok's 1958 *Hellflower* (*Chiok'hwa*) opens with an arresting visualization of postwar Seoul. Tong-sik is just up from the country and lost in the chaos of the cars and people blurring past the train station. He has come to find his prodigal older brother, but his bag is promptly stolen by grim-faced thugs and he is left to wander aimlessly. The scene is intercut with stark documentary footage of dusty streets, crowded markets, and strolling American soldiers, announcing the film's neorealist style. When the camera turns to Tong-sik, it frames him in low angles and long field depth, embedding his humble figure in a faceless, featureless urban space. He somehow manages to spot his brother, Yŏng-sik, and calls out to him, but his brother, in fashionable fedora and flowing linen suit, inexplicably runs off and melts into the crowd. The scene shifts to a strange interior space hung with gauzy curtains and sparsely furnished with a shabby bed and table. Sonia emerges from a back room to help an American GI with his shirt. Giggling softly, she does up a few of his buttons, tells him to come back soon, and sees him out. She then turns languidly to her room, switches on a fan, has a sip of water, and lingers by the bed, humming an enigmatic tune. Her figure is striking: she is dressed in a silky, black halter-top dress, she has a dark mole on her upper lip, and her long hair falls past her shoulders in luxurious curls. She is a base camp prostitute, a "Western princess" (*yanggongju*), one of thousands who serviced American soldiers and anchored the parallel (black) economy of the postwar occupation. And yet everything in Ch'oe Ŭn-hŭi's embodiment of Sonia signals that she is something more than the *yanggongju*; she inhabits the seedy, makeshift brothel but is not of it, leaping out of that space with an abstract, lurid intensity. While Tong-sik and Yŏng-sik are entrenched in the brutal materiality of modern Seoul, Sonia is aloof from it.

The opening scenes of another Shin film from the same period, his 1959 *Sisters' Garden* (*Chamae ŭi hwawŏn*), renders a similar kind of aloofness within a radically different kind of social space. The setting is some bucolic riverside forest, the tall, lush greens dappling the river rocks in shade and framing the action in an ideal repose. Myŏng-hŭi, fitted in an expensive white dress, glows against this background as she poses coyly for a portrait. The dashing painter, Tong-su, with a wild coif and open shirt, applies a few strokes to his canvas and teases Myŏng-hŭi about her pretty smile. Off in the distance, closer to the water, Chŏng-hŭi, elegantly made up in her own summer dress, tends to the picnic fire, the steam from the rice pot billowing around her. The leisure and privilege of the sisters and their suitor are signaled by their clothes and hair, underscored in the luminous glow they exude in these shots, but it is also formalized in the scene's isolated time space, unfolding as a romance linked neither to the country nor to the city, and far removed from the vagaries of war and reconstruction. The sisters are called back to reality when they get word that their father has fallen ill, but the scene has already established the film's aesthetic tone—its removal from everyday reality—as well as its object of sumptuous distraction—the modern woman.

The last of Shin's 1950s melodramas, *It's Not Her Sin* (*Kŭ yŏja ŭi choega anida*, 1959), also quickly pronounces its dissociation from the everyday. Here the departure is realized not only through the sensationalization of the modern woman, though, as in *Hellflower* and *Sisters' Garden*, the shine of Western fashions and commodities is an integral part of the film's visual texture. Rather, the line of flight out of the quotidian is oriented in the way the story, taken up in medias res, is overtly coded in the language of an explicitly foreign film genre. While *It's Not Her Sin*'s thematic core is the predicament of women (especially mothers) in biased social and legal systems, its immediately announced generic mode and visual style is that of the film noir, the femme fatale, and the hard-boiled detective. Yŏng-suk gets out of a taxi at the Ministry of Foreign Affairs and begins to climb the steps to its offices; Sŏng-hŭi follows out of her own cab and pleads with Yŏng-suk to wait. In her haste, she drops her purse and a pistol falls out. When Yŏng-suk shows no signs of stopping, Sŏng-hŭi takes aim and shoots her; Yŏng-suk twists slowly and crumples to the floor. The formulaic sequence, captured in a series of dramatic pans and lurid close-ups, is capped by spinning newspaper headlines publicizing the scandalous though still unexplained crime. The film's opening thus initiates a mystery narrative that will be resolved through the course of police interrogation, confession, and flashback. It also advertises itself as contemporary to the stylized conventions of world cinema—an advance, however awkward or uncanny in effect, on the traditional melodrama/*sinp'a* form.

These films were part of a cycle produced in the latter half of the 1950s—the heyday of what might be called classical Korean melodrama. The key components of these films were standardized in Han Hyŏng-mo's iconic 1956 *Madame Freedom* (*Chayu puin*): a contemporary, largely affluent, setting; a new/tempted/fallen woman narrative; a highly stylized formal mode that actively fetishized women, commodities, and the new. This form of visualizing postwar Korea is bracketed here for what it can tell us about the complex historical moment of the late 1950s, squeezed between the turmoil of the immediate postwar years and the rigid order of the coming authoritarian period. But more important perhaps, the striking, often enigmatic spectacle projected in these films opens a space through which to ground the study of Korean cinema in a more probing theoretical treatment of visuality, mass culture, and global image production. Film critics and historians regularly call attention to the foreign influence in this body of films, tracing it to the overwhelming pressure of American culture and Korea's predicament as a client state.[3] They also argue that the powerful fantasy element of the films' extravagant surfaces reflects the desire to imaginatively, if not literally, escape the material deprivations of postwar reconstruction. These assertions about the encroachment of American mass culture in the postwar period are important and largely correct. However, it seems clear that the alien, escapist spectacle that emerges from these films is too protean to have been produced within a linear and unilateral plane of cultural influence. A wider, intermedial cultural history that takes into account the complex processes of the shift from colonial to Cold War regimes as well as of the array of cultural discourses (literary, neoliberal, or otherwise) surrounding film production is necessary to account for what was happening on screens and in theaters in the 1950s.

Concretely, this chapter pursues three interrelated questions. The first is about the specific kinds of images that circulated in the late 1950s. The tacit assumption here is that what people were seeing, not only in theaters, but also in newspapers and magazines, in cafés and dance halls, and on the streets, was functionally, if not qualitatively, new. The second is concerned with how to account for the appearance and disappearance of those visual forms. Broad historical trends that might have conditioned the production and restriction of the kinds of figures, forms, and stories that were projected, printed, and told will be the primary focus here, but the investigation will of necessity look both to the more specific changes within the film industry and the more elusive shifts in sociocultural memory, nostalgia, and desire. The third question is more speculative, seeking to address the very nature of the image in postwar Korea and its relationship to social and political change. In the course of tracing this problem, I examine the economic and cultural transactions that drove the fashion and popular print industries as well as the troubled, often contradictory public responses to which they gave rise. The chapter's overarching aim, however, is an analysis of the assemblage and projection of the era's fashions, faces, and consumer objects in Shin Sang-ok's work that builds toward an argument that these images, in spite of their oftentimes explicit disavowal of the enlightenment modality examined in the previous chapter, constitute a form of political expression.

It was only in the very last years of the decade that Shin, building on Han's example, made a name for himself with a remarkable series of contemporary, woman-centered melodramas: *Confessions of a College Girl* (*Ŏnŭ yŏdaesaeng ŭi kobaek*) and *Hellflower* in 1958 and *Sisters' Garden, It's Not Her Sin, Ch'un-hŭi,* and *Tongsimch'o* in 1959. At the root of this early success was a consolidation of three key factors of the film industry—the genre, studio, and star systems. The woman-centered melodrama superseded the other major genres of the period—the anticommunist film and the historical epic—hitting home with the largely middle-aged female film audiences. While the advent of a full-scale Shin Films studio would have to wait until 1960, regular staff and funding sources were already established for these films under the auspices of Shin-managed ventures like Seoul Film Productions and Shin Sang-ok Productions. And though she had made her debut in the late 1940s and had begun working with Shin in the early 1950s, Ch'oe Ŭn-hŭi only became a bona fide star with these films. This systematization of film production and the targeting of female audiences in Shin's films were crucial elements in the development of a new form of film spectatorship in the immediate postwar period. Together they informed the local articulation of what Miriam Hansen has called "vernacular modernism."[4] The cinema in postwar South Korea offered an accessible form of entertainment and public gathering that was more fully integrated with the everyday lives of people in both the city and the country than was the colonial cinema or, arguably, any other mass cultural form. At the same time, the cinema played a key role in mediating public discourses on modernity and enlightenment, performing self-consciously modern and cosmopolitan subjectivities in their narratives of personal transformation and social mobility. But perhaps the most radical effect of the new film cultures was to encourage the eye to process in a different manner, to wander in and out of narrative depth and to simultaneously "hover over the surface of images" and "fixate on details." The stylization of images printed in magazines and on posters and projected on screens coincided with and sometimes crystallize what Mary Ann Doane has called a voracious "consumerist glance"[5]; therein, they also articulated the liberatory-utopian promises of postwar reconstruction.

Refinement

There were certainly other spaces and media that provoked or accommodated socially significant visual phenomena in the 1950s. In South Korea, as in so many other countries rebuilding after the midcentury wars, the rapid transformation of cities, the influx of foreign capital and commodities, and the intensification of mass consumption patterns rendered myriad social spaces—from the intimate enclosures of stylish new cafes to the wide-open streets and public parks—as sites of spectacle and visual consumption. New modes of carriage and the new figures themselves (the modern, or, more specifically, "après-guerre" boys and girls) became forms of spectacle and entertainment themselves, the subject of countless reports in news media, both admonishing and celebratory, and engendered the popular pastime of people watching. Nevertheless, the cinema was the dominant medium of mass entertainment and consumption, carrying as it had the powerful investments of state-sponsored filmmaking from the colonial period as well as the "soft" dimension of the postwar American presence. Cinema dominated mass culture not only in unprecedented box office attendance but also by radically reshaping the visual landscape in the diffuse networks through which its promotion and development operated. A number of slick film magazines, which I will examine below, appeared that created a new language of faces and personas. Film celebrity, latent throughout the colonial and immediate postwar periods, advanced through its coupling with print and radio media and through the mobilization of film stars on behalf of commercial as well as governmental interests.[6] The cinema became a powerful social engine in the late 1950s in South Korea when the nation, in the early throes of reconstruction, became more fully integrated with the apparatuses of the world capitalist economy. And while the bulk of this proliferation centered on Hollywood filmmaking, the machinery of production systemization, promotion, and marketing also found an important outlet in Korean cinema.

The film industry as a whole, however, was in the 1950s largely decentralized and fluid: most films were produced by one-off partnerships rather than through established studios. "Rational" and vertically integrated production systems would not appear until they were mandated by the mechanical policies that accompanied the advent of Park Chung Hee's authoritarian developmentalist regime in the early 1960s.[7] The period's generic output was also relatively uneven (the only effective top-down controls worked to censor threats to Syngman Rhee's leadership and the promotion of communist sympathy), though the prevailing filmmaking idiom was historical epics, family and women's melodramas, and urban petit-bourgeois comedies. If there was a dominant figure in the period, it was Han Hyŏng-mo, who made a string of box-office hits throughout the mid- to late 1950s, including the aforementioned and sensational *Madame Freedom*, which capitalized on the anxiety and excitement elicited by the period's radically shifting social values. Han's success, however, depended just as much on the polished stylization of his work, which often featured seemingly superfluous vignettes that highlighted in meticulous form the era's hottest stars and fashions. The long mambo performance in *Madame Freedom*'s dancehall sequence, in which the eponymous protagonist's gaze is glued to a dancer's gyrations, is perhaps the most iconic instance of Han's characteristic spectacle. It is repeated, however, in small form in many of his lesser-known works, such as the striking wide-framing of the glamorous publishing office in *Female Boss* (*Yŏsajang*, 1959), and, perhaps most conspicuously, in the montage sequence of *Pure Love Chronicle* (*Sun'aebo*, 1957) in which the buxom lead changes into one voguish bathing suit after another in search of the man who saved her from drowning (Figure 3). As we have seen, Shin Sang-ok produced work in a similar vein, setting films in contemporary, urban, and largely affluent settings, and maximizing the allure of the vast array of consumer commodities regularly paraded on screen.

The social significance of these films lies of course in the way they manage the predicament of women in the aftermath of war and the sweeping transformations of capitalist modernity. And the bulk of scholarship has rightly concentrated on these themes.[8] But while these symptoms are undeniably compelling, the works by Han, Shin, and a small handful of other filmmakers possess another quality that is crucial to the cultural history that is being attempted here: their technical polish. On a basic level, the films demonstrate a quiet but obvious command over the basic apparatus of filmmaking. The lighting is consistent, rarely under- or overexposed, and is often used for dramatic effect. Editing is also relatively seamless, largely free of the jarring cuts and perplexing gaps that marred many contemporaneous films. And sound is efficiently controlled, with accurate post production dubbing and surreptitiously modulated music levels. In other words, everything in conventional filmmaking is in place. The point of drawing attention to the technical competence of these films, however, is not to advance Han or Shin's excellence as auteurs. Rather, it serves as a way of touching on the material history and significance of technical competence itself and also as a way of thinking through the conditions for the kinds of visuality that are the theme of this chapter. In an interview conducted in the late 1990s, Shin referred to the liberation and immediate postwar periods as "the point where whether you could see or whether you could hear was the real challenge in filmmaking."[9] The pertinence of his assertion is confirmed by even the most rudimentary scan of work from the late colonial period to the 1950s. Whereas many of the "cooperation" films of the early 1940s are strikingly accomplished productions, the films made in the decade following the collapse of colonial power are crude and cheap by contrast.[10] It was only in the mid-1950s, with the merging of a number of factors, that more advanced problems of "seeing and hearing" were solved in South Korean filmmaking. These factors included the incipient circulation of private capital, the rapid resuscitation of filmgoing culture and markets, and the consolidation of regular, if somewhat disorganized, film production companies. Another critical part of this development was, of course, the training and experience many younger filmmakers received

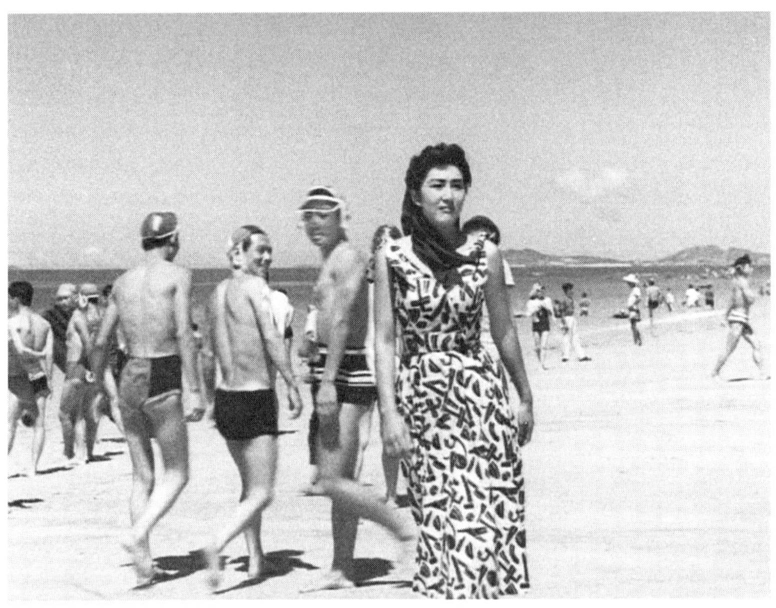

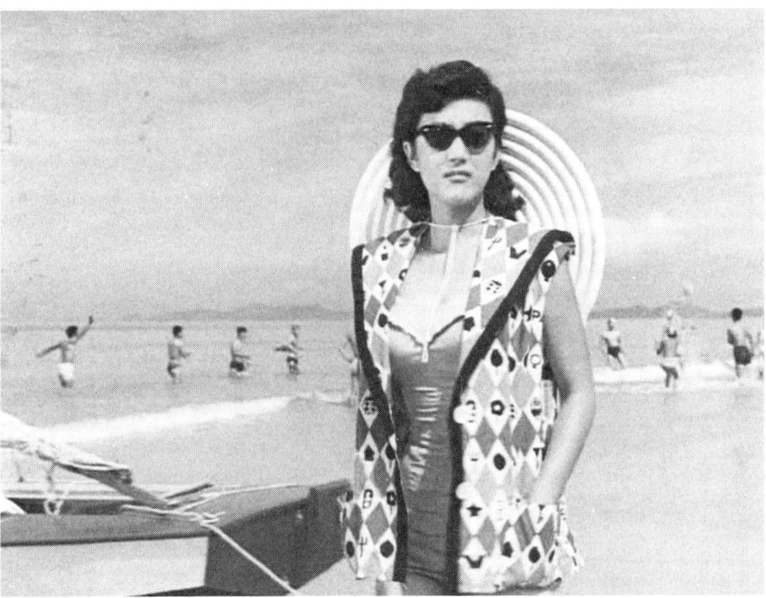

Figure 3. Beach fashions in *Pure Love Chronicle* (Han Hyŏng-mo, 1957). Courtesy of the Korean Film Archive.

under the auspices of American information services. In fact, many of the leading directors of the next decades—Han and Shin, as well as Hong Sŏng-gi and Yi Hyŏng-p'yo—either got their start as directors or first accessed the latest equipment and techniques through these agencies.[11] Additionally, many of the films produced in the immediate postwar years were captured using equipment borrowed, stolen, or otherwise procured through American information and other agencies. The latter half of the 1950s then is the moment that these young directors declared their independence; theirs was not solely or even primarily a political freedom, but a kind of artisanal autonomy, one they exercised by shooting refined—or, in the idiom of the day, "*seryŏn doen*"—pictures.[12]

The roots of this refinement and technical expertise are most easily found in the overwhelming influence of American cultural and technological imports—a situation perhaps best illustrated by the fact that until the restrictions mandated by the First Motion Picture Law in 1961, upward of three-quarters of the films being screened at any given time were Hollywood products. But the 1950s followed sufficiently closely on the heels of the long colonial period that its vestiges, in concrete as well as abstract form, could not be effectively erased, despite the measures taken by successive governments to stanch the flow of Japanese popular culture into Korea. In fact it is precisely these measures—specifically the ban on Japanese films—that enabled a particularly robust form of cultural importation: plagiarism. As Jinsoo An and others have reminded us, 30 percent to 50 percent of the films produced as late as 1962 were thought to be copies or adaptations of Japanese films.[13] In a range of interviews conducted for the Korean Film Archive's oral history project, scores of filmmakers—from prominent directors such as Im Kwon-taek and Yi Hyŏng-p'yo to lesser-known producers like Hwang Nam—testify to the rabid interest in the workings of the Japanese film industry, facilitated through the smuggling of films, scripts, and film magazines (in particular, the professional journal *Eiga Gijutsu* [*Film Technology*], later renamed *Eiga Terebi Gijutsu* [*Film and Television Technology*], the official organ of the Motion Picture and Television Engineering Society of Japan).[14] This close and covert study was driven in large part by the shock of witnessing what is popularly considered the golden age of Japanese cinema in the 1950s, jumpstarted as much by the international acclaim won by Kurosawa's 1950 *Rashomon* and Ozu's 1953 *Tokyo Story* as by the sensational success of the "sun tribe" cycle of the late 1950s. But it was also mediated by the living heritage of filmmakers—stitched closely together by the predominant "master-apprentice" training system of the postwar film industry—that stretched back far into the hey-day of filmmaking in the 1920s and 1930s. It must suffice here to note merely that Ch'oe In-gyu, whom Shin Sang-ok and others credited for doing the most to solve the "seeing and hearing" problems before the war in the late 1940s, advanced his craft under Japanese directors such as Imai Tadashi and in turn trained some of the next generation's leading filmmakers before his alleged capture by the North during the war. The point here is not to question the originality of the early years of Korean film or the nationalist credentials of its practitioners—that argument is made earnestly elsewhere.[15] Rather, it is to call attention to the diffuse and often confused streams of influence, envy, memory, and even nostalgia for Japan that existed alongside the novel stimulus exercised by American cultural power.

Similar cross-purposes and heritages obtain in the fledgling fashion industry of the 1950s. As noted above, the film and fashion industries were closely tied. The refinement and allure of films like Yi Yong-min's *Seoul Holiday* (*Sŏul ŭi hyuil*, 1956) or Shin's *Sisters' Garden* turn largely on their impeccable costuming. The men are invariably dressed in the crisp, fitted suits and narrow ties that echo the French more than the American vogue, lending them the air of the modern intellectual or playboy rather than the salary men or family men that would dominate later filmmaking. But it is of course the women for whom clothing mattered most. They are graced in an often stunning series of the latest fashions: close-fitting suits with oversized buttons, flared skirts that float up with the subtlest movement, sleek black cocktail dresses with extravagant boas. Here, too, it is the French couture of Audrey Hepburn and Givenchy more than the glamour of Marilyn Monroe that is the informing principle. Much of the clothing was designed or pieced together by Nora Noh, an independent designer who had organized some of the earliest runway shows in Korea and who, according to Shin Sang-ok, "was really the only one then who could be called a designer."[16] The intimate linking of fashion and film is hinted at in *Sisters' Garden* where the painter Tong-su (or rather the actor Nam-Kung Wŏn) is captured, in striking footage of the public event, among photographers and other spectators watching models walking in a runway show (Figure 4). It is a striking scene that calls to mind the fact that the leading faces in fashion magazines and runway shows were not professional models but rather film actresses like Ch'oe Ŭn-hŭi, Kim Chi-mi, and Ŏm Aeng-nan.

In fact, the mid-1950s marked the complex beginnings of a fashion industry that cannot be adequately understood through an Americanization framework. Clearly, the massive U.S. military and cultural presence

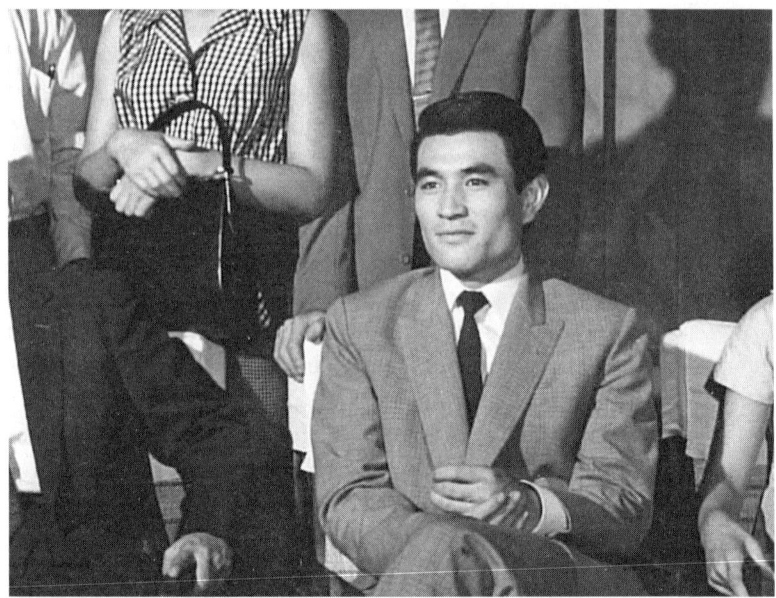

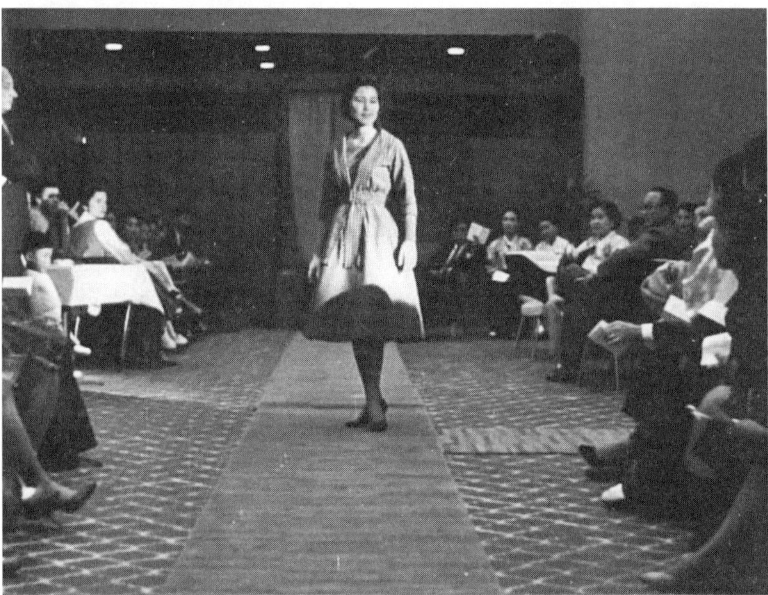

Figure 4. Tong-su takes in the runway show in *Sisters' Garden* (Shin Sang-ok, 1959). Courtesy of the Korean Film Archive.

was crucial. American synthetics like the aforementioned nylon swept into the South following the war, augmenting production efficiency and under-girding both practical clothing (underwear and work uniforms that were durable and easy to clean) and more extravagant dress (scandalously trans-parent blouses that moved like silk). American capital and expertise also facilitated, as it did in so many sectors, the growth of the textile industry, subsidizing, for instance, the incorporation in 1954 of Cheil Mojik, the ROK's first textile company, which would anchor the light industrial sectors that spurred economic development throughout the late 1950s and 1960s.[17] During and shortly after the war, American charity organizations, bring-ing remnant and secondhand clothing in bulk from the United States, would function as a first contact point between many Koreans and Western fashions[18]—a sort of Trojan horse for the import-substitution strategy that would dictate consumption patterns throughout the 1950s. And more insid-iously, the sex workers or "Western princesses" who thrived on the perim-eters of U.S. military installations became vanguards of Western fashion, fostering a secondary industry of itinerant peddlers or *pottari changsu*, who would source American clothes to market at base camps.

But the lines of material importation and aesthetic circulation spilled beyond the borders of the U.S.–ROK dyad. Ch'oe Kyŏng-ja, who opened International Western Clothes (*Kukje yangjangsa*), one of the first and by far the most renowned Western clothing stores in Myŏngdong in 1954, had started her career in Hamhŭng, and then in Pyongyang, learning her craft from and making modern clothes for the considerable Japanese population there through the latter half of the colonial period.[19] After a brief stint in Taegu during the war, Ch'oe became, alongside Nora Noh, the premier cloth-ier to celebrities and went on to found the Ch'oe Kyŏng-ja Fashion Research Institute, dedicated to training designers to meet flourishing demand. In June 1955, Ch'oe, Sŏ Su-yŏng, and other industry players founded the Korean Fashion Federation (*Taehan poksik yŏn'gu hoe*) (later, and to this day, Korean Clothing Designers Federation), a comprehensive organization that included and regulated fields as diverse as flower arrangement, woodworking, and doll making. One of its key early measures was the regularization of fashion and textiles terminology, which to that point was saturated with Japanese. But rather than simply eliminating the so-called loan words altogether, the organization sought to standardize *Han'gŭl* renderings for the vocabulary worth preserving and replace outdated terminology with English or Korean alternatives. Another core initiative was the concerted study of a Japanese fashion industry that, as in its film counterpart, alarmed watchers because of the speed with which it expanded and diversified. Again, federation members found routes around the import ban by smuggling, through third-party nations and international fashion events, Japanese magazines, patterns, and articles that could be used as models for the burgeoning domestic industry.[20]

So while American fashions were indeed the most visible and directly influential source of subsidy and inspiration, "Western" clothing (which could very well be American, European, or Japanese, or some synthesis of all three) was being produced within a complex circulation of stolen gazes, appropriated technologies, and reappropriated styles. A better sense of this may be gleaned from a brief consideration of the fashion craze sparked in part by *Madame Freedom.* On the film's surface, especially from a distant observational vantage, the most radical and presumably alluring transformation is the protagonist Sŏn-yŏng's shift from *hanbok* to *yangjang.* And yet it was in fact the luxurious velvet *hanbok* Sŏn-yŏng and her high society friends wear throughout the first half of the film that proved the greater social sensation. An older and traditionally very expensive fabric that became somewhat more accessible with the advent of more sophisticated looms in the middle part of the twentieth century, velvet was incorporated into the warp of *hanbok* precisely in the mid-1950s. Its popularity was such that a "velvet limitation" law (*pelbet otgam chehan ryŏng*) was passed in 1957 that allotted only one velvet outfit per person per year. This was partly precipitated by the perceived moral danger in the gap between the extravagance of velvet clothing and the devastating scarcity that characterized the immediate postwar years. But it was also a measure aimed against velvet's frequently contraband sources, chiefly Hong Kong for the lower quality bolts, Kyoto for the more refined finishes.[21] This counterintuitive phenomenon prompt a series of reflections about fashion's historicity and function: that it was eminently possible to be modern through ostensibly traditional attire, that America was not the singular object of desire and fantasy, that the consumerist gaze, despite capital limitations and political restriction, could traverse borders in multiple directions.

The New Face of Print

I would now like to consider some of the striking changes that took hold of the publishing industry in the 1950s. The liberation and immediate postwar periods witnessed a remarkable expansion in periodical publishing, with upward of 174 new magazines launched between 1945 and 1954. Many of these folded within a few months and many were either professional publications or monthly editions of newspapers or older periodicals.[22] But qualitatively new forms, with their own protocols and patterns of reading, appeared in these years as well. The most striking of these are the period's film and fashion magazines. While film reviews, gossip about film personalities, and advertisements for new releases had been published in major newspapers since the middle of the colonial period, it was not until the launch of two magazines, *Yŏnghwa Segye* (*Film World*) and *Kukje Yŏnghwa* (*International Film*), in 1955 that writing and representation of filmmaking and stardom found specialized and popular venues for circulation in the postwar period.[23] In many ways, they are fairly typical of the kinds of fan magazines in popular circulation in the same period in Europe, the United States, or other parts of the world. Film celebrities are clearly the primary attraction of the magazines—their faces are printed large on virtually every early page and they are the subject of regular "introduction," "interest," and "gossip" columns. Promotion of new releases is obviously another important component, both in the more straightforward full-page advertisements and in the reviews and "reports" that are often nothing more than narrative summaries and cast introductions. Industry news from home and abroad, in particular about films currently under production or promised for import, and the occasional editorial reporting on trends or themes are regular, though clearly less essential, features. Often taking up the bulk of the pages, however, are full screenplays of recently released films—usually one but at times up to three to an issue—accompanied sparsely by stills from the films. There is some indication that this substantial textual presence may have been mandated or at least encouraged by censors;[24] this seems even more likely considering that the screenplays are almost exclusively for Korean films. But the more compelling and in some ways more obvious explanation is that these screenplays signal the very liminality of the film medium in this particular historical moment, poised somewhere between literate and visual, and highbrow and mass cultures. The weighty presence of the screenplays—drawn primarily, though not exclusively, from the literary (*munye*) genre of films—palpably anchors the cinema in the gravity of older, more serious art forms.[25] There was in these magazines clearly a tension with the promotion and, indeed, celebration of the newly revived medium, indicating that film had not yet marked out a sure position in the art–entertainment spectrum.

Another sign of that delicate balance is in the instructive and often hortatory tenor of the articles in these magazines, itself an obvious symptom of the enlightenment mode in Korean film culture. This is especially apparent in *Yŏnghwa Segye*. Detailed explanations of film terms and techniques—ranging from simpler definitions of the long shot or the fadeout (replete with English renderings) to much more expansive clarifications of generic categories and cinematic styles—appeared regularly in the earlier issues. Each issue in the entire first volume of *Yŏnghwa Segye* seems in fact to have prominently featured in their opening pages a kind of glossary of basic film terminology, starting in the first issue with brief definitions of the role of each member of a credited film company (the producer, the director, the cinematographer, etc.) and progressing, by the sixth issue, to the more complex workings of a typical Hollywood studio. On another level, *Yŏnghwa Segye* is peppered with shorter articles, letters, and single-panel comics that take on the task of creating proper filmgoing manners and ideas. In one letter in the inaugural issue, for instance, a writer complains about the "old-fashioned" (*kusik*) habit of certain members of the audience of talking at the screen—something that is identified with the "outdated" *pyŏnsa*-mediated cinema culture.[26]

Old-timers clearly had to adjust to the new theaters and learn the new conventions of filmgoing. And yet general, presumably younger, audiences too, at least in the eyes of the magazine's editors, needed to be told how a movie was made, what to look for, and how to appreciate what they were watching. All of this pressure on the way to watch films, and to substantiate their cultural position, is especially striking when we consider that films had already been screened in Korea for over thirty years and that Seoul at least had seen an exuberant screen culture as early as the late 1920s. The most immediately obvious way to account for this seemingly excessive exhortation is to consider that virtually a generation—that is, between the nearly complete closure of the commercial film industry in the late 1930s to the reconstruction of the (both local and import) industry in the latter stages of the war in 1953—had been deprived of a bona fide filmgoing culture.[27] But while this is certainly a crucial factor, it is not the whole story. In order to get a better picture of what was going on here in the magazines and in film culture as a whole, we need to look more carefully at the images themselves.

A scan through the pages of these magazines quickly reveals a powerful tendency of filmmaking in the 1950s and the fashion and fan cultures that underwrote it. The eye, reflecting the magnifications of the big screen as well, perhaps, as the increasingly close traffic of the rapidly expanding cities, was being drawn much more consistently and analytically toward the face, primarily, and the body and its clothing, secondarily. Film magazines like *Yŏnghwa Segye* and *Kukje Yŏnghwa* were by their very nature heavily invested in the faces of actors—the production and promotion of stars, and hence of the films themselves, depended on it. The first ten or fifteen pages of every issue, therefore, were made up of full-page portraits of male and female actors, ready for clipping and pasting on walls or circulation among adoring fans. These were not, tellingly, stills taken from film sequences or even promotional shots for specific movies but, rather, were abstracted publicity shots, bereft of any context, serving only to highlight the actor's face and sometimes body—in other words, pinups. Detailed biographical profiles of individual actors in later pages are invariably accompanied by large, similarly abstracted portraits, and even the shorter blurbs sharing gossip about trysts and other significant tidbits are rarely published without smaller, cleanly framed (the standard oval shape) face shots. The abstract format of these portraits gives some indication of the cultural work of the film magazine. That is, that the culture of celebrity, and therein the orientation of the eye toward the face, in some ways exceeds or escapes the prosaic function of film promotion. And in this work, the film magazine was clearly at the forefront. For, while the 1950s saw the establishment of a number of popular magazines, none of these, not even the highly popular and explicitly commercial monthlies such as *Sinch'ŏnji*, *Arirang*, or *Modŏn Chosŏn*, approached the pictorial saturation of the film magazine.

Tellingly, it was only *Yŏwŏn*, the leading women's fashion magazine launched in 1955, that could rival *Kukje Yŏnghwa* or *Yŏnghwa Segye* in this bald foregrounding of the image. In fact, that magazine was the first in Korea to feature offset pictorial printing and to feature advertising prominently.[28] By the April 1958 issue, the magazine featured full-page advertisements for OB Lager, which leveraged the image of leisured women in quiet repose to appeal to *Yŏwŏn*'s apparently aspirational readership. But the magazine had already staged a more signal departure in its inaugural issue with the advent of "Mode," a multipage special section that featured the era's most recognizable film stars wearing the latest fashions. The full-page images that constituted the spread were accompanied by captions indicating celebrity and designer names or providing tips on how or when to wear specific styles. The first iteration showcased a young Ch'oe Ŭn-hŭi on the cusp of greater stardom, posing in the latest autumn fashions (Figure 5). The captions here draw attention to pertinent details of the outfits, transliterating their terms ("one-piece," "flare," etc.), highlighting the effects of specific cuts ("slimming for both thinner and thicker ladies"), pointing out construction details (bias

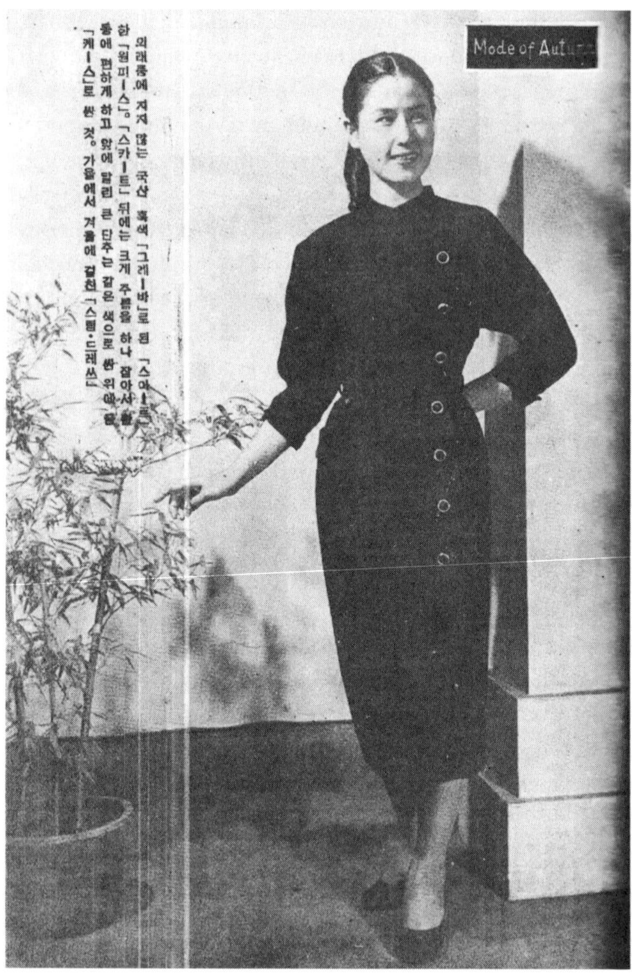

Figure 5. Ch'oe Ŭn-hŭi's "Mode" spread in *Yŏwŏn*'s inaugural issue (1955).

cut, offset buttons, etc.), and, perhaps most tellingly, trumpeting the local provenance of the garments—the caption on the spread's third image begins, "a smart domestic [*kuksan*] one-piece of black grebe that could stand up to any foreign design." By all indications the spread and the magazine as a whole marked a shift in the sensorial engagement with Korean publishing, instantiating not only a sharper focus on the image but also a keener processing of the social and material import of those images. *Yŏwŏn* therein actively participated in the intensification of the "consumerist gaze" in popular media, and its stakes for women in the face of a burgeoning culture of consumption was radically ambivalent—exposed and liberated, the subject and object of desire, exquisitely aware of fashion's ephemerality and social disparities.[29]

But like its film counterparts, *Yŏwŏn* throughout the period maintained a text-heavy profile, rich with short stories (leading female author Pak Kyŏng-ni was a regular contributor) and articles ranging in subject from the challenges of motherhood to the joys of Western classical music. Fashion was only one, albeit expanding, component of what was a comprehensive women's magazine, one that had few viable competitors and thus little reason to specialize in a particular thematic or stylistic direction.[30] Later *Yŏwŏn* editions, especially toward the late 1960s, would shed some of this textual weight in favor of more lavish photo spreads and celebrity profiles, just as the film magazines would eventually cut their multipage screenplay reprints. But it is important to stress here that the magazines' forms in the 1950s did not constitute a transitional stage en route to becoming bolder, less self-conscious visual media, but rather that they embodied the tensions central to early postwar cultural discourse. As a comprehensive magazine, *Yŏwŏn* suspended in its pages a high cultural sensibility (represented best perhaps by its regular full-color reprints of Impressionist paintings, or its multipage "etiquette" pictorials illustrating, for instance, the proper mechanics of Western-style fine dining), and the burgeoning mass culture modes of reception and consumption. Structurally, magazines like *Yŏwŏn* and *Kukje Yŏnghwa*, despite their mass cultural foundations, resisted the full embrace of low cultural escapism, an index of which is the fact that nothing like the overt sexuality of contemporary American or Japanese women's magazines like *Seventeen* or *Josei Jishin* (*Ladies' Own*), or the invasive leering of fan magazines like *Movie Story*, *Screen Romances*, or *Eiga Fan* (*Film Fan*), ever made it into the Korean publications. At the same time as they took the lead in training the eye to process static and moving images and in coaxing their readerships into taking greater initiative in assuming new social identities, the magazines maintained an affinity to older cultural sensibilities seemingly possessed of more gravitas. They committed to paper the radical and at times comic collisions—tips on applying eye makeup next to a report on the April 16 demonstrations, analysis of Italian Neorealism followed by giddy celebrity gossip—that came to characterize the decade's mass cultural production.

Camera, Fashion, Space

The six films that make up Shin Sang-ok's classical melodrama series, *Confessions of a College Girl*, *Hellflower*, *Sisters' Garden*, *It's Not Her Sin*, *Ch'unhŭi*, and *Tongsimch'o*, are tied together by their concern with the predicament of women in the aftermath of war and the sweeping transformations of capitalist modernity.[31] The institutions of marriage and family are threatened by dramatic shifts in gender identity (feminized men, masculinized women) and the intrusion of money into all social relationships, and the narrative arcs of these films oversee the struggles of women to variously confront or yield to those changes. The films are also characterized by their contemporary, largely urban, settings. This is notable when we consider that Shin Sang-ok's work has been popularly defined by historical dramas such as *Sŏng Ch'unhyang* (1961) or *Prince Yŏnsan* (*Yŏnsan'gun*, 1961). The films embody, albeit unevenly, the technical polish that was described above, which allowed Shin to effect a significant shift in the way that his films engaged with reality. This is not to say that his 1950s pieces represented reality more accurately than it had been in the past; in fact, social or documentary realism was not the primary goal of the filmmakers of this period. Rather, skill with the technical apparatus of filmmaking allowed Shin to, in André Bazin's formulation, "aim at" reality—that is, to confidently construct sequences of shots or fabricate settings and moods that could be presented as reality.[32] Italian neorealist auteurs and Korean postwar directors were clearly pursuing different kinds of projects, but they shared a common approach to exploiting the cinematic apparatus to forge a particular, stylized, version of the real. Filmmakers in Korea from the colonial period to liberation had used images to yield specific senses of time and space appropriate to the narrative demands of their subjects. But it was not until filmmakers like Shin Sang-ok, possessed of more sophisticated equipment and trained in its use, that Korean cinema saw the full-fledged advent of self-conscious realism.

What Shin was "aiming at" in nearly all of the films from this short period was a special sort of look, which we can label with the voguish term defined above, the *seryŏn*. This is embodied in the overall atmosphere of these films, with their clean, low-key lighting schemes, efficient but leisurely pacing, and quiet scores composed of romantic classical works or sophisticated jazz pieces. A sort of apotheosis of this refinement is achieved in *Sisters' Garden*, which narrates the plight of two sisters coping with the realities of modern life following the sudden death of their wealthy father.

The younger Myŏng-hŭi is courted by the suave painter Tong-su, and we are given a relaxed, lingering portrait of his studio apartment hung with Impressionist landscapes and still lifes. The medium, low-angle framing effectively blurs the line between the figures they cut and the paintings that surround them, and they are thus rendered as the ideal modern couple, removed from the vagaries of postwar Seoul. The older Chŏng-hŭi is wooed by the wealthy businessman Mr. Pang. Always respectful and well-mannered, he takes her to a series of elegant cafés where he pledges to honor the memory of her father. In a memorable scene, Chŏng-hŭi is captured against the dark, painted walls of the café at an oblique angle and in richly contrasting light that signals not the noisy popularity of the contemporary coffee house (*tabang*) but the rarefied space of the contemporary elite. One of the stylistic as well as the affective high points of the film comes at about the halfway point, when Myŏng-hŭi announces to her sister that she will marry Tong-su, a match that worries Chŏng-hŭi. The two women are captured kneeling in a plush bedroom, and the bright, high-key lighting of the scene adds a brilliant luster to their hair and an ethereal glow to their gauzy nightgowns. Myŏng-hŭi accuses Chŏng-hŭi of being jealous, but the older sister quietly assures her that she only wants to be certain that it is real love and that the child-like Myŏng-hŭi will be able to look after her future husband. The scene works to underscore the tension between the sisters, but its formal construction is most heavily invested in intensifying the allure of the two women. Their femininity and abstract beauty is the very subject of Shin's meticulous, painterly framing.

The refinement of this scene, as it is in virtually all of the films under review here, is further enhanced by costuming. As we saw above, *Sisters' Garden* is saturated with a veritable runway of alluring fashions. The force of clothing is also nakedly displayed in the lurid scenes in *Hellflower*, where Sonia slinks her way from one revealing evening dress to another, barely hidden behind a gauzy partition. The quiet opulence of costume design had multiple effects and purposes throughout Shin's work. It was of course a major factor in the construction of character and social class, marking off the sisters in their isolated garden or the mother and daughter in *Tongsimch'o* as neither the traditional lady of the inner quarters nor the laborers and housemaids of the semipublic sphere, but rather the worldly modern woman. Fashion also functions, in conjunction with the high gloss of Shin Sang-ok's camera, to mark off these films as different and more sophisticated than all prior or even contemporary productions. Ch'oe Ŭn-hŭi's face, popularly considered to be "traditionally beautiful," is transmuted by the suit jacket and the noirish lighting scheme as the epitome of the new. And finally, in the incipience of an independent fashion industry, and indeed before the material accessibility of couture, these films perform as venues for the consumption of modern fashions, and the worldly personae and affluence they suggest. Fashionable women are a central component of the fetish—for the foreign, for the refined, for the modern—that operates at the very surface of these films.

Fetishism, or at least a sort of lurid fascination, is also conducted compellingly in the relentlessly modern and often opulent commodities and spaces that are screened in these films. In fact, the visual field here is rarely colored by anything resembling the premodern. Only in *Tongsimch'o*, built as it is around the theme of conflict between the old and the new, does an old *hanok* enter the frame. But even in that film, the "traditional" is caught inescapably in the modern: the grand house is the object of an anonymous economic transaction (when an uninvited outsider moves to buy it from underneath the family), and the resplendent *hanbok* worn by the wealthy women are cut and patterned in a self-consciously modern style and accessorized with diamond jewelry and smart leather handbags. The consumption and use of new luxury products—a glass of expensive whiskey, Western clothes and baubles, gleaming foreign cars, and even Lassie-esque dogs—are pulled to the surface of the films via close framing, overt spotlighting, or by the sheer uncanniness of their presence. Much of the action also takes place in fresh settings: a new, compartmentally organized office building, alien law offices, the Ministry of Foreign Affairs, a multistory Chinese restaurant with private rooms, slick cafés (both popular and elite), and, notably, public parks and boulevards. But the most emblematic structure is the modern house, poised in virtually every film as the seat of social privilege and modern life. In *Confessions of a College Girl*, Senator Kim's mansion is an imposing, ivy-covered structure abstracted from its surroundings.[33] It is the home of political power, and so appropriately dark and aloof, its interior reminiscent of Victorian opulence more than postwar modernism. But it is also the site of a renovation in social relations, for the senator will soon welcome Sŏk-hŭi into his family as his daughter, despite the fact that she has lied about her blood ties. New dimensions of the house—a heavily trafficked foyer, a communal dining room, and Sŏk-hŭi's sprawling private bedroom—structure the relations of the modern family. The house featured in *It's Not Her Sin* is also an imposing structure, similarly cordoned off by a high iron fence, indicating the rarified domain of the well-traveled and seemingly flexible social elite. The entry is attended by a young housemaid, and the interior is furnished with the spare modernist furnishings of the period. The living room features a baby grand piano and a television set, two of the quintessential objects of the modern, cultured class. The plush grandiosity of the Western-style house was the icon of modernity and refinement; before the advent of the apartment complex, it was the site and object of social fantasy.

The height of the fetishization of the spaces of modern affluence though is achieved in *Sisters' Garden*, where there is seemingly nothing outside the enclosed world of material comfort. This is boldly projected from the film's first frames in which Mr. Pang, alone in his window seat, touches down in a Korean Air jet and is met by a line of shiny Cadillacs and chauffeured to a clean, private clinic owned by his friend Dr. Nam. The setting shifts to the scene sketched at the start of this chapter, a picturesque waterside clearing where butterflies can be caught in giant nets and the landscape presents itself for painting. Much of the action of the rest of the film takes place in jazz bars or elegant cafés, spaces marked not only as eminently modern but also as preternaturally cool. One of the more striking views we are given is of Mr. Pang's house, a building that, in contrast to the Victorian mansions alluded to above, is the model of modern, Bauhaus architecture: white, spare, and boxy, and similarly aloof from its invisible surroundings. The interior is comfortably furnished with a striking collection of modernist pieces (a Barcelona lounger, an Eames desk, etc.), and jazz plays casually from a sleek turntable. This space is further outdone by the "mansion" Mr. Pang owns, a house for "entertaining" VIPs with hostesses and where Chŏng-hŭi will soon function as "madam." The sprawling building is a blend of traditional and modern architecture, its rooms connected by covered walkways and tiled roofs, and is elegantly furnished with both large European couches and low-slung Korean tables: it is the kind of opulence that will not be seen in Korean cinema again for decades. But perhaps the most explicit, literal iteration of this grammar of consumption is in the furniture store where Myŏng-hŭi and her husband Tong-su shop to ornament their newlywed life. Myŏng-hŭi prances through the store, fingering pieces, enumerating prices for plush sofas and glimmering chandeliers; we later see the effect of this spending spree when the massive poster bed awkwardly invades the master bedroom. This radical and irrational renovation is financed somehow by the sale of Tong-su's paintings, but also by the displacement of the sisters from their late parents' house and, eventually, of the house itself.

Stars and Spectacle

But if fashion was the signifier and object of material fetish, the most complex sites of fantasy were the faces and bodies of female stars. While a number of popular, attractive stars peopled Shin Sang-ok's early films—especially Ch'oe Chi-hŭi, who played Myŏng-hŭi in *Sisters' Garden* and was a sensation throughout the late 1950s and early 1960s, and Yi Min, who took minor roles in these films (including as Yŏng-suk's new flame in *It's Not Her Sin*) and was perhaps the leading male idol of the period—undoubtedly, Ch'oe Ŭn-hŭi was the central icon of Shin's films. It is possible to argue in fact that Ch'oe structured Shin's films, prescribing both the themes he was able to treat and the modes in which they were visualized through the complex, often contradictory meanings of her face and persona. This is clearly the case with the films from this period, all of which are more about women than even their ostensible plots would allow. That is, while the six films are drawn from different generic modes—the family melodrama, the crime drama, the exploitation picture—they are more properly understood as venues for the exploration and consumption of women in modern society. And what Richard Dyer calls the "structured polysemy" of Ch'oe's persona,[34] the complex and often contradictory significations of her on- and off-screen lives, lends to the films an especially rich way of visualizing postwar modernity.

Largely through the success of the films discussed here, by the close of the 1950s, Ch'oe became positioned in a relatively short line of Korean female film stars. Interestingly, men tended to dominate the screen through the colonial period, far outnumbering their female counterparts. Nevertheless, a handful of women—notably, Sin Il-sŏn, who had starred in a number of Na Un-gyu's films, Yi Wŏl-hwa, who was the epitome of the modern girl, and Mun Ye-bong, who took leading roles in many of the late colonial films—had become recognizable public figures.[35] In the immediate postwar period, women, as we saw above, become much more the focus of film celebrity, reflective of a profound shift in the gendering of commodity consumption. Ch'oe rose to fame with films like *Confessions of a College Girl* and *Hellflower*, a few years later than other actresses like No Kyŏng-hŭi and the aforementioned Kim Ŭi-hyang, but she became the first bona fide superstar of the postwar period, featured in more films and the kinds of interest pages, profiles, and gossip columns discussed above than any other actress over the next decade. But her stardom in the late 1950s was structured through a complex merger of temporalities, cultural identities, and social significations. The image that she projects in films like *Confessions of a College Girl* and *Sisters' Garden* hearkened back before the late colonial period and construction of patriotic femininity to the radical and dangerous sexuality projected by the modern woman of the late 1920s and 1930s. Ch'oe, in other words, embodied the sort of nostalgia for colonial sophistication that animated the *seryŏn* imagination described above. At the same time, in films like *Hellflower* and *It's Not Her Sin*, she projected a persona that was clearly inflected by the brash sexuality and mystique of the Hollywood leading lady. Yet, unlike Kim Chŏng-rim, who rose briefly with her leading role in *Madame Freedom*, or Kim Ŭi-hyang, whose career, as we have seen, was a short-lived cycle of one-dimensional sexpot roles, Ch'oe Ŭn-hŭi's career endured precisely because of the multiplicity of meanings—a kind of productive dissonance—contained in her body. And these found their fullest expression in the films here in a way that made the films a powerful conduit for fantasizing the possibilities of modernity.

The epitome of this productive dissonance is projected in *Tongsimch'o*. Ch'oe plays Madame Yi, a single mother widowed by the war who is torn between at least three poles: the memory of her husband and the social customs that relationship entails; the material and ethical debt she owes to Kim Sang-gyu, who bailed her out of a difficult financial situation; and the desire they mutually share for each other that is muted beneath those obligations. The action centers around a grand house in the affluent Seoul neighborhood of Hyehwa, both the site for and object of Yi's conflicts, which is contrasted to the modern world of busy streets and bustling offices that is associated with her daughter on the one hand, and the timeless countryside home in Choch'iwŏn that is a station of family and tradition on the other. The narrative is in many ways similar to *The Houseguest and My Mother* (*Sarangbang sonnim kwa ŏmŏni*, 1961), a film Shin would direct two years later and with which Ch'oe would be closely identified, but is distinguished precisely in the mode by which this archetypal *yeŭi* vs. *chŏng* (duty vs. feeling) conflict is played out. Where the conflict in *Houseguest* exists at the interpersonal level between the neo-Confucian ties that bind the mother to her late husband and mother-in-law, on the one hand, and the romantic longings that connect her to the houseguest, on the other, the conflict in *Tongismch'o* is configured more explicitly at the social level, between the forces that enclose Madame Yi into her roles as widow and mother (the old mansion, the rural home) and the new material venues (the retail business venture, the sale of the old mansion) that promise to release Yi from her social bondage. For, despite the fact that she is dressed in the traditional *hanbok* and sports conservatively parted hair in every scene, Yi is in fact firmly embedded in the modern: in the sorts of spaces mentioned above (the chic Chinese restaurant, in the back of a gleaming Cadillac) and in her active enmeshment in modern capitalist relations (she actually went into debt trying her hand in a Western goods store). This is perhaps visualized most explicitly in Yi's many journeys on foot throughout the city and by rail between Choch'iwŏn and Seoul: she is active and mobile in a way unthinkable for the housebound mother in *Houseguest*. Thus, despite the fact that the affective center of the film lies in whether Madame Yi and Kim Sang-gyu will be able to consummate their love, the visual surface constructs a picture story of the woman's negotiation with modern spaces and social relations.

Ch'oe Ŭn-hŭi mediated and crystallized these conflicts between the traditional and the modern and between obligation and feeling more aptly than anyone else working at the time. Ŏm Aeng-nan, who plays Ch'oe's forward-thinking daughter in *Tongsimch'o* and who, as we have seen, was often compared to Audrey Hepburn, rose to fame precisely for her modern looks and "fit" (*ŏullim*) with modern fashions. The other major star of the period, Kim Chi-mi, who was celebrated for her unusually "Western" looks, took on a number of leading roles in contemporary films but could never, for that reason, succeed with period works. Ch'oe, on the other hand, became known for her performances in historical dramas such as *Sŏng Ch'unhyang* and *Prince Yŏnsan*, to which she brought a different sort of tension. But the strange, often uncanny clash her persona brought to the modern roles of the 1950s projected a particular brand of femininity that both embodied the predicament of women in this fraught historical period and acted as a venue for women and men to imagine otherwise. Her reputation was split between public rumors that she had worked as a sort of entertainer for the military during the war and the minor scandal that she had divorced her husband in 1957, and remarried Shin Sang-ok in the same year, and her face and figure (characterized by her smooth round face and downcast eyes) that so aptly fit the picture of the traditional, Chosŏn-era woman. When this split was again displaced onto the urban, contemporary roles she played in the 1950s, the "structured polysemy" of those on- and off-screen poles did not make failures of the portrayals (as did Kim Chi-mi in her own iteration of Ch'unhyang) but rather functioned to enhance the public legibility, resonance, and imaginative power of those roles.

The clash between Ch'oe's public persona, the on-screen image she cultivated, and the roles that she took on in the period is most highly pronounced in *Hellflower*. As sketched at the top of this chapter, Ch'oe plays Sonia, a base camp prostitute pictured from the very first frames in the service of American soldiers. What little remains of contemporary reviews indicates the general consensus that the role was a mismatch for Ch'oe, who had recently starred as the dedicated daughter in the Silla-period film *Shadowless Pagoda* (*Muyŏng tap*, 1957) and as the bookish student turned lawyer in *Confessions of a College Girl.* Interviews with Ch'oe and Shin confirm the "difficulty" and "awkwardness" of the characterization, though both concede that they were satisfied with the outcome.[36] But while the general consensus of the principles and critics is that the film works despite the dissonance, it is possible to see that it works precisely because of that dissonance, which yields a picture of modern femininity and sexuality that is appropriately uncanny and surprising.

The film pushed the limits at once of Ch'oe's range and the bounds of what could be screened in contemporary Korean theaters. The narrative is fairly complex, pitting Sonia between the innocent Tong-sik and his older brother Yŏng-sik on the one hand, and a series of action sequences featuring highly orchestrated black-market heists on the other. Sonia elects the reluctant Tong-sik over his brother and deflects the latter's wrath by informing on the heist, leading to its failure. The film ends badly for both, as Yŏng-sik succumbs to wounds sustained in a gun battle with police, but not before he has tracked down Sonia in a muddy field and stabbed her to death. The convoluted plot carries with it its own drama and suspense—a sort of homage to the American potboilers of the late 1940s—but it is also fabricated precisely to accommodate the spectacle of the heist and of the women of the camptown. Returning to the opening scene, it is worth reiterating the jarring, disjunctive quality of its framing and of Ch'oe's presence within it. The real revelation of the scene lies not in picturing Ch'oe with the American soldier and in the sordid circumstances of the camp town, but in the way all of the energy of both the performance and the camera is directed at rendering Ch'oe a sex object that leaps out of her surroundings. The revealing black dress, oversized earrings, and heavy makeup, as well as the sway of her hip and her slack-jawed gum-chewing, all work to create a performance of the Western princess. Once the soldier leaves and Sonia is left to linger in the sordid space, the camera pans to follow her movements and only lets go of its full body framing when it tracks in luridly toward Sonia's upper body and face as she stares almost directly at the camera, back at the gaze of her on- and off-screen audiences.

But as suggested above, and as is in some ways typical of the femme fatale, Sonia is never fully trapped in the gaze of her suitors/victims nor is she fully embedded in her surroundings. Partly, this is the paradoxical effect of the camera's exaggerated leering. The framing and staging of many shots luridly align the gaze of different men with the camera's view. We see Sonia slowly changing out of her dress behind the gauzy partition as Tong-sik ogles helplessly; she moves seductively toward Tong-sik and into the camera so that her lips fill the frame; Yŏng-sik, in a jealous rage, slaps Sonia, but when she turns back to him the full force of her disgust and derision is directed obliquely toward the camera. Further, the camera frames her sexuality in such a way as to push the limits of censorship. Two years after the first kiss scene in Korean cinema (in Han Hyŏng-mo's *Hand of Fate* [*Unmyŏng ŭi son*]), Sonia is rolling around with Yŏng-sik on a mosquito-net–covered bed, and later in the fields, or the motions of her lust rock the small boat they sail on a lake. She is clearly the object of obsession and, indeed, despite her manipulations, her fate is decided in the end at the murderous hands of men. Yet the camera makes clear that she is also the subject of her image and of her sexuality, self-consciously performing for the frame and staring back at the gaze.

Interestingly, the film is constructed in a loosely neorealist style, making liberal use of documentary footage, splicing images of American soldiers on the streets or embedding shots of busy public spaces (train station, market) with more formally staged sequences, and filming almost exclusively on location. The film also economizes the use of other media, entrusting almost the entirety of the "score" to a haunting solo harmonica. While Shin claimed that this cinematic form was the inevitable result of budget constraints, it was nonetheless highly appropriate to the film's social and physical space in the sordid, makeshift base camp. But more relevant to the argument at hand, the film's stark neorealist framing also works to highlight its fetish-fantasy dimensions, furnishing a palpable context for the abstract fetishization sketched above and in a sense making a spectacle-fantasy out of reality. And this is where the skill with the technical apparatus converges with the manipulations of fashion, space, and persona converge, and where the effect of these films is conjoined. For *Hellflower* does not, of course, aim at the same sort of look of refinement that is so explicitly a point of the *Sisters' Garden* or *It's Not Her Sin.* But it does work to signal, in an equally powerful way, the fact of its own as well as its subject's modernity, through the production of spectacle and fantasy.

This is perhaps nowhere more apparent than in a riveting scene halfway through *Hellflower* that conjoins two kinds of visual spectacle, women and action, and brings together the two narrative strands of the romantic triangle and the heist. The sequence is ingeniously constructed. A group of Korean thugs, who inhabit the base camp and who are essentially the pimps to the prostitutes who work there, orchestrate a heist, using the occasion of a dancehall show and party, as well as the women themselves, as diversion. As the scene opens, we are presented with footage of a dance party on the base; the camera pans back and forth across the couples, American military officers and their Korean women partners, dancing cheek to cheek. The field then jumps to the base's fringe, where the thugs cut through barbed wire and crawl through, hiding themselves between trucks and behind barrels. Cutting back to the party, the camera reveals that a show has begun, a line of women dressed in revealing one-strap sarongs swaying onto the dance floor accompanied by a lively mambo band as the seated officers look on. With their attention glued to the choreography, the officers fail to notice that a few of their "hostesses" have signaled each other and slipped out of the hall. Once outside, the women send different kinds of signals to soldiers guarding the perimeter, luring them away with their satin-draped figures and trails of cigarette smoke. With the coast clear, the thugs pounce out of hiding, working in teams to hit their targeted cargo, loading it onto a wooden cart. Meanwhile, the officers in the hall are treated to an even more lurid spectacle: accompanied by a lyrical electric guitar and organ piece, a performer dressed in a strapless, legless gown with a trail of feathers has entered the spotlight, rotating her hips and staring out at the crowd. She moves around the space with strides drawn from both the ballet and the burlesque, her hair, frame, and style roughly reminiscent of Josephine Baker and the Moulin Rouge. The camera lingers over her seductive dance, tracking in on her feather-covered pelvis as she tilts it to the rhythms of the guitar. The scene climaxes as the thugs run off with their contraband and the dancer turns her back and spreads her feathery train, fluttering her body and arching her back to complete the orgasmic spectacle.

At once we realize that there is a doubling of gazes, a complicity between the officers who are distracted from their work by the dancers, and our own attention, which is absorbed in the whole display. Indeed this is part of the audacity of the construction of the scene. There is also a special kind of voyeurism at work here, one that leers into the closed space of the foreign as well as the hybrid. The film grants access to the storied sordid space of the American base and the sanctioned shameful transactions—the black-market, the sexual—that are processed there. But mostly, the sexualized performance exists as a spectacle of its own, presented as an absorbing performance diverted from the rest of the film. This is somewhat similar to the celebrated dancehall scene in *Madame Freedom*, likewise structured around a lurid burlesque performance and similarly transcendent, in visual terms, of the film narrative. But whereas that earlier performance was staged with a high polish (using one of the earliest crane shots in Korean cinema), lending the dance a classic MGM quality, the performance here, shot within the dark, alien space of the army base, has a deeply erotic, perhaps even pornographic, quality. This is clear in the saturated sexuality of the frame. The suggestive feathers of the dancer's costume, her long legs spread and pelvis tilted toward the camera, and the rhythms of her gyrations constitute a spectacle whose explicitness would not be seen again in Korean cinema for decades. The scene invites the "rapt, mindless fascination" of the pornographic. This is the flower that blooms amid the hell of postwar devastation, marketing the utopian within the dystopian mess of prostitution, crime, and miscegenation.

Imaginary Depth

The film and fashion worlds of the 1950s, particularly in their refined and extravagant iterations, were largely derided by serious contemporary critics and their status remained contested until the late 1990s. The bases for this negative assessment are numerous, but generally converge on two central ideas: that they were not Korean enough, and that they were not art. While praising their exceptional technical accomplishment, critics were especially tough on the appropriation of foreign material in the era's films. A review of Shin Sang-ok's *It's Not Her Sin* in the *Seoul Sinmun*, targeting the work's French origins, argued for instance that the "unnaturalness" of the translation (*pŏn'an*) was only slightly mitigated by the appeal and acting skills of the two leads, Ch'oe Ŭn-hŭi and Chu Chŭng-nyŏ, concluding that "while Shin seems to have gotten the hang of producing adaptations, taking up the fruits of other people's labor can never be art."[37] And a reviewer of *Ch'un-hŭi* in the *Han'guk Sinmun* claims that "with *Confessions of a College Girl, It's Not Her Sin*, and other translated works, Mr. Shin's films this year amount to nothing more than mannerisms."[38] This sort of appraisal continued in various ways throughout the following decades. While much more open to the fact of translation, leading film critic and historian Yi Yŏng-il complained in 1969 that many of the films of the late 1950s, including Shin's, were "ethically vacuous."[39] He also categorized the majority of the period's films as *sinp'a* derivatives, implying that they were marked by the emotional excess, narrative improbability, and social clichés that were the conventions of that form. Filmmakers themselves, reflecting on that phase in their careers, tended to dismiss or downplay the work of that period: Yu Hyŏn-mok, in his history of the Korean film industry, wrote that his 1950s work was largely "naive" (*sobak han*) and "derivative" (*p'asaeng toen*)[40] and Kim Su-yong "confessed" in his autobiography that he was not proud of his "juvenile" films.[41] In interviews and statements made throughout his career, Shin Sang-ok quietly directed attention away from his earlier work and toward the accomplishments of the 1960s. With the exception of *Evil Night* (*Akya*, 1952), his first film, and *Hellflower*, celebrated as a neorealist masterpiece at home and abroad, Shin largely seemed to want to forget the "cheap" work of the 1950s.[42]

Critics in the 1990s, informed by feminist film theory and new sociological research, began to reappraise the period's films. Rather than engaging strictly with the films' expressions of cultural identity, they began looking more closely at the politics of spectatorship and reception, as well as the social life of melodrama as a cinematic form. While skeptical about the patriarchal discourses in films such as *Madame Freedom* and *Hellflower*, they saw those films as potentially radical and empowering events for the lower-class middle-aged women who made up the majority of audiences. "There must have been a special kind of pleasure," argued Yu Chi-na, "for those women in seeing the new, dangerous women on screen, no matter that they were always punished in the end."[43] The closed narrative structures and affective excess that defined melodrama and *sinp'a* were also seen as latent sites of unruly identification and solidarity. Following theorists like Linda Williams and Christine Gledhill, Chu Yu-sin called attention to the "emotional catharsis of seeing other women damaged, abused, repressed."[44] The melodrama and *sinp'a* of the 1950s were thus recast as "women's films" and read as venues of relief from the hardships of postwar reconstruction and patriarchal domination.

Both of these critical streams—rejection as foreign and/or crude, and sanction as affectively and/or politically affirmative—converge around two approaches to film: the notion of film and mass culture as distraction, and the search for meaning underneath the surface of the image. Both, in different senses, disavow surfaces and attempt to uncover art or social significance in any place but the image—literary form, civic spirit, emotional surplus, psychological identification, and so on—a critical trace, perhaps, of the enlightenment mode of reading cinema. These have informed an enormously productive approach to Korean film history, but they have also tended to overlook the significant shifts that were suggested above. What distinguishes the films of this period, especially those of Han and Shin, is precisely a capitalization on and play with surface. That this play covertly mimicked the contemporary images of the former colonizer and took unbridled pleasure in highlighting a new constellation of faces and fashions belied the radical symbolic work of the films—a point missed by both nationalist and feminist critics and elided in the stark high–low cultural tensions of the film and women's magazines. The period's films do not simply erase the physical destruction, ideological conflict, and overwhelming poverty that characterized early postwar Korea; but neither do they represent that history in any direct way. At the core of the undeniable escapism of the era's melodramas and romantic comedies was the push to imagine a qualitatively different reality from the one promised by American liberalism and its South Korean adherents. In the literary field, this dissatisfaction with the present took the form, in fits and starts, of an existentialism-tinged prose of despair.[45] In film, it took the form of an ambivalent critical engagement with Hollywood's offerings, typified in the faint praise for the 1955 *Seven Brides for Seven Brothers*, in which the reviewer noted its impressive cinemascope spectacle while acerbically applauding its "American-style odorless pleasures."[46] It also took the form of the mode proper to the medium: fantasy. But rather than otherworldly or psychic withdrawal, the fantasy time–space of Korean films was a just out-of-reach bourgeois society of sexual intrigue, gender reversal, comic confusion, and lavish consumption. And, given the crude desolation of Seoul's postwar landscape, it is no coincidence that filmmakers turned to the quickly rehabilitated neighborhoods of Myŏngdong and Ch'ungmuro, or even better, to the easily controlled architecture of sets, and, more crucially, to the faces of stars and the fashions of Europe, Japan, and America to mediate that critical fantasy.

Taking into view the palimpsest historicities and desires of the film and fashion worlds of the 1950s, it is possible to offer here a provisional conclusion: the escapist and apparently mimicked aesthetics of the period were not only the repressive effect of the American cultural machine, or only a venue of distraction and pacification. Rather, the self-conscious identification with America also contained the radical fantasy of transformation and difference, the desire to realize a new sociocultural identity. Simultaneously, the sophisticated luster of fashions and cinematic imagery in this period reached back implicitly to the refinement of the colonial period, when most of the filmmakers had apprenticed and enjoyed the material, if not moral, support of major, largely state-sponsored, Japanese studios. After a ten-year hiatus that saw the evacuation of Japanese capital and expertise as well as the full-scale destruction of the most active sites of film production, Shin Sang-ok and the young filmmakers of the late 1950s turned back nostalgically to the urbanity and style of their youth, projecting that memory onto the screen in the form of the slickest, most refined, and technically accomplished images possible. The modern fantasy of 1950s Korean cinema was therein a palimpsest visualization of Japan and America, old and new, and East and West—one that could condition the imagination of a new Korean modernity.

  AUTHORSHIP AND THE LOCATION OF CINEMA

In the Region of Shin Films

Author

One of the predominant themes in Shin Sang-ok's own writings as well as the published interviews and scholarship on his work is the tension between the concept of the filmmaker as artist and the vicissitudes of the filmmaker as entrepreneur. On the one hand, Shin seems to have granted the existence of creative and independent authorship in Korea. Reflecting on his career in 1997, Shin mused:

> There are two kinds of film authors. The first is the sort that begins with his own stories; the other is a technician who brings other people's work to life. We can recognize Na Un-gyu in those terms as having been a real author. Clearly, he had Japanese support. . . . The important thing with *Arirang* though was that its espirit was Na Un-gyu's. Yes maybe some Japanese person worked on it as the cinematographer, but directors weren't really much back then so that's not really an issue. . . . If you see the artistic sensibility of films like *P'unguna*, which he made himself after *Arirang*, you'd be able to recognize *Arirang* as Na Un-gyu's own work. His spirit is there, so even if you say he didn't have the technique, it wouldn't be a stretch to see him as the very first director to have been driven by a real spirit of authorship.[1]

On the other hand, Shin seems to have been deeply cynical about the possibility of animating that artistic spirit within the scope of an under-developed industry:

> I see our generation as having worked at a time when we couldn't make claims about creating art. That was a point where filmmaking was just being established as an industry, so there was that fateful shortcoming. A director in the strictest sense must be a producer as well. A really good director must

be his own writer and his own producer. That's why I like Chaplin the best. He wrote, acted, directed, and even did the music himself. I think we have to see Chaplin as the most perfect in the world.[2]

And if Charlie Chaplin stood at the zenith of Shin's idealization of authorship in Hollywood, at the core of his cynicism about Korean filmmaking was the pressure to maintain the critical mass of a studio that was apparently the requisite for making meaningful films:

> There's a reason why a studio begins as an independent and then ends up as a major: you've got to become a major to pull together the things you need to make all the films you want to make. . . . Strictly speaking, it's fine to go independent and make films with an artistic spirit, but movies don't really get made that way. You can't make the films you want to make that way.[3]

But Shin reserved his sharpest skepticism for those contemporaries who sought to overcome these pressures and assert their independence: "I really despise these pretensions to being an artist. I do my best to avoid it. And pretending to have some sort of social conscience, that's just the worst."[4] Thus, the film artist must, as Chaplin apparently had been, be in near total control of the process of production or, as in Na Un-gyu, be able to project a distinctive spirit through the realization of his own work via a third party (whether this be a technician or a borrowed apparatus). In this familiar formulation, the author is a solitary creator bringing life to work removed from or perhaps in opposition to his sociopolitical milieu. At the same time, authorship itself is inextricably linked to the material world, mediated by the need to control technology and finances in a merging of the roles of the director and the producer. Thus, Chaplin is for Shin the most perfect film artist for having been uniquely immune to the contingencies of history, politics, and economics. This is precisely why, in one moment, Shin allows for the existence of authorship in Korea while, in another, he suggests that, in the midst of postcolonial/postwar reconstruction, the freedom of an independent studio was unattainable and the notion of artistry fundamentally illusory. Against the "fateful shortcomings" of an only half-formed film industry, the autonomy of a Charlie Chaplin (or, elsewhere, an Orson Welles or a William Wyler) becomes the pretension of the Korean filmmaker posing as an artist. For Shin, independent filmmaking is built on the primacy of the studio. The artist is endangered without the machinations of the entrepreneur.

It is easy to glean in these and other statements he made toward the end of his career that Shin Sang-ok felt driven to account for the disparity between, on the one hand, the legacies of contemporaries such as Yu Hyŏn-mok, Kim Ki-yŏng, and Yi Man-hŭi, who had come to be recognized as important modernist or realist voices in postwar filmmaking, and, on the other, his own reputation as a savvy businessman whose chief contribution had been the expansion of the filmmaking industry through the production of conventional genre films. For indeed, while Shin was variously celebrated and reviled throughout the postwar period for the unbridled ambition with which he built not only the era's leading studio but also helped to shape the policies governing the film industry, his ambivalent reputation as an author was generated just as film history and criticism were piecing together a fuller picture of Korean cinema. Already in the 1970s the preeminent historian Yi Yŏng-il had fixed Shin's status as a "genre master," foregrounding his producer's role in the calculation of box-office profitability over his director's identity in the crafting of original work.[5] This broad figuration was taken up more recently by another influential critic, Kim So-yŏng, who as we will see more closely in chapter 4 argued that Shin's corpus was defined by heterogeneity and discontinuity—a symptom of the priority Shin had apparently given to technical over expressive development.[6] Even the most charitable of his commentators struggled to account for the broad unevenness of his work. In a recent interview, the august film historian Kim Chong-wŏn reflected with an uncharacteristic lack of eloquence that,

> Back then, having to appease the whims and tastes of audiences or regional investors, and without even pointing to specific films, there was yes . . . a sort of rough and tumble aspect to the quality of things. Well actually more than quality it was that there was a preoccupation with quantity, and you see that in a lot of the films. In that respect there was deep disappointment. So on that point Shin Sang-ok sort of shuttled between shadow and light.

Kim later rounded out his thoughts on the "great filmmaker" with his oft-quoted line that Shin Sang-ok "would have jumped down to hell if he had to in order to make movies."[7] In similar fashion, Shin himself was torn between claiming the film author mantle (from heroes like Chaplin and Welles) and retreating to the logic of historical determinism (in which the author could not exist in Korea of the 1950s and 1960s). Shin grudgingly acknowledged the creation of respectable work (Kim's *Housemaid*, Yu's *Stray Bullet*), but at the same time suggested that they were the coincidental outcome of a system that did not, perhaps could not, engender sustained artistic production. Shin clearly craved the auteur title as much as he wanted the license to dismiss pretensions to it; at the same time, he wanted to direct attention to the impediments of filmmaking in Park-era Korea and the remarkable and necessary achievement of his studio.

It is important, I think, to see something more in Shin's shifting and ambivalent reflections than a ragged defense of his career or the desire to safeguard his legacy. Rather, they suggest not only the contradictions in Shin's own thinking about art and authorship in postwar Korea but also the complexities and historical contingencies of the very idea of film authorship. We might begin to pursue these complexities by considering how Shin's formative years coincided with the formulation around the world of new ideas about cinematic art and authorship (which Shin himself seems to have acknowledged in his passing suggestion that directors "weren't much" in the early twentieth century). Crystallizing in the 1950s around the work of Italian and then French filmmakers, and then moving quickly through global critical discourses, the "politique des auteurs" did not so much foment the idea of the film author as effect a shift in its values in the light of postwar mass culture. In many ways the crucible of that shift was in the pages of magazines like *Cahiers du Cinema* where practitioners and critics like François Truffaut and André Bazin asserted the primacy of a synthetic cinematic style over literary tradition and quality.[8] But further, as Dudley Andrew has noted, in moving against the seriousness of social-problem films or literary adaptations, the proponents of the new postwar cinema opened to a complex embrace of both the iconoclasm of low culture and the classical values of romantic humanism.[9] This was the basis on which the auteur theorists celebrated, not historical or contemporary European masters, but rather American filmmakers who had produced, within the Hollywood production system, work from which distinctive expressive structures could be deciphered. As we have already seen, Shin's work, as in the broader mass cultural field of the postwar period, marked a corresponding departure from the quality of literary and classical culture—that is, away from both the romanticism of "pure art" as well as the seriousness of "social consciousness." And it is precisely in the realm of these complex contemporaneous discourses that we might more profitably read Shin's slippery embrace of populist filmmaking and mass production as well as his rejection of artistic pretension. For, of course, Chaplin was as much a hero to the proponents of the "new cinema" as he was to Shin Sang-ok.

Thus, while much of the writing about film authorship has concentrated on ontological and political questions—that is, about when and what made possible the discourse of authorship and about the ideological effect of that discourse—I am more inclined here to consider Shin Sang-ok's ideas in light of the specific historical practices around which they were formed. For while the breadth of Shin's directorial corpus certainly presents an interesting challenge to the standards of consistency and singularity upon which classical notions of authorship are anchored, the broader scope of his career as director, producer, and impresario presents a vital opening through which to explore the broad material bases of the concepts of art and authorship. These exist in two overlapping dimensions. First, the conditions in which Shin and the other filmmakers of his generation brought their artistic ambitions to bear—specifically, an underdeveloped industry and market, heavy state intervention, and a radically uneven relationship to American, European, and Japanese cinemas—necessitated compromise of those ambitions and an often sobering recognition of the limitations on filmmaking in Korea. At stake here is a cross-cultural politics of the very notion of film authorship that, in spite of the apparent universalism of the iconoclastic romanticism alluded to above, owed its existence to the relative stability and privilege of the European and American culture industries. Second, Shin Sang-ok's career occasions a more sustained consideration of the connection between authorship and those elements from which it is commonly sifted: the pressures of the market, the collective processes of studio production, the conventions of genre, and the contingencies of political control. Rather than attempting to isolate his authorial signature from the noise of these elements, we need to look at how those elements conditioned the sort of films Shin created and, by extension, how the concepts of art and authorship variously cooperated with and counteracted the forces of market, studio, and genre.

With this in mind, this chapter offers a history of Shin Films studios, from its inception in 1960 through the transfer of the bulk of production to the massive Anyang studios in 1966 and to its collapse in 1975. Shin directed approximately thirty-six and produced over one hundred films for the studio, an extraordinary but by no means unparalleled output.[10] The films, true to Shin's reputation as a "genre master," are highly diverse, ranging from the standard women's and family melodramas, period pieces, and war pictures to experiments with horror, western, and slapstick comedy forms. They seem, further, to demonstrate little formal consistency in either atmospheric or technical terms, swinging wildly between the understated framing of the domestic dramas to the garish tilts and zooms of the horror and action pictures. Such inconsistency is not surprising given that, for most of its existence, Shin Films was a hierarchically organized and producer-centered system whose often prolific output (more than twenty-three films in a year)

Shin oversaw at the same time as he applied his hand to the films bearing his directorial signature. It is the very diversity of the studio that makes the continuities of Shin Sang-ok's corpus surprising and worthy of extended consideration. And indeed, a more careful consideration of this body of work reveals certain consistencies within the apparent miscellany. The generic range of Shin's films, first, is somewhat more limited than customarily assumed, dominated in fact by the period-historical drama and the domestic melodrama, eclipsing the war film and entirely precluding the "youth" (*ch'ŏngch'un*) picture. The idiom, further, is overwhelmingly melodramatic, the codes of social conflict and affective excess animating nearly every film. And finally, the films are inhabited almost exclusively by a familiar set of faces—the contract players of the studio, led by Ch'oe Ŭn-hŭi and Sin Yŏng-gyun—that mobilize a stock dramatis personae—the middle-aged woman and the middle-aged man—that stage two central themes, the conflict between men and women and between the private and the public in the Confucian social order. To a certain extent these factors are conditioned by Shin's overt entrepreneurial populism: the studio produced largely conventional melodramas about families for the lower- to middle-class middle-aged women who until the late 1960s made up the bulk of movie going audiences in the urban as well as the crucial rural markets. But they were also the narrative and affective structures through which Shin as a filmmaker, caught up in the pressures of mass production and, perhaps most important, his intimate links with the Park Chung Hee administration, could sustain a critical and creative conversation with the repressive domains of postwar Korean society and culture.

Studio

The first few years of the 1960s saw political power in South Korea change hands twice, resting finally with the Park Chung Hee regime that would hold it in increasingly oppressive fashion until the dictator's assassination in 1979.[11] As we will see in more detail in the next chapter, the military coup staged by Park and his junta of officers aimed to sweep away what it saw as the moral and financial corruption, dependency, and stagnancy of the Syngman Rhee political world. Following an efficient and relatively bloodless purging of the old guard, the new administration, dubbed the Supreme Council for National Reconstruction (SCNR), fielded an army of technocrats and quickly drafted and implemented an extensive set of reforms under the "fatherland restoration" and "modernization" banners. The showpieces of these reforms were the series of five-year economic plans that set the course for rapid industrialization, starting with the improvement of agricultural output and development of light industry in the early 1960s and culminating in an overhaul of the rural economy and the expansion of heavy industry by the early 1970s. The point here is that this push for enlightenment and rationalization extended beyond the economy and manifested in sweeping social policies and cultural reforms. These came down in the form of highly structured, rigorously calculated codes and regulations designed to strengthen South Korean cultural output as productive industries.

The new regime was met with mixed though largely enthusiastic response from public intellectuals, many of whom were drafted to help fashion social and cultural policy. Under the auspices of a set of restructured administrative offices (the Board of Education, the Ministry of Culture and Information), the SCNR and its subsequent civilian manifestation under President Park instituted a series of laws—the Public Performance Law, the Recording Law, the long-standing Cultural Assets Protection Law, and others—that actively sought to regulate public (and by explicitly stated extension) private culture. Given its centrality as the premier mass cultural form as well as its relative economic significance, filmmaking was a focal point for the Park regime. On September 11, 1961, less than four full months after tanks had rolled through Seoul, the SCNR announced its new policies for motion picture production companies, proposing to enforce the new act by the end of the month and eliminate any firms that were not in compliance. It is worth noting here that these measures put an abrupt end to Korea's first nongovernmental film regulation body, the Civilian Film Ethics Committee, which had assumed oversight of the industry only less than one year earlier during the "spring" of the April revolution.[12] Shin Films, established on a comparatively large scale in early 1960, was the only entity to meet the SCNR's stringent requirements and register officially. The regulations went into legislative effect in the form of the First Motion Picture Law the following January, giving leeway to those few companies with adequate means to restructure and meet code, and were given punitive force in a first major revision in March 1963.

As we saw in chapter 2, the South Korean film industry was robust in the latter half of the 1950s, turning out an annual peak of over one hundred films by 1959. The lightly regulated market thrived largely on venture capital; the majority of films were financed and produced as one-off projects (where studios would make an average of only 1.5 films in 1959), finding their way to exhibition through informal channels. This inevitably resulted in a number of bad deals and bankruptcies, would-be directors and producers absconding with funds, or investor insolvency putting abrupt halts to production. We also saw that foreign films, despite the institution of the first screen quota in 1958, dominated the market through massive importation as well as through the not necessarily less obvious channels of mimicry and plagiarism. The early film laws of the Park regime sought to address these problems and strengthen the domestic industry through *"kiŏp'hwa"*—translating literally as "enterprization" but implying something closer to industrialization and rationalization. The absolute number of imported films fell from 135 in 1960 to an all-time low of 51 in 1964 through the institution of import quotas, the designation of separate theaters for foreign film exhibition, and the establishment of a system whereby only registered production companies could obtain licenses to import foreign films.[13] But while the statistics certainly reflected a shift in import quantity, lax enforcement and the continued popularity of foreign films with urban audiences meant that the quota and license systems fell short of the goal of strengthening local production companies. That burden then fell to an equally well-intentioned but similarly misguided set of production quotas.

These measures were in fact the centerpiece of the early film laws and shaped the film industry for the next two decades. Under the new system, films could be produced only by studios that had registered with the Ministry of Education and Information and that met an array of conditions. Those set minimums for personnel—at least three full-time contract directors, three full-time contract cinematographers, a sound engineer, ten male and ten female contract actors, and so on—demanded that the studio space itself be at least two hundred *p'yŏng* (approximately 7,200 square feet), and that the company possess a broad spectrum of equipment, including three 35 mm cameras, lights totaling at least 200 KWs, and modern sound recording facilities.[14] Of the sixty-five studios extant in late 1961, none save Shin Films could pass muster; the rest were forced to close their doors or consolidate with other entities before the 1962 deadline, leaving only sixteen studios nationwide.[15] The most troublesome regulation, however, proved to be the registered studio's obligation to produce at least fifteen films per year, an overwhelming task made even more onerous by the abruptness of its implementation. Many studios resorted to lending their names to independent studios, which would otherwise be unable to produce films, or were forced to grind out cheap productions quickly in order to meet the quota.[16] The stakes were raised even further by the attachment to those quotas of the foreign film import licenses, ultimately the most lucrative side of the film business. When stricter enforcement of the quota began in the first half of 1963, the number of extant studios fell in that year to an all-time low of only six, returning to ten and then to nineteen in the following years, stabilizing at around twenty for the next decade.

Domestic film production numbers soared over this period, increasing gradually from a low of 86 feature films in 1961 to a peak of 229 in 1969. But while the decade certainly saw the release of a number of diverse and often challenging films, the result in quality overall tended to diminish with the quantitative proliferation, ebbing into formula and repetition. And further, while Korean films tended to perform reasonably well at regional events such as the Asian Film Festival, the industry as a whole never managed to achieve the international prestige or export profitability that was at first the tacit and then later the explicit aim of the Park administration. These short-comings, as film historian Pak Chi-yŏn has argued, were largely the result of the implicit contradiction between regulation and promotion within the regime's legislation, despite the fact that the overall aim was market capital-ization.[17] There was, Pak suggests, an unmanageable "imbalance" between the "politicization of culture," which translated into inescapably stricter forms of censorship, and the rapid development of the industry, which was implemented via the mechanical regulations and quotas outlined above. Films, in other words, did not function in the same way as the textiles and small crafts that were leading the nation's export-led growth in the 1960s. While the Park regime's overall goal of industrializing and rationalizing the film industry was welcomed by filmmakers and critics alike, this was, Pak concludes, an effect of the "pseudo-consensus" that had been forged around the concept of "modernization" and could not be converted into a sustain-able cultural force.[18] When the developmentalist flush of the early 1960s faded, the film industry became a highly productive but creatively con-stricted factory.

To a certain extent, this astute assessment (crystallized by Pak but made in different forms by a number of other prominent critics) works as a cri-tique of Shin Films, by far the most productive studio of the Park era. But while Shin Films has come to be synonymous with the heyday of Ch'ungmuro (South Korea's Hollywood), it is important to note how and where Shin's company diverged from the industry and the enablements and constraints placed on Shin's own filmmaking as a result of the particular forms the stu-dio took over the decade. The first thing to note here is that Shin had already acquired significant cultural and financial capital in the late 1950s and built a major studio before the advent of the Park regime. With the success of the sophisticated melodramas discussed in chapter 2, particularly with *Confessions of a College Girl* (*Ŏnŭ yŏdaesaeng ŭi kobaek*, 1958), Shin had established himself as a dependable hit-maker, put together networks of distribution and exhibition around the country, attracted the interest of leading star talents and technicians, and saved up the funds to invest in an independent production company. Built as a major expansion on the Seoul Film Company studio, Shin Films was launched in early 1960 and its first production, *Romance Papa* (*Romaensŭ ppappa*, 1960) a light though impeccably produced family comedy, fixed the studio's reputation for high quality filmmaking with mass appeal.[19] This was immediately followed by a remarkable string of generically diverse films that defined Shin's legacy: *Madame Whitesnake* (*Paeksa puin*), *Until the End of This Life* (*Yi saengmyŏng tahadorok*), *Evergreen*, *Prince Yŏnsan* (*Yŏnsan'gun*), *Sŏng Ch'unhyang*, and *The Houseguest and My Mother* (*Sarangbang sonnim kwa ŏmŏni*). All of these films were produced before the 5.18 coup and screened well in advance of the SCNR's film policy legislation. In other words, Shin had already achieved a measure of industrialization and rationalization before it was mandated by the state.

As we have seen, "*kiŏp'hwa*" had been a keyword in public discourse, and in writing about the film industry, in fits and starts since the 1930s. Bemoaning the "shabby" (*ch'orahan*) look of Korean films when compared to imports, a December 1958 editorial in the *Kyŏnghyang Sinmun* suggested that:

> Among the fifty or so production companies out there, the only ones that show any kind of vitality are Sudo, Samsŏng, and Han'guk Yŏnye. These are the only places to find the stability and health of a real enterprise [*kiŏp*]. The rest are just small fry that make one or two films and disappear.[20]

Another editorial in the *Chosŏn Ilbo* (June 1959) noted that, "while the sheer production numbers of our film industry have shot up with astonishing speed, the preponderance of one-hit wonders ("*ilsa iljak*") shows that we are still in the cradle as far as enterprization goes."[21] The new policies of the Park regime only occasioned a shift in the rhetoric toward more explicitly stated nationalist concerns; writing in *Yŏnghwa Segye* in 1962, the director Yun Pong-ch'un argued that, "we filmmakers finally have a part to play in national reconstruction. Industrialization means that we must take up our duties and make all the effort and sacrifice for the cause."[22] For the film industry at least, the Park regime did not install the "pseudo-consensus" of modernization but rather instrumentalized and codified it as (albeit mechanical) law. Shin Films was one of the few companies to achieve "the stability and health of a real enterprise" without government intervention; it was able to turn out full-scale blockbusters through its own regular production system and distribution-exhibition networks. Shin Films as a *kiŏp'hwa* forerunner did not, contrary to popular belief, benefit from the reforms so much as receive sanction and endorsement through them.

Shin Films was built explicitly on the (by that point defunct) Columbia Studios model, and by 1962, well exceeded the benchmarks set out in the First Motion Picture Law. Given the pressures it would exert on production, it is worth considering for a moment the sheer scale of the studio. The Yongsan complex where the bulk of production would happen until Shin Films took over Anyang studios in 1966 totaled close to two thousand *p'yŏng*, ten times the minimum requirement, housed two full-scale stages, two recording studios, and a multistation editing room. The studio also owned six 35 mm cameras of various makes and was the first or early adopter of every technical advancement of the period: color cinemascope, zoom lens, sync sound recording, and others. By the mid-1960s Shin Films employed more than 250 staff, which at any one time included contracts for at least six screenwriters, five directors, six cinematographers, and numerous actors and actresses.[23] The studio's center of gravity, though, seems to have been the extensive infrastructure of production and management. Personnel were driven onto the lot on shuttle buses, ate at communal mess halls, and showered and often slept in the company quarters.[24] The costume design department had its own wing and storage facilities and was charged with the manufacture and maintenance of the costumes used not only in the many Shin Films period productions but also rented out to smaller studios.[25] Actors were also heralded into a studio where the senior players were encouraged in their spare time to apprentice the many younger faces that were frequently recruited by the studio; later, this developed into regular acting classes and then, at the Anyang site, into a bona fide acting school.[26] Directors, cinematographers, sound engineers, and the many other trades had their own forms of apprenticeship, and Shin Films became a veritable training ground for a generation of filmmakers. In its vertically integrated production system and strict division of labor, Shin Films operated like a midsized corporation, a hierarchically structured enterprise with a broad but not limitless set of products.

But while Shin Films dwarfed competing studios and easily met all of the regulations set out by the new legislation, it was far from free of the structural constraints of the industry itself: the limits of censorship on the one hand, and the heterogeneous demands of the market on the other. The first of these constraints was systematized quickly in 1961 along with the first film policies and set up for administration via the newly created Office of Public Ethics. The mandate given to this body over filmmaking and other public media was broad and ambiguously articulated and aimed at "protecting" the "public morals" of citizens and ensuring that no public performances would endanger the health of the state.[27] While a standard set of prohibitions was mobilized—such as those against "lewd acts," threats to the state, and "incorrect" depictions of the past (i.e., the colonial and war periods)—the power the office wielded was flexible and tended therefore toward both arbitrariness and increased stringency with the intensified oppressiveness of the regime itself. After a series of censorship scandals in the mid-1960s (most famously the seizure and destruction of Yi Man-hŭi's *Seven Women POWs* (*7-in ŭi yŏporo*), most studios, including Shin Films, backed off from sensitive or challenging material.[28] At the height of the studio's powers in 1965, the Shin Films picture *Queen Min and the Sino-Japanese War* (*Chung-il chŏnjaeng kwa Minbi*) was halted from screening by the board, which cited the film's portrayal of murderous Japanese as a dangerous conflict with the state's recently announced and violently controversial normalization plan with Japan and was only released when Shin contacted the Blue House directly to request a reprieve. Critics have taken this as an obvious indication of Shin's coziness with power. But while Shin certainly enjoyed friendships with high-ranking officials (including Kim Chong-p'il and perhaps even Park himself), the episode in fact illustrates the studio's vulnerability to surveillance and regulation. In fact, 1965 marks a point where Shin's period films took a soft turn toward the remote and abstract and away from narratives and historical themes that could arouse negative and possibly costly attention.

But perhaps the most important condition for both the operational viability and the expressive sensibility of Shin Films was the regional investment and distribution system that powered the postwar Korean film industry. It is worth spending some time here to expand on the workings of that system, given not only its centrality to Shin Films but also its usefulness in understanding the film cultures of the period more broadly. On the one hand, the system is clearly not without precedent or analogy. The U.S. block-booking program, for instance, or the Japanese advanced payment systems, both of which are examined further below, come immediately to mind as comparable forms through which film financing, distribution, and exhibition were secured. But, on the other hand, the Korean regional system differed from those forms in ways that are illustrative of the cultural economics of small postcolonial developmentalist states. The core of this economics is of course the unevenness that marked urban and rural as well as local and global socioeconomic structures. And indeed, the system is broadly depicted by the period's practitioners and observers as well as by contemporary scholars as something of a historical necessity, albeit an efficient and profitable transitional measure before the fuller development of a properly modern direct distribution system.[29] In the great number of articles, editorials, and interviews that address the processes of distribution, the system is described as working in the face of a lack: of a more easily coordinated transportation and rotation system, of the availability or viability of multiple prints, of a more homogeneous mode of penetrating rural markets. Or it is bemoaned for not working well at all, for exposing producers to the vagaries of calculating returns and to the stark divergences in urban and rural markets. In many ways this gap between the "enterprization" ideal, for which the U.S. and Japanese film industries stood as models, and the contradicting realities of the postwar economy is symptomatic of the enlightenment thought that was detailed in chapter 1. But further, the regional investment and distribution system had a profound effect on both the kind of films that were made and how they were produced. It lay at the core of the improvisational, inventive, and often fraudulent practices that in many ways defined the workings of the postwar Korean film industry—which is also to say that it informed the uneven brilliance of the period's films. If the successive iterations of the motion picture laws (and their attempted circumventions) form the core pillar upon which filmmaking practices were governed and controlled, it was the regional investment and distribution system that made postwar filmmaking possible and even legible.

The archival record yields few clues about the precise origins of or rationale for the regional system, though its beginnings are marked sometime in the mid-1950s and its demise in the mid-1980s. The distribution and exhibition system inherited from the colonial period was one that swung wildly between ad hoc and sometime heroic individual ventures (best typified perhaps by the figure of producer Im Su-ho circulating prints of *Arirang* throughout the country on the back of his motorcycle)[30] and the more regimented networks of state and corporate distribution (which ranged from mobile projection units that screened films in remote rural markets to the state-managed theaters in the cities). The broad contours of the postwar system, however, are well known. From the late 1950s, distribution was segmented into six regions: the Seoul outskirts, Pusan and South Kyŏngsang province, Kwangju and Chŏlla province (which included Cheju), Taegu and North Kyŏngsang province, Ch'ungch'ŏng province (encompassing Taejŏn), and the combined Kyŏnggi and Kangwŏn provinces. Each of these regions was overseen by a principal agent, of which there were between three and six per region, who not only managed films for the major first-run theaters in the larger cities but also coordinated distribution for the urban second- and third-run theaters as well as the smaller rural theaters that constituted those agents' chains. These agents were largely theater owners, though some markets were managed by independent middlemen with ties to either the theaters or production companies. Many of the chains, particularly at the height of studio agglomeration in the 1960s, were associated with one or two production companies and exclusively exhibited the in-house and licensed import films of those studios; a few of them, as in the Taejŏn and Taegu networks of Shin Films that will be described further below, formed more formal distribution chains managed directly out of the studios' regional offices.

This regional or "indirect" distribution system greatly facilitated the circulation of film prints into diverse markets at a historical juncture where underdeveloped communications and transportation routes essentially prohibited centralized distribution for all but the most sprawling production companies. By the early 1960s, distribution was managed into a relatively strict system wherein the print (one of which was ordinarily struck for each region) would screen for a set time frame (usually one or two weeks for the larger theaters and bigger productions, more briefly for smaller venues) before cycling off to succeeding nodes on the chain. The importance of these markets and their colonization cannot be underestimated: through the 1960s and 1970s, and despite the centrifugal force of Seoul postwar expansion, anywhere between 80 percent and 90 percent of box-office numbers were drawn from regions outside of the capital.[31] So while the ethnographic record abounds with anecdotes about the rough and improvised operations of many of these chains (prints were often moved from one city to the next by taxi by agents who would regularly sleep in nearby motels, while box-office numbers were manipulated wildly for distributor and exhibitor advantage),[32] the system effectively facilitated the formation of rigidly tiered national film markets and cultures.

But the real importance of the system was financial. The capital raised from the regional distribution networks accounted for 80–90 percent of the cost of production. It was garnered in successive stages of production— ordinarily 20 percent upon presentation of the script and other rudimentary elements (director and actor names, etc.), 50 percent halfway through production, the rest upon delivery—and shared not only among the regions but also within each of those markets.[33] One effect was to reduce risk for both the production companies as well as individual exhibitors. But the system's more fundamental salience lay in the fact that, before the intervention of *chaebŏl* and venture capital in the 1980s and 1990s, the collective fundraising of the regional system was the only reliable source of film financing. As we saw in chapter 1, one of the core complaints about the state of the Korean film industry at any given point, but in particular the postwar period, was the relative weakness of finance capital. And indeed, the prospect of moving beyond the apparent vagaries of the regional investment and distribution system is a minor touchstone of the era's "enterprization" discourses. One of the crucial points to be made here is that while the Korean distribution system functioned in broadly similar ways to the monopolistic and heavy-handed Hollywood "block-booking" system of the 1930s and 1940s, it was not only or even primarily a leveraging tool for the studios.[34] The so-called *ipdo-sŏnmae* (sale before harvest) system did not require exhibitors to blindly pay for a studio's output, but rather was a means, indeed the only means, through which a studio could raise capital in advance of production. This is also the Korean system's difference from the Japanese *chŏndogŭm* (前渡金) practice, in which the emphasis lay on assuring distributor and exhibitor access to particularly sought-after studio films.[35]

The ramifications of this system for particular studios or for specific practitioners are only dimly suggested in the archival and ethnographic record, whose substantive emphasis is weighted toward the challenges and deficiencies of the system. Nevertheless, it is possible to glean two crucial implications for Shin Sang-ok and Shin Films. The first, an easily measurable point, serves to distinguish Shin Films within the broader map of the industry's workings. The studio's output, and in particular Shin's own directorial work, was among the most coveted by regional investors. The bankability of Shin's work, seen as consistently polished and associated with the industry's biggest names, is a common refrain in both contemporaneous reviews and the historical reflections of investors. The chains were prepared to essentially blind-book Shin's films, advancing to Shin the maximum capital to finance his own as well as the other work across the studio. At the same time, Shin Films was one of only a small handful of studios that could transcend, if simply in a few markets, the regional distribution system. Pak Haeng-ch'ŏl, who worked variously in the Yongsan (central Seoul) Shin Films headquarters and in regional offices in Chŏnju and Taegu, has described a complex formula wherein the investments took on the form of promissory notes that were balanced against the shared calculation of box-office returns.[36] This more direct distribution system proved to be more profitable for Shin Films (partially circumventing the ruses many theaters used to fudge numbers), although it put more pressure on the company to raise funds or defer its dues. Throughout the 1960s, the studio's importance to the regional markets, as well as the value of those markets to the studio, was rivaled only dimly by one or two other production houses. When the fact that a broad swath of the postwar industry subsisted primarily on films made exclusively for the second, third, and most remote markets is taken into account, the stature of Shin Films in this period becomes even more pronounced.

But the more interesting point is that the system exerted influence on the kind of films the studio would produce. This may seem obvious enough given the simple calculation that would have been required to determine the financial importance of the regional markets, even for filmmakers or studios that implicitly or explicitly targeted the apparently more exclusive and highbrow first-run Seoul circuits. However, the more concrete ways in which the filmmaking of studios like Shin Films were conditioned by the regional system are elusive and beg speculation. Attendance records, particularly for rural and second-run theaters, are notoriously inconsistent, and the picture they project allows only two broad conclusions: that the rural markets tended to sway toward genre cinema and that Shin's own films, especially in contrast to those of the other directors working under contract with Shin Films, enjoyed consistent success throughout the 1960s and early 1970s. We draw closer to the point when broad differences in urban and rural taste are considered, the most striking fact perhaps being the uneven numbers associated with foreign films. As we have seen, where the Seoul and surrounding theaters accounted for approximately 35 percent of the overall market, at the same time, it represented well over half the national market for foreign films. According to distributors and investors active in the postwar period, particularly those who specialized in imports, foreign films were a difficult sell in the rural markets (and more difficult the more remote the theaters) at a point when literacy rates remained low in rural areas and the distance with world cultures remained vast. Attracting the older women who formed the core of rural markets was apparently as easy as projecting "a clean print with easy-to-understand Korean"—or in some cases, interestingly, employing all-but-defunct *pyŏnsa* to narrate films, doing away with the need for reading obscure subtitles.[37] The plainness of this sociological fact of the geographic unevenness of postwar development levels only becomes provocative when weighed against the critical importance of foreign films to the way studios were run and for how film production and exhibition were managed legally. Indeed, the profitability, if only in the urban centers, of foreign films was substantial enough that many companies deployed a range of creative tactics to satisfy the import restrictions put into effect in the motion pictures law detailed above, from the studio nameplate "borrowing" practice to patched-together international coproductions (some of which were notoriously fake) that, under the rabid expansionism of the government's film policies, could earn import licenses for the studios.[38] Given its complex links with the Shaw Brothers and other leading Asian film companies, Shin Films was, as we will see in more detail below, certainly one of the most deft operators within these mercurial production and import systems. Nevertheless, the regional markets, provincial as they may have seemed, remained the studio's bread and butter throughout its operational heyday, and Shin Sang-ok turned to it reliably to generate the capital or, sometimes, the political goodwill necessary for the more ambitious and cosmopolitan projects that he strove to put at the heart of his studio.

And it is on this point about the centrality of the regional markets that a more cohesive picture might be drawn about Shin Sang-ok, both as a director and as a producer. Specifically, if, as the broad consensus suggests, Shin prioritized market calculation, political acquiescence, and creative conservatism, his motivation may have lain not, as is generally argued, in the blank growth imperative of the studio (which Shin the producer is presumed to have fought for ruthlessly), but rather in the complex forces of the regional market. But what distinguished the demands of the regional from the central urban markets? It is crucial to note, first, that the evaluations made in the production and distribution processes were conditioned by investors, middlemen, and theater owners, and not, as in Seoul where most major companies either owned outright or held exclusive contracts with first-run theaters, solely by the studios or by paying customers.[39] While audiences may have voted with their feet, estimates about what would work throughout the smaller chains and presumptions about what sorts of films would "raise" customers fell largely within the province of the distributors' financial calculations. While there is little evidence to suggest that even the most brash and successful regional investors put overt pressure on studios to generate specific kinds of films or to use particular actors or directors (though, not withstanding this lack, it is entirely plausible that such pressure coursed through the closed-door and gray areas of the industry), the very structure of the production and distribution system—where capital was courted and furnished, and a commitment to screen films made, in key and successive stages of production—seems to have placed considerable priority on a small range of elements: genre, name value, track record.[40] As Kim Il-su, a prominent Kwangju distribution agent put it succinctly, "the box office was guaranteed with companies like Shin Films or Segi because they put out good work by well-known directors."[41] Recognizable actors and actresses, of course, were also critical factors, and Shin Films was especially effective in scouting, training, and putting under contract the leading faces of the era, and in general those faces tended to be safer, older, and more "classically beautiful."

But, as was suggested above, the Shin Films nameplate and its star roster were not enough to guarantee investor interest. It was also the generic features of films that were broadly scrutinized for their marketability. And this is where the specific tastes of rural audiences, or rather the calculation of those tastes, becomes most salient. Throughout the 1960s and 1970s, it was the "conventional" (*t'ongsok*) melodramas principally, and the spy or Manchurian action pictures, secondarily, that would dominate regional theaters. These films would do well in Seoul too, of course, but the range of genres that could succeed in that more heterogeneous market tended to be broader, allowing for foreign and youth films to register more consistently at the box office. Further, work with art film leanings (or, what were broadly seen as pretensions) proved a tough sell. Kim Wan-bae, a central player in the postwar second-run and Seoul-surrounding markets, offers an intriguing assessment: "In the past, art films wouldn't work at all in the regions. They only screened in Seoul. So the regional investors wouldn't look twice at art films. This was more the case the further you went into the country. Those were just the times. So domestic films did very well until the mid-1970s."[42] Kim's passing equation here between art and foreign films is noteworthy, especially in light of the populist critical attitudes toward adaptation we saw in the context of Shin's 1950s melodramas: the artiness of films could make them as alien to rural audiences as their linguistic or cultural foreignness. It might be possible to locate here one of the roots of a broader symptom of postwar Korean film culture, namely, the relative paucity of modernist cinematic forms and, further, the virtual absence of avant-garde or experimental work. With the exception of films such as Kim Ki-yŏng's *Housemaid*, say, or Yi Man-hŭi's *Black Hair* (*Kŏmŭn mŏri*, 1965), the spectrum of formal innovation and technical experimentation in Korea tended to be narrow, especially when projected alongside the voluptuous modernism that arose in Japan, Europe, and pockets of the United States throughout the 1950s and 1960s. But the more focused point here is not only that Shin Films presented this symptom, which it did in spades, but also that Shin positioned his work in an uneasy but often productive relationship with the category of art cinema. As we will see below, Shin carved out a seemingly natural though elusive niche between the art and genre ends of the filmmaking spectrum— what we might call avant la lettre of the "Korean wave," *well-made genre films.* Borne out as much by the consistent rigor of the films as by the common descriptive language of their contemporaneous reviews (which highlighted the films' "smoothness," "polish," "authenticity"), this stylistic character can be traced back to the 1950s melodramas and forward to the apparent grindhouse horrors of the late 1960s. But it is also an index of the location of Shin's authorship, its coordinates on a map of global filmmaking practices and local cinematic consumption. Shin Films amply demonstrates that while the circuits and resources of cinema are irreducibly global, its contours, depths, forms—and even the concepts of art and genre that subtend them—are shaped domestically, in the regional theaters.

In certain ways, the fate of Shin Films in the 1960s is the familiar story of a small business incorporated: along with massive expansion and opportunity came greater responsibility to and integration with multiple interests. Producing more than twenty-four films per year at its peak, the output of Shin Films was, on the one hand, generically and even politically diverse but, on the other hand, restricted by the (albeit profitable) regularization of the studio system (contract directors, actors, costumes, etc.), the watchful eyes of the censors, and the real or imagined tastes of rural audiences. While the vertically integrated, industrialized studio is certainly an emblem of the Park-era modernization push, it is not its direct product, nor, as will be elaborated below, are Shin's films themselves a simple outcome of the cultural protocols of the period. Shin Films came into the 1960s and through the First Motion Picture Law nearly fully formed. The really significant shift over this period, rather, was the one that saw Shin Sang-ok himself transformed from an urban to a *regional* filmmaker, from the director of the slickly modern works discussed in chapter 2 to the maker of earthier and more broadly resonant period pieces and family melodramas. The city and the modern continued to appear in his work, and his films maintained a fraught though critical stance toward the Confucian social order. But as the premier director of a studio in the throes of continual expansion, Shin married his abiding interest in the predicament of women and the family to largely ahistorical figures and narratives that reached out to his most important viewers in the steadily receding country.

Market

In another set of interviews he gave toward the end of his life, Shin Sang-ok, in his characteristically elliptical way of speaking, put his finger on the tension peculiar to Shin Films and stressed the studio's indebtedness to multiple interests:

> We broke away from Ch'ungmuro once we became fully industrialized. Something like opposed mountain ranges. We didn't do the sorts of Manchurian action flicks people like Chŏng Ch'ang-hwa or Ch'oe Wan-gyu did. We only did what you might call artful work or things with really national-popular [*kŏkuk*] appeal. It probably seemed to people on that side [Ch'ungmuro] that we were just lolling around in an ivory tower. But the fact is that we weren't a really solid independent but were actually running on other people's money (*chŏnju rŭl murŏ kajigo*), which meant that we could only go with what they demanded. That's the way moviemaking is, isn't it? And within a capitalist system especially, you've got to use popular stars, and if melodrama's worked in the past then you've got to do it again. In that sense, they're films that are made with other people's interests, not ones that a producer has made.[43]

Shin herein highlights the calculated populism that is the implicit (and sometimes explicit) charge of film critics and historians who have attached labels like "genre master" and "master of the mise-en-scène."[44] But it is also important to note the tension, indeed the seeming contradiction, between that populism and how Shin characterizes the identity of his studio and of his films. Clearly, Shin Films did not make art films; the "historical fate" of postwar South Korean industrialization precluded that for the studio as it did for virtually the industry as a whole. But neither did Shin himself make cheap or lowbrow material—a range that would include the Manchurian action pictures as well as the cut-rate horrors and screwball comedies that proliferated from the mid-1960s through the 1970s.[45] Rather, Shin argues here that his films differed from the usual Ch'ungmuro fare by at least tending or aspiring toward artistic work—which he enigmatically equates here with the "national-popular" (*kŏkuk jŏk*)—notwithstanding the inevitable compromise with commercial interests. The ambivalence of the term *kŏkuk* itself, somewhere between mass and national, suggests the complexity of

Shin's appraisal of the cultural position of his films. While the studio was not quite an ivory tower, it did attempt to produce mass art with national, perhaps universal, significance. So while Shin's filmmaking shifted its appeal toward the regional in the 1960s, it nonetheless sustained a commitment to highbrow artistic sensibility; his films targeted rural audiences without pandering to them.

A high-gloss, high-value treatment of popular material characterizes Shin Sang-ok's work of the 1960s more accurately than the somewhat nebulous "genre" or "mise-en-scène master" appraisals mentioned above. This is borne out vividly in the episode that marked the real breakout of Shin Films, sealed Shin's reputation as a leading filmmaker, and in many ways inaugurated the *kiŏp'hwa* of the South Korean film industry: the decisive Ch'unhyang battle.[46] The competition was waged between Shin and Hong Sŏng-gi, fellow alum of Ch'oe In-gyu's Koryo Film Productions studios and another major filmmaker of the late 1950s. The battleground was the *Ch'unhyang* story, the *p'ansori* folk tale narrating the conflicted relationship between Sŏng Ch'unhyang, daughter of a *kisaeng* mother and *yangban* father, and Yi Mongryong, full-blooded *yangban* scion.[47] Production on both films, Hong's *Ch'unhyangjŏn* and Shin's *Sŏng Ch'unhyang*, began in 1960, and the brewing rivalry generated a small frenzy within the film industry and beyond. The stakes were raised by the fact that both films were shot in the then novel color cinemascope format, tallied unprecedented production budgets, and starred each of the director's respective muse-wives, Kim Chi-mi for Hong and Ch'oe Ŭn-hŭi for Shin, by far the biggest stars of the day. Hong's Hong Seung Kie Productions owned Seoul's largest movie house (named, despite the fact that it was dedicated to domestic films, *Kukje Kŭkjang* or International Theater) and had an extensive network of regional investors that readily put up substantial funds for the proposed epic. Released to coincide with the New Year holidays, *Ch'unhyangjŏn* premiered first but exited the theaters after only fourteen days, falling well short of projected ticket sales, effectively ending Hong's career. *Sŏng Ch'unhyang*, however, despite its delayed release (one month later than planned), packed the Seoul Myŏngbo theater for seventy-four days, pulling in a record 380,000 viewers over that span, a remarkable success at a time when Seoul's population was hovering around 2.5 million and the average attendance for a film stood at less than 35,000.[48]

A contemporary review in the *Han'guk Ilbo* suggests, with some (perhaps unintentional) complexity, the advantage Shin's film may have had:

The most striking impression was the forceful shared emotion and excitement between the full audience and the screen. It seemed that the commoner housewives with their babies on their backs were breathing in unison with the film. The image of Ch'unhyang that people had cherished in their minds was faithfully projected on the screen. Put another way, it is clear that the film found the highest common denominator for everyone in the audience. In terms of technique, while the color composition was quite strong it might have been better had the camera been somewhat more active.[49]

Another review in the *Han'guk Ilbo* argued "*Sŏng Ch'unhyang* was more substantial than *Ch'unhyangjŏn*, its comic and tragic elements more convincing and entertaining," and that despite its bland interpretation of the narrative, "it had great mass appeal."[50] In their suggestion that *Sŏng Ch'unhyang* appealed especially to lower-class women and rendered an ideal version of the folk icon-heroine, these reviews are broadly symptomatic of prevailing contemporary opinion as well as the critical discourse surrounding the episode in academic scholarship. Older film historians such as Yi Yŏng-il and Kim Hak-su merely note that Shin's version was more broadly popular, tacitly suggesting the film's greater mass legibility or visual draw.[51] More recent scholarship has suggested in various ways that *Sŏng Ch'unhyang*'s resonance was social: for Jinsoo An, the film's conclusion communicated to its audiences the possibility of public justice while for Paek Mun-im, the Ch'unhyang realized by Ch'oe Ŭn-hŭi was a more affirmative representation of female subjectivity.[52] Looking to the pleasures of the film itself, critic Chŏng Chong-hwa has argued that it was in fact the supporting actors, Hŏ Chang-gang and To Kŭm-bong, in their comedic roles as Pangja and Hyangdan, which appealed to contemporary audiences.[53] Shin Sang-ok's own view was that his film was more "truthful," both in the way that it got to the essence of the original narrative and in the historical accuracy (or what he elsewhere calls the *kojŭng*, or historical materiality) of its costumes and fittings. "Hong Sŏng-gi failed," he claimed wryly, "because he didn't do his homework."[54]

These assessments to varying degrees help to sketch the social and cultural discourses in which this significant cinematic event occurred. Undeniably, the majority of *Sŏng Ch'unhyang*'s audiences were low- to middle-class women who might have been moved by the suffering and eventual triumph of the beautiful and courageous Ch'unhyang. And the bright colors of the screen and the energetic performances of all the actors could only bolster the film's popularity. But Hong Sŏng-gi's film did not lack these features in any serious way. *Ch'unhyangjŏn*'s target audience was identical and its star, Kim Chi-mi, was often labeled "the most beautiful woman in Asia." The conventional historiography comes up short in interpreting how these two films, born of the same filmmaking tradition and within identical production systems, could have such diametrically opposed commercial outcomes. In a crucial way, an authoritative explanation is simply not possible; the vagaries of the mass cultural market, as any realistic producer or critic would know, are not completely predictable. A more guileless (but possibly accurate?) approach would simply call *Sŏng Ch'unhyang* a better film, more accomplished in its formal finish, and more satisfying in the flow of its story telling pace, though, interestingly, even contemporary journalistic reviews do not venture far into this territory. But a more rigorous address might start by taking Shin's own seemingly trivial and offhand remarks more seriously. For on one level, while equally unquantifiable, it would be a mistake to underestimate the importance of historical sincerity, if not accuracy, for the audiences of period pieces. Presumably, the vast majority of audiences would likely care very little whether a particular hat was originally made out of horsehair or fashioned out of straw. Nevertheless, the costume and set details, not to mention what Jinsoo An has called the "irreducible historical indexicality" of the location shooting,[55] hangs together in *Sŏng Ch'unhyang* and at the very least guards against, in Shin's words, the "threat of awkwardness."[56] But more concretely, the film's *kojŭng* is a reflection of the filmmaker's seriousness. In the course of making a film with mass appeal that "found the highest common denominator," Shin worked with a measure of easily palpable professionalism that, whether or not it registered consciously with his audiences, spoke to the respect Shin paid to his viewers as well as to his own craft.

This professionalism, furthermore, was not limited to props and costumes, but also found more conspicuous expression in the film's photography. This is suggested in the first review cited above which rightly, though uncharitably, points to the economy of the camera's movement in *Sŏng Ch'unhyang*.[57] This is apparent early in the film, especially at Kwanghallu where Mongryong pours drinks for his manservants and the modest scene is captured at medium length through a virtually static lens. Shots of this sort are repeated throughout the film, allowing the camera-viewer to take in the action, or the colors and details of the costumes and sets, or the locations and comfortably tamed landscapes that ground the proceedings (Figure 6). More than composing a painterly or dramatic mise-en-scène (which he nevertheless certainly does), the strength of Shin Sang-ok's direction here

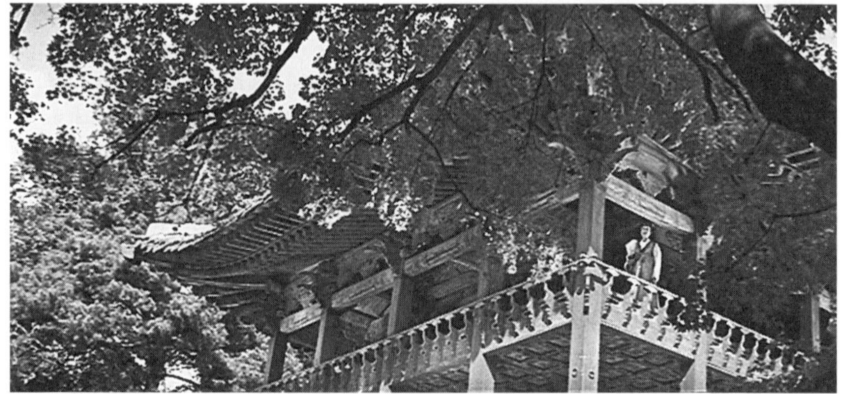

Figure 6. An emblematic long shot in *Sŏng Ch'unhyang* (Shin Sang-ok, 1961). Courtesy of the Korean Film Archive.

is in making the most of the new apparatus, the color cinemascope lens. The Ch'unhyang films were certainly not the first iteration of color cinemascope in Korea (the format having been introduced via foreign films well in advance), but they furnished the first real occasion to view Korean subjects through that hypersaturated and expanded form of seeing. And the diverse, often leisurely movements of Shin's camera—a mix of long and medium shots and slow tracks and pans—took better advantage of that novelty than the busy darting and medium-close shots that dominated Hong Sŏng-gi's framing. This was especially germane to the subject itself, a narrative of loyalty, filial piety, and justice that, however speciously, claimed to represent the beauty and spirit of Korea. And this is perhaps what accounts most convincingly for *Sŏng Ch'unhyang*'s success: a blending of careful craftsmanship and earnest primitivism that allowed it to become a *kŏkukjŏk'in*, or national-popular, event, equally legible to urban crowds and rural masses on the cusp of full-scale industrialization.

Genre

Much of Korean film criticism over the past decade or so has worked within a methodology of ideological analysis, advancing a critique of the sexual politics of melodrama,[58] the social significance of female stars,[59] or the symbolic work of the historical drama.[60] And certainly, readings of *Sŏng Ch'unhyang* or any number of Shin Sang-ok's films from the 1960s must take serious account of this approach if their sociohistorical significance is to be

grasped in any significant way. The present study, in fact, has sought to con-
tribute to that critical investigation precisely by pausing to consider some of
the more basic mechanisms by which the ideological coding of the modern
Korean state found its way into films and how those in turn found their way
back into public discourse. Studio operations, market pressures, and formal
innovations have thus far been the focus not because they are, as formalists
may claim, the primary inducements of filmmaking, but because they
have so often been ignored by recent critics or cast aside as discrete from
ideological processes. A tacit assumption of much of the above-referenced
criticism has been that Korean films from the 1960s are the product of
factory-like studios and that they could therein only directly reflect state
"discourses of power" in that mechanical industrialization–rationalization
process. A corollary assumption has been that audiences, even the low- to
middle-class women whom critics seek to salvage from the discursive violence of conventional filmmaking and film historiography, were duped
into their modern authoritarian subjectivities at least in part by the seductions of the Ch'ungmuro dream factory. And finally, as we have seen, Shin
Sang-ok has often been singled out as particularly culpable, his prolific
manufacture of archetypal (read, formulaic) genre films, excessive com-
mercialism, and intimacy with the Park regime seen as antithetical to the
socially conscientious filmmaking (i.e., Yu's *Stray Bullet*, Yi Man-hui's *Seven
Prisoners*, Kim's *Housemaid*) that at the very least troubled the censors
charged with policing the moral and political content of films. But while
Shin's films were often complicit with, and at times explicitly championed,
the discourses of state power, the production processes of his studio were
more complex and the dialogue his films invoked with both their audiences and the state more multifaceted, than has been allowed by recent
scholarship. A fuller critique of the ideological dimensions of the period's
films will take these into account.

With this more developed sense of its intellectual stakes, we can now
return to the argument that was begun in the first half of this chapter by
turning briefly to the question of genre. As mentioned above, the generic
range of Shin Sang-ok's body of work in the 1960s is fairly limited. Of the
thirty-six films he directed, nineteen could be classified as either period
or historical dramas (*sidaegŭk*), though that number rises to twenty-one if
films set in the colonial period (*Houseguest* and *Samnyong the Mute*) are
included. This category of films is sometimes broken down into subgenres
such as *kungjung* (royal court) or *sagŭk* (history), and crosses over substantially with horror films, which are invariably set sometime in the Chosŏn or

Silla periods, as well as the broad *munye* (literary adaptation) genre, but such narrow classifications are not stable and are not helpful to the present discussion (a different sort of grouping will be suggested below). Outside of this overwhelming majority, the rest of the films are spread out rather evenly across three broadly defined genres: four or five enlightenment or military films (which include *Evergreen, Rice* [*Ssal*], and *Red Muffler* [*Ppalgan mahura*]), three action films (a belated and short-lived series of Manchurian action pictures such as *The Wanderer* [*Musukja*]) and four horrors. A handful of other films do not easily fit into any of these categories; *Romance Papa*, despite its being emblematized as a 1960s family melodrama, seems to belong as much to the modern dramas discussed in chapter 2. *Romance Gray* (*Romaensŭ kŭrei*, 1963) a sophisticated social satire, and *A Woman's Life* (*Yŏja ŭi ilsaeng*, 1968), an exceptional *sinp'a* forerunner to the popular *I Still Love You* (*Miwŏdo tasi hanbŏn*) series, are relatively autonomous.[61]

The point of this listing is not merely taxonomic but rather intended to suggest the continuities and instabilities of both Shin's work and the genre classification system itself. Two things are immediately apparent here: Shin's output in the 1960s was dominated by the period piece and is bereft of anything resembling the youth (*ch'ŏngch'un*) film. This latter fact is especially striking considering the commercial popularity of films like Kim Su-yong's *Classroom of Youth* (*Ch'ŏngch'un kyosil*, 1963) and Kim Ki-dŏk's *Barefoot Youth* (*Maenbal ŭi ch'ŏngch'un*, 1964) throughout the decade, and the fact that Shin Sang-ok had "discovered" the leading actor of this genre, Sin Sŏng-il, in one of his famed talent searches of the 1960s.[62] This lacuna in itself, further, complicates a reading of the preponderance of the period film in Shin's filmography, for if the string of mostly profitable period films was substantially motivated by the dependability of their commercial success, the evasion of the youth film is perplexing. There are a number of possible explanations. The first, and most basic, is that Shin Sang-ok and Shin Films as a whole specialized in a set of genre films and chose to capitalize on both that reputation and the considerable investment in the particular enablements of that style of filmmaking (i.e., costumes and sets for the historical dramas as well as the staff that quickly became experts in filming them). At their peak and to some degree thereafter, the major Hollywood studios of course were associated with particular genres and even appearances (i.e., the glittery MGM musical style, the gritty Paramount crime dramas). The second explanation, suggested above, is that Shin and his studio had by the early 1960s reoriented toward the regional markets, flooding the screens with well-made iterations of easily palatable material. The broad assumption that must be made here is that the youth film would have been more popular in Seoul and seemed somehow alien or unpleasant to regional audiences, and vice versa for the period film. Finally, we are compelled to contend with the possibility that the preference for the period piece over youth film was Shin's own, an authorial "signature."

The stakes and implications of that signature will be elaborated below. At this juncture, however, it may be useful to pause and consider how genre filmmaking—not only the period film but the action and horror films as well—was inflected by the specialization of Shin Films as a regional studio and Shin's directorial tendencies. While it was something of an anomaly in terms of its investment structure and its level of preparation, *Sŏng Ch'unhyang* is emblematic of the overall tenor of Shin's productions. Most, but clearly not all, of the films are made to a standard of professionalism that, for regular filmgoers, would have been readily apparent. Not only did Shin utilize the latest technological innovations—the color cinemascope and zoom lenses, sync sound recording, and so on—but he invested significantly in keeping his studio up with the latest trends, subscribing regularly to American as well as the ostensibly banned Japanese film magazines, and inviting Japanese filmmakers and technicians to visit with his crew. It was thus not only screen composition that marked off Shin's "golden age" films, but the whole surface of technical polish detailed in chapter 2 (smooth edits, subtle lighting, etc.) applied to a larger scale of filmmaking. Furthermore, Shin's films were continually populated by the era's top stars, an ensemble cast led by Ch'oe Ŭn-hŭi, Sin Yŏng-gyun, and Hŏ Chang-gang, who were easily identified with the roles they were assigned.

Another critical inflection is that the films Shin produced in each of the three minor genres were latecomers to the screen, following well behind the first flush of novelty and therefore positioned to refine or reconfigure the codes in various ways. As Jinsoo An has pointed out, the cycle of Machurian action films—"westerns" set in the vast Kando and Manchurian plains in the colonial period—began in 1962 with Im Kwon-t'aek's *Farewell Tumen River* (*Tuman kang'a chal ittkkŏra*) and reached a peak in 1964 and 1965 with the release of a new picture nearly every month.[63] The trend had eventually played out by 1967, so that by 1968, when Shin's *The Wanderer* was released, it must have seemed incongruous or even nostalgic. And indeed its portrayal of a weary and embittered fighter in place of the committed and patriotic soldier of the classic films signaled a major shift in sensibility. Yet, it was *The Wanderer*'s gritty but minimal look, as well as its relaxed pace, more knowingly resonant with both the Japanese samurai and Italian western traditions that were the genre's obvious sources, which set it apart from its cheaper and more action-packed predecessors. Shin's 1969 and 1970 horrors, too, shaded the genre in novel ways. While ghosts had haunted Korean screens from the inception of domestic filmmaking (the 1923 *Changhwa Hongnyŏn*), the horror genre (at first *koedam* or *koe'gi* [ghost tale] and then *kongp'o* [horror]) would not revisit theaters in any substantial way until 1963 with Yi Yong-min's *People from the Grave* (*Mudŏm esŏ naun saram dŭl*).[64] The form was adopted by a number of accomplished filmmakers such as Yu Hyŏn-mok (*Han*, 1965), but the genre only exploded in 1967 with Kwŏn Ch'ŏl-hwi's bombastic *Public Cemetery under the Moon* (*Wŏlha ŭi kongdong myoji*). Shin Sang-ok's entries, *Dead Woman* (*Sa'nyŏ*) and *Thousand Years Fox* (*Ch'ŏnnyŏnho*) in 1969 and *Yi Dynasty Ghost Tale* (*Yijo koedam*) in 1970, were not anachronistic (the cheap and relatively profitable genre would guarantee regular production into the late 1970s), but called special attention to themselves as oddly refined and challenging work. *Thousand Years Fox*, in particular, hyperbolized the genre's latent themes of repressed female sexuality and installed a hitherto foreign dimension of lyrical pathos into the conventional narrative of possession and revenge. Both the Manchurian action films and the horrors, then, were Shin Sang-ok's ventures into explicitly B-movie genres, and both saw him capitalize on and then refine their codes, luring them modestly closer to the imagined Shin Films ivory tower.

But it was, of course, the period film for which Shin mobilized his studio's assets most fully and established the particularities of his authorial signature. We have already seen how the coalescence of forces—the growth and reorientation of Shin Films, the overwhelming success of *Sŏng Ch'unhyang*—set Shin on a course of commercially lucrative specialization in the genre. But what is it that made Shin's films so popular with his regional viewers? Certainly, their formal superiority to contemporaneous films was a chief factor. This is crucial, of course, not only in the inherent visual pleasure that it affords, but also because of its suspension of a high-culture sensibility within an eminently accessible entertainment form in a way that regional (that is, peripheral) audiences could value. It also, conversely, suspends within the fantasy of the various splendors or horrors of the past a sense, however illusory, of the authenticity of representation. The long, static takes of *Sŏng Ch'unhyang* or the long landscape shots that evoke the premodern village of *Chastity Gate* (*Yŏllyŏmun*, 1962) are not only, of course, experimentations with the long or cinemascope lenses, but were for Shin the most compelling way to visualize a cultural heritage that was quickly evaporating or being repressed by the machinery of modernization.

All of this seems to have endowed Shin's period fabulations with a sort of authority—a significant counterweight to the folk popularity of the narratives his films appropriated.

This visibility and legitimacy would have mattered very little, though, were the films illegible socially or thematically to contemporary audiences. In her detailed study of Shin's period films, Kim Ho-yŏng argues that they were important "social texts" precisely because they "show how traditional Korean culture and modern Western culture collide and fuse and create disorder"—exactly what those in the smaller regional cities and towns as much as those in Seoul were experiencing firsthand.[65] Taking a wide view, we can see that Shin was dealing broadly with two gendered forms of social conflict. The first conflict centered on men and the confrontation with family trauma, or an incommensurably alien social-political sphere. The second conflict concerned women and the seemingly irreducible tension between sexual-sensual desire and Confucian social codes. These two strands told different stories, had different functions, and were aimed at different audiences. The representative male-problem film is *Prince Yŏnsan* (1961), about the monarch driven mad to uncover the truth about and then avenge his mother's tragic demise in the face of royal court power struggles. The central struggle here is between the private and public realms, between the affective and psychological ties that are forged in blood and the formal obligations and roles that are set in the Yi royal lineage—formalized in the discourse of the king's two bodies. Shin returned to this thematic in rapid succession: first with the bloodier follow-up, *Yŏnsan the Tyrant* (*P'okgun Yŏnsan*, 1962); and then with *A Reluctant Prince* (*Kanghwa toryŏng*, 1963) and *Ch'ŏljong and Poknyŏ* (*Ch'ŏljong kwa Poknyŏ*, 1963), both about averse country bumpkins called on to forsake their first loves and take the throne; and, later, with *The Eunuch* (*Naesi*, 1968), which narrates the seemingly inexorable violence of petty courtier power struggles.

Against the grain of earlier interpretations, Jinsoo An rightly points out these films were not strictly allegorical portrayals of the contemporary political scene.[66] Both the sadistic and vengeful Yŏnsan and the figure of a sincere buffoon-turned-king certainly echoed elements of Park Chung Hee's leadership, but neither characterization was commensurate with Shin Sang-ok's relationship to the regime circa 1962. The films, rather, come much closer to articulating the regime's rhetorical position in relation to the politics of both the Chosŏn kingship and the Syngman Rhee era, namely, that both festered with stifling and irrational bureaucracies that obstructed strong and responsible governance. As we will see in the next chapter's analysis of *Evergreen*, this discourse was attached to a pastoral retrospection for the imagined innocence of the country, often figured as a longing for the affective attachments of family and first loves. Here the male-centered period films can be seen as complex treatments of the past that are inescapably modern and political, bearing a nostalgia for, variously, the innocence or grandeur of the past at the same time as they implicitly suggest a freer, less traumatic future (or present). Married to Shin's bold formal designs, this critical reflection on the past resonated with both the public discourse of enlightenment and development and the stubborn desire to catch an extravagant glimpse of the nation's past.

Shin Sang-ok's treatments of women through period films, by contrast, appear deliberately apolitical and ahistorical, despite their haunting and often radical critique of the oppressive structures of the past. Following *Sŏng Ch'unhyang*, these films, nearly invariably starring Ch'oe Ŭn-hŭi in roles as beleaguered women, dominated Shin's output and public image. They ranged from the minimalist melodrama of *Chastity Gate* to the formal experimentations of *Cruel Stories of Yi Dynasty Women* (*Yijo yŏin chanhoksa*, 1969) to the playful explorations of horrors like *Yi Dynasty Ghost Tale*. But within this stylistic diversity, the films were conjoined by the figure of the woman made to suffer physical or emotional violence or to repress sexual desire by various manifestations of Confucian social custom. At the same time, the films do not suggest a political or historical solution to women's predicament; they suggest, rather, that oppression lives as inescapably in the present as it did in the past. Shin Sang-ok's often contradictory reflections on this work suggest why his period narratives about men and women would diverge in this way. For on the one hand, he implies that he started with social critical intent:

> When I took *Houseguest* to the 1961 Asian Film Festival as a panelist, I recognized that the only place the kind of morality or Confucian tradition the film portrayed existed anymore was Korea. I really had no choice but to go with women's films, given the severity of the restrictions (*cheyak*). I would have liked to do more modern material, but the Confucian morals and ethics really left me no choice.[67]

On the other hand, Shin has consistently deflected positive suggestions that his films are feminist:

> With *Chastity Gate*, people were saying that it had a critical consciousness about Confucian society, but despite whatever was in the material I myself

personally admire Confucianism. The idea that the film called for human or women's liberation is just wrong . . . I believe that perseverance is a virtue.[68]

To a certain extent, these remarks reflect Shin's efforts to shape his legacy as a filmmaker. In nearly every one of his interviews, Shin attempted to turn attention from the social dimensions of his period and women's films and direct it toward either the films' formal properties or to a discussion of altogether different films, preferably to what he called his "social pictures" (*sahoe mul*)—or, alternatively, "men's stories" or, as above, "modern" material. This is presumably because he felt that the feminist reading of his films would merely bolster the perception, popularly held since the late 1950s, that he was only a women's (or in the implicitly derogatory usage of the day, *komu sin* [rubber shoe]) filmmaker, apt to make maudlin *sinp'a* for lowbrow enjoyment. Shin was comfortable with his reputation as a mass cultural producer, as long as he could claim the masculinity of social conscientiousness.

It is clear, however, that more is at stake than Shin's reputation, for even in the remarks referenced above he betrays an awareness, if not serious interest, in the critical utility of his women-centered films. In nearly all of his work, women must either repress their need for emotional fulfillment or sexual pleasure or are punished for their transgression of social restriction. In *Madame Whitesnake, Houseguest,* and *Chastity Gate,* widows are forced, in the face of patriarchal authority (commanded, typically, through the figure of the mother-in-law), to forsake the possibility of meaningful connection to their beloveds: Madame Whitesnake to her earthly lover, Madame Yi to her dashing houseguest, and the nameless daughter-in-law to both her servant-lover and long-lost son. Queen In-mok and the court lady Cha-ok in *The Eunuch* are punished and eventually killed for their sexual excesses, as are Queen Chin-sŏng and the possessing female spirit in *Thousand Years Fox.* Yet in contrast to the explicit political signification of *Prince Yŏnsan* or *The Reluctant Prince,* the pathos of physical or emotional trauma does not translate into a more fundamental critique of the social order. For Shin, there is no contradiction between an "admiration" for Confucianism and a consciousness or even abhorrence of the predicament in which it leaves women. Rather, it is the moments of surplus repression—excesses grounded in but not necessarily integral to the basic repressions of the harmonious Confucian social hierarchy—that awaken both his social and mass cultural consciousnesses. But rather than developing into protest, both the basic and surplus repressions are projected as undifferentiated pillars of social stability, and more relevantly, presented for the aestheticization of the market. The irreducible melancholy of the unrequited loves in *Houseguest* and *Chastity*, and the macabre fates of weary or wayward women in *Cruel Stories* or *Thousand Years Fox* are leveled, transformed into eminently consumable images, tragic and primitive.

Cruel Stories, in fact, is a fascinating text through which to consider the multiple factors conditioning Shin Sang-ok's treatment of women. The film was produced at a juncture when, after a major expansion into the sprawling Anyang studios complex and subsequent subdivision into smaller units, the large-scale period piece was no longer profitable or feasible for Shin Films. The studio sought different, more quickly profitable projects, and Shin found himself directing more films than he had ever done in the past, shooting seven films in 1969. Like *The Wanderer* and *Thousand Years Fox*, *Cruel Stories* was something of an experiment, though here the play was not with genre but with form. The film takes an omnibus structure, split into four distinct narratives that are conjoined by their coarse, brooding style and their common exploration of the cruelties visited on women under Chosŏn rule.

The first, roughly translating to "Wives Must Follow Their Husbands" (and archaically titled in the original "Yŏp'il chŏngbu"), narrates the fate of a young woman whose adolescent would-be groom has died, but who is nevertheless obligated by prior contract, enforced by the stern commands of her own pious father, to enter into the manor as widowed daughter-in-law. When she can no longer endure the pressures and sexual deprivations of being a virgin widow and quietly escapes, she is slain by her father to protect the family name. Her body is dragged to the boy's gravesite, creating the illusion that she killed herself to follow her husband. Her seeming sacrifice is honored by the erection of an imposing *yŏllyŏmun* (literally, virtuous or chaste woman's gate). The film closes with the image of a young girl brought by her grandfather to admire the gate, her expression an ambiguous blend of awe and doubt.

The second, "The Seven Sins of a Wife" ("Ch'ilgŏji'ak"), is the story of an older wife who after ten years of marriage has committed the cardinal sin (among the seven legitimate justifications for divorce): not bearing the family a child. She ironically redeems herself when, on an outing, she abruptly seduces her mute manservant in an exquisitely conflicted scene and becomes pregnant. After the long-awaited baby is born, however, her husband discovers that he has been sterile since adolescence and confronts his wife; fearing for her baby and for her honor, she stabs herself in the mouth and, swearing the manservant to secrecy, dies grotesquely. In his rage and grief, the husband threatens to smother the baby but is stopped by his father, who had known of his son's sterility all along. The film's last image is a tableau of the family's peculiar patriarchy: the lineage-obsessed grandfather, the sterile son, the mute father, and the cherished scion.

The third and last extant installment,[69] "Hidden Desires of the Royal Palace" ("Kŭmjung pisaek") is set among the society of palace ladies who serve the unchecked cravings of a Yŏnsan-like monarch. Middle-aged Madame Yi, whose sole task is to observe and report on the activities of the nocturnal royal chamber, is doomed to a maddening suppression of sexual arousal. When she is pushed beyond endurance and dashes beyond the palace walls, she is ravished in the woods by a faceless stranger and becomes pregnant. Despite repeated attempts to abort the pregnancy, her predicament is discovered by the senior palace ladies, who are nevertheless convinced to protect Yi and help her bring her child into the world by hiding her in an abandoned storeroom. On one of their trips to the storeroom, they spy the baby's father and, mistakenly fearing for their reputation (being discovered outside the palace walls is a sin punishable by death), join together and kill him. The story ends well, however, for the ladies pack Yi and her baby into a coffin (that is, the only vehicle through which a woman can leave the court) and send the single mother out free into the world.

Cruel Stories is unique within Shin's oeuvre and in the canon of Korean film in a number of ways. In addition to its omnibus structure (which was, further, intended to be color-coordinated), it is, generically, neither a typical period piece nor a melodrama; rather, it contains elements of both and infuses the macabre sensibility of the horror film. And while, as mentioned above, it is a much more modest production than the period pieces of the early 1960s, it is reminiscent of the way *The Wanderer* and *Thousand Years Fox* invested a higher level of sophistication and complexity into a seemingly minor and luridly sensationalist film. The cast, in fact, is made up of nearly all the leading female faces of the 1960s (Ch'oe Ŭn-hŭi, Kim Chi-mi, Chu Chŭng-nyŏ, To Kŭm-bong, Hwang Chŏng-sun, etc.), a high-value list that was nonetheless compromised by the fact that nearly all of them were in the twilight of their careers (which imparts the subtle sense that the film as a whole is somehow a last gasp at greatness). *Cruel Stories*, nevertheless, is lively and novel; the short, elliptical episodes are fast and engrossing and give the archaic (and to an extent absurd) stories a dimension of playful enjoyment. The film, to the studio's pleasant surprise, was a minor hit, successful on its first release and especially popular in its second run. Though it could not be extended to future productions, Shin's experiment worked on both creative and economic levels.

The film's approach to women under Confucian patriarchy, however, is largely conventional. On the one hand, the caricature of the social codes of the *yangban* elite is devastating: the pathos of women who die to protect their families' names is intensified by the emptiness and hypocrisy of the patriarchs who kill them or the monuments (the gate, the illegitimate child) that honor them. There is nothing, only death, for women beyond the servility of being a daughter, wife, or mother and/or the repression of sexual desire that is the requisite of virtue, service, and loyalty. And yet, as was suggested above, the cataloging of suffering does not amount to a critique of the structures of the injustices (i.e., the Confucian strictures of the episode titles) nor does it project a means of escape from them. Even the freedom of life beyond the palace walls cannot be visualized: the sunrise into which Madame Yi stumbles with her baby is marginally positive but symbolically empty. The primitiveness of the social codes, underscored by the titles and by the authority of the male narration and by the crude and gruesome violence to which the characters are driven, seems to suggest that they exist only in the ancient past. And it is this temporal distancing, the relegation of the basic and surplus repression to the past, that is the apolitical and ahistorical action of Shin Sang-ok's films. *Cruel Stories* facilitates a pleasurable spectatorship of the past and its irrational gendered violence while turning away from the present and the presumed timelessness of Korean women's pain.

And yet it is also possible to detect a shift in *Cruel Stories* toward a more critical engagement with the Park regime, if not the patriarchal codes that structure it. Heretofore, the problem of power was deflected via abstract representation as universal law or through an assignment of blame to imperfect human hands. Here, though, the upholders of hollow law and the perpetrators of irrational violence are for the first time embodied concretely in the figure of the patriarch: the two fathers and the king. As in the projection of premodern bureaucracy and stagnation in *Prince Yŏnsan*, there is the suggestion that this representation of the inhuman authoritarianism of the Chosŏn monarchy could also double as a critique of the present. By the late 1960s, whatever idealism the Park regime promised in its seizure of power had been completely dispelled, leaving only the dull routine of industrial developmentalism and the brutal expansion of state power. At the same time, the regional investors and markets were covering smaller portions of the cost of production, and the prolific machinery of the Shin Films-Anyang studios had started to become a productive engine of steady losses. The professional conversation Shin had had with his mass audiences would finally become a weary argument with the status quo.

Demise

In 1976, the last film that Shin would put his hand to in the Shin Films era, *Female Prisoner 407* (*Yŏsu 407-ho*), was released to middling box-office returns. It was a blatantly exploitative film that followed the sensational twists in the eponymous Sŏ Kang-hui's life: her lover wrongfully accuses her of subversive activity and she is thrown into a colonial prison; she escapes along with a mob of other female prisoners; she finds her traitorous lover and shoots him dead; a fellow escapee takes the fall. These outrageous turns are punctuated by long and leering shots of the women's prison where, in one scene, the prisoners' naked bodies are just barely concealed by steam rising from the communal showers and, in another, a sudden cut just barely denies a full glimpse of two women making love. Shin in fact wanted to make the entire film much racier, having banked on the draw such exposure could generate in export abroad, but was foiled by the increasingly proactive censorship codes alluded to above. Ultimately, the film never reached the United States, its intended target market, and instead played in a series of second- and third-run theaters before engendering an even more absurd sequel, *Female Prisoner 407, the Sequel* (*Sok Yŏsu 407-ho*).

But in fact, by the time of the film's release, Shin Films and all of its spin-offs had already been shut down. In the screening of a preview for a Shin Films–Shaw Brothers coproduction, *Wild Dog and Rose* (*Changmi wa tŭlgae*), a three-second kiss scene that had been ordered cut in the prerelease review stage was seen by a group of high school students that had come to watch the feature. The story made most of the major newspapers, causing a minor scandal and forcing the hand of the authorities who, citing a violation of the public morals code, stripped Shin Sang-ok of his production license on November 28, 1975. This put an end for Shin to more than twenty unbroken years of filmmaking and effectively signaled the end of an era for the Korean film industry. While Shin had weathered a number of legal proceedings, suffered through personal scandal and, as we shall see, witnessed the slow decline of his studios, the shuttering of the Shin Films offices in Myŏngdong—long a locus of power in the Korean film world—came as a serious shock. But the end of Shin Films did not, of course, come unpredicted out of the film review committee barrel. Indeed, Shin and others closely connected with the company have hinted that *Wild Dog*'s kiss scene was half-consciously leaked in a gesture of either mild resistance or, perhaps most tellingly, fatalistic indifference.[70] The writing on the wall appeared as early as 1970 when the four puppet companies under Shin's control could muster together only seven films—a dramatic drop from the thirty-two films, nearly all made under the Shin Films banner, that were put out in 1969. Shin managed to pull the numbers up respectably for the following few years, but signs of wilting were also obvious in the films Shin made himself in the early 1970s. As in *407*, many of the movies were sensationalist quickies (one may think of the 1973 *The Half-Soul Woman/The Ghost Lovers* [*Panhonnyŏ*], a conventional and very loud horror film, as an example) or, like *Wild Dog*, one of a variety of odd products that Shin put together in cooperation with major Hong Kong studios (such as the virtually unwatchable *When Tae-kwondo Strikes* [*Hŭkgwŏn*, 1973]).

In some important respects the process of this decline can be read through a simple narrative of diminished visibility and intelligibility. Shin Films was the product of a specific historical juncture in which, on the one hand, domestic rural film markets remained dominant and largely receptive to the conventional melodramas in which Shin had come to specialize and, on the other, the South Korean state was powerfully invested in the construction of stable native industries built on strong technical bases and rigid production quotas. In the early 1970s, Shin failed to close the burgeoning gap between his studio and the changed filmmaking and filmgoing environments, precipitating a fall in box-office numbers for which no entrepreneurial schemes could easily compensate. This increasing irrelevance underlines the arguments made above about the material bases of Shin's cinematic style and also helps to account for how some filmmakers and studios (albeit a minority) thrived within the new film cultures of the 1970s while others faltered (though it is crucial to note quickly here that the careers of most of the filmmakers with whom Shin had cut his teeth, Han Hyŏng-mo, Yu Hyŏn-mok, Yi Man-hŭi, etc., had also effectively ended by the 1970s). And indeed, the 1970s is a decade characterized within the existing historiography as a radically distinct cinematic period, largely associated with the overall decline of the industry and a surge in the youth and pink cinemas of the "visual generation" (*yŏngsang sidae*) that was its new core. But while this gap between Shin's authorial sensibilities and that new core forms a compelling account of the studio's decline (which is, furthermore, essentially affirmed by Shin himself), it is vital, I believe, not to reify Shin's cinematic style or to reduce the complexity of either the era's filmmaking laws or its cultural habits. Toward a fuller picture of Shin's position within the film cultures of the late postwar era, I want to offer, in the closing pages of this chapter, a synthetic account, at times necessarily speculative, of the material and aesthetic forces subtending the decline of Shin Films.

If, as we will see in the next chapter, the early postwar years and even the first half of the Park Chung Hee regime witnessed a complex, overlapping, and often contradictory meeting of politically repressive and culturally productive forces, the 1970s marked a hard turn toward more comprehensive systems of state control. These were anticipated in the late 1960s by the institution of programs like *kyoryŏn*, which mandated militaristic training in schools, or the more comprehensive civil administrative apparatuses like the 1968 national registration system. At the heart of the new systems, however, was the *"Yusin"* constitution. Drafted in late 1971 and ratified by a 1972 referendum universally considered a sham, it granted Park not only unrestricted electoral stability by virtually eliminating term limits and effectively precluding oppositional candidacy but also an unprecedented concentration of power over theretofore autonomous bodies such as the National Assembly and the Supreme Court. Observers had to exaggerate very little in claiming that *"Yusin"* converted Park's presidency into a legal dictatorship."[71] But the expansion of power extended beyond the executive and into territories that had only been grazed by the pressures of state developmentalism. The New Village Movement, which we will encounter more closely in chapter 4, was the most concrete form of this expansion, reorganizing as it did rural social structures and affecting a shift in both the agricultural and light industrial modes of production across the country. The state also moved as far as ever into everyday life in both the city and country, implementing new family planning and public hygiene practices, shifts in dietary patterns toward apparently more modern and efficient wheat-based staples, and, perhaps least surprising, regulations in public fashions that targeted the usual suspects: long hair, blue jeans, miniskirts. These programs were facilitated by the proliferating state-controlled media outlets as well as the increasingly docile private media interests, which broadcast a variety of public awareness and messaging campaigns and internally stifled hard-edged criticism of the government.[72] Parallel to these relatively soft measures of control, of course, were the more primitive means of political persuasion, exacted through the exponentially expanded powers of the Korea Central Intelligence Agency and by the enhanced instrumentalization of the police and military in campaigns of intimidation against "national security enemies." These latter, overrepresented among liberal intellectuals, Christian leaders, social activists, and opposition officials, were largely snared in the ill-defined and largely indiscriminate nets of the era's multiplying anticommunist campaigns. The 1973 extraterritorial kidnap and torture of the vocal opposition leader Kim Dae Jung in Tokyo and the 1975 life sentence given to the dissident poet Kim Chi Ha are but two of the most well-known expressions of an ethos that earned the state its "republic of torture" moniker.

But in spite of the suffocating closeness of the state in virtually every aspect of daily life, Korea in the 1970s was not quite a totalitarian state. Protest and opposition persisted throughout the decade, even in the face of willfully violent suppression. For every one of the measures listed above—the institution of *kyoryŏn*, the sacking of journalists, the trimming of hair, and especially the ratification of "*Yusin*"—waves of public demonstration and outrage pushed against the government. Of course, this stubborn resistance inspired extraordinary counteractions by the Park regime, capped by the May 1975 "emergency measures" that sought to manage the state as a prison, but these measures in themselves were a clear indication that state power fell short of hegemonic rule. For indeed, the brutalization of figures like Kim Dae Jung and Kim Chi Ha was a reflexive and in many ways nonideological response to the existence of articulate censure. Despite the government's best efforts to instill "spiritual patriotism" and to create a "new national subjectivity," ardent labor activists continued to protest, conscientious writers continued to publish, and righteous teachers continued to educate, although nearly every one of these figures would eventually suffer for their causes.

The point here is not, of course, that the Korean 1970s were free or without intolerable repression. Undeniably, Park's Korea had few contemporary rivals in terms of its policing functions. Rather, the purpose of alluding to the decade's dissensual practices, however weak they were, is to indicate that governmental control was not total and thus that it had uneven effects on political and cultural expression. The Fourth Republic's ideological goals were brutal and narrow, focused on a continual strengthening of the economy built on the backs of a physically and morally disciplined citizenry. If anticommunism, lent legitimacy by the instabilities of the Cold War, was primarily an arbitrarily instrumentalized policing discourse, the Fourth Republic's one true faith was exports. Faced with a growing sense that the ROK could not, especially after Nixon's 1972 China visit, depend on continued and robust aid as a client in the global Cold War system, the Park regime invested heavily in industries that it forecast could bring in foreign currency and, in turn, buttress a wholly sovereign economy. A new series of five-year economic plans in the 1970s prioritized heavy industry and essentially created export sectors where none had existed or even, arguably, belonged. Seed money, interest-free loans, and bailouts for major corporations were accompanied by the institution of a range of softer incentives such as prizes (cash, trophies, etc.) for small and medium firms that had surpassed export benchmarks. The fuller brunt of state repression centered on movements or initiatives that could endanger this all-out effort (which accounts for the government's near total appropriation of labor unions until well into the next decade as well as its particularly harsh treatment of Kim Chi Ha, who had satirized the cronyism and corruption at the heart of the developing economy) while applying a comparatively lighter hand to other areas of cultural and political expression.

Beginning in the late 1960s, analysts with the Ministry of Culture and Information, abetted by cooperative private agencies like the aforementioned Korean Film Producers Association, argued that the developmentalist strategies of the first two iterations of the Motion Picture Law had been all too effective and had led to an oversaturation of films on the domestic market. It thus reversed the tenor of the production quotas, placing a limit of five films annually per registered studio—a measure that would have a particularly deleterious effect on companies like Shin Films, which by 1966 had taken over the massive Anyang Studios with an eye to expanding its operations even further. Shin would minimize the blow by creating three shadow companies, Shin-a, Tŏk-hŭng, and Anyang, but this clever move had the unforeseen and perhaps more insidious effect of watering down the Shin nameplate. The most transformative policy changes, however, came down in the form of the 1970 third and 1973 fourth revisions to the Motion Picture Law, which were aligned unerringly with the export-first philosophy sketched earlier in this chapter as well as the blunt implementation methods of the five-year plans. The new laws introduced three major provisions: a wholesale change to the import–export and production licensing system, a proviso that the right to freedom of speech could be suspended with regard to the state's emergency measures, and the creation of the Motion Picture Promotion Corporation. These last two provisions have received the most attention from critics trying to account for the overall decline of the film industry in the 1970s. Indeed the hypersensitive and deeply conservative censorship codes created such a harsh environment for filmmakers that many simply withdrew to other careers. The MPPC (Motion Picture Promotion Corporation, now the Korean Film Council), established on the premise that it could "foster and promote the growth of Korean cinema" by "rationalizing" investment, distribution, and exhibition structures, became quickly involved with the production of notoriously propagandistic and mind-numbing "national policy" films.[73] The severely constricted expressive range of films as well as the steady diet of national policy pictures at the theaters drove audiences even more emphatically home to the rapidly expanding pleasures of television.

But it was in fact the changed licensing system that had the greatest direct impact on the film industry, especially for major companies like Shin Films. While, as we have seen, the existing provisions had tied lucrative import rights to production quotas and to achievements at foreign film festivals, the new revisions shifted those obligations to film exports and coproductions with foreign companies. In order to preserve its import license, a "foreign film import–export company" was required to export six films within its first registered year and four annually thereafter. The licensed company could work toward these quotas or otherwise import films through cooperation with foreign entities on coproductions, which the laws defined as films in which at least two Korean actors/actresses and two Korean production staff were involved for exports and two foreign actors/actresses and staff involved for imports. Additionally, the law stipulated that the proceeds from these exports had to amount to a minimum of US$30,000 annually. The mechanical absurdity of the laws, which while intended to promote the export and profitability of cultural products in the same fashion as automobiles and chemicals, is readily apparent in its consequences: a further fetishization of imports and a lasting devaluation of Korean cinema abroad. But in his rigorous study of the "economic history" of the period's film industry, Sangjoon Lee has amply demonstrated that the laws also had heterogeneous effects, both wildly lucrative and farcically disastrous. On the one hand, they gave greater sanction and incentive for major firms in their transactions with foreign companies. Shin Films, which had already built robust relationships with Shaw Brothers, through which it laid unprecedented distribution networks throughout Southeast Asia, stepped up its production of films for export, primarily in the period dramas and war films that performed consistently in the region. More important, these films functioned as barter for the often tremendously popular and profitable Shaw Brothers martial arts features such as *The One Armed Swordsman* and *The Golden Swallow*, which Shin imported in 1968.[74] The new licensing system also occasioned ingenious practices such as what Lee calls the "counterfeit co-productions" for which, say, Shin would splice a few Korean faces into the print of an otherwise wholly Hong Kong film or attach the names of a few well-known Hong Kong directors to films produced entirely in-house.[75] And in spite of this ingenuity and the not infrequent box-office successes engendered by the new system, many studios like Shin Films fell into bankruptcy and ruin within a few years of the new laws' institution. Following on the testimony of industry insiders, Lee concludes that the era's capricious laws and a series of ill-timed investments, particularly in export-targeted films, were the principal factors in the demise of Shin Films. The failure of the era's savviest film entrepreneur to thrive within the new system was a clear indication—at least in retrospect—of the law's shortsighted and dim view of cultural production and, it might be argued, the true repressiveness of its aims.

But Shin was not a passive victim of the 1970s legislation. While his studio did not score the triumphs it had achieved so consistently in the early 1960s, it adapted quickly to the new filmmaking environment and pushed out a remarkable number (a peak of sixteen in 1973) of films that, as the critic Yi Yŏn-ho noted in her interview with Shin, even looked foreign.[76] Further, the existence of inventions such as the counterfeit coproductions, among a host of other ploys, demonstrates that there was ample play within the *"Yusin"* film laws, despite the fact that Shin and others would be caught and prosecuted for precisely those practices.[77] That this play was primarily entrepreneurial and only minimally creative is nevertheless a critical point. The most salient argument to be made here, however, is that Shin's work remained remarkably consistent through the last days of his South Korean career. That is, despite the magnified powers of the film censorship committees, and in the face of a geographically expanded market, Shin continued to make films that looked and sounded much like the work on which he had built his popularity in the 1950s and 1960s. Of the thirteen films he put together in the decade, three were war films, three were period pieces or historical treatments, three were women's melodramas, two were horror films; one musical and one revenge farce round out the list. This is an even genre distribution that is roughly analogous to Shin's output of the 1950s and 1960s. The work was also characteristically uneven politically: while some could be read as conservatively acquiescent (Yu Chi-na, for instance, argues that the 1973 *Three Days' Reign* [*Samil ch'ŏnha*] marked a turn toward heroic patriotism themes in his period films),[78] others were radically ambivalent. For instance, his 1974 *Boy, 13* (*13-se sonyŏn*) bears none of the anticommunist rhetoric of *The Han River* (*Han'gang*), made in that same year, nor does it rest on the mildly surprising pacifism at the bottom of his 1964 *Red Muffler*. About a boy orphaned by the war and taken in by an ostensible enemy soldier, the film patiently and quietly follows the strengthening bond between these strange allies. In many ways, the film comes closest to Shin's 1961 *Until the End of This Life* in its earnestly humanist treatment of individual triumph over the tragedies of war. The point of drawing attention to this odd consistency in Shin's work is not simply to underscore his distinctiveness as an author, but is a way to speculate about the precise ways in which Shin negotiated not only the changed film cultures of the 1970s but also his creative relationship with his own studio. For while he seems never to have affirmed this pattern, and in fact warned consistently and convincingly against such a reading,[79] it appears that for his own directorial work, Shin preserved his attachments to the domestic regional markets while shifting the rest of his studio's operations toward the new markets in Southeast Asia and beyond. This division of labor likely grew from Shin's recognition that his name as well as his directorial style continued to be reasonably bankable assets in the albeit shrinking regional and urban market for domestic films. In this respect, the creative structure of Shin Films in the 1970s was roughly analogous to what it had been in the 1950s and 1960s, although, notably, instead of the largely B-grade genre films that had filled the Shin Films lineup in the past, it was a new set of quasi-foreign B-grade films against which Shin would distinguish his own films. The really critical difference, however, was that the market for domestic films, in both the country and the city, had itself taken on new features.

One of the last films that Shin made in South Korea, *I Love Mama* (*Ai rŏbŭ mama*, 1975) should suffice to illustrate this point. Comparatively epic in scale, it was touted as the nation's first movie musical, made in the tradition of films like *The Sound of Music* and *My Fair Lady* (both of which, while released ten years earlier, continued to enjoy, as they did in other parts of the world, enormous popularity in Korea through revivals, television broadcasts, and original soundtrack recordings), though it perhaps came closest in style to the 1973 cult hit *Jesus Christ Superstar*. It featured a cast of relatively unknown young actors (many of whom would go on to successful careers in music and film[80]), drafted straight out of the new acting schools such as Anyang for their relatively uncommon triple-threat talents, and starred Ch'oe Un-hŭi in one of her rare 1970s ventures with Shin Sang-ok. It was also advertised brashly as one of the era's rare 70 mm films, though it was later revealed that it was in fact shot simply with a 35 mm anamorphic lens.[81] The film's real selling point, however, trumpeted across its marketing media, was the top-notch creative staff associated with its production. Yi Hyŏng-pyo, who had at that point moved decisively into television production, was brought back as "technical adviser" on what most could recognize was a technically challenging production.[82] But more significantly, Sin Chung-hyŏn, the legendary rock musician who had made a name for himself on U.S. base-camp circuits and then as one of the leading lights of the 1960s and 1970s music scene, collaborated on *Mama* as lead composer and accompanist.[83] The soundtrack album, it may be worth noting, proved remarkably successful, though tragically, Sin Chung-hyŏn would be jailed later that year for what were eventually revealed to be largely trumped-up charges of marijuana possession and all of his recordings were banned until 1987. *Mama*'s budget totaled more than 800 million won, nearly four times the average for contemporaneous films, an investment that was amply reflected in the film's scale, topped by a dazzling final sequence that featured tightly choreographed numbers, enormous sets, and a cast of hundreds.

Mama, however, flopped at the box office, attracting just over 20,000 admissions in a short one-week run in Seoul and faring little better in the second-run and regional markets. Neither Shin Sang-ok's drafting of Sin Chung-hyŏn, a bold move clearly aimed at attracting the young *"t'ongbŭl"* (acoustic guitar, blue jeans) crowd that made up the core of the era's mass culture market, nor the all-out extravagance of the film could yield a turn-around for the studio. But while this was presumably disappointing, the failure could not have come as a complete surprise. As noted above, the filmgoing market as a whole had dried up by the mid-1970s, as the generation that had sponsored the "golden age" of the 1950s and 1960s stayed home to watch the growing range of period, melodrama, and spy series conveniently broadcast on television. The contracted Korean theater market, despite constantly shifting quotas and restrictions, was dominated by foreign films, in particular by American and Hong Kong action films. What remained of domestic production skewed toward the aforementioned "youth" films of a younger generation of directors (represented by Ha Kil-jong's 1975 *March of Fools* [*Pabo tŭl ŭi haengjin*] and Yi Chang-ho's 1974 *Home of the Stars* [*Pyŏl dŭl ŭi kohyang*]) and to the new and often quasi-pornographic "hostess" genre of films (the most iconic being Kim Ho-sŏn's 1975 *Youngja's Heyday* [*Yŏngja ŭi chŏngsŏng sidae*]). But more fundamentally, while Shin Sang-ok seemed to gesture at accommodating the demands of the new market with *Mama*, behind its folk-rock score and bell-bottom fashions, the film remained classically Shin Sang-ok. Not only did it have the hallmarks of, on the one hand, Shin's sly manipulations (i.e., the 70 mm misrepresentation) and, on the other, his tireless technical and genre experimentations (the film remained Korea's only full-bore musical until the late 1990s), its core sensibilities were closely aligned with those expressed in Shin's work of the late 1950s and 1960s. *Mama*'s narrative follows the efforts of three lively sisters to find a match for their widowed mother. The core, though admittedly somewhat meager, pleasures of the film derive from the various ruses they employ with the help of their boyfriends to have the demure middle-aged woman meet an aged though still dashing Nam-Gung Won. While this playful openness signals a departure from the tenor of Shin's many widow films (*Houseguest*, *Chastity Gate*, etc.), where the widow's desires could only be stifled or punished, the familiar grappling between dimly alien social and moral codes and individual desire remains the film's dominant problematic. Shin's rather tongue-in-cheek assertion that "patience is a virtue" is affirmed in *Mama*, even despite the fact that the mother eventually agrees to the new match: it is the very struggle to move beyond the memory of her husband and her duty/identity as his wife that confirms her moral worth. Put another way, while it is her individual happiness that is celebrated in the film's rousing finale, that freedom to embrace a new beginning is only possible because she has, throughout the film, so earnestly labored against it.

And it is here, in the basic consistency of Shin's treatment of women in Korean society, that we can ascertain that it was not vestigial neo-Confucian sex and gender codes that Shin championed, but rather a more universal though perhaps equally conservative set of values that lay at the base of his films: the primacy of family and social harmony; the necessity, virtue, and even beauty of suffering; a vaguely melancholic but affirmatively pragmatic acceptance of the contemporary state of affairs. These imbue Shin's period dramas as much as they do the contemporary enlightenment melodramas and genre treatments. That these values are often only subtly articulated or even untraceable in Shin's corpus is an effect of their heavy inflection by the more immediately effective set of values that Shin brought to his career: the priority of formal and technical polish, the importance of populist appeal; the fundamental imperative of making more and better films. A high-gloss genre treatment, technically advanced and superficially hip, *I Love Mama* was the last major work to express Shin's complex filmmaking synthesis. But while these values resonated with the regional audiences that formed the core of the first few decades of the postwar market, by the 1970s they became, as a result of the transformations outlined above, far less legible within the broader terrain of Korean cinema. Perhaps not surprisingly, it is in the moment of its eclipse that the sharper outlines of Shin's authorial vision can be most clearly discerned.

But more important, it is when his studio and his films become invisible in South Korea that the more fundamental politics of Shin Sang-ok's career can be defined. These politics are inextricable from the forces that made his work visible in the first place. As we have seen, the field of this visibility was demarcated, on the one hand, by both the vicissitudes of the regional market and the rough and sometimes arbitrary controls of the state and, on the other, by the flexible, creative, and even proactive ways in which Shin and other producers crafted their films within those changing systems. The manner in which the subtle experimentation and sophistication of the 1950s gave way to the protean populism of the 1960s melodramas and, finally, to the proliferating pink and policy cinemas of the 1970s describes a slow contraction in the scope of political expression over the twenty years of Shin Sang-ok's South Korean career. That Shin could thrive throughout this period, despite some significant setbacks, is an index not only of his flexibility but also of the broad legibility, across cultural and political lines, of his authorial tendencies. While his work oscillated loosely between an uncanny alignment with administrative and increasingly authoritarian power and an abstract critique of the excessive repression of Korean state and society, it remained throughout the postwar decades the very emblem of Korean cinema and its possibilities. This centrality, as I have tried to argue, was securely anchored to the postwar space of the market and the state that regulated it; when that space shifted, Shin would begin the most radical unmooring of his career.

4 MELODRAMA AND THE SCENE OF DEVELOPMENT

Complicit Images

The political and generic heterogeneity of Shin Sang-ok's films should be unsurprising when we take into consideration that he was initiated into filmmaking in the tumultuous years of liberation from nearly a half-decade of colonial rule, shot his first films in the throes of a horrific and nearly total war, built his industry-leading studio within the sphere of a militarized developmentalist state, and closed the most productive years of his career precariously straddling the dangerous antimonies of the Cold War. Indeed the resourcefulness reflected in his career finds uncanny resonance with that of the icons of the postwar age of "heroic entrepreneurialism," figures like Chŏng Chu-yŏng, who built Hyundai into one of the nation's most powerful conglomerates through early ventures in an unlikely range of industries and through multifarious collusion with government interests. But filmmaking was not a straightforward *kiŏp*, notwithstanding the clumsy efforts of the state to make it one, and, plainly, the politics that conditioned its operations and the politics to which it gave expression were often circuitous and unpredictable. In this sense it is perhaps not surprising that the filmmaker to whom Shin himself referred most often was not a celebrated contemporary like Kurosawa Akira or Douglas Sirk but, rather, William Wyler. Easily one of the most commercially and critically successful American directors (though largely disregarded in more recent film criticism), Wyler set a model for Shin in the generic range of his work (which included westerns, historical epics, and fast-paced comedies) and the reputed perfectionism he applied to his films (which earned him the nickname "90-take Wyler"). Perhaps the more striking parallel, however, which Shin seems not to have stressed, was Wyler's ability to make films that were eminently legible in the diverse historical moments of the prewar years as well as the heady first decades of American hegemony—a consistent visibility that was amply underwritten by the still robust Hollywood studio system.

However, the most telling correspondence of Shin's career in my mind is with Mizoguchi Kenji, a filmmaker whose geographic and historical proximity to postwar Korean cinema nevertheless did little to significantly register his work with Shin or any of his contemporaries. I do not mean to suggest an analogy on a formal level, not least because it might be considered a minor heresy—plainly, Shin would not bring his cinema to match the rigor and subtlety of Mizoguchi's work. Rather, the two filmmakers share similarly heterogeneous filmographies (and, to be sure, the specific points of overlap are uncanny—on the women's melodramas, folk horror tales, historical epics, etc.) that were, further, similarly conditioned by the wild swings in the social and political history in which their careers were embedded. Additionally, and despite the fact that Mizoguchi's career opportunism is perhaps rightly overlooked in the close attention paid to his films, both were eminently entrepreneurial, ready to compromise on the political fidelity of their work if such adjustments meant that they could enjoy making more and better films. For these icons of East Asian filmmaking, the cinema was a religion whose pious and prolific practice came through the dual blessings of the state and market. For Shin, as it was for Mizoguchi, the complex overlap between these forces in the early years of postwar developmentalism bequeathed enough freedom to produce films that could signify not solely through the esoteric language of art cinema, but via the mechanisms of affect and the borrowed forms of ideologically opposed cinemas.

In a brief but compelling essay, leading Korean film critic Kim So-yŏng argued that Shin Sang-ok's films are characterized not by stylistic or thematic uniformity, but rather by "mutually contradictory and discontinuous itinerancy."[1] This itinerancy and the heterogeneous identities, religious confusions, and sociopolitical instabilities that animate the diverse body of Shin's work, she suggests, are reflective of the tumult of the 1960s in which, borrowing Marx's phrase, "all that is solid melt[ed] into air." For Kim, Shin's film world is either apolitical and populist, or, when politics do break through to the surface, essentially conservative. Desperate crises that threaten to fracture family and social structures or unhinge gender relations are neatly resolved or pasted over with comic or melodramatic flourish. Further, she contends, there is no "future vision" in Shin's films, "only the present trapped in the past or the past as seen through the present" and all of this screened without any glimpse of a community to replace the oppressive and violent but ultimately secure Confucian social order that has been lost. And yet this conservative nostalgia and what Kim calls Shin's "Foucauldian" heterogeneity are not marks of his personal vision but are instead symptoms of the shared concerns of the period's artists and cultural elite. What in the end distinguishes Shin's cinema from that of his contemporaries, Kim argues, is its emphasis on visuality over narrative and its meticulous construction of mise-en-scène. Referring to Shin's statement (albeit tongue-in-cheek) that he would have liked to have had his films screened backward to counter the supremacy of the plot, Kim concurs that it would be a shame indeed to forget the striking visual pleasures of Shin's filmmaking.

There is, to a large extent, a consensus of opinion in critical writing on this assessment of Shin Sang-ok as a filmmaker who privileged his craft, the popular appeal of his films, and the success of his studio over political engagement and social criticism. Shin's drive to build a major, Hollywood-style film studio as well as the strong hand he played in enacting legislation to modernize the Korean film industry alienated many of his colleagues and earned him a reputation as an opportunist comfortably in bed with political powers.[2] As early as 1978, the film historian Yi Yŏng-il argued that any study of Shin's work would have to take into account, with "great sympathy and forbearance," both the pressures of the Park administration's developmentalist policies and Shin's near-fanatic dedication to the art and science of making movies.[3] For Yi, any questions of Shin's auteurship and politics, conservative or otherwise, are subordinate to the larger issue of his entrenchment in the politics of the film industry in which Shin "did anything and everything to get his films produced." While Yi rates Shin as a filmmaker somewhere below contemporaries such as Yu Hyŏn-mok or Kim Ki-yŏng, he nevertheless praises Shin as a "cinematic being" whose work elevated the formal practices of Korean cinema. As with Kim So-yŏng, the core value and interest of Shin's cinema lies for Yi in two distinct but related areas: the way in which his career mirrored the orthodoxy and status quo of culture and politics in the 1960s, and the formal, primarily visual, pleasure of the films themselves.

More recent studies have contributed to varying degrees to a well-informed and highly historicized understanding of Shin Sang-ok's cinema.[4] Clearly, one of the most fascinating aspects of Shin's work as both a film producer and director is how he colluded with the Park government to establish his studio and to produce films that in various ways became emblematic of the "allures and chaos" of the 1950s and 1960s.[5] Regardless of how we come to assess Shin's politics, no study of his filmmaking can ignore this remarkable and largely unprecedented imbrications with authoritarian power. Nevertheless, there are a handful of subtle but serious difficulties that these studies encounter to different degrees in projecting an image of Shin as a collusive and essentially conservative filmmaker whose movies can be read as symptomatically exposing the ideological and discursive structures of the period.

This chapter seeks to address the question of the politics of Shin Sang-ok's filmmaking, in part by rethinking the terms by which it has previously been formulated. At the core of this study will be a consideration of the discourses circulating around and within two of Shin's less celebrated but in some ways most important works, *Evergreen* (*Sangnoksu*, 1961) and *Rice* (*Ssal*, 1963), both considered standard bearers of the enlightenment modality examined in chapter 1. The logic of selecting these films is twofold: first, they are the most overtly "political" in Shin's corpus (with the possible exclusion of two of his North Korean films, *Salt* [*Sogŭm*] and *Record of an Escape* [*T'alch'ulgi*]), and come in the period that marked both his greatest professional success and closest collaboration with the Park regime; and second, the striking formal qualities of both films speak forcefully not only to the critical technical advances of the period but also to the interpretive challenge posed by the ideological porousness of global cinematic traffic. My aim here is not simply to counter the arguments of the scholars cited above. Certainly, it would be pointless to turn away from Shin's enmeshment in the authoritarian politics that came to dominate Korea in the 1960s or to deny the reactionary dimension of the melancholic celebration of Confucian social principles that was the thematic nucleus of so many of his films. Rather, I want to argue first that the politics of even the most explicitly ideological and partisan of Shin's films should be read against the radically unstable and contradictory political discourses and practices of the period. The enlightenment movements that *Rice* and *Evergreen* portray were not the sole prerogative of the Park regime's developmentalism but were instead highly overdetermined historically and signified a number of different, often competing, social and political projects. This chapter proceeds with a synchronic historical account of how the films take up the dominant social and political discourses of the period. It then moves to an engagement with specifically cinematic pleasures, suggesting that the films' melodramatic modality and affect as well as their mass cultural appeal inflect and redirect the explicitly didactic thrust of the enlightenment genre. The study then concludes with a reflection on the political dimension of style. Seizing on a set of images and visual codes, I argue that Shin's films not only participate in the production of national discourse and the attendant transformations of South Korean postcolonial/postwar subjectivity, but that they are also in dialogue with a broader spectrum of global image-making in a way that challenges conventional definitions of Shin Sang-ok's politics.

The State, the Revolution, and I

While they are both structured around a classic *vnarod* plot, the narratives of the two films are fairly distinct. *Evergreen* remains faithful to its literary origins in narrating in relatively straightforward terms the lives of its two educated protagonists, Ch'ae Yŏng-sin and Pak Tong-hyŏk, and their work to enlighten and empower the rural poor.[6] After meeting at a Christian youth rally in Seoul, where Pak demonstrates his fervid commitment to lifting the *minjung* out of poverty and Ch'ae her moxy in defending women's equality, the two resolve to escape the stagnant and hypocritical world of Seoul intellectuals (embodied in the polite YWCA dinner where the merits of enlightenment are debated) and go directly to the people in country villages. Pak returns to his own hometown to get his hands dirty in leading communal agriculture projects while Ch'ae finds her way to Ch'ŏngsŏkgol, a poor farming village where she sets up a variety of literacy classes for children and adults. The film's emotional core is of course its love plot, which grows as the two take turns visiting the other's villages and as they witness the depth of the other's political dedication, but which ultimately remains platonic. However, the dramatic energy of *Evergreen* lies in the gradual, sometimes troubled, but ultimately rewarding progress Ch'ae makes in her efforts to attract Ch'ŏngsŏkgol's villagers to her classes and to build a school to accommodate them, variously enchanting the children with accordion music or earning the respect of the women by gamely helping out in the fields. Despite the interference of a local dandy just returned from his studies in Tokyo, Ch'ae manages to pool the village's resources to build the humble but sturdy one-room school, but the strain of her cause takes its toll and she falls irreversibly ill. Meanwhile, Pak himself struggles to combat the meddling of the local landowner in his projects, and through a series of unfortunate events he is wrongly accused of arson and arrested. Upon his release from prison, he rushes to Ch'ŏngsŏkgol to be with Ch'ae, only to find that he is too late and that she has already succumbed to her disease. Emotionally shattered, he rises the next day and stoically rings the school's piercing bell, which goes out like a clarion call to the weary villagers. Their love is symbolically consummated as Pak carries forward Ch'ae's commitment to hope and enlightenment.

Rice is based on an original script (which nevertheless has recognizable precedents in depression-era American film and Stalin-era Soviet cinema) penned by Kim Kang-yun, a prolific scenarist who worked under contract at Shin Films, who also, interestingly, adapted *Evergreen* for Shin. Opening sometime in the late 1950s, the narrative follows Yong, a recently discharged soldier crippled in the war who, upon hearing that his father is terminally ill, returns from Seoul to his backward and destitute hometown, Muju, in south Ch'ungch'ŏng province.[7] Though his father (who is dying, as are many others in the village, from want of rice) orders him from his deathbed to move the family out of the lifeless village and back to Seoul, Yong pledges to stay on. With the support of his mother (who sells the family's last plot for funds), his sister (who eventually prostitutes herself to sponsor him), his old flame Chŏng-hŭi (the independent-minded daughter of the local landlord), and his loyal friend Kŏn-bae, Yong proposes to bore a tunnel through a mountain to divert river water that could irrigate the parched and wasted village fields—a scheme, we learn, first developed and then abandoned in the colonial period by the Japanese. In a rousing speech detailing his well-researched plan, Yong convinces the villagers that Muju will finally have rice in the five years it will take to complete the project, and the work proceeds apace with the labor of many volunteers. However, the plan is opposed by Chŏng-hŭi's father, Song, the local landowner and industrialist, who only stands to profit from the village's poverty and who spreads rumors that Yong and the volunteers are communists. It is also opposed by the village shaman who, at Song's bidding, spreads her own rumors that the mountain spirits will punish Muju for its trespasses. But the most serious obstacle proves to be the bumbling and ineffective local and federal bureaucracies that recognize the value of the irrigation project but do not have the means to grant it any meaningful support. The fate of the village, and indeed the narrative thrust of the film itself, turns precisely on the problem of the government's competence. Just at the nadir of Yong's fortunes, when the project has been all but abandoned and the villagers recruited to work at Song's mine, the May 16 military "revolution" sweeps aside the former Syngman Rhee–Chang Myŏn regime's red tape and throws its efficient and benevolent force into helping the village blast through the mountain. The film closes with the jubilation of all the villagers at the sight of the torrent that spills out of the tunnel and promises rice for everyone.

While neither *Evergreen* nor *Rice* were quite the box-office sensations Shin Sang-ok's other films from the period (such as *Confessions of a College Girl* [*Ŏnŭ yŏdaesaeng ŭi kobaek*], *Sŏng Ch'unhyang*, or *The Houseguest and My Mother* [*Sarangbang sonnim kwa ŏmŏni*]) proved to be, they both in different ways enjoyed significant critical and commercial success.[8] With its well-loved narrative and casting of two of the most recognizable stars of the era, Ch'oe Ŭn-hŭi and Sin Yŏng-gyun, *Evergreen* fared well with audiences, placing eighth in box-office receipts in a remarkable year that saw the release of a number of heavyweights, such as the three listed above and also Hong Sŏng-gi's *Ch'unghyangjŏn*, and scored, however dubious they may have been, a handful of prizes at the first Grand Bell awards.[9] The film also earned notorious praise from Park Chung Hee himself, who, as is often recounted by Shin and by his critics, reportedly cried during a screening. In an interview given on the occasion of *Evergreen*'s special invitation to the Cannes Film Festival in 2003 (the only one of his films to be shown there), Shin claimed that the film was in fact his favorite and most representative work.[10] *Rice*, while largely forgotten by film historians or dismissed by critics as pure propaganda, was an even bigger hit than *Evergreen* when it was released on the eve of the handover of power from Park's military rule to his "civilian" administration. Beating out even well-loved weepies like Yu Hyŏn-mok's *Pharmacist Kim's Daughters* (*Kim yakguk ŭi ttaldŭl*, 1963) at the box office, it also swept a number of awards at the Grand Bell and Asian Film festivals.

What was it, then, that led to the success of these films? Clearly, *Rice*'s all-star casting (which featured not only Ch'oe and Sin, but a broad spectrum of the period's celebrities including Hŏ Chang-gang, Kim Hŭi-gap, and To Kŭm-bong) and the remarkably high production values (including one of the earliest uses of the zoom lens) contributed to the popular appeal of the film, as they did for *Evergreen*. Yet, as even the casual observer of the film industry knows (and as Shin himself witnessed with the failure of his heavily invested 1957 epic, *Shadowless Pagoda* [*Muyŏng tap*]), big budgets can never be a guarantee of commercial success. Further, while Shin refers to the films as "social pictures" (*sahoe mul*), both were given the generic classification of "policy film" (*chŏngch'aek yŏnghwa*), a label that proved to be a turnoff for moviegoing audiences, especially in the nation's growing cities, who largely sought to escape the rural settings and the often didactic and formulaic themes that were conventionally the chief components of that genre. At the same time, it is clear that these films, which traced in different ways the struggle to lift the nation out of poverty, resonated emotionally and intellectually with audiences who, at a basic level, were caught between the harsh realities of their own poverty, the enduring national division, and the urgent debate over what path the nation could take to achieve some measure of security and prosperity. If *Evergreen* could squeeze tears out of Park Chung Hee and if *Rice*, as has been claimed, is a paean to Park's program of "national reconstruction," would it be possible to conclude that the films managed to capture the spirit of the times and to reconcile, aesthetically, the desires of the masses with the will of the leader? Or alternatively, if *Rice* (and we may extrapolate to include *Evergreen*) is, as film critic Chu Ch'ang-gyu argues, a projection of the elite bourgeois nationalist fantasy of enlightenment and development, was this a fantasy shared by moviegoing *minjung* as well? In short, what are the terms by which contemporary audiences understood and engaged with these films? The point here is not to try to faithfully reconstruct the way contemporary audiences understood the films. Rather, this line of questioning is forwarded as an attempt to reconstruct synchronically how explicitly ideological filmmaking could function as popular entertainment in a period that gave rise to the first properly modern mass culture industry in South Korea.[11]

Even the cursory review of the narrative structures of these films above should suggest the extent to which they resonate with the conflicted and contradictory but undeniably revolutionary spirit of South Korea in the early 1960s. The central themes of these works—cultural and intellectual enlightenment, rural revitalization, national reconstruction, community solidarity, and self-sufficiency—were crucial concerns shared, though of course hotly debated, by nearly the full spectrum of Korean society.[12] The four- or five-year span in which these films were produced was perhaps the most turbulent in Korean history, even by the standards of its compressed modernity. Whereas the seven years following the end of the Korean war, a period overseen by a grossly corrupt administration, saw little economic growth and only marginal expansion of civil liberties, the April 19 (or, popularly, 4.19) student revolution signaled the start of a new era of hope for national regeneration. While political power ultimately shifted first into the hands of the old guard opposition party, and then into fists of military leaders, 4.19 spawned a new spirit of public activism and construction that could be co-opted and absorbed but never erased. Most relevant to a consideration of these films, a new *vnarod* movement, surreptitiously dubbed "native land development" (*hyangt'o kaech'ŏk*), sprung up, replacing the Rhee-backed and transparently propagandistic organizations like the 4-H clubs, that mobilized intellectuals to spread literacy and "democratic citizenship skills" to heretofore isolated rural populations.[13] Immediately following Rhee's resignation and throughout the brief but comparatively liberal Chang administration era, intellectuals and religious leaders debated vociferously the merits of different forms of democratic government, the efficacy of various economic structures, and even invoked the idea of peaceful national unification in their attempts to formulate viable future paths for the country. While there was little resolution to these arguments, all were agreed on the desperate need to revitalize the country from the ashes of war and the stagnation of the Rhee era.

The May 16 (or, 5.16) military coup was not, of course, what anyone, neither the student movement leaders nor the old guard conservatives, had in mind. While the coup itself was relatively bloodless, the junta led by Park and the Supreme National Reconstruction Council (SNRC) that was to rule until the handover to "civilian" rule in November 1963 was brutal in executing scores of "national traitors" and ruthless in silencing political dialogue. Yet despite the chasm that separated the ideological and spiritual goals of the 4.19 student movement and the 5.16 military coup, there remained at least for the first few years of the decade considerable ambiguity and overlap in the conceptual if not practical relationship between the two "revolutions." While established intellectuals almost uniformly expressed concerns about the dangers of military rule, their writings, in leading journals like *Sasanggye* (*World of Thought*) and *Sedae* (*Generation*), also gave voice to their hope that the strong hand of the new government could institute much needed reforms and provide the strong push necessary to rehabilitate the country. Even staunch defenders of democratic principles, such as the Quaker leader Ham Sŏk-hŏn, could not at first reject the coup out of hand; given his well-known call for a "surgical" transformation of Korean society, he held out hope that the coup leaders could, as "flowers" to the *minjung*'s "tree," act as life-giving blooms that fall in due course.[14] For their part, the country's new leaders tried to project an aura of continuity and vindication. In two books published less than a year after the coup, as well as in his numerous public addresses, Park argued that the "supreme objective" of his own revolution was for it to become "the successor of the 4.19 revolution."[15] He also astutely appropriated much of the discourse the students had used, identifying the coup as a "common people's revolution" that would "restore" the "national spirit," and pointed out that many of the SNRC's imperatives (i.e., anticorruption, economic reconstruction, national unification) were in fact those of the student movement itself. This combination of striking physical force and shrewd rhetorical manipulation helped the coup leaders consolidate their power with a population that was, on the one hand, aching for broad social transformation, and on the other, wearied from the upheavals of the postliberation/postwar decades.

If the discursive field in this period was unstable and fraught with ideological ambiguity, the material transformations enacted through the ambitious and often brutal planning of the SNRC presented a clear and palpable sign of a radically changed Korean society. Under various slogans such as "Korea first, economy first," or "Construction on the one hand, national defense on the other," the push for national reconstruction touched virtually every area of life in the country, from the reorganization of the public education system and realignments in the banking sector to reform of laws governing land ownership and corporate governance. While in some ways the terms of the first five-year economic plan were not as oppressive as the controls that would be instituted in the 1970s, the effect they had on people's lives was certainly more sudden and sweeping. And while much of the planning focused, as it would throughout the next two decades of the administration, on the industrial sector, its vision for a strengthened agricultural economy and rapid urbanization fundamentally altered realities in rural areas where, as late as 1963, 80 percent of the population lived. But even here the line separating the April from the May revolution was sometimes blurry. For, within the overarching "Patriotic National Reconstruction Movement," the overarching program of the SCNR, sprang the "People's Reconstruction Movement" (*kungmin chaegŏn undong*), a relatively short-lived campaign that sought to build democracy from the bottom up through a number of rural programs that emphasized adult literacy, mutual aid for community projects, and even hygiene. Sent out under the slogan, "Let us attain revolutionary tasks with our own hands," the largely educated youth who were the "vanguards" of the campaign worked closely with local governments to initiate their tasks. While within a few years the movement hardened to eventually form the highly bureaucratic Office of Rural Development, its early goals and methods merged unmistakably with those of the "native land development" campaigns of the 4.19 radicals and their *vnarod* project. Further, both of these movements themselves echoed similar initiatives taken decades earlier by elite urban intellectuals who, in the aftermath of the March First Independence Movement, returned to their rural hometowns to bring enlightenment and civilization, as well as political empowerment.

The Melodrama of Development

The experience of these upheavals form the basis of the engagement of *Evergreen* and *Rice* with the popular imagination. While set in two distinct historical frames, *Evergreen* in the middle stages of the colonial period and *Rice* in the three or fours years leading up to the 5.16 coup, both films implicitly speak to the ethos of rural revitalization, national reconstruction, and stubborn self-reliance that imbued popular, intellectual, and political culture in the early 1960s. But before looking more closely at how the films took up both the ideas and experiences of the period, it is imperative to underscore how, as mainstream narrative films, they depended for their appeal and impact on specifically cinematic pleasures. Clearly, the capacity of commercial movies to register affectively and to call on the desires of audiences is at least as vital to their commercial success (and to whatever political effect they may aim toward) as their social, cultural, or ideological legibility. And here again, even in the light of his most didactic films, reflection on the work of melodrama is fundamental to a grasp of Shin Sang-ok's cinema. As we saw in the previous chapter, throughout his many interviews and personal memoirs Shin worked strenuously to distance his legacy from the family or women's melodramas that ultimately became the mark of his filmmaking. Both *Evergreen* and *Rice* were centrally important for him in this task, being the films he most consistently pointed to as the truest expressions of his directorial vision (i.e., most unencumbered by commercial pressures). And yet it is clear that the melodramatic features of both films, albeit to varying degrees, are integral to their mass cultural effect, that is, the potential of the film narratives to make an impression emotionally and work politically. Melodrama does not inhibit, enhance, or exceed the social realism Shin covets, but seems rather to be the core experience of his films.

The veracity of this claim can be more easily tested in *Evergreen*, in which the tragic love plot is more prominent as the film's key emotional register. At first, only the subtext to the dominant *vnarod* narrative, the relationship between the principals Pak Tong-hyŏk and Ch'ae Yŏng-sin assumes its pronounced position through an archetypal progression from emotional suppression (and innocence) to ecstatic (though platonic) consummation and to tragic (because too late) incommensurability. It is worth noting here that the tension between the story's personal and political features was central to the literary original and its contemporary and historical critical receptions. Written by Sim Hun in response to a call by preeminent man of letters Yi Kwang-su for a literature that would capture the realities of the rural enlightenment movement, the serialized novel was mostly praised for its nationalist spirit. But it was also criticized, especially by writers of the disbanded left-wing writers guild KAPF (*Korea Artista Proletaria Federacio*), for its sentimentality and romanticism. *Evergreen* was canonized after the war with the advent of the national educational institution as a representative Korean literary work and was often (and indeed continues to be) introduced in textbooks as a classic anticolonial narrative. Nevertheless, its enduring popularity owes as much to the distilled tragedy of its love plot, so reminiscent of other iconic modern Korean romances like "Sonagi" (Hwang Sun-won, 1959) or "Samnyong the Mute" (["Pŏng'ŏri Samnyong"], Na To-hyang, 1925) as to its lauded representation of colonial social movements. And it would not be stretching the imagination to surmise that this quality is precisely what made the novel ripe for adaptation to film, both by Shin and later, in 1978, by the central figure of the next generation of Korean filmmakers, Im Kwŏn-taek.

The protagonists' mutual attraction is sparked initially at the youth rally where they are each roused by the other's defiant political speeches and is later cemented when, in an isolated stand of trees, they profess their desires to abandon city life and devote themselves to the rural poor. Consummation of this romance (to the extent that this was possible given the boundaries of the heavily Christian-influenced original narrative and the censorship codes of the 1960s) comes in the middle of the film, when Pak and Ch'ae come to see each other's passion for their enlightenment work (Pak on his farm, Ch'ae in her school): against a backdrop of bleak mudflats, they speak their declarations of political commitment and personal love with the same breath. The heightened melodrama reaches its apex not coincidentally with the most politically charged sequences of the film, when as a result of his incarceration by colonial authorities Pak is not able to be with Ch'ae in her dying moments. The pathos of this classic incommensurate time–space serves to intensify the anticolonial layer of the narrative, but obviously it also serves its own end, namely, in the dramatic force of pathos.

Shin Sang-ok amplifies these melodramatic pleasures throughout the film in a way that belies his subsequent public disavowal of the melodramatic mode. He shrewdly capitalizes in this adaptation on the cinematic form to draw out the sentimentality that is latent in the politicized sequences of the literary original. His formal approach to the love plot is largely orthodox (though the staging, as in the mudflat sequence, is sometimes unusual) but dramatically effective, framing the aforementioned scenes in the kind of emotive close shots and swooning score that are the hallmarks of popular melodrama. This melodramatic mode of telling is repeated in small form throughout the film in flashes that make a spectacle of the enlightenment process. The tribulations Ch'ae must endure in recruiting students for her class are represented in a dynamic montage that cuts scenes of conflict with the community together with close shots of Ch'ae's pained expressions. This conflict is addressed and resolved at different stages with two striking scenes: the first in which the child Ok-pun, newly literate, reads a letter to her illiterate elders, whose stunned faces are captured in a beautiful, dramatic slow pan; the second in which Ch'ae, overwhelmed by the excess of new students crying out for learning, must teach them through the school's windows, spectacularizing enlightenment with oversize chalk marks.

Referencing Peter Brooks's assertion that post-Enlightenment melodrama is most centrally about assigning public guilt and innocence, Linda Williams concludes that for cinema, melodramatic "pathos and action are the two most important means to the achievement of moral legibility."[16] At *Evergreen*'s thematic core is the moral responsibility of privileged intellectuals to bring enlightenment and empowerment to the rural masses, a normative good that is constrained by the evils of the colonial authorities and their native sycophants; its affective core then is the protagonists' ultimately doomed struggle to reconcile this moral struggle with their relationship. While Williams makes the radical claim that realist narratives often serve spectacles of pathos and action (rather than being interrupted by them), it seems that with *Evergreen* the relationship between melodramatic pathos and (social) realism is more complex, overlapping, and multidirectional. The pathos of the love plot serves the moral imperative as much as the narrative of rural enlightenment serves the dramatic impact of the love plot, highlighting the radical incommensurability of the personal and the political under the "black umbrella" of colonial rule. It seems that this generic variance may stem in part from the sociocultural boundaries of Williams's critique, underscored in her conclusion that "it is thus in ever modernizing forms of melodrama, not epic, not 'classical realism,' that *American democratic culture* has most powerfully articulated the moral structure of feeling that animates its goals of justice"[17] (emphasis added). My purpose in highlighting this cultural specificity is not to fabricate some charge of Euro-American centrism; Williams is much too rigorous in consciously aligning her revision of melodrama within the Western dramatic tradition. Rather, it is to suggest that a distinct form of melodrama is at work in *Evergreen*, one that builds upon the Western cinematic heritage that it undeniably inherits, but that is also marked by the different social and political conditions of its production. Taking up and redirecting anthropologist Nancy Abelmann's suggestions about class, gender, and narrative in contemporary Korea, I would like to name this form a *melodrama of development*.[18] But instead of locating the form only in Shin Sang-ok's work or in South Korean cinematic culture (where it is nevertheless prominent), I would suggest that it is a form peculiar to a larger postcolonial context where the social (repression and/or resistance of the colonized), while not inseparable from the personal, has often deliberately and explicitly found dramatic and politically potent narrative representation within it. What marks this form in my mind is precisely how the nation's development, figured variously as enlightenment, development, or modernization, is narrated through the personal within the conventions of popular melodrama.

In *Evergreen*, the melodrama of development is latent in the ill-fated love affair as well as in the struggle for enlightenment. The complex chemistry of the film's personal and political themes is given keen cinematic pleasure not only through the kinds of formal manipulations alluded to above but, perhaps most viscerally, in its casting of principal actors, Ch'oe Ŭn-hŭi and Sin Yŏng-gyun, in roles with which they have become synonymous. These popular, melodramatic modes of representation are what separate Shin Sang-ok's filmmaking from the more staid works that make up the enlightenment or policy film genre in contemporaneous Korean cinema. But whereas *Evergreen* is in some ways the archetypal melodrama of development, *Rice* is perhaps even purer in its distillation of personal pathos and social development. The film shares with *Evergreen* its investment of dramatic energy in the passionate but ultimately platonic relationship between the male and female protagonists, again played by Shin Yŏng-gyun and Ch'oe Ŭn-hŭi. And in this film too the "moral structure of feeling [animating] goals of justice" weighs negatively on the landowning class that seeks to profit from the complacency of a corrupt regime (the stagnant postwar Rhee administration). But in *Rice*, the seat of affective pathos and action is placed more emphatically in two areas of the social realm outside the love binary—in the ideological conversion (enlightenment) of ordinary citizens and the dramatic transformation of the political regime—turning what is a didactic and essentially policy narrative into popular melodrama.

Elements of conventional melodrama are certainly an important part of *Rice*'s appeal. The figure of the protagonist as a crippled war veteran returning to his home village to relieve his late father's resentment and suffering (*han*), subjected to further trial and humiliation at the hands of both feudalistic and modern bureaucracies, forms the basis of the classic postwar male melodrama. Present here as well are the suffering women emblematic of the "golden age of South Korean melodrama," including Yong's mother and sister, who each sacrifice dearly for the irrigation project, and especially Chŏng-hŭi, who renounces not only her class privilege to be with Yong but also, to some degree, her femininity to labor in the tunnel. As in *Evergreen*, these generic codes are given explicit sociopolitical signification (again, too explicit to be allegorical) wherein the spectacle and pathos of development is the core emotional experience of the film. But the affective high point of *Rice*, as indicated above, has little to do with either Yong or Chŏng-hŭi, but is focused instead on a relatively minor character and on the largely unseen but palpable change in political order. The village shaman, the eccentric but nonetheless socially important vestige of premodern Korean life, colludes with Song, the wealthy landowner and government official, in return for heaping bowls of white rice. She first warns villagers against the dangers of Yong's engineering project, invoking the specter of angry spirits that will lead the village to starvation and death. Later, she helps Song spread the rumor that Yong and his band are communists, convincing mothers and wives to send their men to labor instead in Song's mines. The first crack in this unlikely ideological-religious conspiracy appears when Song, now nearly successful in sabotaging Yong's work, rejects the shaman's pleas for more rice. But the major blow comes when the shaman's daughter Kap-sun, the village fool, driven by the metaphorical promise of the rice she believes will flow from the tunnel, falls and drowns while helping out at the site. In a moment of spectacular and manic conversion, the shaman neither rushes to her daughter's body nor curses the project but, instead, marches into the tunnel, grabs a pick and, wailing in remorse, smashes at the rocks (Figure 7). The potent drama of this scene of personal transformation—a mixture of spiritual enlightenment and radical politicization—is heightened by vivid camerawork (the film's tightest shot, on the shaman's hysterical face), histrionic music, and a sweeping countershot of the faces of villagers stunned by the spectacle. The formal and affective investment of this scene is remarkable given that it is relatively unimportant in terms of the overall narrative.

The other big scene, of course, comes at the close of the film, when the long-awaited river water gushes out of the tunnel, welcomed ecstatically by the entire village. This is the culmination of the efforts of Yong and the newly converted-enlightened inhabitants of Muju, but also of the intervention of the military regime that has seized power and swept away red tape and corruption. No mention, interestingly, is made of Park Chung Hee

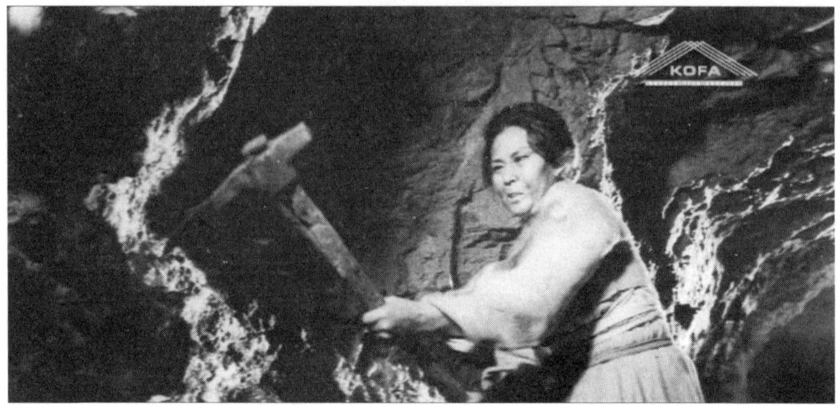

Figure 7. The shaman zealously joins the cause in *Rice* (1963). Courtesy of the Korean Film Archive.

directly; the 1961 coup instead is symbolized by Yong's old army buddy Ch'ŏl who, though crippled himself, has risen to a position of authority in the new administration.[19] With Ch'ŏl's help, explosives are trucked into the village and promptly used to blast through rock, completing the project in nearly one motion and giving the villagers the means with which to grow their long-cherished rice. As in the shaman's conversion, the scene is marked by a number of striking formal applications: rousing score, sweeping pans of jubilant villagers, and especially the shots of the water itself, at first a small flow and then a startling torrent that threatens to overwhelm the scene's staging. And its pathos is exaggerated by the anguished cries of the shaman who calls out to the now dead Kap-sun to come and eat her fill. This closing sequence in fact brings together the two thematic problems of the film—that is, how to enjoin the villagers to work on the tunnel, and how to enlist the help of the government for the project—and solves them by dramatically enclosing everyone (the enlightened shaman, the redeemed and redeeming soldier Ch'ŏl, and even the now recalcitrant landowner Song) in the same frame, foregrounded by the life-giving waters. In *Rice*, as in *Evergreen*, a melodrama of development, arising not solely out of the experiences of women under repressive social conditions or men under the strains of warfare, but rather out of the experience of the postcolonial/postwar developmentalist state, sutures the personal and political by dramatizing development itself. The popularity (i.e., commercial success) of the films is not a measure in itself of either the spirit of the times or the political orientation of Shin Sang-ok's filmmaking. Rather, it suggests that South Korean mass culture of the early 1960s was conditioned by neither one of the national development ethos at the height of both the "native land development" and "people's reconstruction" movements or by the intoxications of Western media and culture, but rather a complex mix of both wherein the nation was mediated through a melodramatic modality.

The Style of Developmentalism

A recent exchange of papers published in two leading Korean scholarly journals, *Yŏksa Pip'yŏng* (*Critical History*) and *Tangdae Pip'yŏng* (*Contemporary Criticism*), between two of Korea's leading intellectuals, Yim Chi-Hyŏn and Cho Hŭi-yon, crystallized a long-running debate over the Park Chung Hee regime and the nature of its forms of control. The gap between their opposed conceptual approaches opens a space to think through the political orientation of Shin Sang-ok's cinema and its relationship to the shifting ideological discourses of 1960s South Korea. In his first piece, "The Fascism within Us," Yim argues that critics in large part have overstated the instrumentality of not only the systems of physical violence and subjugation but also the direct reach of the Park administration's state apparatuses.[20] The period certainly gave birth to new forms of hegemony, he suggests, but those did not flow solely from the top-down structures described by revisionist-nationalist historians but from a more insidious, extensive, and total bottom-up domination he labels the "dictatorship of the masses." Drawing on George Mosse's study of German "mass nationalization" as well as on Michel Foucault's theorizations of power and subjectivity, Yim contends that the "fascism" of the Park regime was rooted in the consent of the people themselves, consent that was nevertheless generated in the everyday seductions of modernization and capitalization. Cho Hŭi-yŏn counters that any kind of complicity or collusion the masses seemed to demonstrate was rooted only in what he calls a "pseudo-consensus."[21] While postwar administrations set up anticommunism and state developmentalism as the dual master discourses upon which to build power and control, they never formed the basis of what could be called political legitimacy. Thus "only violence and coercion," he argues, "and not agreement and consensus, were left as the instruments of power."[22] The proof for Cho lies in Park's consistently weak voting record in elections (where, despite ramped-up red scare mongering and grandiose economic plans, the ruling party won only scarce majorities) and in the regular use of police and military force to put down labor and student resistance. Cho charges Yim with irresponsibly deflecting blame for fascist rule to the masses themselves, concluding that the only really progressive critical position is to clearly mark the opposition between authoritarian power and mass resistance. Yim responds to this critique with a reiteration of his notion of the function of ideology and culture that is worth repeating at length:

> Ideology must be understood as the mythological structures through which the mutually reinforcing discourses of desire and illusion are disseminated. Further, the problem of the "consent" of the masses must be addressed with a thorough questioning of the everyday of the masses. From the point of view of the masses, one must question how rule is made possible, and how that fact transformed the lives of the masses, what the mechanisms are through which dictatorship is made functionally attractive, and at precisely what point the masses were repulsed from it. Any hope of engaging with these questions cannot rest with looking at voting tendencies or trying to locate the political positioning of the masses, but requires analysis of the cultural politics and everyday of the masses.[23]

Yim contends that political and social power is not found solely or even mostly in official, governmental processes, but in "the school, the army, newspapers, magazines, television, radio, the movie theater, museums, monuments, cemeteries, memorials, gymnasiums, etc."[24]—in other words, in the basic experiences and practices of the masses.

I am not inclined here to try to intervene in this important conversation about postwar Korean authoritarianism; I also have no interest in revisiting the other implicit debate over the ideological status of popular culture generally and cinema specifically. My concern rests instead with locating Shin Sang-ok's popular dramatization of development between the poles of Yim's notion of complicit mass dictatorship from below and Cho's arguments about violent pseudo-consensus from above. Korean films of the early 1960s, especially those churned out by Shin Films, fell much more definitively under the sway of financial investors and paying audiences than under the direct hand of censors or those wielding any form of political power. While the newly enacted motion picture laws did set both moral and political guidelines for films themselves (although as we have seen, the emphasis there was placed much more decidedly on production facilities and operations), Ch'ungmuro was not yet in the business of making propaganda films.[25] But while the politics of Shin's filmmaking do not belong to any such direct forms of manipulation, they obviously took part in the kind of cultural politics that made developmentalism, if not quite dictatorship, "functionally attractive." The commercial popularity of *Evergreen* and *Rice* testify to the extent to which, in the very early years of the Park government, development and modernization discourses were already broadly legible and apt to resonate with contemporary audiences. From the evidence of the films themselves as well as their reception, it seems that any kind of consensus that existed around those discourses was not quite "pseudo"—but neither can we say that developmentalism functioned as the sort of fascistic "mass dictatorship" Yim finds in modern Korea generally. As I will attempt to argue below, an acute political ambivalence splits the films, rendering problematic any attempt to assess what ideological position they stake out. This splitting does not contradict the notion that state developmentalism is the master-signifier linking the film narratives with the policies of the Park regime; as Kim Tong-ch'un has argued, modernization-as-capitalization became an irrefutable precept in the 1960s, and Shin's films replicate it faithfully.[26] Rather, the tension arises between the implicit nationalist-developmentalist thrust of the films, rendered, as I have argued, in a melo-dramatic mode, and their explicit formal surfaces, which evoke a different, seemingly opposed, set of ideological assumptions. In Shin's "enlightenment" cinema, pseudo-consensus animates full-hearted melodramatic affect, and mass dictatorship is sometimes projected as a dictatorship of the proletariat.

As most critics readily point out, both *Evergreen* and *Rice* screen the dominant codes that structured the "androcentric" authoritarianism of the Park administration. The films precisely reproduce the nationalist rhetoric circulated in the kinds of official publications and speeches we traced above. While in some ways less overtly propagandistic than the anticommunist films that were produced shortly after the end of the war and that flooded the screen throughout the next few decades, the enlightenment film genre became synonymous with official rhetoric and later became an important component of the centrally managed National Film Production Office. Even as both films are structured intimately around the village unit and little direct reference is made to the nation, the construction of a powerful and deeply felt nationalism is the obvious subtext, perhaps even supratext, of the narratives. Repeated mention is made throughout *Evergreen* to the *minjung*, as in the early scene where Pak delivers a rousing speech calling for rural activism; and the protagonists, especially Ch'ae, make frequent use of the emotive article "we" (*uri-dŭl*). Sim Hun's narrative, we may remember, was an outgrowth of both the "cultural nationalist" school of writing that was prominent in the late 1920s and early 1930s and the agrarian "return" (*kwihwang*) or "to the people" (*vnarod*) movements of the mid- to late 1930s. This latter literary form invariably featured the return of an urbanized/ radicalized intellectual from either Seoul or the Japanese metropole and figured rural peasantry as the true locus of the Korean national spirit. Pak Tong-hyŏk and Ch'ae Yŏng-sin work toward the anticolonial objective of shedding the taint of their privileged and complicit education as well as toward the nationalist goal of capitalizing on that education to enlighten and mobilize the masses. The film's more dramatic sequences—as in the child Ok-pun's reading the letter or an earlier scene where Ch'ae lectures to a rapt audience of village elders on the importance of learning ("knowledge is power" she says)[27]—signal the link between education and political empowerment, with the implicit message that enlightenment is the only path to national strength and independence.

Rice, with its sweeping images of the countryside and rapid montages of the village population, as well as in its direct references to the 5.16 coup, evokes nationalist spirit even more overtly. The film is prefaced with an explicit, textual framing of the national implications of the narrative that reads:

> This film is based on research covering the development of farmland in Pangu-ri, Puri-myŏn, Kŭmsan-gun, Ch'ung-nam. Further, the film has added to it the tale of the "evergreens" that exist in each corner of the country. As such, this is not the narrative of any specific village, but rather is a story that could and in fact should happen anywhere in the country. We have made this film with the hope that our nation's people will live with such diligence and earnestness.

Yong, then, is the archetype of the postwar subject, the village an emblem of national reconstruction, and the irrigation project a model of the nation's development. The film projects a militarized solution to the nation's problems, which are captured acutely in the bureaucratic confusion Yong must negotiate in Seoul to find support for his cause. Reminiscent of the village women's zigzag through the civil service complex in Kurosawa's *Ikiru* (1952), Yong limps dejectedly from one gray civic office to the next, only to meet a succession of pencil pushers who each intone that Yong must go on to another bureau. This stands in sharp contrast to the swift decision making of the new military government's authorities who immediately throw their weight behind the project and turn over the local-level corruption embodied in Chŏng-hŭi's father Song. *Rice* therein explicitly affirms the social worth of the 5.16 coup, reproducing in cinematic terms the official rhetoric of the strong, militarized state solution. Furthermore, it is no coincidence that both films could win Park Chung Hee's personal, if not official, sanction. As we have seen, appropriating preceding forms of nationalist struggle (including the March 1 and agrarian independence struggles of the colonial period), revolutionary movements (chiefly the spirit of 4.19), and social activism (the *hyangt'o kaech'ŏk*) was a centrally important rhetorical strategy of the Park regime.

But the way in which these films participate in the politics of the Park regime goes beyond these direct reproductions of official discourse. As in the clear majority of the films of the "Golden Age," *Rice* and *Evergreen* uncritically articulate the social and cultural codes that moor the ideological structures of postwar South Korea. In her study of *Rice* and another agrarian return film, *Ttosuni*, film critic Pyŏn Chae-ran argues that repressive gender norms were produced in the postwar period through the ascendancy of a patriarchal nationalism that situated women as both the object and instrument of development.[28] She contends that Shin Sang-ok's filmmaking, while notably sensitive to the suffering of women under Confucian patriarchy, faithfully replicated these postwar gender norms. This is certainly apparent in the two films under consideration here: women are habitually sacrificed for the sake of the hero, the village, and the nation. Ch'ae Yŏngsin in *Evergreen* literally dies (one of Ch'oe Ŭn-hŭi's many onscreen deaths) for the enlightenment cause and Pak is left to carry on her work. Her narrative arc, taking her from shrill and hysterical feminist to faithful servant to both the village and her beloved, would have fulfilled, if not for her untimely death, the dual feminine ideal of good wife, wise (community) mother.[29] *Rice* is simpler and more unrelenting in its gender divisions. Yong is surrounded by women who sacrifice themselves for the irrigation project. His mother, to the outraged protests of her brother, sells the family's last plot of land to get the seed money for his plans. His sister, at the opening of the film realized as a simple-minded country girl, goes to the city to sell her body at a bar when Yong's project is at its nadir. The crushing reality of this sexual labor in postwar Korea is strikingly visualized here in a fleeting glimpse of the bar's sordid scene, the sister suddenly transformed into a cackling hostess at the service of leering men in business suits. Chŏng-hŭi, as we have already seen, renounces her class privilege and to some extent her femininity itself for Yong, hiding out in the gloomy cave one moment and taking up the hammer the next. The shaman's sacrifice is perhaps the greatest, losing as she does not only her hapless daughter Kap-sun but also her spiritual beliefs to help rice grow in the village. Under the terms of what Pyŏn names the system of "material westernization and psychic/cultural Koreanization," women remain tethered to traditionalized forms of domination at the same time as they are summoned to surrender themselves to the development of the nation.

Social differences, while highlighted in the narratives, are in different ways resolved by either being subsumed into or expelled from the totality of the nation. When Pak stoically strikes the school bell to close *Evergreen*, the call goes out to everyone in the village, even to the local colonial police officer and the landowner who had opposed the project. This mirrors the final scene in *Rice* where the entire village, including Song the landowner, comes out to celebrate the water that gushes from the finally completed tunnel. This is especially striking given how forcefully the film draws class lines in the language of hunger: earlier, while the village children were driven to tear the bark off of trees to fill their stomachs, Song absentmindedly spoons his dogs clumps of pristine white rice. In fact, when the military government takes power and arrests Song for his abuses of power, it is Yong himself who steps in to plead for clemency. In the essay referenced above, Chu Ch'ang-gyu correctly points out that this social leveling, brought about as it is through the agency of an outside intellectual (in *Rice*, Yong has returned from the war and years spent in Seoul), is fundamentally a bourgeois fantasy of national leadership and unity. Both films are reiterations of the colonial period enlightenment narratives that imagined a nationalist vanguard of the bourgeois elite while eliding the genealogy of class privilege and collusion with colonial rule. This paradigm is salient across the broad political spectrum of colonial period writing (in Yŏm Sang-sŏp's *Three Generations* [*Samdae*] as much as in Yi Ki-yŏng's *Native Soil* [*Kohyang*]),[30] in the intellectual dialogue of the postwar period (even in the "liberal" writings published in *Sasanggye*), and, of course, in Park Chung Hee's own rhetoric.

The third form of sociocultural renovation rendered in the films is a nostalgic distancing between the country and the city. The idealization of the rural hometown, people and lifeway is in some ways intrinsic to the experience of colonial modernization; as the imperial city became the point of extraction and collusion, the country came to be imagined as the seat of national essence and resistance. The terms of idealization shifted in the postwar period as rapid urban expansion and development and rural decline created a less overtly politicized longing for the country. *Evergreen*, as a colonial narrative produced in the postwar period, complexly echoes both forms of distancing. Seoul is the locus of enlightenment and radicalization as much as it is the closed space of the privileged and oftentimes compromised elite. The Christian youth rally where Pak delivers his opening speech is closely watched by the colonial censor, whose disapproving glance has the power to stifle dissent. And when Ch'ae invites Pak to dinner at her boarding house at the prestigious YWCA, we see that the overfed intellectuals there are somewhat too comfortable in their judgments about the future of the nation. This is immediately contrasted to the wide-open spaces and lush foliage of the country, where the honest villagers know only the language of seasons and rice. But even here, while rural folk can learn to appreciate the hard work and sacrifice of the "returned" intellectual, hardened vestiges of the dark Confucian/Chosŏn past prove to be obstacles to development. The pipe-puffing elders (that is, before their conversion) scornfully reject any notion of learning, especially for countrified women, and keep their children at home to learn to farm. A similar rejection of the city for an imperfect (that is, to-be-enlightened) country is at work in *Rice*. While the film's action takes place for the most part in Muju, its first shots, as though lifted from another film, are glossy images of the city at night as seen through the window of a cab, set to a swinging rendition of "It Had to Be You." The drunken soldiers (including Yong) who harass the bar girls are clearly a symptom of Seoul's corruption, and the only real escape is to the country, projected here as desperately poor but ultimately redeeming. The keenest urban–rural contrast of the film, however, is perhaps between Yong and the suitor Song's parents have arranged for Chŏng-hŭi. This latter modern boy, who snaps photos of the unfamiliar country houses, who warbles quotations from Shakespeare, and whose legs fall asleep during the short course of conversation, is eclipsed by the stocky war veteran Yong, whose loyalty and determination more than compensate for his injuries. And yet, as in *Evergreen*, the country is also rife with the problems of the past, as in the folk superstition the shaman invokes to impede the project and in the old social customs that subordinate the village to the landowning neo-*yangban*. This ambivalence is directly traceable to the unofficial discourse of the Park regime, whose leadership circle largely consisted of country boys who scorned the effete modern boys who survived the colonial and war periods. Park's writings at the same time fiercely attacked the legacy of Chosŏn social and political structures as an obstacle to modernization and sought to replace folk culture with a robust "androcentric" culture of militarized development.[31] This was in some ways the foundation for the "material westernization and psychic/cultural Koreanization" that characterized the modernization of the Park regime.

And yet there is still within this classic patriarchal nationalist formula considerable ideological and formal ambiguity that resists the tragic or triumphalist narrative closures in these films. As outlined above, the work of intellectuals and activists "returning" to the country or hometowns (*kwihyang*) was fraught with overlapping and often competing social and political interests. We should remember not only, say, the distinction between the grassroots "native land development" and the official "people's reconstruction" movements but also that the *vnarod* concept itself originated in populist socialist movements of the late nineteenth century. It should also be pointed out that a crucial tension in the South Korean developmentalist push was its endeavor to compete with the communist North, whose own economic plans (the successive two-year, five-year, and *Chŏllima* plans) by the early 1960s helped its economy to outpace that of the South. This ambiguity is given different kinds of expression in the films. In an early scene in *Evergreen*, Pak's passionate speech calling for rural activism is cut short by the disapproving gaze of a colonial official; later, Ch'ae's efforts to teach the village children is jeopardized when a local dandy, just returned from Tokyo, reports the school to the colonial police. The enlightenment campaign in this light is figured as an anticolonial and to some degree antiintellectual nationalist movement aimed at empowering rural populations against exploitation and oppression. While it is possible to see it, as Chu Ch'ang-kyu does, as an elitist undertaking, this is certainly not the only register *Evergreen* would have hit on, either in the original 1935 publication or the 1961 adaptation. Interpretive flexibility is even greater with *Rice*. The crew of men and women who stay loyal to the tunneling project are labeled communists ("*ppalgaengi*") by some of the villagers after they devise a plan to fairly share their resources and labor. This is as much an indication of the broad political intolerance prevailing in Cold War Korea as it is of the very fineness of the distinction between the kind of cooperative community labor encouraged by national reconstruction policies (which were to be even more capitalized under the Saemaŭl or "new village" push of the 1970s) and the kind of cooperative community labor that characterized socialist economic restructuring. The film flirts with this instability further when Song, who already runs the mines where many of the village's men are employed, offers to buy out the irrigation project once he sees that it may actually work. Yong rejects the proposal as an attempt at "labor exploitation," insisting that the work that he and his men are doing must be for the benefit of the whole. Thus while the film's most explicit intertextual references are the agricultural reforms and national reconstruction campaigns of the early Park era, the implicit reference to the industrial advances, cooperative economy, and socialist discourse of the communist North cannot be completely expunged from the text.

The discursive ambiguities that are captured in the diegesis of these films also find subtle though unmistakable expression in their formal dimensions as well. Always an avid student of world cinema, Shin Sang-ok not only introduced a number of technical advances to Korean film but also boldly adopted and popularized a range of stylistic modes and characteristics from Japanese and American as well as Chinese, Mexican, Soviet, Italian, and whatever other national cinemas he could access. While it is more pronounced in *Rice*, these influences on Shin's filmmaking are just as important in *Evergreen.* There is a distinctive style in these films that uncannily echoes the look of cinema with an ostensibly different ideological orientation. We might consider two of the more prominent visual themes in both works: the mass pan and the labor montage. With the relative financial flexibility won through the consecutive box-office successes of the early 1960s, Shin was able to hire a vast cast of extras, replete with highly detailed costumes, through whom he was able not only to portray realistically the population density of a typical village, but also to evoke, in slow pans, an image of the mass, of a people, of a collective. The effect is striking and largely unprecedented in Korean cinema.[32] In the first half of *Rice*, the village mass is twice captured, all dressed in luminous white, perched closely together in a remarkable bit of staging between the craggy peaks of the region's mountains (Figure 8). A sense of precarious beauty is lent to what is

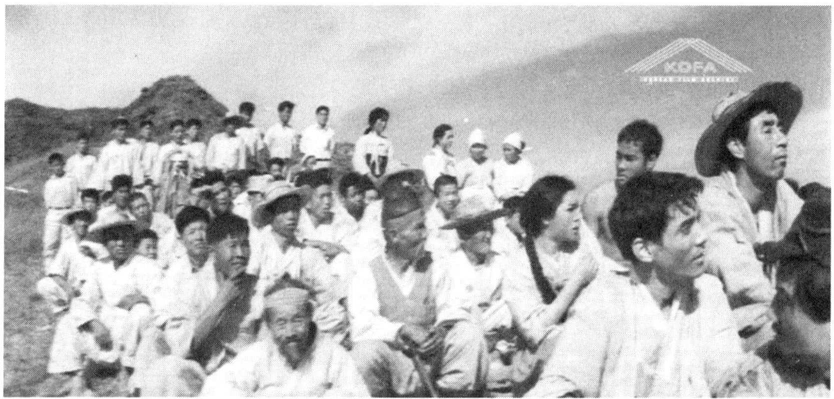

Figure 8. The villagers mass on the peak in *Rice.* Courtesy of the Korean Film Archive.

implied to be the traditional communal gathering space where the whole village is called upon to meditate on community issues. This imagining of the collective is spectacularized in the closing sequence of the film when word spreads that the mountain has finally been breached. Villagers young and old stream out of their houses and toward the site and mass at the tunnel's opening to watch the water surge forth. The sweeping pan of their variously jubilant and awestruck faces, as indicated above, dissolves the class and social antagonisms that divided the community, uniting all into a collective celebration of rural development. The final scene in *Evergreen* is almost exactly the same, a pan of villagers heeding the call of the school bell, gathering en masse to mark not only the passing of the school's founder but also the bright promise of their own enlightenment.

Equally significant are the lively montage sequences that represent progress and labor. In *Evergreen*, Ch'ae Yŏng-sin's project reaches a turning point when the village's men and children finally volunteer to help build the school, a decisive moment that is highlighted by a lively sequence: hauling timber, fitting beams, reinforcing walls (Figure 9). In *Rice*, a string of shots—irons cast in fire and then cooling in water, hammers striking stone, bundles of wood and rocks on backs, close shots of laborers—is used twice, once when the tunneling project begins, and again when it is restarted with the help of the military. Perhaps the most memorable examples of this form highlight the brute physicality of the project labor, the first, a vivid shot of Chŏng-hŭi, sweat dripping from her face and sleeves rolled up to reveal bulging arms, striking at the rocks with stony determination. And toward the close of the film, Yong and his faithful friend Kŏn-bae, swinging their picks from opposite sides of tunnel, break through in a rapid sequence of shots cutting back and forth between them until the wall's final ecstatic penetration.

These two visual themes, the mass pan and the labor montage, accord to some degree with the ideological demands of the "elite bourgeois" developmentalist state: the mass stands in for the nation and the vigorous labor for national reconstruction work. But I would argue that they also resonate in an uncanny way with the tropes and figures formalized in Soviet socialist realist filmmaking and taken up not only in Mao-era Chinese cinema and Italian neorealism (where, obviously, it was greatly altered), but also in the kind of cinema style that burgeoned in North Korea throughout the late 1950s and 1960s.[33] Clearly, visualization of the masses does not belong to any one cinematic camp; the frenzied collective has been appropriated with as much regularity in European fascist filmmaking as it has in the dogmatic

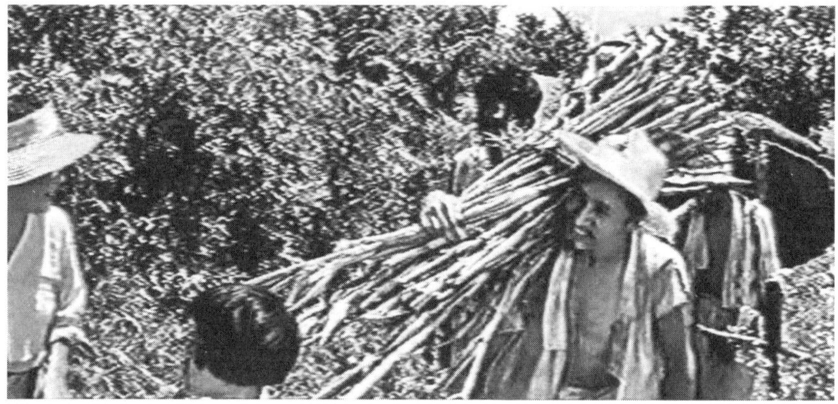

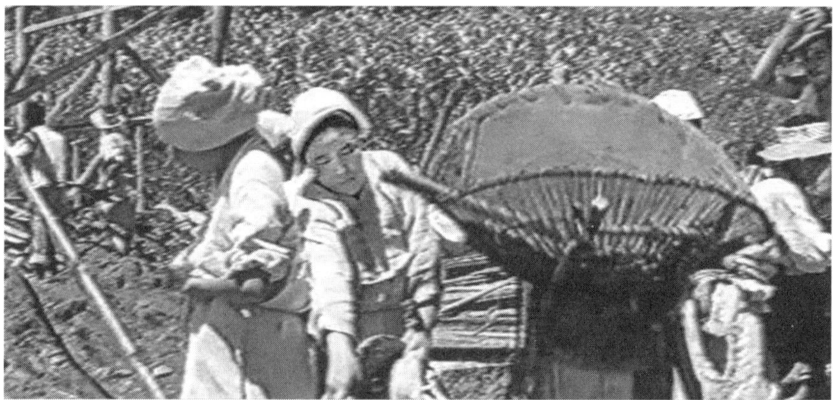

Figure 9. The village's collective efforts captured in a lively montage in *Evergreen* (1961). Courtesy of the Korean Film Archive.

imagery of Cold War American movies. But the specific components of Shin Sang-ok's mass pan, which frames the machinery of development (the waters, the school) against the backdrop of newly converted peasantry, create the same *look* as many of the iconic films of revolutionary Soviet cinema. In early takes such as Aleksandr Dovzhenko's *Ivan* (1932) or *Earth* (1930) or Sergei Yutkevich's *Golden Mountains* (1931), long-suffering peasants are saved by the collective purchase of a tractor or the triumphant return of a prodigal party cadre.[34] Chinese filmmaking from the early Mao period, while overwhelmingly didactic, nevertheless makes extensive use of progress and labor montages that are "suspended" from the narrative and form

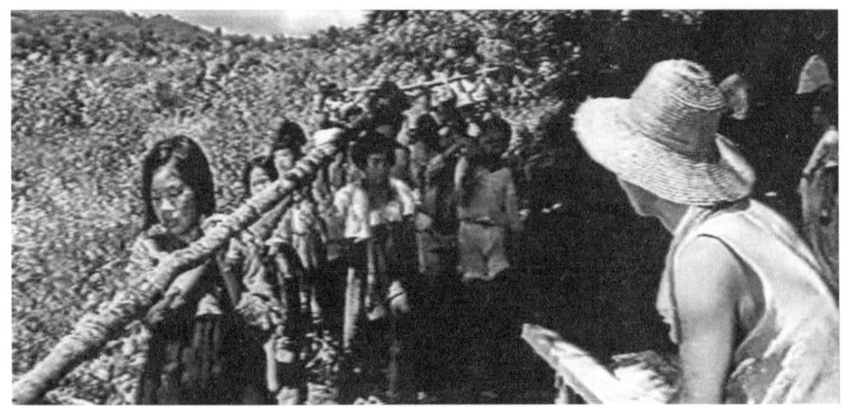

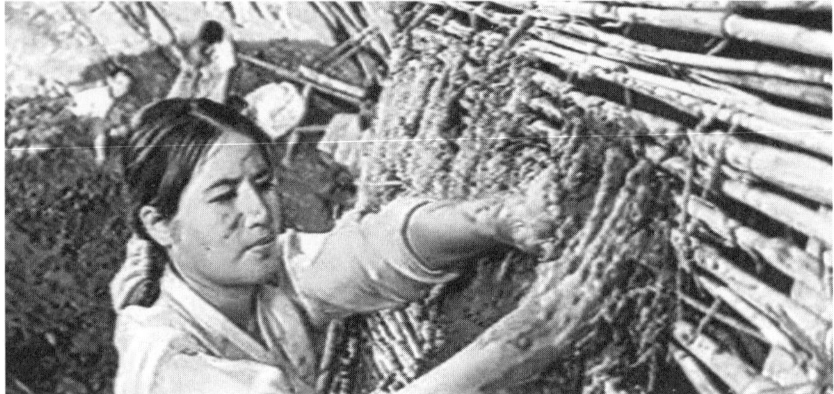

Figure 9. (continued)

their own paradigm.[35] The sequences flashing through the primitive instruments and sheer force of labor evoke the preindustrial revolutionary scene of twentieth-century communist states.

My claim here is not that Shin Sang-ok borrowed these stylistic elements intending to make socialist realist films, nor is it that these formal codes belong only to a particular ideology. In fact, in some ways, it is the exact opposite. To the extent that it is possible to argue that ideology can impinge on a film's narrative and overall content, the visual surface of the film can also reflect the ideological contests and material conflicts in the offscreen world as well as mediate the way audiences negotiate and identify with the depth of a film's ideological import. Elite enlightenment and civilization rhetoric of the colonial period contend in *Rice* and *Evergreen* with both the radical, even socialist, rural activism of the *minjung* culture movement and the centrally administered rural reconstruction campaign of the Park regime to claim ownership over the meaning of the country classroom and life-giving community project. Global cinematic institutions and codes are appropriated and transformed within the particular pressures of postcolonial/postwar Korea to render what I have called a melodrama and aesthetics of development. In these the most "political" of Shin Sang-ok's films, form and content merge to construct, and in the same movement unsettle, the ideological contours of postwar South Korea.

5   **"IT'S ALL FAKE"**

Shin Sang-ok's North Korean Revisions

A Culture Industry?

Following the collapse of his studios in the late 1970s in the South, Shin Sang-ok crossed over to North Korea in 1978. Until his return in 1986, he established a sprawling studio through which he directed seven films, produced at least ten others, and laid plans for a number of projects, most of which were eventually realized. According to his memoirs and the numerous interviews in which he recorded his experiences, the films themselves were not only wildly successful but also marked a profound shift in North Korean film practices and cultures. These claims are largely supported by the informal testimony of defectors, fledgling research into North Korean film history, and the scant remains of North Korean publishing on this episode in Shin's life. This dramatic border crossing has defined his public image, likely at home and certainly abroad, more vividly than the prolific filmmaking career that he forged in the preceding decades. The episode, however, remains enigmatic, captured amid a series of competing discourses: the complex promotional and protective impulses of Shin's own testimonies, the "national interests" of state agencies and institutions, and the sensationalist and sometimes orientalist interests of domestic and international media and scholarship. Furthermore, few outside of North Korea have seen any of these films, which were barred from public exhibition in the North in 1986.[1] This chapter does not, indeed cannot, aim at the truth of the episode; the record is incomplete and any answer would rely on speculation into the sincerity of Shin's testimonies. Rather, the present study is guided by a different set of questions: How could a filmmaking practice refined in the South function in the North? How might this inflect our understanding of the ostensibly opposed ideological structure of the two states? And does the episode prompt us to think any differently about the relationship between mass culture and ideology?

I begin this investigation of Shin Sang-ok's North Korean period with these more abstract questions about mass culture in order to offer an alternative to the more easily available approaches to making sense of the story. These, present in a range of scholarly and journalistic writings, can be divided into two broad streams: the technical and the cultural. The first, drawing on Shin's own accounts and grounded in a general understanding of the conditions of both the South and North Korean film industries, presents Shin as a multitalented technician whose expertise was essential for bringing North Korean cinema to some minimal parity with world cinema. Shin's centrality in the development of the South Korean film industry, as we have seen, would have given him a broad skill and knowledge set that, presumably, was lacking in the North. The logic of this stream also informs an understanding of Shin's personal motivations as an ambitious entrepreneur, robbed in the South of the means of making movies, for going north. The second stream, rarely explicitly articulated but coursing through many accounts, assumes a space of common cultural knowledge upon which ideological differences could be bridged. Shin was, of course, fluent in not only the sort of folk and historical narratives that were selectively appropriated in the North but also in the broader neo-Confucian social codes that are argued to have survived in both Korean modernities.[2] Accordingly, Shin was recruited by the North for his aptitude for bringing Korean cultural sensibilities to life on film. These two streams of reasoning coalesce at a common point: the assumption that ideology is secondary or, alternatively, exterior to the nucleus of filmmaking, the core elements of which are technological and cultural. The politics of a film is measured by the degree to which it expresses ideological messages on a scale between explicit polemic and implicit symbolization. Shin Sang-ok's border-crossing performance can be read from this point as a bold but simple trick of ornamenting a technically advanced and culturally specific filmmaking practice with ideological messages tweaked to fit the North's politics. The account is compelling, not least because it provides a supplement to Shin's popularly imputed lack of any political or ideological commitment.[3] Yet it is one that can do very little to account for the intelligibility and, indeed, sensation of Shin's films on both sides of the political divide. This is because the legibility of his work depended not on its overt political message—and indeed, the political message in his North Korean films is sometimes ambiguous at best—but rather on a convergence of formal and aesthetic conventions that were forged within specific historical contexts and themselves the subject of divergent political articulations. But further, this convergence not only discloses the real proximity of North Korean film and mass culture to that of South Korea but also, as I hope to demonstrate below, effects a careful reconsideration of the affective mechanisms, narrative configurations, and performative logics that inform North Korean political subjectivity.

There has, of course, been no shortage of writing on the traversal of mass culture—whether popular literature, music, or film—across ideological borders. In fact, one may argue that the theme of convergence is the critical supplement to the theme of divergence in the analysis of mass culture from the mid-twentieth century through the Cold War. This stems at least partly from how the relationship between mass culture and ideology was formulated in culture theory in terms of a split between popular and institutionalized art forms on the one hand, and modernist and avant-garde forms on the other. Among the earliest and in some ways still most influential reckonings of mass culture and modernism, of course, was Theodor Adorno and Max Horkheimer's critique of the extensive, if not total, commodifications of the "culture industry."[4] They saw in the magazine and the paperback, in popular music (particularly jazz), and especially in the cinema the obverse to the older artistic forms that, they claimed, contained a dialectically structured resistance to capitalist materialism. Therein was an accounting for how the arts of modern socialist states, while opposed ideologically to U.S. liberal capitalism and possessive individualism, were nevertheless conjoined with the arts of their geopolitical rivals. The culture industries of both capitalist and socialist states, each absorbed into and instrumentalized within the sphere of the economic, served only to facilitate conformity, homogenize local difference, and co-opt resistance. We might remind ourselves here that, for Adorno and Horkheimer, the culture industry was not the disfigured heir to the authentic, autonomous, and potentially critical aesthetic forms that had existed prior to the global triumph of authoritarian and monopoly capitalist states. Rather, both authentic popular culture and bourgeois high art were, by the twentieth century, wholly displaced by the mutually productive and antagonistic spheres of the culture industry and of modernism, neither of which existed outside of what Andreas Huyssen encapsulates as "the commodification of art and the aestheticization of the commodity."[5]

The core assertion about the culture of the Cold War is that the arts of both democratic capitalist and socialist states are defined by the imperatives of duplication and advertisement. While this deeply pessimistic view of mass culture was certainly not original to Adorno and Horkheimer, the panoramic view across regional and ideological boundaries that their articulation enabled made it a broadly influential modality of reading postwar mass culture. One of the earliest American proponents of this critical modality, Dwight Macdonald, pursued its implications to their endpoint, concluding that "the Lords of kitsch, in short, exploit the cultural needs of the masses in order to make a profit and/or maintain their class rule—in Communist countries, only the second purpose obtains."[6] Reading twentieth-century mass culture in these terms, it becomes possible to argue that Shin Sang-ok slipped comfortably between the political boundaries of North and South Korea not because the cinemas of both states simply shared a common cultural heritage, but because they were conjoined in the instrumentality that is their raison d'être: the maintenance of social and political stability. Here, the translation required for legibility on either half of the peninsula is quite simple, a matter of substituting at the last moment the specific signs of political allegiance.

But while this reading takes more careful heed of the historical coordinates of Korean mass culture, it remains caught within a reductive theoretical perspective that must dismiss a priori the possibility that Shin Sang-ok's border traversal could have signaled novelty and even transformation in the peninsula's cultural politics. As I hope to demonstrate in this chapter, such a dismissal would be regrettable, a short-sighted preemption that reflects the limits of Adorno and Horkheimer's critique of mass culture. These limits, of course, are vexed subjects for even the most sympathetic critics of the Frankfurt school, who must confront the deep pessimism and stubborn elitism that apparently lie at the core of the very concept of the culture industry.[7] Fredric Jameson has arguably done the most to recuperate Adorno's rigorous critique of modern capitalist culture, sifting out, even within the most apparently debased or mechanical cultural forms, the layers of affirmation and critique that are the means through which the culture industry both manages mass consciousness and allows for the possibility of dissent.[8] I follow Jameson here by, on the one hand, seeking to exploit the critical potential in a dialectical reading of Adorno's culture theory and, on the other, looking to the contradictions and instabilities across North and South Korean cinemas that could allow Shin Sang-ok's work to signify politically as both acquiescence and reproach on both sides. My own conclusion, neither pessimistic nor optimistic, will be that the novel and often counterrevolutionary elements of Shin's films could sustain their visibility through, on the one hand, their complex absorption in preexisting narrative and affective conventions and, on the other, even more radical transformations in the North's political aesthetics.

But before examining Shin Sang-ok's negotiations with North Korean cinema more closely, it may be worthwhile to consider briefly the implications, for an analysis of North Korean cinema, of Adorno and Horkheimer's apparently elitist rejection of the critical possibilities of all but the narrowest nonrepresentational and avant-garde forms of art. For while the conjoined ontologies of the culture industry and modernism within twentieth-century monopoly capitalism is a central tenet of *Dialectic of Enlightenment*, Adorno, especially, continued in his subsequent writings to explore the political potentiality of work by modernist artists like Arnold Schoenberg, Bertolt Brecht, and Samuel Beckett. Of course, for Adorno the cinema could hardly be the locus of even ambivalent forms of political expression. More fully self-conscious and informed modalities of artistic invention were simply not compatible with the brute mimetic processes of film—or at least of the kind of films that Adorno had taken into view. But how does this bifurcation of mass culture and modernist art obtain in relation to postwar Korean cinema? As I attempted to show in chapter 3, South Korean filmmaking throughout the postwar era was almost wholly absent of the experimentations in visual realism or narrative continuity that are the most easily detected marks of modernist cinema. Made virtually illegible by the pressures of the market and the insidious effects of state policy, avant-garde filmmaking proper could only erupt in rare flashes in the mainstream or lurk in marginal films, giving way to the near total hegemony of the commercial film industry. Similarly, the North Korean film scene is to an extent defined by the state's conscious and rigorous evacuation of what its cultural policy castigated as the decadence and mystifications of prewar modernist arts, nominal though these may have been. Its socialist and then *chuch'e* realist aesthetic principles coded in official terms the defining feature of Adorno's view of twentieth-century arts: the absorption of all preexisting practices and discourses of art into the singularity of the culture industry. Redundant then would be the search for anything like, say, the nauseating repetition and self-referentiality of Oshima Nagisa's early work or even the monstrous excesses of Kim Ki-yŏng's representation of stifled sexual desires in *The Housemaid* (*Ha'nyŏ*, 1960). So too then would be the search for filmmaking with anything like a politically critical capacity, entirely absorbed as virtually all motion picture production was under state management. Thus, if we follow Adorno through an analysis of North Korean arts, we can only conclude that it was constituted within a state monopoly of the culture industry. But rather than furnishing a conclusion, this analysis is in fact where the most radical questions of this chapter are located. First, given the stark rigidity of these artistic regimes—where modernist experimentation in the South was rendered all but invisible and in the North was formally purged—what made it possible for Shin Sang-ok to traverse the border between them, precisely on the plane of mass culture that was the exclusive territory of political instrumentalization? Second, if the politics of film are something more than the dramatization of slogans or the censorship of criticism, how must we revise the coordinates, which I have here attributed to Adorno, but which of course are embedded in a broader tradition of social analysis, given to mass culture, modernism, and politics, especially in light of the often-puzzling continuities across Shin Sang-ok's South and North Korean corpus?

History, Affect, Time

Despite the fact that the films themselves are rarely seen outside its borders, North Korean cinema is far from being an unknown entity. This is due as much to the critical importance of filmmaking to the sociopolitical life of the isolated state as it is to the centrality of the image and of spectacle in the apprehension of the state by foreign observers. The picture of North Korea, especially in the West, is dominated by a neat dyad of the leader and the mass: the figure of the variously devious, debauched, or insane Kim Jong Il against the hypnotic vision of the military procession, the orchestrated mass games, or the zealous performance of the child stars.[9] Film figures crucially in the representation of this totalitarian nightmare, not only in the assumption of a monolithically propagandistic cinema but also in the cinephilia by which Kim Jong Il's leadership and sanity is commonly mocked.[10] Shin Sang-ok, of course, plays a vital role in this representation; his abduction and forced filmmaking accord vividly with the total coerciveness that is the hallmark of North Korean political life and it was his recollection of Kim Jong Il's vast personal archives that first drew public attention to the leader's film fanaticism. Even sociological and foreign policy research works off the assumed conflict between image and reality, tacitly assuming an empty posturing in the regime's negotiating brinksmanship.[11]

The centrality of film to political and cultural life in North Korea is a fact, however, that exceeds its sensationalization in journalistic discourse. Thanks to volumes of official North Korean writing on film, records of a broad sampling of defectors, and incipient scholarly research, a clearer picture of the links between film and political administration and control has begun to emerge.[12] The very scale of official North Korean publishing on film, ranging from abstract musings on its political role to minute instructions on makeup and shot selection, appears to substantiate the seriousness of Kim Jong Il's assertion, echoing Lenin, that film is the most important of the arts.[13] Kim Il Sung, of course, is credited with the creation of a number of "revolutionary operas" and theatrical plays and is also listed as executive producer (where Kim Jong Il is named as director, writer, or other key personnel) on a selection of key cinematic works from the liberation period through to the 1970s. This crediting is absurd at the literal level; its rationality speaks more to the centrality of film than to the logic of production. Other marks abound. Inside the monumental Film Museum, part of a sprawling network of buildings just outside of Pyongyang dedicated to cinema, is a remarkable mural depicting Kim Jong Il directing an army of filmmakers—an image that effectively collapses the fictional and actual realities under his command (Figure 10). Further, some issues of the one-won bill, presumably the most commonly traded currency, were stamped with images of the three classics of North Korean cinema, *Sea of Blood* (*P'ibada*, 1969), *Flower Girl* (*Kkot panŭn chŏ'nyŏ*, 1972), and *The Fate of a Self-Defense Corps Soldier* (*Han chawi taewŏn ŭi unmyŏng*, 1973) (Figure 11). And research has shown that, as recently as the early 1990s, North Koreans were likely watching more films than any other people in the world, not only

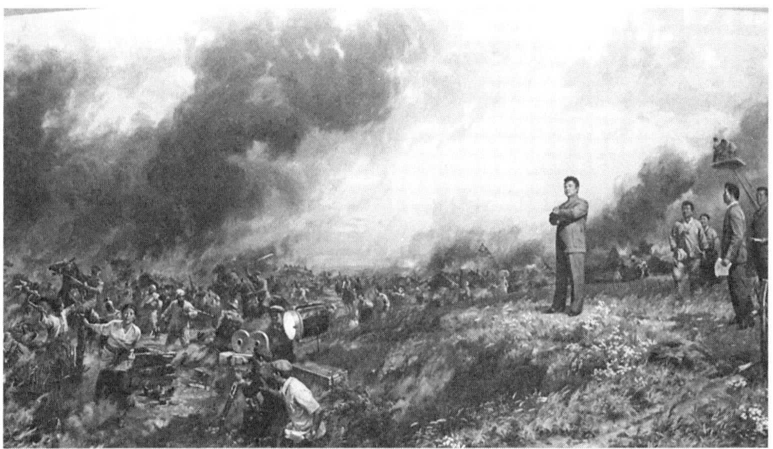

Figure 10. A Pyongyang mural depicts Kim Jong Il directing an army of filmmakers. Photograph by and courtesy of Jin Heon Jung.

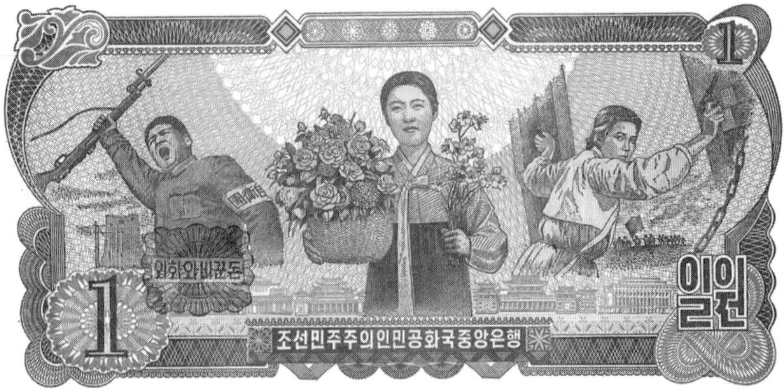

Figure 11. A pantheon of film heroes on the North Korean one-won note. Photograph by the author.

in theaters (with an average of thirteen visits per year), but on television (broadcast regularly on state television) and throughout the countryside (through the equivalent of the Soviet agit-trains), workplaces, and public spaces.[14]

Shin Sang-ok did not simply feed his work mechanically through this already productive machinery, but neither did he unilaterally transform its operations to fit with the filmmaking techniques he had mastered in South Korea. Rather, his filmmaking practices became legible in North Korea through often creative negotiation with existing stylistic practices and discourses about film. Accordingly, an examination of two distinct features of North Korean cinema—one historical, the other aesthetic—is crucial for thinking through that negotiation. We might begin with the first by problematizing the notable convergence between the official history of cinema in the Democratic People's Republic of Korea (DPRK)—specifically, the version that has assumed a hegemonic position since at least the late 1960s— and the progressive historiographic revision undertaken by researchers in the Republic of Korea (ROK) since the loosening of political tensions in the late 1990s. While there are certainly important differences in these accounts, particularly in terms of their critical tenor, it is possible to trace the shared contours of this genealogy. Specifically, two major ruptures that figure as central coordinates—the first marking a break between the colonial and liberation eras mediated by Soviet intervention in 1945, the second signaling the gradual canonization of *chuch'e* ideology in 1967—are represented as empirical facts.

It is largely agreed that the Soviet occupation period witnessed a wholesale renovation of filmmaking practices and discourses.[15] And the evidence for the overwhelming influence of Soviet ideas in this transformation is undeniable: filmmaking immediately became a privileged domain of revolutionary thought and action and was centralized and overseen by state agencies such as the North Chosŏn General Arts Federation (directed by Han Sŏl-ya); a number of active and influential agencies—for instance, the Chosŏn–Soviet Cultural Society, the Soviet Foreign Cultural Exchange Committee, the Soviet Film Export Agency—were established to facilitate the exchange (though in most cases the cultural influence was unidirectional) of Soviet and North Korean ideas and cultural forms; more than six hundred ethnic Korean students were sent to Moscow to learn about film between 1946 and 1949; the occupation government enacted a screen quota mandating that more than 60 percent of exhibitions be Soviet productions; a 1948 Soviet film festival brought eighty-eight Soviet films (a balance of feature narrative and documentary work) to forty different cities, utilizing theaters where available and setting up makeshift "agit-prop" screening facilities where they were not.[16] Stalinist filmmaking principles, most notably the socialist realist forms that had gained ascendancy in the 1930s, came to dominate, directing North Korean cinema toward the basic goal of representing the truth of class conflict and its overcoming via the agency of the party.

The key point here is that the line separating filmmaking discourses of the colonial period and its aftermath is drawn too starkly. Despite the fact that most active members of the filmmaking world were almost uniformly former "southern faction" KAPF (*Korea Artista Proletaria Federacio*) members active in the colonial film industry, any possible influence is broadly effaced in both historiographic traditions.[17] The logic of this erasure in the North is mapped quite easily: in the formative stages of *chuch'e* ideology's development in the late 1950s, the preceding period's filmmaking was cast as the work of intellectuals too reliant on Soviet ideology; and in the official systematization of *chuch'e* policy in 1967 the output of the 1940s is attributed, as most forthcoming cinematic work would be, to Kim Il-Sung.[18] Commensurate with the official national narrative, the history of film articulates a process of maturation, under Kim's benevolent guidance, from dependence on foreign (advanced or "*sŏnjin'guk*" communist) power to self-reliance and cultural independence.

This firm demarcation in South Korean historiography is less closely tied to a political program and so the stake of its logic is somewhat more elusive.

Writing recently, Song Nak-wŏn neatly encapsulates the predominant bifurcation: "North Korean cinema was not connected in any way with the Japanese colonial period, and rather than organic internal development it was foreign Soviet influence—in the multiple forms of personnel, technique, equipment—that was decisive."[19] To bolster this claim, Song rehearses the material and organizational developments referenced above, and then highlights, through a reading of *My Hometown*, formal departures from colonial filmmaking structures and tropes, chief among them the narrative resolution to formerly uncontested social iniquities through vigorous guerilla struggle. This interpretation, recurring throughout the extant literature, in essence casts North Korean ideological and cultural formation as a primarily if not solely foreign intervention. This reading is tellingly consonant with the anticommunist rhetoric that would dominate writing about North Korea throughout the Cold War years. But the possibility of collusion between these critical perspectives on film history and strategic nationalist interests is beside the point here—though indeed, the odd fit between this collusion and the ostensibly progressive political orientation of more recent North Korea research is worth further examination. Rather, my concern here is for the specific terms of an argument that, on the one hand, hews closely to the official North Korean version, and, on the other, drastically reduces the complexities of cultural and aesthetic transformation. For, by construing the film cultures of the late 1940s as without connection to the colonial past, the robust history of socialist engagement with filmmaking is written out of the story, as are the troubling revisions and disavowals those discourses underwent in the closing, militarist years of colonial rule.

The critical shortcomings of this conjoined historiographical framework might best be recognized by returning to one of the *locus classici* of Korean socialist film theory, Im Hwa's reflections on the politics of Chosŏn cinema. Throughout the 1920s Im, along with Pak Wan-sik and Sŏ Kwang-je, was at the forefront of disseminating Marxist theories of economics and culture under often-beleaguered KAPF auspices. Specifically, Bolshevik ideas about filmmaking, which encompassed larger notions about the political efficacy of film as mass culture (i.e., film as weapon) to smaller questions of form (with an emphasis on the montage), lay at the core of Im's early thought and were put into diffuse practice in the short-lived "tendency" school of filmmaking with which he was associated. But as we saw in chapter 1, from approximately 1936 onward, Im's writings effected a turn toward a critique of what he described as the "crudeness" and "artificiality" of socialist theory and culture. Investment in the enlightenment of the masses did not disappear from his prescriptions for filmmaking but shifted to an apparently more mature and pragmatic recognition of the local imperatives of entertainment and popularity. Im's "overcoming" of the primacy of ideological conflict, we may remember, was not simply an appropriation of the logic of imperial assimilation, but rather a displacement, within an enlightenment conceptualization of the "culture industry," of the optimal conditions for political visibility and cultural identity. The point here is not to turn away from the influence of Soviet institutions and aid in the formative years of North Korean filmmaking and film theory. Rather, it is to indicate that Stalinist "socialism" was being absorbed in and worked through a field of discourses and practices in which it was already eminently visible and intelligible. As Song and others have pointed out, the earliest North Korean films differed from both the KAPF productions and the pro-Japanese militarist pictures of the early 1940s in their explicit recognition of Kim Il Sung's leadership. Yet the two axial terms of Im's conceptualization of film under imperial rule, popularity and localism, span in important ways the film discourses of the KAPF group and early North Korean film. Film theory in the North would return repeatedly to this topos, though, of course, popularity and the local would again be translated into highly politicized terms (i.e., "the people" [*inmin*] and "the state" [*kuk'ga*]), but it would retain the basic reorientation instantiated in the early engagements with socialist thought: visibility of the local masses and articulation of the subaltern for the sake of vanguard political ends. In dozens of roundtable discussions and indeed in the official reviews attributed to Kim Il Sung himself, the stress was placed on depicting realistic (though, tellingly, not yet heroic) characters through which to illustrate class conflict. These otherwise ideologically differentiated discourses are commensurate with the "enlightenment modality" examined closely in chapter 1. Clearly, it would be a mistake to ignore the socialist aims that gave specific expression in North Korea to this general mode, as it would be to downplay the sweeping effect of saturated exposure to Soviet technology and films. Yet, precisely because they do not correspond to the pronouncements that inaugurate successive political regimes, the continuities highlighted within the enlightenment film modality are more compelling than the changes in personnel and organizational affiliations cataloged in prevailing North Korean film histories.

My examination of the enlightenment modality of Shin Sang-ok's North Korean films, salient as much in the classical socialist awakening pieces as in the bold experiments with minor genres, will lay bare the complex convergences and divergences those films traced in relation to South Korean and preexisting North Korean films. For the moment, I will close this reconsideration of North Korean cinema genealogies by suggesting a critical amendment to the historiography of the second major break signaled above, the conquest of *chuch'e* realist discourse in the 1960s. The essence of that narrative, of course, is that, beginning around the end of the 1950s, *chuch'e* arose as a political and cultural master code that both described and rationalized the growing and often violent gap between Kim Il Sung's regime and what remained of the competing factions of the North Korean revolution as well as the state's ideological and economic sponsors, the Soviet Union and the People's Republic of China (PRC). *Chuch'e*-realist film theory, accordingly, displaced the older socialist and Soviet and Chinese protocols as well as any trace of Euro-American filmmaking styles. *On the Art of the Cinema* (*Yŏnghwa yesul ron*), attributed to Kim Jong Il, crystallized with remarkable detail the techniques of properly *chuch'e* filmmaking.[20] Filmmaking should, according to Kim, project models through which to grasp the revolutionary nature of the present historical stage, understand *chuch'e* or self-determination as the condition of that revolution, and recognize Kim Il Sung's and the Party's leadership as both the manifestation and instrument of *chuch'e*. Filmmakers must therefore fully master *chuch'e* principles themselves and plant this "seed" (*chŏngja*) in all of their work. So while it shares with conventional socialist realism the task of representing class contradiction, North Korean film must also screen a reality—a "visual textbook"—in which self-determination is the only real solution to social problems.

Neither *On the Art of the Cinema* nor any of the commentaries that preceded or followed it articulate a detailed conceptualization of cinematic *chuch'e* realism. Rather, *chuch'e* serves as a critical foil by which the success or failure of a scene or a screenplay or an actor's performance in communicating its apparently amorphous and situationally defined substance is gauged. In other words, while it instituted, as cinematic goals, recognition of the primacy of self-determination and sublimation of revolutionary desires through the agency of the Party, and further, while it occasioned the production of undeniably novel narratives of socialist heroism, *chuch'e* never became a theoretical model. It was, rather, a political and heuristic apparatus that disciplined North Korean film by radically narrowing the narrative and stylistic range through which the predominant enlightenment modality could be realized. In this way, the *chuch'e* rupture is less radical than is advertised in the official North Korean historiography. Interestingly, this is the same conclusion reached in the revisionist history, which finds in *chuch'e* only minor modifications to the Soviet socialist realist tradition or characterizes it as an empty placeholder for the enforcement of the Party's administrative authority. But I want to argue that while the continuities across postwar North Korean filmmaking instrumentalities are undeniable, qualitatively new modes of filmmaking did in fact coincide with the rise of *chuch'e* realism. These were substantiated as formal techniques and narrative practices that modify both classical and socialist norms of cinematic realism in politically expedient, if not quite radical, fashion. And in a complex, though indisputably instrumental, echo of the modernist reaction against the reifications of representational realism, these modes instantiate shifts in two fundamental areas of cinematic continuity: affect and time.

The first of these inhabits the seemingly redundant explications about film and the often absurd injunctions to specific formal practices in Kim Jong Il's writing on art and film. It also exists vividly, perhaps too obviously, in the films themselves, manifesting in an extreme magnification of affective spectacle. Often precisely the object of critical derision outside of North Korea—particularly for the use of ostensibly retrograde techniques (frequent zooms, dramatic coincidence, maudlin score, etc.)—this insistence on emotional force is curious for the way it introduces a productive binarity to the concept of realism. On the one hand, the selection and proper treatment of subject matter, toward the reproduction of revolutionary realism, is cardinally important to North Korean filmmaking; *On the Art of the Cinema* contains specific instructions for actors ("there should be no affectation in speech or action"), cinematographers ("filming should be realistic"), and even set designers ("the sets should reflect the times"), and the full range of filmmaking staff on how best to render realistic scenes. On the other hand, the treatise devotes considerable space to the manipulation of events, shot angles, and even props toward yielding the maximum emotional impact. The stakes of such construction are obvious but spelled out nonetheless:

> The delineation of emotions is not merely intended to create tension in the audience or amuse them, but to amplify the ideological and emotional impact of a film. The delineation of emotions is meaningless if it makes no ideological impression on the audience. Emotional scenes in a film have to be subordinated to the profound expression of the idea of the production.[21]

And because emotion is political, there is also a correct way of managing it:

> The strength of the emotions must be built up and there has to be a motive for their coming to a head. . . . Emotions which come to a head without any buildup or motive are either unnatural or false. The force of the characters'

emotions should build up as the drama develops and the motive for the emotions to be expressed has to be supplied at precisely the right moment. If the
buildup is excessively prolonged, the emotional current is weakened and the
film becomes boring.[22]

Thus the ideological effect of filmmaking depends on emotional impact,
which in turn depends on the proper phasing of emotional events. *On the
Art of the Cinema* thus mandates a nonmimetic measurement of affective
timing that will make or break a film.

This measured temporality, the second novel feature of *chuch'e* filmmaking, works both in the historical setting of the vast majority of the films
as well as in their pacing. Most of the feature films made until at least the
end of the 1980s were confined to the narrow period between the mid- to
late 1920s and the end of the war in 1953. Not only the great canonical
works, stretching from *My Hometown* through *Sea of Blood* (1969) and *Star
of Chosŏn* (*Chosŏn ŭi pyŏl*, 1980–86), but even the massive serials such as
Nation and Destiny (*Minjok kwa unmyŏng*, 1992–present) rarely move back
beyond the March First movement or forward to anything like the present.
In fact, the bulk of production infrastructure is invested in replicating the
late colonial, early liberation, and civil war periods: costumes, architec-
tural fittings, and train claddings at the February 8 Film Studios were
measured almost exclusively for those historical stages, and the sprawling
Chosŏn Art Film Studios has one permanent set that is a faithful replica of
a medium-sized town under Japanese colonial rule. The span is clearly the
revolutionary time–space of the North Korean regime, after the shame of
dependence on China and annexation to Japan and before the mundane
but often violent processes of nation building. Filmmaking returns ceaselessly to this historical moment to mine it for new heroes and phases of radicalization or slightly reconfigured ways to tell the same revolutionary tales.
But further, the narratives rarely move beyond the conditions of revolution
or the process of radicalization. Rather, the films dwell continuously, though
sometimes episodically, in the phases of darkness, suffering, and repression,
only to end precisely at the moment of enlightenment, recognition, and
release. It is a temporality that is more regressive than messianic, dwelling
in pain more than in anticipation of redemption. Release, of course, does
come, or is at least suggested, in the films, but the way to liberation is rarely
projected, either because the free space is already too well known, or somehow for that reason unrepresentable. Here too, the ideological imperative is
clear. Film art captures the conditions for and process of grasping revolu-

tionary relations: specifically, of recognizing the unceasing injustice of the landlord, the foreigner, the other, and the importance of self-actualization (whether this is realized in an act of vengeance, the agitation of a group or mob, or in the shining example of a leader). This, of course, is the corollary to the affective excess sketched above. The release from that mode of suffering and the advance from the time–space of instruction is climactic but almost incidental; the real action and pleasure in North Korean cinema works through returning to the moment of humiliation, dwelling in injustice, and drowning in tears.

Flower Girl, produced ostensibly by Kim Jong Il in 1972 and based on a revolutionary opera credited to Kim Il Sung, is perhaps the most iconic of North Korean films. It not only made a national hero of its lead actress and forged a set of songs and images that entered deeply and enduringly into popular consciousness, it is also referred to repeatedly in Kim Jong Il's and subsequent film writing as the exemplary piece of filmmaking. It tells a story precisely the way we would expect, in perfect alignment with the principles of *chuch'e* filmmaking. Flower (*Kkot-bun*) cuts flowers on the mountain plain and sells them from her basket on the busy streets of a country town in the colonial period. Through the device of a fortuneteller's synopsis, we learn that Flower's father has passed away, her brother has been taken off to prison, her mother is ill, and her little sister, Suni, is blind. Much of the family's troubles have come at the hands of the wealthy landlords from whom they rent their land and for whom they work. Suni, in fact, was blinded when the matriarch, enraged at the little girl for sneaking a taste of sun-dried peppers, pushed her into a kettle of boiling water, scalding her face and eyes. Enraged by the injustice, the older brother, the family's pillar, set fire to the landlord's storehouse, resulting in his imprisonment and the family's eternal indenture to the landlord. Despite her virtual enslavement to endless hours of excruciating labor, the mother protects her eldest daughter from her own fate by sending her out to sell flowers. This eventually takes its toll and the mother collapses; the medicine that Flower and Suni scrape to buy comes too late and she dies. Left in utter despair, Flower goes off in search of her brother, only to be told, after the month-long journey, that he had died in prison years before. Upon returning to the village, she receives another blow: Suni has gone missing, likely kidnapped or killed by the landlord's henchman. When Flower goes to confront the landlord and matriarch, she is clubbed for her trespasses and locked in a storeroom. This numbing string of tragedies is broken, finally, by the entry of a savior: the brother, who, it turns out, had escaped from prison and spent the years since in the mountains as an anticolonial guerilla. Upon his return to the village, he discovers Suni safe with a mountain hermit, and hears of his family's woes. Rousing the villagers, he leads them on an assault on the landlord's house, tearing down the walls, thrashing the inhabitants, and rescuing Flower from her entrapment. United after so many years, Flower is torn between joy and rage at her prodigal brother. He, for his part, addresses their woes with a fervent speech calling all to see that the nation's enslavement is the root cause of their suffering. Flower is awed and the next day her bountiful, colorful flowers sell on the sunny streets with renewed vigor.

Flower Girl is a remarkably closed text. All aspects of its character construction, moral trajectory, and emotional impact build inexorably toward the momentous, if absurd, catharsis of the brother's radicalizing return. Enemies and comrades are clearly delineated: the cruel landlords, ready to strike and slash for the barest infractions, and nefariously connected to the coldly uniformed colonial authorities, are pitted against the laboring masses, short of means but ever ready to share food and a helping hand. Suni's blinding, the brother's arrest, and the mother's relentless toil and catastrophic demise pile together layers of resentment that beg for a release that can only be targeted at the landlords. And the release is in fact foretold at the beginning of the story by the fortuneteller, who assures Flower that a savior (*kwi-in*) will solve the family's problems, thus structuring the film as a messianic fable. Were this a contemporary American drama, we might expect that Flower, through some sort of positive transformation, would herself become that savior. Or, unaware of the allegorical tendencies of North Korean filmmaking, we might anticipate the entry of Kim Il Sung himself. In *Flower Girl*, as in virtually all North Korean films, the *kwi-in* is at the same time all of these figures—the radicalized prodigal brother, the awakened masses, and enlightened Flower herself—and none of them: it is the principle of *chuch'e* itself, allegorized and mobilized in the act of mass insurrection and personal self-realization.

And yet, while *Flower Girl* does not present overt resistances to or fissures within this closure, the very weight of its narrative, moral, and emotional trajectory can tell us about the paradoxically less obvious mechanisms of North Korean filmmaking. While cinema under Kim Jong Il is, as we have seen, governed by the absorption and transmission of the *chuch'e* idea, *Flower Girl* is almost wholly caught, temporally as well as affectively, in the moment before self-realization and deliverance. It could be argued, of course, that this dwelling in suffering and helplessness only prepares the ground more fertilely for the intervention of the *kwi-in*. Nevertheless, it is important to see this excess on its own terms and to think seriously about its formal as well as ideological implications. The film functions for its better part as a cataloging of the sufferings of the *inmin* (people), amplifying primal scenes of humiliation, pain, and death to the fullest cinematic extent. The most powerful of these scenes represent the mother's toils. The intense physical exertion of washing clothes and linens—hauling a load out of the kettle, drawing cold water from the well, beating cloth with a heavy mallet— is a drawn-out spectacle, narrated by the mother's own unspoken thoughts about wanting to die. Her endless hours grinding grain at the millstone are mirrored by the camera's incessant return to the stone itself. And later in the film, when the landlord's wife is abruptly haunted by remorse for her wrongdoings, the mother's suffering is projected in a vivid collage that synchronizes scenes of labor and the numerous thrashings she endured at the hands (or cane) of the landlord. But the apex of this suffering spectacle (and indeed of the film as a whole) is the mother's death, accompanied by a series of catastrophic images and sounds: a quickly darkening sky torn with lightning, waves crashing violently against a jagged cliff, trees shaken madly by a powerful wind. The heavens literally fall at her demise.

The film is also broken by a number of lyrical, painterly frames that do not strictly serve the forward motion of its narrative. The most striking of these is the picture of Suni wailing, first for her mother at the beginning of the film, and again for her sister toward the end. Shot in a stark, horizontal tableau next to a withered tree, Suni sings the flower girl theme or alternately calls out to her family in incomprehensible sobs. These scenes of suffering and waiting do not serve the narrative in a strict sense and do not prepare any further for the emotional impact of the finale. Rather, they exist at the affective heart of the films themselves as, it might be said, the crucial node of its enjoyment. But what is most suggestive is not that they resist the film's overall ideological content, but that they are so nonspecific in their character. While the mother suffers at the hands of the landlords, there is nothing in that suffering or its representation in itself that anticipates or necessitates *chuch'e* or the communist revolution. The inherent critique of feudal exploitation could belong to either the socialist or modernizing discourses of the colonial period. Further, Suni's plaintive calls for her family, or the waiting for the *kwi-in*, again, are not aimed at the coming of the communists. The film exists in the prerevolutionary moment in more than one sense. And in tarrying so long in the moment of suffering, its political impact more closely resembles that of the early left-tendency literature of the colonial period: ill-defined ideologically (i.e., not part of a program or strict class analysis) but highly invested in the basic structure of suffering and release. *Chuch'e* is the lesson of the film if only it is anticipated as such; its most powerful moments, however, lie in the magnification of suffering.

These sensationalized modes of representing suffering and dwelling in the moment of waiting pose no challenge to the ideological closures of North Korean film or political discourse. Whether the savior's entry is presented as an abrupt deus ex machina or whether the moment of enlightenment is implausible, the production of the film within the enclosures of *chuch'e* realism renders whatever happens in the end literally a foregone conclusion. What matters, as official North Korean discourse repeatedly reminds us, is that the construction of the film will be good enough to move and instruct its audience. Affective surplus and temporal thickening both constitute, then, the political aesthetics of North Korean film. In other words, while well-defined *chuch'e* messages are indispensable, the politics of *chuch'e* realism are embedded in the basic grammar of this lachrymose, bloated visualization of revolutionary conditions. And it is precisely in light of these political aesthetics that the terms of Shin Sang-ok's intelligibility and, ultimately, effect in the North become more distinct. For, on the one hand, those aesthetics in themselves are protean, open to application to unconventional genres and even retrograde narratives. But, on the other hand, their distinct coding of reality explicitly highlights the difference of other filmmaking forms (Soviet, American, South Korean, or otherwise)— differences that, integrated into its own practices, could prompt a shift in those political aesthetics themselves. As I hope to demonstrate below, Shin's adventures in the North, far more than confirming this political dexterity, show the heterogeneity of North Korean film culture and its complex engagement with classical realism. The mass effect of his translation in the North suggests the instability of the culture industry in North Korea,[23] and, at the same time, the perhaps surprising flexibility of the North in coping with transformation.

Shin Films, North

While filmmaking and to a certain extent reception during the period of Shin Sang-ok's North Korea period is documented by a number of sources, the events of his departure and return, as well as the details of the eight years spent there, are only recorded by Shin himself. As a result, suspicion has long prevailed over his and Ch'oe Ŭn-hŭi's claims that they were abducted, forced to produce films, and then managed to defect in a dramatic episode in Vienna. This was only bolstered by Shin's perhaps intentionally provocative claim sometime after his return that, had he not been allowed to produce films in the South in the 1960s, he "would have gone North on [his] own two feet."[24] North Korean authorities for their part claim that Shin and Ch'oe defected to the North voluntarily and that they embezzled millions when they sought amnesty in 1986.[25] The validity of their accounts is not the concern of this chapter. However, a summary of the episode told in their memoirs and interviews is necessary both to contextualize the films and to draw out their wider implications.

As we have seen, the latter half of the 1970s saw the demise of Shin Films amid a string of box-office flops, the unwieldy expansion of the studio to Anyang, and a falling out of favor with the Park regime that saw Shin unusually vulnerable to a string of scandals, first with a bribery count for which he was acquitted and later for a censorship battle, which his studios eventually lost. Lured to Hong Kong by the possibility of a new production deal, Ch'oe disappeared there in January 1978; following leads in his search from old partners in Hong Kong, Shin was taken in a bizarre series of events through Beijing to Pyongyang. While Ch'oe was welcomed warmly in North Korea, accommodated in comfortable isolation at luxury villas, and eventually met Kim Jong Il (who praised her as the mother of Korean film), Shin was subjected to harsh treatment from the start and, owing to a series of failed escape attempts, spent the next five years in bleak internment camps and was subjected to reeducation programs. Released abruptly in 1983, Shin was reunited with Ch'oe and met with Kim Jong Il at an elaborate reception. In a meeting that Shin managed to record, Kim espoused his views on cinema and explained why they had been "forcibly invited": he hoped that, backed by his resources and authority, they would take over filmmaking in North Korea and elevate it to international standards. Taking over control of the existing February 8 and Chosŏn Art Films studios and reincarnating a North Korean Shin Films studio (officially named "Shin Films Motion Picture Studio" [*Sin pillŭm yŏnghwa chwaryŏngso*]), Shin and Ch'oe collaborated on at least twenty films over the next three years. The production scale was vast, fielding up to seven hundred in staff that included technicians from Japan and Hong Kong, and filming on location around the country and in parts of Northeast China and Eastern Europe. Many of the films were screened at film festivals abroad; Ch'oe Ŭn-hŭi won prizes for direction at the 1984 Karlovy Vary Film Festival (for *The Secret Emissary* [*Toraoji anŭn milsa*], which Shin directed but which he credited to Ch'oe) and for acting at the 1985 Moscow Film Festival. Location shooting and negotiation for distribution afforded them relative freedom to travel, and in March 1986, on a trip to Vienna to source exhibition venues, they eluded their handlers and declared amnesty at the U.S. Embassy. After a course of investigations within U.S. and South Korean diplomatic bureaus, the two were released and found their way back to Seoul in June.

Upon their return to Korea, Shin and Ch'oe were pressured to give a full account of their experiences both by parties suspicious about their claims of abduction and escape and by those curious to glean inside information from their unique double border crossing. They held press conferences and gave a series of public interviews, where their consciously glamorous posturing (Ch'oe in her trademark oversized sunglasses and Shin decked out in his usual ascot) gave the lie to many about their harrowing experiences. Shin returned to filmmaking in 1990 with *Mayumi*, about the 1987 bombing of a Korean Airlines jet, which Shin claimed he was compelled to make to confirm his political identity and loyalty.[26] They also published a series of memoirs on the episode: *The Kingdom of Kim Jong Il* (*Kim Chŏng-il wang-guk*) in 1988, *My Name is Kim Jong Il* (*Nae re Kim Chŏng-il imneda*) in 1994, and finally *We Haven't Escaped Yet* (*Uri ŭi t'alch'ul ŭn kkŭtnaji anattda*) in 2001, which included material from the previous books, new reflections, and an open letter to then president Kim Tae-jung. The majority of this writing is focused on re-creating the events of their capture and escape, as well as on broad speculations about the fate of the North Korean regime. Most intriguing is the long conversation (essentially a monologue) with Kim Jong Il recorded in the second book, which Shin apparently taped using a machine bought in an officer's supply store and somehow smuggled into the meeting. The global visibility and prestige of North Korean cinema seems to be Kim Jong Il's central concern; the ideological effect on domestic audiences only secondary. He laments that where early North Korean filmmaking, produced by staff trained in the Soviet Union, was promising, subsequent work, with few exceptions, has been largely "embarrassing" and unworthy of the world stage. Kim dwells at length on his thwarted desire to host an international film festival, and while it is clear that he is concerned about what his people are watching, he couches his concern more in terms of the formal quality than the ideological content of the films:

> [S]o despite what our people may want, there's a reason why we can't show foreign movies on television. Chinese and Soviet films, and even American films are really good. There are even good historical treatments, but because of that we can't really put it out there or else it will invite comparison, com-

parison with what we've got I mean. And because we've got these university educated types. With people at their level, at that level, if we're not careful things could turn nihilistic, so our propaganda department's got to be careful and that's why our television's so rigid and staging the same things days and night.[27]

Kim's point (as poorly articulated as it is throughout the text) is that the native film industry must come to rival world filmmaking, both for the artistic and political satisfaction of that development in itself, as well as for the positive effects this would have on social order and the maintenance of *chuch'e* ideals. Shin's task here is not to make the best socialist-*chuch'e* realist films, but to make quality films that would implicitly speak to the fact of self-realization.

By almost all reports, Shin's films instantiated broad changes in the North Korean film industry, created a cultural sensation and did penetrate the world (if only that of the communist bloc) market. The memoirs call attention to the accomplishments repeatedly: the first "private" film studio, the first time filmmaking staff were fully credited (*The Secret Emissary*, 1984), the first screen kiss (*A Million Li along the Rails* [*Ch'ŏl kil ttara ch'ŏnman li*], 1985), the first utterance of "love" as well as the first time a film instigated ticket-scalping (*Oh My Love* [*Sarang sarang nae sarang*], 1984). The work was also well received by Kim Jong Il, who was especially ecstatic about the international film festival prizes, as well as by Kim Il Sung, who for instance praised *The Secret Emissary* as having the look of a European film and *Record of an Escape* (*T'alch'ulgi*) for its dramatic power. A recent survey of one hundred defectors placed a number of Shin's films in the "Top Fifty" North Korean films—*Hong Kil-dong* (1986), for which Shin claimed development credit, was number one, while *Oh My Love*, placing twelfth, was fondly remembered for its scandalous scenes.[28] Another defector, writing anonymously in the *Daily NK* on the occasion of Shin's death in 2005, wrote that Shin's new releases would cause such a commotion in Pyongyang that jobs in movie theaters became wildly popular.[29] Shin's works, the article reflected, were welcomed as "movies that were really like movies" and brought love and energy to an otherwise dry and sterile cinema.

Shin's North Korean films, then, had a significant mass cultural effect. They altered modes of production, installed a producer-centered studio system, shifted the horizon of expectations for film audiences, and opened North Korean filmmaking to a sort of cinematic internationalism, as limited as that may have been. This certainly furnishes a way of thinking about

Shin's translation from the South to the North. In effect, Shin crossed a border between two ideologically opposed, but identically authoritarian developmentalist regimes. The state capitalism of the South, integrated within the world capitalist economy, early on facilitated, indeed demanded, cultural production that was fully articulated with (though continually forced to "match") Hollywood and the West. The centrally administered economy of the North, robust in its first few decades, was driven into increasing insularity by the continual withdrawal and liberalization of the communist bloc, yielding cultural production that could no longer bear "comparison." Shin's hallmark technical rigor and sensitivity to sociopolitical zeitgeists allowed his filmmaking to become the most spectacular, though by no means singular, instance of peninsular border crossing. But further, as we have seen, this traversal is conditioned in less material and more enigmatic ways by the often overlooked codes of pre-Shin North Korean filmmaking. The particular forms of spectacle, affect, and temporality that governed iconic films like *Sea of Blood* and *Flower Girl* inhabit Shin's films in complex and diverse ways. While the episode certainly marks a sensational fracturing in Shin's life, it also signals continuity within the larger, cosmopolitan scope of Shin's cinema.

Enlightenment, Revised

Given the eclectic body of work Shin produced over three decades of filmmaking in South Korea, it comes as little surprise that his North Korean films are generically, stylistically, and thematically heterogeneous. As in his work throughout the 1960s, the films he produced under the auspices of the North Korean Shin Films come out of a studio system that aimed at, as was its explicit mandate, films with mass appeal. As sketched above, Shin directed seven films: an early modern historical epic (*The Secret Emissary*), two films based on colonial period literary works (*Salt* [*Sogŭm*]), *Record of an Escape*), a classic enlightenment film (*Breakwater* [*Pangp'aje*]),[30] a folktale rendered as musical (*Oh My Love*), a folktale rendered as fantasy (*Simch'ŏng-jŏn*), and a folkloric monster film (*Pulgasari*). Films made under the Shin Films production label include a number of enlightenment films set in the colonial or early liberation periods (*A Road* [*Kil*], *A Million Li along the Rails, Until We Meet Again* [*Hae'ŏjyŏ ŏnje kkaji*]), war films (*Red Wings* [*Pulgŭn nalgae*]), and a hagiographic sports film (*Run Chosŏn Run* [*Tallyŏra Chosŏna*]). And before his appearance in Vienna, Shin had also planned out two period pieces, the martial-arts-inflected *Hong Kil-dong* and the multi-part historical epic, *Im Kkŏk-jŏng*.

Salt, Record of an Escape, Breakwater, and the other enlightenment films constitute the most coherent set and are most closely attuned to the North Korean *chuch'e*-realist standard. At the same time, they are closest formally as well as thematically to the melodramatic development films we examined in chapter 4. Shin Sang-ok, in fact, often referred to these films, especially *Record of an Escape,* with *Rice* (*Ssal*) and *Evergreen* (*Sangnoksu*) in the same phrase, regarding them as his best work. The continuity is not at all surprising on the aesthetic level, given the primacy of realism in Korean film criticism (South and North), or on the political level, given the shared authoritarian developmentalism of the two states. A line of demarcation, though, can be drawn in terms of the peculiar temporality-affect structure sketched above. For where the South Korean films pushed relentlessly forward, dramatizing labor, progress, and overcoming, the North Korean films idle in suffering, returning again and again to moments of pain and humiliation. In a sense, this stagnant temporality reflects the sensibility of the leftist literary works they adapt.[31] But given that the majority of the works of that school were forsaken and its leaders (Yi Ki-yŏng and Han Sŏl-ya) purged by the North Korean regime in the 1960s (though they would make a return in the late 1980s), the structuring principle of these films is perhaps more complex.

Record of an Escape is based on the classic 1924 Ch'oe Sŏ-hae short story of the same title and employs the original's epistolary form to construct its voice-over narration (though it departs immediately from this, as discussed below, in its suggestive opening shots). The early scenes establish the setting as the early colonial period and seem to promise the unfolding of an archetypal enlightenment narrative. Diligent, thoughtful Sŏng-ryŏl abandons his studies and brings his pregnant wife Sun-sil to live with his mother and father in their country village. A neighboring cousin who holds the deeds to the surrounding property suggests that Sŏng-ryŏl and his family expand the work on their modest plot to include the wild fields he owns, promising to take only a small percentage of the harvest. Work clearing the fields begins in earnest, the entire family hauling stones, digging irrigation ditches, and planting shoots in a quick montage accompanied by a rousing score. Sŏng-ryŏl and Sun-sil also find time to enlighten the village, conducting night classes for the adults and, echoing *Evergreen*'s classroom scenes, literacy classes for children under the shade of an old tree. Months pass and their arduous labor pays off in a lush, sprawling field of rice. The idyllic portrait collapses quickly, however, when the cousin reveals that he has sold the land (and its harvest) to Japanese colonial interests; Sŏng-ryŏl's protesting father is slain by a ruthless Japanese officer and the family is left with nothing to show for their labor.

The scene shifts to the northern stretches of Kando, the promised land of the early colonial period, where Sŏng-ryŏl has brought what remains of his family in search of security and prosperity. Instead, Kando offers only an unending series of disappointments, reversals, and tragedies, starting on the very first day when they are accosted by bandits. When the family carves a humble mud-house out of the earth, they are harassed by the local land manager. Exposed to the elements, they suffer bitterly and the newborn baby falls ill; unable to afford treatment or medicine (the landowner offers only a tiny advance on the harvest), the family is helpless and watches him die. Traumatized, they burn down their house and move to the city, where Sŏng-ryŏl tries his hand and fails at a string of jobs: as a scribe (where he is unable to bribe the patrolling police), as a water delivery man (where he is muscled out by the competition), as a chimney sweep (where he is harassed by a local widow), and as a woodsman (where he is arrested for trespassing on newly acquired Japanese land). Meanwhile, his mother and wife struggle to make do with what tiny funds trickle in, taking in laundry and milling grain on an old stone. The lowest point comes when the pregnant Sun-sil, desperate for nourishment, gnaws on mandarin orange peels she finds in the neighbor's garbage. But the tragic climax is in the frail mother's mauling at the hands of a local businessman's dogs. Bleeding and unconscious, she is refused help by doctors and pharmacists who turn Sŏng-ryŏl away at the sight of his filthy clothes. Enraged, Sŏng-ryŏl refuses to simply watch his mother die; picking up an axe, he smashes the pharmacy to pieces in a long scene captured almost entirely in lurid, slow-motion photography. He is arrested, abruptly accused of being a communist, and taken away to execution. The story then takes a sudden turn. On the train, headed presumably toward labor camps, Sŏng-ryŏl is liberated by armed gunmen who then welcome him into their anonymous party. To the closing voice-over explaining his sudden conversion to communism, the film ends with a spectacular shot of an exploding train, the culmination of the repressed, humiliated energy of Sŏng-ryŏl, his family, and the people.

Salt, based on the 1934 Kang Kyŏng-ae novella, is also set in Kando, but in its later colonial iteration, already torn by multiple layers of strife between local landlords, bandit factions, colonial authorities, and communist guerrillas. Again the opening is promising, if not quite idyllic: a small family rents a farming plot from a landlord and manages to send their son Tongsik (who seems to be tarrying with communists) to school. While conflicts break out on the outskirts of the village, and sometimes into their house (a wounded partisan seeking protection), the family's life is simple and comfortable, afforded the modest pleasures of a handful of salt and the occasional clump of *toenjang* (bean paste). Things fall apart quickly, however, when the father is caught in the crossfire between the landlord's guards and what seems to be a band of communists (but later turns out to be rogue colonial police forces) and dies. Tongsik is then arrested on suspicion of communist alliances; he is bailed out by his mother who unwittingly inculpates Tongsik's girlfriend. Tongsik runs off in anger, leaving his mother and sister to fend for themselves. The mother then turns to the landlord for help, appealing to the fact that her husband was killed while trying to protect him. The landlord, a Korean-Chinese draped in fine Chinese silks and replete with a sinewy mustache, agrees to take in the mother and daughter, but attempts to rape the mother soon after. On his second attempt, a sordid scene embellished metaphorically with overturned urns of liquor, he is accidentally killed by a falling beam. While the authorities believe her story, they nevertheless intern her and put her to work in the prison to protect their own public image and because of the lingering suspicion of her son's involvement with the communists.

However, the mother's miseries continue when she discovers that she is pregnant with the dead landlord's offspring. In two appalling scenes, she tries to abort the pregnancy first by throwing herself down a dark set of stairs, and second by swallowing a bar of laundry soap. Despite these efforts, the pregnancy is carried to term and, in another dismal scene set in a roofless, abandoned stable, she fights through labor herself and gives birth to the unwanted baby boy. She tries at first to kill him, squeezing his throat with her still bloody hands, but then collapses in pain and despair. To endure her burdens and raise her two children, the mother takes a job as a nursemaid in a wealthy household. The work is demeaning, subjecting her to the whims of the haughty birth mother, and perilous to her family, forcing her young daughter to take care of the baby boy alone for days on end. Eventually, the children succumb to their squalid conditions and are infected by some unnamed epidemic virus; the local *hanyaksa* (oriental medicine man) and Western doctor, despite the mother's desperate pleas, refuse to help and the children die, carted away in their tiny coffins. Pushed to her limits, the mother attempts to hang herself, but is saved by her neighbor, who then suggests a venture that appeals to the mother's desire to escape everything:

salt smuggling. The long final sequence mirrors that of *Escape* in its abruptness and spectacle. The mother, loaded with a sack of precious salt, treks over precarious mountain passes and through icy river torrents with a band of weary smugglers. They are suddenly attacked by an attachment of the Powi-dan, the quasi-official force that patrols the borders and was responsible for the husband's death, who arrest them on smuggling charges. In a sudden reversal, however, the attachment is itself attacked and run off by a fleet gang of communist guerillas, who then announce to the band that they will protect them as they protect all the suffering *inmin*. Gazing up at the fighters, the mother awakens dramatically to the fact that her husband had been a victim of colonial violence and that her son, rather than running off with hoodlums, had sacrificed his family for the *inmin* and become a hero. Leaving her commodity sack behind, she turns back to Kando, determined to find her son and true calling.

Both *Escape* and *Salt* bear the archetypal elements of North Korean socialist realism. Chief among these is the broad polarization between the ruling-landed-wealthy classes and the laboring-peasant-poor people. This is established in the earliest scenes in *Escape*—Sŏng-ryŏl's father hauls buckets of water yoked to his back through steep village streets only to be scolded by the household madame for making too much noise. She takes the opportunity to deride the old man's endeavors to educate his son (saving him from backbreaking labor like his own) as the hopeless pretensions of a *sangnom* (peasant). The moral bankruptcy and malevolence of the upper classes is then repeated throughout the film: Sŏng-ryŏl's wealthy cousin is the first to sell out to the Japanese; the Kando landowners exploit their desperate tenants; the doctors turn away Sŏng-ryŏl's dying son; and the pharmacist refuses even palliative medication to the penniless family. *Salt* also reads as a cataloging of the cruelties of the landed classes: the landlord's sexual violence, the wealthy employer's cold indifference to the mother's difficult situation, and the doctor's fatal refusal to administer basic medication to the children. This cruelty is balanced of course against the generosity and solidarity of the poor. In *Escape*, Sŏng-ryŏl and his family are surrounded by a community that is seeded by the literacy classes but also bands together to celebrate the birth of Sŏng-ryŏl's son on one occasion and to mourn the death of his father on another. Toward the end of the film, after a long absence, the poor appear spontaneously to help Sŏng-ryŏl carry his broken mother to the hospital, and even accost the wealthy neighbor to live up to his responsibility for the attack. Peasants and poor neighbors appear sporadically throughout *Salt* as well, typified by the warmhearted friend who lends the family salt, takes in the mother after her release from jail, cuts her down from her noose, and suggests the salt trade as a form of escape. Thus, both films cleanly, if somewhat inconsistently, set up the Manichean social structure that the protagonists will eventually come to recognize.

Another crucial, perhaps uniquely highlighted, dimension of the North Korean socialist realist world is the antagonism between foreigners (and their conspirators, lackeys, and sycophants) and the native *inmin*. In *Escape* these are the Japanese who buy up the land (the country farm as well as the forested hills) and who murder Sŏng-ryŏl's father, and the Chinese land-lords and police who exploit their labor and harass them for bribes. *Salt*'s Kando is torn apart by ethnic conflict that victimizes innocent Koreans literally caught in the crossfire. The Chinese bandit groups steal from tenant farmers and the Powi-dan are mobilized only for Japanese colonial interests. The *inmin* are thus doubly colonized, subject to the whims of the native ruling classes as well as the brutality of the foreign soldier and entrepreneur. Therein, the films take up the standard *chuch'e*-realist model, anticipating a revolutionary awakening to the absolute restrictions of modern colonial society and its feudal social structures. Sŏng-ryŏl and the mother, suffering a string of tragedies at the hands of the rich, move inexorably closer ("ripening") to proper class-consciousness.

But if the films structure social relations in the archetypal, albeit exaggerated, socialist realist fashion, they ultimately come up short in carrying those arrangements through to their ideological conclusion. We can see this as a function of the ambiguous political orientation of the literary works from which they are adapted as much as of the mass cultural effect they were intended to achieve. For while Shin Sang-ok referred to Ch'oe Sŏ-hae's story as "a point of origin" for Korean communism,[32] the relationship between the early socialist literature and postwar North Korean ideology is at best problematic. For even those early literary critics, such as Im Hwa, who were enamored of socialist thought tended to regard Ch'oe's work as iterations of "vulgar communism" and closer in spirit to anarchism. Indeed, the majority of Ch'oe stories narrate a last-minute explosion of rage and are largely bereft of class analysis or any politically organizing principles. Kang Kyŏng-ae's ties to communism are even more tenuous. While her writing contains some of the bleakest, most horrifying portraits of life under colonial rule, their radicalizing moments often only apply a lesson of basic human solidarity. It is no coincidence, however, that Shin chose these pieces as among his first projects in North Korea. Their political fluidity as well as their thematic proximity to the enlightenment films he produced in South Korea provided fertile ground for the compelling cinema he pledged to bring to North Korea. His experience rendering enlightenment as melodrama and spectacle, in other words, was easily translated in these ideologically ambiguous texts. But in some ways, his treatment of *Escape* and *Salt* highlights the tension between cinematic pleasure and political edification that is latent in model films like *Flower Girl*. On the one hand, as we have seen, the abruptness of *Flower Girl*'s conclusion is mitigated by the formalization of codes of waiting and longing (the foretold *kwi-in*, the plaintive song). *Salt* and *Escape*, on the other hand, tip the scale toward cinematic pleasure and in so doing aestheticize the process of suffering and maximize the suddenness, indeed artificiality, of communist enlightenment.

Shin approached the films as socialist realist texts. As we have seen, in his reflections on his career, he returned repeatedly to *Escape* as his best "social picture" (often code for realist). And indeed, the films are quieter and relatively less embellished than other North Korean films, minimizing the use of music and going with longer shots and takes. Meticulous care was also taken in *Salt* to re-create Kando's social fabric, not only the detailed sets but also in the use of regional dialect. Nevertheless, the films are produced as entertainment, and toward this end Shin employed a number of tools to magnify the spectacle. The films make liberal use of the zoom, a technique Shin had exploited early in career, for its (cost-effective) dramatic effect, zeroing in on pained faces and implements of suffering (the noose, the dogs, etc.).[33] Further, he also staged major spectacles, ranging from the awesome landscapes of the northern stretches of the peninsula, to mob scenes, to the celebrated train explosion (which Shin referred to as the highlight of his career). And finally, and perhaps most significantly, he exploited Ch'oe Ŭn-hŭi's stardom. For while there were certainly stars in North Korean filmmaking before Shin Films, none brought with them Ch'oe's signifying power and depth. Her presence in *Salt* especially serves to narrow even further the affective and temporal focus on the picture of suffering, held patiently, sometimes torturously, in the camera's frame. Ch'oe's performance is perhaps unprecedented in North Korean cinema in its naturalism and complexity, an indication not solely of her skill but of how Ch'oe mobilizes acting practices (including the first use of regional dialect) uncommon in North Korean film and evokes the compelling force of a return to the suffering-woman roles she took on in South Korea in films like *Until the End of This Life* (*I saengmyŏng tahadarok*, 1960) and *A Woman's Life* (*Yŏja ŭi ilsaeng*, 1968).

The prolongation and magnification of suffering, then, is a part of the pleasure of conventional North Korean filmmaking that Shin appropriates for these films. But while this pleasure is ultimately transmuted into revolutionary enlightenment in *Flower Girl* and theorized-mandated as the proper maturation of the emotions toward ideological recognition in *On the Art of the Cinema*, it becomes subtly troubled and excessive in Shin's iteration. For while *Flower Girl*, however artificially, politicizes affect, *Salt* and *Escape* sensationalize it in the fashion of a big budget studio picture. The effect is a greater absorption and even stagnation in the affect–spectacle itself, and a greater abstraction, though by no means departure, from the ideological lesson. Whether or not this was Shin's intention is unknowable and largely irrelevant. Rather, it is a clearer indication of the sometimes inarticulate lines of continuity and discontinuity between "engaged," purpose-driven filmmaking and ostensibly "pure" art cinema, both within and between North and South Korean cinematic formations.[34] Enlightenment narratives conjoin the ideological trajectories of the two developing states; the spectacle–affect of the enlightenment film meets but also exceeds the bounds of the ideological.

War and Love, the Remake

The porosity and excess of the ideological is also apparent in sometimes surprising ways in the other generic modes through which Shin Sang-ok produced films in North Korea. Shin revisited a number of works that he produced in South Korea as classic, (culturally) nationalist and patriotic films, reconfiguring them in various ways for North Korean production. These included a return to the 1964 blockbuster air force picture *Red Muffler* (*Ppalgan mahura*), reimagined in 1985 as *Red Wings*, and, most famously, a revision of his 1961 *Sŏng Ch'unhyang* as the folk musical, *Oh My Love*. And here, as we can perhaps anticipate by this point, the return does not tell a simple story of infusing the original works with the proper ideological content. For while the North Korean "versions," as some critics have pointed out, certainly heighten the class conflicts that are latent in the film or literary originals, they also introduce more complex affective ties and mobilize cinematic pleasures that exceed easy ideological categorization.[35]

Red Muffler was a major box-office success and one of the first South Korean films to perform well in foreign markets (primarily Hong Kong and Singapore), owing primarily to its impressive aerial photography and compelling battle scenes. While it is set in wartime, the film is firmly ensconced in the patriotic militarism and industrialism of mid-1960s South Korea, taking up in its fighter pilots perhaps the most romantic of military forces and depicting crucial but unspecified advances against the communist North. *Red Muffler* revolves around the gruff but kindhearted commander nicknamed "Wild Boar" and his fraught relationship to Kap-sun, a hostess working in the local base-camp bar. In an early flashback, we learn that Kapsun's husband died while on a mission under Boar's command, leaving Boar to assume responsibility for her well-being. He sets her up with Kim, a virtuous soldier in his company; when Kim is downed behind enemy lines, therefore, Boar goes all out to rescue him in the film's most spectacular sequence. Boar is later fatally shot by enemy fighters but somehow manages to fly his disabled jet into the targeted bridge, blowing it and himself up in a blast of kamikaze heroism. The film closes with heightened pathos when Boar's mother comes to greet the company and, at her son's funeral, acts as a surrogate for all the weeping flyboys.

Red Wings is set, predictably, in the late colonial, revolutionary, and war periods and tells a more complex story than *Red Muffler*. The first half of the film is set in Japan, where Mun-ch'ŏl, despite his racial shortcomings as a Korean imperial citizen, is the top cadet in the Imperial Air Force Academy. He is in love with So-hyang, the daughter of a wealthy Korean businessman who runs a transport company in Tokyo. The father, who hopes that his daughter will marry the son of a Japanese business partner, opposes the relationship, but So-hyang, somewhat reluctantly, elopes with Mun-ch'ŏl. Months pass and Mun-ch'ŏl has graduated from the academy, but he is injured along with the many other Korean pilots who are pressed by unsavory Japanese officers to test experimental fighter planes. Unable to fly, Mun-ch'ŏl returns with his family to Seoul and, borrowing one of his father-in-law's cars, works as a taxi driver, chauffeuring fat Japanese businessmen and their cackling Korean consorts. Miserable with his emasculation, he intentionally drives his car through the window of a store. The fallout is dire: he loses the car as well as So-hyang, who, taking their young son, leaves her embittered husband and goes back to her father. Mun-ch'ŏl returns to Tokyo to work as an airplane mechanic.

War breaks out, announced by blaring headlines and footage of the Japanese attack on Pearl Harbor. Mun-ch'ŏl is recruited to fight for the Imperial Army but is shot down in the Pacific and spends the rest of the war in a prisoner-of-war camp. With the war's end, Mun-ch'ŏl returns to his wife and son in their hometown Sinŭiju (in northern Korea) but finds them in desperate straits: So-hyang's father has been accused of treason by the revolutionary authorities. But while her heart is still with Mun-ch'ŏl, So-hyang elects to accompany her father to the safety of reactionary Seoul. In a sudden twist, however, it is revealed that So-hyang's father is in fact not her biological father. The truth of this is immediately confirmed in the next sequence: the father has sold his adopted daughter to a Seoul hostess bar in return for the deed to a bookstore. Traumatized by this reversal, So-hyang throws herself in the Han River, only to be saved by Mun-ch'ŏl, who has come to Seoul just in time. Reconciled to the facts of her parentage and to the debauchery of Seoul, the couple decides to return to Sinŭiju. In another incredible twist, however, So-hyang is shot dead by an American soldier as they cross the thirty-eighth parallel, and Mun-ch'ŏl alone rejoins their son, Tong-sik, who has himself become a fighter pilot for the North Korean army. With the outbreak of war, Mun-ch'ŏl (as ground support) and Tong-sik (as fighter pilot) are, somehow, assigned to the same assault mission on an American armament. When Tong-sik is shot down by South Korean forces, Mun-ch'ŏl takes up his son's plane (which has miraculously landed safely nearby) and is himself shot, but not before he is able to fly into the armament, destroying it in another blast of kamikaze heroism. The film closes some years in the future: Tong-sik commands the impressive new North Korean air fleet, watching with pride as the gleaming planes launch in perfect formation.

While the generic parallel of the two films is somewhat tenuous, owing to the breadth of the air force genre (narrower than the war film, but less codified than, say, the enlightenment film), the correlations are obvious. Both *Red Muffler* and *Red Wings* exploit the romantic fatalism of the fighter pilot, translating the heroism of that dangerous duty into self-sacrificing patriotism. The machinery of the aircraft, the pinnacle of modern technology, stamped boldly with the markings of the respective armies, is an unmistakable sign of the progress and strength of both nations. It is no wonder that the respective military regimes granted their generous support for these films, paeans as they are to military, industrial, and economic development. The films also equally exploit that support, presenting vivid footage shot out of actual fighter cockpits, re-creating the speed and confusion of the aerial dogfight. But the points of departure are equally obvious. Where the enemy in *Red Muffler* is clearly the North, they are figured as a faceless horde of ground infantry or masked behind shaded helmets. The antagonists in *Red Wings*, on the other hand, are myriad and manifest: the Japanese officer, the Korean collaborator, the American soldier, the American armament (interestingly, though, the South Korean opponent here is also faceless: the long-lost little brother cannot be demonized). And while the only social tension in the enclosed world of *Red Muffler* is between the pilots and their girlfriends, the drama of *Red Wings* is driven by the class conflict splitting Mun-ch'ŏl from So-hyang and her wealthy father.

And it is precisely this configuration of affective ties that provides the most complex and interesting contrast between the two films. The political finds more compelling expression in the representation of family relations in these films than it does in the overt projection of the faces of the enemy. *Red Muffler*, on the one hand, articulates the typical kinship structure of postcolonial/postwar South Korean film: an absent father, a strong, sacrificing mother, a remasculinized son. But given that Wild Boar's mother appears only at the conclusion, when it is already too late, it is possible to see the family as altogether absent in the film. In its place are the paternalizing-infantilizing relations of military order and its brotherhood of powerful homosocial bonds. Even the sexual relations here are tenuous, tying together soldiers and bar hostesses as lovers; and while Kapsun marries twice, the marriages are formalized in perfunctory, unseen ceremonies that serve material more than emotional needs. In *Red Wings*, on the other hand, traditional family ties are fraught but deep and intensely important: Mun-ch'ŏl and So-hyang's troubled though mutually faithful marriage, So-hyang's loyalty to her father, and Mun-ch'ŏl's close relationship with his son, Tong-sik. When So-hyang learns of her father's true identity, the crisis is as much political as personal, at once rendering the father illegitimate, immoral, and traitorous. The link between father and son is much more abiding and fruitful, not only building a lineage of fighter pilots but also guaranteeing victory in the war.

So whereas the social space of *Red Muffler* is inhabited by individual actors stitched together by the circumstances of the war, these kinds of contingent, functional relationships fall away in *Red Wings*, leaving correct political alignments in their wake. Within the narrative, the bare fact of So-hyang's father's collaboration with the Japanese is not politically significant in itself; the burden of that crime is actually subordinate to the sin (and those stemming from it) of his illegitimacy. The moment So-hyang recognizes the absence of blood ties with her father is her moment of radicalization, when she can throw herself in the river to be reborn as a North Korean. And in some ways the fact of their alignment with the North Korean army is coincidental to Mun-ch'ŏl and Tong-sik; hereditary transmission and heroic fatherly care make up the central theme (in fact, it is not immediately clear in the film which side Mun-ch'ŏl chooses to fight for after his wife's death, owing to the elliptical structure of the film's denouement). So while the films are certainly distinguishable in terms of the degree to which national enemies and social conflicts are highlighted, it is, perhaps counterintuitively, the differential politics of the family that separates them most emphatically. Shin Sang-ok's North Korean reiteration of the air force film mobilizes spectacle in the same way as *Red Muffler* but reconfigures affect to make ideology more legible. On the one hand, this is not entirely astounding given the centrality of the family, symbolically as well as structurally, in North Korean sociopolitics; by the early 1980s, we might note in passing, Kim Jong Il was quietly being groomed to succeed his father (though subsequent power struggles would ultimately complicate the picture). On the other hand, the family also played (and indeed continues to play) a crucial role in the authoritarian culture of the South; the early 1960s especially marked a kind of high point of family-centered political discourse.

A similar suggestion is made in the space between Shin Sang-ok's two versions of *Ch'unhyangjŏn*. As we saw in chapter 3, the *Ch'unhyang* story has occupied a privileged position in the historiography of Korean film and a special place in the consideration of North Korean cinema in the South. While it was formalized as a literary text sometime in the nineteenth century, its origins are likely as *p'ansori*, the folk oral dramatic form, and thus especially amenable to adaptation to modern theatrical and cinematic forms. Among the first feature film productions of the colonial period (1923), there have been at least sixteen film versions in one form or another: three productions in the 1950s, four in the 1960s, one each in the 1970s, 1980s, and 1990s, and the latest in 2000 by Im Kwon-taek. *Ch'unyayng* has become a rich cultural-historical text, both in its latent presentation of problems of gender, class, and political ethics and in its enduring popularity and openness to adaptation and revision. There have also been at least three productions of the *Ch'unhyang* story in North Korea, Kim Ryŏng-gyu's *Ch'unhyangjŏn* (1959), Yu Wŏnjun and Yun Ryŏng-gyu's *Ch'unhyangjŏn* (1980), and Shin Sang-ok's *Oh My Love*.[36] The complex issues raised by the ostensible conflict between the shared folk-narrative tradition and the opposed modern cultural-political spaces of its production have proved irresistible to film critics. While other stories, such as *Hong Kil-dong-jŏn* and *Simch'ŏng-jŏn*, have also been produced on both sides of the border, the latent social-class critique of the *Ch'unhyang* tale and therein its availability to North Korean propaganda has attracted the most critical attention. In her chapter comparing North and South Korean versions, Hyangjin Lee argues, for instance, that ideological differences are manifested in the narrative revisions, concluding that the

North Korean versions aim to "intensify class antagonism."[37] In a more recent essay, Wang Sun-nyŏ structures her arguments in much the same fashion, though with a more sophisticated eye to how the text is overdetermined by gender relations.[38]

Shin Sang-ok's particular inflection on the *Ch'unhyang* historiography in some ways typifies the arguments laid out by Lee and Wang but in others exceeds the margins of their analysis. As we saw with the South–North air force pictures, the points of convergence and departure in film are not necessarily plotted along the more easily defined borders of political discourse. The first fact to note about both *Sŏng Ch'unhyang*, Shin's South Korean version, and *Oh My Love* is their exceeding commercial popularity. *Sŏng Ch'unhyang*, we will remember, was born of a rivalry between two leading director-producers (and lead actresses) and the incipient industrialization of the film industry. Its unprecedented success heralded the development of the Korean blockbuster and owed much more to its production scale (all-star cast, color-cinemascope photography, expensive costume and set management) than its particular representation of feminine virtue. In terms of mass appeal, *Oh My Love* created an even more significant relative impact than its South Korean predecessor. A huge color-cinemascope production that mobilized hundreds, if not thousands, of extras, *Oh My Love* seems to have been the first North Korean film to have instantiated surplus value: that of ticket prices (the aforementioned scalping) and of lurid spectacle. Having debuted on television with *The Secret Emissary* and *Record of an Escape*, Shin had begun to build cultural capital by the time *Oh My Love* was released in theaters. The real sensation, however, was created by the film's title, the first explicit mention of "love" in any public art work, and through word of the unprecedented explicitness of its depiction of sexual relationships. What Shin brought to both *Sŏng Ch'unhyang* and *Oh My Love* was more than an auteur's stamp or a particular cultural-critical voice; he also marshaled a production system and an enthusiasm for mass visibility that fit both sides of the peninsula in different though equally significant ways.

Oh My Love preserves *Sŏng Ch'unhyang*'s narrative structure with little revision or embellishment. Ch'unhyang is the same virtuous daughter of a *yangban* father and *kisaeng* mother and equally subject to Mongnyong's sexualizing gaze. When the latter abandons her to follow his father to Hanyang (Seoul), she rebukes him for his weakness and bemoans the injustice of the class system. She takes an equally strong stance with Pyŏn Hak-do, the corrupt and licentious new provincial governor, challenging his trespasses with her command of Confucian ethics. And when Mongnyong returns to restore justice, she meets him with the same mix of joy and reproof. Hyangjin Lee remarks with some surprise on how few concessions *Oh My Love* makes to "North Korean ideological forces," in contrast to an earlier North Korean production (Yu and Yun's 1980 *Ch'unhyangjŏn*) that liberally reprogrammed the tale to read as a stark conflict between proletarian and bourgeois virtues (while preserving, in accord with North Korean social values, the patriarchal strictures of the original narrative). But, determined to discern the "cultural and ideological" difference of the North Korean text, Lee points out that there is an unresolved "competition between traditional and socialist perspectives concurring in Ch'unhyang's actions [that] is clearly felt in the clashing images of the heroine as a *kisaeng* and simultaneously as the virtuous wife of a *yangban* man." Lee argues that this "oscillation" is a drawback that leads the film to "suffer from inconsistency in characterization and theme."[39]

But while this conflict between the alluring *kisaeng* and faithful *yangban* wife is certainly apparent in *Oh My Love*, its presence has less (if anything) to do with "socialist perspectives" than with the contradiction endemic to the traditional perspective itself. One of the challenges of producing the *Ch'unhyang* tale in any sociopolitical context has been, primarily, in reconciling the spontaneous passion of the couple's "first night" with the enduring chastity of the rest of the narrative and, secondarily, the inconsistencies of a *yangban* social order that torments but can also liberate women. Contrary to Lee's assertions, these conflicts, especially the disagreement between Mongnyong's departure and return, are sutured in *Oh My Love* not by resort to higher authority or the grafting of socialist perspectives but by a return to the family. For if there is a significant revision in *Oh My Love*, it is the expanded role given to Wŏlmae, Ch'unhyang's mother, and her warnings about the dangerous allures of *yangban* courtiers. This apprehension, moreover, does not entail an abstract critique of class prejudice, but is rather expressed in the plain language of motherly care—warmhearted Wŏlmae wants to protect her daughter from her own sorrows. And it is Wŏlmae who smoothes over the awkward tension of the conclusion—an awkwardness that is intensified by Mongnyong's (devious?) delay in revealing his true identity to the still-shackled Ch'unhyang. When Mongnyong finally puts aside the special investigator's mask, it is Wŏlmae who pushes through the crowd and raucously welcomes him back into the fold. Slapping him on the chest and confirming her (actually shaken) faith in her son-in-law, Wŏlmae declasses Mongnyong, prioritizing his personal virtue over his rank. It is also Wŏlmae who enjoins the gathered masses to celebrate the new social order, making the restoration of *yangban* control seem like a jubilee of true social justice. With Lee, we might recognize the conflict between the folk narrative and socialist values; however, we also see that it is resolved within and not outside of the family.

But the real difference of Shin Sang-ok's northern rendition of the *Ch'unhyang* tale, glossed over by Wang and neglected altogether by Lee, is its overwhelming entertainment value and spectacle. For *Oh My Love* is not solely a period melodrama but a musical production made in the tradition, if not the spirit, of the story's *p'ansori* origins. The breakout into song and dance numbers was perhaps not entirely jarring in North Korea either generically or diegetically, given the close ties there between opera and film, but their effect is nonetheless striking. Perhaps the most celebrated sequence in the film is Ch'unhyang and Mongnyong's performance of the title song "Love, Love, My Love" after they have consummated their "first night." The song is a lyrical modern duet and the dance is choreographed in a flowing ballet style (made up of classic *kisaeng* movements). Beginning in the small bedroom, the number breaks out (as walls slide away) to reveal a sprawling set hung with backdrops painted with classical poetry and land-scape renderings. The singing couple winds between a series of painted screens, and they finish their song under the bow of a painted tree. The sud-den abstraction of the scene is striking, at once calling up a live theatrical performance (replete with tracking spotlights) and the dream sequences of filmic fairy tales (one imagines that, if resources allowed, the scene would resemble the spectacular sequences in *The Sound of Music*). The scene is matched by two numbers that come at the close of the film. The first, a dance performance staged for a boisterous party given by Pyŏn Hak-do, and the second, the final celebration sequence picturing what seems like the entirety of the cast. These are captured from a variety of high angles and make a spectacle out of the sheer volume of actors. Moreover, the uncanny precision and synchronicity of the choreography mirrors (or anticipates) the haunting meticulousness of the military procession or the mass games, re-presenting the image of physical mastery as mass entertainment.

The ultimate drawing power of the film, however, stemmed in all likelihood from the thrill of seduction and the celebration of love itself. Once Mongnyong has secured Wŏlmae's consent, he wolfishly closes in on Ch'unhyang in the seclusion of her room (Figure 12). Smoothly undoing the sash on her *chŏgori*, he gets as far as taking it off her shoulders but, sensing her unease, he turns to the lamp and blows out the light. The next we see of the couple, they are lounging in the dimly lit space and before long they

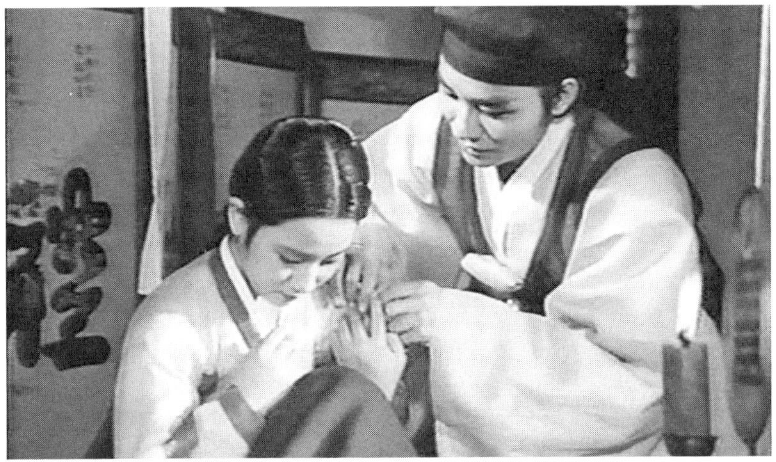

Figure 12. Mongnyong moves scandalously in on Ch'unhyang in *Oh My Love* (Shin Sang-ok, 1984).

break into the aforementioned song. The "first night" seen, then, is elliptical but daring, pushing the bounds of representation with the clear suggestion of disrobing and lust. It should be noted, however, that the seduction sequence is broken by comic snippets in which Pangja recites nonsense verse and doodles sketches of his beloved Hyangdan while covering for Mongnyong (who should be studying). This incongruous cutting mitigates the shock of seeing the lovers, likely making it more palatable to censors; it has the effect, though, of rendering their relationship as play. Love takes on a lighter, more whimsical tone that balances against the darker thrill of seduction. This is continued in the following number where the song performed by Ch'unhyang and Mongnyong merely testifies, with the fluffy repetitiousness of its pop-song-like lyrics, to the "truth" and "delight" of their love for each other. The question of Mongnyong's sincerity (indeed dubious in any rendition of the tale) and Ch'unhyang's virtuousness is not resolved by the song but rather eschewed by it. And this is perhaps Shin Sang-ok's most radical intervention here: unburdening love and sex, if only for a moment, of its deeper and more serious sociopolitical attachments. The difference between Shin's South and North Korean Ch'unhyang's is certainly political; but, as in his South and North Korean pilot pictures, complex manipulation of affect and spectacle—in other words play—is suspended within that difference.

Extravagance, Play, and the Monstrous

With films like *Record of an Escape*, *Salt*, and *Breakwater*, Shin Sang-ok demonstrated a way of working firmly within the ideological as well as the affective–temporal codes of socialist realism while subtly troubling them, magnifying their implicit contradictions through spectacle. In his reprisal of earlier successes such as *Red Wings* and *Oh My Love*, Shin again produced ideologically coherent films but reconfigured the axes of politics and affect to prioritize the power and pleasure of private, emotional investments over larger or more abstract political ones. In a number of other films, especially toward the end of his tenure under Kim Jong Il, Shin staged an even more radical departure from North Korean cinematic convention. These were, again, not screened as resistance to mainstream political rhetoric; neither did the films diverge from his mandate to renovate the industry toward greater global visibility and esteem. In fact, with films like *Hong Kil-dong* and *Pulgasari*, Shin's work achieved a kind of apotheosis of both demands; in so doing, however, he demonstrated their tenuous viability but ultimate contradiction.

Elements of this muted challenge are already discernable in Shin's first North Korean film, *The Secret Emissary*, which seems to have been the only film for which Kim Jong Il's approval was sought. The film loosely re-creates the history of Emperor Kojong's "secret emissary," Yi Chun, and his tragically failed mission to plea for Korean independence at the 1907 Hague Peace Convention. The narrative unfolds through the recollections of Anna, a Dutch woman who had hosted Yi and his associates, as told to a North Korean traveler who has come to pay his respects at Yi's gravesite after the war. The first half of the story takes place in Japanese "protected" Chosŏn with Kojong under the thumb of Ito Hirobumi and his armed guard. Yi Chun, a dedicated family man and patriot, is contrasted to Yi Wan-yong, the spineless bureaucrat ready to serve the needs of his Japanese benefactors. Succeeding in an elaborate plot to sneak past the palace guards and gain audience with the Emperor, Yi Chun convinces Kojong to send him to the Hague Convention with declarations of sovereignty and of the nullity of the Ŭlsa Treaty.[40] But while Yi and his partner Yi Sang-sol manage to make it to the convention, aided along the way by the American missionary Homer Hulbert and a Chinese delegate, they are blocked from full participation by a collusion of the Japanese and American delegates. Nevertheless, Yi gives an address about Chosŏn's plight to a formal dinner gathering (where the response is mostly supportive) and later manages to force himself into the convention hall. Before the assembly, Yi delivers a fiery speech on Chosŏn's five-thousand-year history and the injustice of its current occupation. However, the Japanese delegate challenges Yi's (and Chosŏn's) legitimacy and has guards remove him from the hall; Yi responds by pulling a knife from his coat and slashing his stomach, dying as the horrified convention participants look on. The film closes with the assurance that Chosŏn has staged a revolution and, after long struggle, shed itself of Japanese tyranny.

While Shin Sang-ok claims to have been sorely disappointed in the final product (leading him to assign directing credit to Ch'oe Ŭn-hŭi), *The Secret Emissary* is certainly a strikingly different film from the North Korean norm. For while the first half of the film is possessed of the austerity and simplicity of typical North Korean reproductions of the early colonial period, the second half is sumptuously detailed and expansive and furnishes an unprecedented glimpse into a foreign time–space. Long takes of the present-day (and likely little-changed) exterior of the Hague establish the exotic setting; location shooting in Czechoslovakia, while architecturally, historically, and culturally inaccurate, enabled the re-creation of a cosmopolitan European city, enhanced by long, wide shots, slow pans, and maximum field depth. Further, hundreds of Czech extras, dressed in turn-of-the-century finery, stood in for the delegates of the Euro-American sphere. The actors standing in for Theodore Roosevelt, Hulbert, and others are also Czech (while those playing Japanese and Chinese are likely North Korean) and almost certainly give their dialogue in Czech, which is then dubbed into Korean. While this serves to facilitate legibility for domestic audiences, the effect is, on the one hand, uncanny, reversing the conventional burden of translation/representation, and, on the other, narcissistic, creating a Korea(n)-centric space where the foreign is adapted to the native. Kim Jong Il, according to Shin's recollection, was ecstatic at the outcome, matching as it did his filmmaking ambitions. "I'm really happy with this," he said as he held Shin's hand. "I don't have any complaints at all. It was like watching a European movie. I'll have to show it to the Supreme Leader. . . . This is going to make a lot of guys jealous when it gets out there [on the international scene]."[41] And indeed, the film performed well outside of North Korea (if only within the shrinking communist bloc) where, as mentioned above, it brought home the first-ever film festival prize for a North Korean film (the special director's award at the 1984 Karlovy Vary Film Festival).

Kim Jong Il's comments are telling for their (at least momentary) erasure of the second goal of filmmaking, the strengthening of nationalist-socialist spirit among the people. Part of this is clearly the excitement of seeing a "world-class" North Korean film, glittering on the surface with the marks of European sophistication, but it also stems from the ideological neutrality, or at least ambiguity, of the film itself. For the accuracy with which *The Secret Emissary* reconstructs the visual surface of the Hague Convention is undercut by the manipulation of the historical events. And it is clear that this manipulation is motivated more by cinematic than political interests. While the lionization of anticolonial heroes is a standard trope in North Korean filmmaking, the hero is conventionally anonymous, or embedded within a larger community of activists (or, alternatively, in the service of *chuch'e* principles). Even the celebrated film *An Chung-gŭn Shoots Ito Hiro-bumi* (*An Chung-gŭn Yitŭng Pakmun ŭl ssoda*, Ŏm Kil-sŏn, 1979) ostensibly about the actions of an anticolonial assassin, resists the appeal of glorifying the individual and submits genuine political resistance to the leadership of Kim Il Sung. In *The Secret Emissary*, however, Yi Chun has the support of his family and friends but ultimately takes heroic action upon himself; his sensational public suicide, an embellishment on the historical Yi Chun's equally tragic death from consumptive illness, renders him a martyr in advance of the guerilla struggle. Further, the class status (landed aristocratic) of Yi Chun and his partners, ordinarily a marker of moral and political bankruptcy (belonging to the traitorous-powerless intellectual elite), is unquestioned. And finally, the emperor and his faithful ministers (with the exception of Yi Wan-yong) are represented as committed anti-Japanese nationalists, restricted in their patriotism only by the superior military strength of the Japanese invaders. *The Secret Emissary* naturalizes, and tacitly commends, the feudal structures and heroic individualism that are normally expunged from North Korean film texts. The film benefits from a cleaner division between the repressed nation-empire and the repressive empire, out of which springs the dramatic figure of the self-sacrificing hero. Thus, while its politics in other hands would almost certainly have been attacked by North Korean censors, the Hollywood heroism and European styling of Shin's *Emissary*—in other words, its extravagance—compensate for its political incorrectness.

Shin brought a similar sort of extravagance to bear on future productions to diverse effect. For instance, he directed a musical version of the folk *Tale of Simch'ŏng*, the meandering story of the filial daughter of a blind beggar who sacrifices herself to the spirit of the seas only to be returned to the king in the form of a lotus. While the film was unavailable for the present research, interviews and concise reports suggest that it was similar in production scale to *Oh My Love*, though screened with fantasy sequences commensurate with the dreamlike nature of the folktale. In his recollections, Shin underscored the worldliness of the production, pointing out that much of it was filmed at the Munich Bavaria studios and that the special-effects team that worked on *The NeverEnding Story* (1984) helped with *Simch'ŏngjŏn*. An even more worldly and lavish production was the 1986 *Hong Kil-dong*, completed under another director following Shin's exit from North Korea, but born of Shin's production company. Based on the Korean Robin Hood story in which the outcast son of a *yangban* official leads a band of virtuous mountain bandits who steal from rich travelers and feed the poor, the film was ripe for North Korean production. The story's latent social critique is amplified in the film by inventing a subplot wherein Kil-dong, as a half-caste commoner, is forbidden to marry the daughter of a *yangban*, though they are madly in love. And the vague parallels to anticolonial guerrilla struggle are spelled out by inserting a Japanese invasion, which only Kil-dong can repel, into the narrative. But the truly remarkable dimension of this film is its appropriation of Hong Kong martial arts film codes. For Kil-dong is not simply a skilled swordsman driven to banditry but a flying warrior trained from a young age by a bearded mountain hermit in mystical martial arts. *Hong Kil-dong*'s training and battle sequences are imbued with Hong Kong convention (the laughing master, the broken sword) and employ similar special effects (speeded-up film, wire work). Further, the Japanese invasion is led by a group of ninjas, contrasting the spectacular though honest fighting styles of Korea against the dark and devious arts of Japan. Shin Sang-ok called on martial arts film specialists in Hong Kong (choreographers, cinematographers) and had imagined *Hong Kil-dong* as the first Korean "kung-fu" picture. Though it was completed by other technicians, the film struck a by now familiar balance between fantasy and *chuch'e* interests and went on to become one of the most popular in North Korean history.

But perhaps the richest of these later extravaganzas is *Pulgasari*, the tragic-comic monster film Shin made just before his departure. It is not clear whether the film was released publicly in North Korea (though there is some indication that it was screened for Kim Jong Il and other cultural and news officials). It is one of the rare North Korean works, however, that was released commercially, distributed by the Japanese filmmakers who collaborated on it sometime in the early 1990s, and screened in Japan, South Korea, and other parts of the world to a wide range of audience reactions, from the incredulous to the cult fanatical. *Pulgasari* is one of the only North Korean films to be seen outside the peninsula and has been the subject of a relatively large volume of criticism (mostly fan-based but some scholarly), though strangely it has not attracted much attention in South Korea. Referring to *Pulgasari* as the North Korean *Godzilla*, many critics point to the similarities between the Japanese ur-monster as well as to the fact that Satsuma Kenpachiro, one of the later actors to don the Godzilla suit, was brought in to play the title character.[42] The tendency has thus been to view the film as a peculiar copy and to see North Korean political rhetoric faithfully reproduced within it. More nuanced readings have discerned a subtle critique of that rhetoric, citing the monster's insatiable hunger and its deleterious effects on the poor, and attribute that resistance to Shin Sang-ok's personal resistance to a regime from which he was preparing to escape. But while there are certainly measures of propaganda and censure in the film, it seems more productive to see those as grounded in the mechanisms of cinematic pleasure and populism at which Shin, even in the North, always aimed his work. If there are slippages in *Pulgasari*, they are not only the sly manipulations of the author but the consequence of the contradictions of Shin's (and Kim Jong Il's) cinematic project.

Pulgasari is set sometime in a Koryŏ period torn by strife between the tyranny of the king and a peasant insurgency. An old blacksmith is ordered by the local governor to forge weapons for the king's army, but when he discovers that the iron he is given for his work has been plundered from the poor farmers of his village, he refuses and is promptly thrown in jail. In his cell, he is beaten to a pulp and deprived of food; however, when his young daughter, Ami, throws rice through the bars, he stubbornly refuses to eat while his village suffers. Instead, he molds a tiny figurine out of the rice and, with his dying breath, imbues it with the redemptive spirit of the people. Ami later recovers the figurine and when she accidentally pricks herself with a sewing needle, the drop of blood brings the tiny monster to life. She and her brother, Takse, fawn over the adorable Pulgasari and marvel as he consumes the needle and any other metallic objects he can find. Over the next few days, however, they are stunned to find that, eating more and more metal, he has grown to full adult size. Meanwhile, the local governor's forces round up any possible insurgents in the village and arrest Inde, the blacksmith's apprentice, and his mother. Just when the executioner is about to chop off Inde's head, however, Pulgasari appears and eats the executioner's sword, scaring away the guards. Pulgasari then becomes the village's protector, terrorizing the governor's men into submission. When word of the monster's trespasses reaches the king, the imposing General Hwang is dispatched to quell the growing threat. General Hwang launches a series of attacks and schemes to destroy the monster and put down the rebellion, but Pulgasari by this point has become so overwhelmingly large that nothing succeeds. When the monster is finally subdued (with the help of a hypnotizing shaman!) and buried in a massive ditch, another drop of Ami's blood brings him back to life. With Pulgasari in the lead, a huge peasant army launches an assault on the king's palace; they overrun the king's army, and Pulgasari, after destroying the palace, squashes the tyrant under his massive foot (Figure 13). However, the villager's troubles do not end with the coup; Pulgasari's insatiable appetite has left them without the tools to tend their farms. In a bizarre series of events, Ami climbs inside a bronze temple bell and tricks Pulgasari into eating her, causing the monster to self-destruct. In the film's closing scene, a once again tiny Pulgasari zaps himself into Ami's lifeless body, presumably bringing her back to life.

In terms of its overall narrative, *Pulgasari* actually owes less to the Godzilla pictures than to the ancient Jewish golem tale in its depiction of a monster culled from humble materials (rice substituting for mud) and turning (at

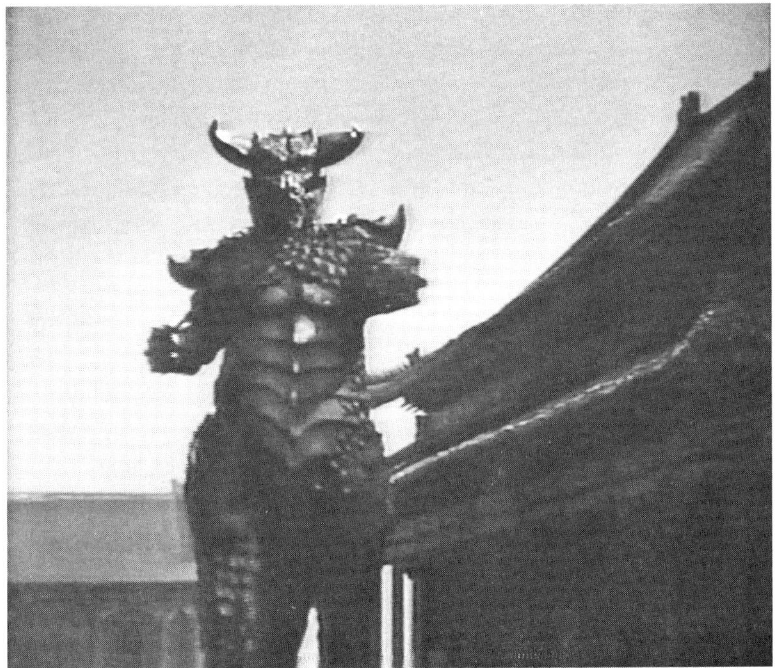

Figure 13. Pulgasari menaces the royal palace in *Pulgasari* (Shin Sang-ok, 1985).

least figuratively) on its creators once the task of defense is complete. Further, while Godzilla is often figured as the incarnation of the atomic attacks on Japan or, alternatively, as the return of the repressed in genteel and effeminate modern Japan, Pulgasari is, at least ostensibly, a more straightforward allegorization of antifeudal (and by implication anticolonial and anticapitalist) history. Pulgasari is the (literal) incarnation of the spirit of *inmin* resistance, a fantasy of agrarian (and then proletarian) revolt against aristocratic tyranny, carried through to a gruesomely logical conclusion in the crushing of the king. That he consumes metal is, presumably, the monster's revolt against the instruments of suppression—a point driven home when he eats a cannonball, chews it up, and spits it back at the king's guard. The thesis of the allegorization is made clear when, after Pulgasari has smashed the palace and killed the king, the people of village (and the peasant insurgents) gather for a raucous party to celebrate their liberation.

Yet the allegory is nowhere near seamless, just as the golem story celebrates Jewish resistance as much as it provides a lesson about hubris. In *Pulgasari*, the moral lesson is not for the peasants but has more to do with the monster itself. For when the party is over, Pulgasari's hunger does not subside but rather drives him to eat up all of the villager's tools. It is only Ami's sacrifice—which is at the same time a more literal consumption of the *inmin* and a sort of matricide—that stops the monster. This postrevolutionary exploitation of the *inmin*, of course, can easily be read as an attack on the ruling elite in North Korea, that is, a revolutionary force born of the masses but becoming a cannibalistic and even suicidal exploitation of its labor, livelihood, and spirit.[43] This, of course, is precisely how Shin Sang-ok would characterize Kim Il Sung's regime in his "letters" to Kim Jong Il and Kim Tae-jung. In fact, the tenor of Shin's memoirs (i.e., the suggestively titled *The Kingdom of Kim*) encourage another reading of the film wherein the despotic though ultimately helpless king stands in for the Supreme Leader himself. This is suggested in the film by the long, wide shots of the tyrant's palace, filmed at least partly in the Forbidden City, and uncannily reminiscent of the monumental architecture of contemporary Pyongyang.

The two allegorical interpretations do not, of course, mesh in any logical manner—the monstrous subject of revolution cannot squash the feudal tyrant of mass dictatorship. And to a certain extent the true meaning of *Pulgasari*, relying as it would on the assumption of a reluctant and slyly defiant author, is unavailable, if not irrelevant. In its stead is the agency of the cinematic apparatus itself, overdetermined, radically open to alternative analyses, and resistant to discursive closure, in spite of the authority, repetitiveness, or command of theory and criticism. For as in the enlightenment films and the remakes, Shin produced an ostensibly politically correct film with *Pulgasari*; its danger arose in the play and extravagance of its unique pleasures as a monster film. And there is perhaps no need to assume that any of its spectators were duped by the duplicity of Shin's works. When Shin finally met Kim Jong Il upon his release from prison, the future leader apparently took his hand and, pointing at a performance praising the regime, declared, "it's all fake." Shin, of course, was "invited" to the North not to make something real, but to bring everything he had learned in Japan, and the South, and America, and to make the best possible fakes around.

Out to the World

North Korea experienced a number of significant transitions from the late 1970s through the late 1980s. The steady economic growth that had been built on the back of a vestigial colonial industrial infrastructure, strategic trade arrangements with the USSR and the PRC, and a series of carefully managed economic master plans had reached a plateau, and it was becoming apparent that South Korea was poised to surpass the North, both in terms of economic strength and international standing. The regime more actively sought the support and assistance of the USSR and the PRC, convening a number of talks throughout the early 1980s, many of which Kim Il Sung himself would secretly attend. But while the forthcoming cooperation was more symbolic than material, the two ostensible allies were certainly more receptive than in the Khrushchev era or the immediate aftermath of the Nixon–China talks. The North also began to cultivate relationships with a series of Third World or "nonaligned" nations, receiving the heads of Libya, Egypt, Congo, and even Palestine in elaborate ceremonies throughout the 1980s. The state came to be seen as a model for the postcolonial version of the "socialism in one country" thesis and Kim Il Sung a highly respected figure of sovereign strength, an albeit limited international prestige the regime energetically worked to amplify through orchestrated cultural and ritual exchange. But perhaps the most substantial development of the period was the rise to visibility of Kim Jong Il, culminating in his official designation as successor in 1980. Taking on the "Dear Leader" and "Party" designations, Kim moved through a series of vital posts in the Politburo and Military Commission in the process of consolidating his image and power. The 1980s was for the DPRK a period of postrevolutionary internationalism—perhaps the last such light it would see for decades.

It is essential to think about Shin Sang-ok's performance in North Korea through this political history. The very fact of his border crossing, regardless of whether it was voluntary or coerced, was enabled by North Korea's efforts to resituate itself geopolitically and by the need to consolidate symbolically the power that had been conferred officially on the heir to the throne. The regime's relationships with Japan, Hong Kong, or even China and the USSR were far from being normalized; nevertheless the 1980s witnessed the spinning of tenuous networks of communication and exchange on which Shin's internationalism would be authorized to travel. And despite the looming fact of South Korea's ascendance and the decline of Communist power, the DPRK, after two decades of economic growth and the formalization of *chuch'e* discourse, was by the 1980s relatively self-assured and open to moderate social change and novelty as well as the influx of foreign cultural capital. Shin Sang-ok proved to be an apt fit, both in his political flexibility and the facility with which he commanded the full apparatus of the cinema. He did not, of course, bring mass culture to North Korea; rather, he helped to develop, on an extant industrial infrastructure, a kind of production system that met but then exceeded the bounds of the existing cultural-ideological machine. Shin's work was not that of a radical auteur, but the kinds of films he produced—high(er) quality, entertaining films that could perform well on the international circuit and that aimed explicitly at mass pleasure and enjoyment—could not but sometimes bear an implicit critique of the cultural-political practices of the regime. It was a critique, however, that the regime could not only absorb but flaunt in its controlled flirtation with the outside world.

THE TUMULTUOUS YEARS following his return from North Korea in 1986 saw Shin Sang-ok bring his career to a close in the same way that it had begun: shuttling between nations, embroiled in controversy, living for the thrill of watching, planning, and making films. But before he could again, in the Korean parlance, pick up the megaphone, he would have to pass through a gauntlet of intelligence investigations, bureaucratic adjustments, and public scrutiny. He and Ch'oe Ŭn-hŭi spent most of the late 1980s in the United States, giving testimony to American and Korean agents about their adventures in the North and winning back the right to enter and work in South Korea. At press conferences and in interviews, Shin narrated in notably cinematic terms the twists of their captivity and, ultimately, their dramatic dash toward the freedom of the U.S. Embassy in Vienna. The sense that there was something disingenuous in their account was inescapable, fed as much by the couple's glamorous public grooming as by the proliferating rumors that they had come away with millions in North Korean funds. And yet, they returned to the fold as some of the last surviving protagonists of the waning years of the Cold War, perhaps because the very hyperreality of their story made it more easily intelligible as a sign of the past's unreal polarities.

Shin managed to squeeze out seven more films before his passing in 2006. Developed with funds sourced in characteristically inventive ways, they were produced in traffic between Seoul and Hollywood and were each testament to Shin's seemingly bottomless capacity for improvisation and exploitation. Two of these, *Mayumi* (1990) and *Disappearance* (*Chŭngbal*, 1994), were produced in South Korea with the explicit aim of recuperating Shin's reputation as a faithful adherent to the conflicted freedoms of democratic capitalist society. But they also shared with Shin's American productions, *Galgameth*

(1997) and, especially, the *3 Ninjas* series (1994, 1995, and 1998, respectively), a cosmopolitanism and entrepreneurial savvy that should, by this point, provoke little surprise. The three films in the series, for which Shin resurrected his studio nameplate (though this time as the Anglicized "Sheen Productions") and directed under the name Simon Sheen, enjoyed wildly divergent degrees of success, the second and third installments being picked up by majors (Disney and TriStar, respectively), while the first virtually bankrupted Shin and his private investors.[1] Germinated from a scheme to create an Asian *Home Alone*, the series (the last of which inexplicably starred Hulk Hogan) ultimately won over sizable audiences with its formulaic but largely inoffensive charms. Like the two South Korean testament pictures, it was meant to prove Shin's filmmaking credentials and set the stage for the production of the epics Shin had been dreaming about since his studio's demise in the 1970s. Among these would be a treatment of Genghis Khan, about whom Shin presumably felt he had gained expertise both in operating under the dictatorships of the Korean peninsula and, perhaps, through his own outsized filmmaking ambitions. Nevertheless, the closest he would come would be the production of *Galgameth*, a cut-rate and unimaginative retelling of *Pulgasari* that hardly registered in any market. Despite shopping the Genghis Khan script tirelessly and bringing it up in nearly every one of his public appearances, Shin would instead close out his career with *Winter Story* (*Kyŏul iyagi*, 2005), a small and maudlin film about the disappointments of growing old.

In one sense, the disappointments of Shin's last decades were an unavoidable outcome of the displacement of the political milieu in which his filmmaking style had been formed. While the symbolic end to the Cold War would arrive, of course, with the fall of the Berlin Wall in 1991, signs of the demise of the era's monolithic polarities were already visible precisely in the years Shin spent in North Korea and immediately after. Of course, the Korean peninsula, divided to this day, would have to endure the antimonies and continuing violence of the Cold War through the following decades, but the clear economic triumph of the South's fitful attunement to global capitalist hegemony affected an irreversible shift in discourses not only about the North but also about the salience of ideology itself. Over the course of the 1990s and 2000s, the stark moral difference of the North as well as what Alain Badiou has called the twentieth century's "passion for the real"—the committed politicization of reality into opposed ideological spheres—were displaced in Korea by a confidence in the obsolescence of ideology and the ascendant importance of economic "survival."[2] Shin's seeming detachment from any explicit ideological commitment, socialist, capitalist triumphalist, or otherwise, promised him greater visibility in this "postpolitical" era. Indeed the burgeoning "new wave" of the late 1980s and 1990s had begun to craft figures and narratives that escaped and often overturned the old binaries (communist vs. nationalist, Western vs. Korean, artistic autonomy vs. social engagement, etc.) that had defined Cold War cinema.[3] Characteristically, the films of the last phase of Shin's career are politically and stylistically heterogeneous, tilting from *Disappearance*'s dark though perhaps disingenuous critique of Park-era corruption to the light escapism of the *3 Ninjas* films. And yet, his work was met, at least in Korea, with blasé dismissal as remnants of a cinematic past irrelevant to the new cultures of postauthoritarianism and globalization. Though many of the films rivaled in scale and budget the work of Shin's heyday, they could win only short, unsuccessful runs in the era's new multiplexes and grudging broadcast on late-night television.

But while Shin, like the virtual entirety of his generation of "golden age" filmmakers, had undoubtedly fallen out of step with the new film cultures, it was not his vestigial Cold War political worldview that conditioned his obsolescence. Contrary to the critical rhetoric of his day, it was in fact the old conflict between Shin's developmentalist imperatives, on the one hand, and his authorial ambitions, on the other, that put him out of touch with the mainstream of both Korean and global cinema. The coup that he had scored with *3 Ninjas* might have translated into sustained and efficiently profitable success with small-genre filmmaking; instead, it fueled an ambition for a return to the greater scale and artistic freedom of his heydays in the South and North. Such well-made films would come in the 2000s, of course, but they took up not the epic ambitions of Genghis Khan but rather the more ironic and local monstrosities of Bong Joon-ho's *Host* (*Koemul*, 2006) and Park Chan Wook's *Oldboy* (2003). The point is that Shin's work became outmoded not simply by the dulling of Cold War antimonies, but through the transition from a state developmentalist organization of public culture to a postmodern "becoming cultural of the economic, and the becoming economic of the cultural."[4] Shin continued to court the state, if only cynically, with the production of films of national political significance at a point when the state was busy ceding cultural production to the interests of private capital. In fact, it is possible to argue that it was the very cynicism that lay between the increasingly dampened pressures of the state and Shin's own cinematic vision that was most idiosyncratic to the new filmmaking cultures. A reading of one of Shin's most maligned, but at the same time most commercially successful, films, *Mayumi*, will bring this incongruity into greater relief.

Mayumi is a synthetic and in many ways idiosyncratic treatment of the 1987 bombing of a Korean Airlines jet that killed more than two hundred passengers and crew on its way to Seoul from Abu Dhabi—an appalling event made all the more outrageous by the surreal theatrics of the investigation that followed it and by its close proximity to the watershed 1988 Seoul Olympic Games. The film is split into complementary parts. The first, shot in an ostensibly documentary style, follows several strands in the days leading to the bombing, including the adventures of some its colorful passengers (among whom are an intrepid long-haul truck driver and some oil construction engineers) as well as the preparations of two North Korean agents who take on new Japanese identities for the mission, as "Hachiyama Shinichi" and "Mayumi." The pace is frenetic, tracking both the truck driver and the agents separately as they negotiate the bureaucracies of a series of mostly Eastern Bloc countries (each filmed on location) on their way to boarding the flight. The first half closes with a drawn-out, crude, but detailed re-creation of the midair bombing that depicts chunks of the plane ripping apart and bodies, as Shin had expressly envisioned, "flying away like pieces of paper."[5] The film's second half is similarly fast-paced but its tone is sober. Shrewd sleuthing by KAL employees and by an unspecified South Korean agent leads to the capture of "Mayumi" in Baghdad ("Shinichi," who had apparently been terminally ill anyway, managed to take a cyanide pill and kill himself just at the moment of capture). Work then begins by a team of seasoned South Korean intelligence agents to "restore Mayumi to her humanity" and coax her into a public confession. Exposed to the grief of the victims' families and, more dramatically, to both the splendors of modern-day Seoul and the ostensibly democratic processes of the 1987 South Korean presidential elections, "Mayumi" reveals her real name, Kim Hyŏn-hŭi, and, in an uncannily faithful re-creation of the indelible media event, delivers a tearful apology to a throng of press and onlookers.

With the exception of a handful of reviews that applauded the film's documentary qualities, critical reception of *Mayumi* was largely derisive. The negative views of audiences and reviewers were best crystallized by an MBC television executive who, explaining why the station had rescinded its contract to broadcast the film, argued that the film was "no different from the anticommunist and *saemaul* broadcasts of the 1970s."[6] Shin was himself perhaps the film's harshest critic, characterizing it in later interviews as an anticommunist picture merely outfitted in documentary clothing. He explained that he could not but make the film to "confirm [his] identity" as a loyal South Korean citizen and to win back the right to make movies in the country.[7] And in many ways, *Mayumi* was eminently fit to such a purpose. The plain outrage of the bombing is intensified in the film through an unambiguous moral division between the South and the North, embodied best in the contrast between the earnest, can-do spirit of the trucker whose sole aim is to bring home wealth and honor and the cold though often fumbling calculations of the North Korean agents who seem driven only by the promise of inciting violence. The film also projects a celebration of the complex freedoms of the South, splicing together footage of the presidential campaigns with images of fierce street demonstrations that ostensibly testify to the authentic democracy that has taken root. And if Kim Hyŏn-hui's basic humanity threatens to destabilize the neat normative division between the South and the North, it is redeployed in the film to highlight both the monstrous brainwashing tactics of the North and the deep empathy of the Southern agents who see Kim as a victim of the North's manipulations. This seemingly obvious point is driven home in the film's final sequence in which an extreme slow-motion shot of a repentant and suicidal Kim is over-dubbed by the intonements of an invisible male authority who gently reasons that she must live in order to appease the ghosts of the victims and to bear witness to the tragedy of national division. Any semblance of documentary style is undermined in these moments of the film that recycle the familiar tropes and retrograde figures of the Cold War policy picture.

But a more grim critique of the film stemmed not from its seemingly simpleminded representation of Kim Hyŏn-hui and the North but from the way it abused the images of the victims and their survivors in the South. According to statements given by representatives of an ad hoc Surviving Family Association to the press immediately following the film's release, Shin Sang-ok had apparently won the rights to the story and permission to use documentary footage with the promise of making a film that would honor the victims. *Mayumi*, they declared, did no such thing, but rather exploited the victims with its "blood-soaked death scenes."[8] The association brought a deceit and defamation suit against the film, attempting to garnish what was forecast to be its unprecedented profits in local and foreign markets. The real insult for the survivors must have been how *Mayumi* conjoined the bloody bombing sequence with documentary footage of their own anguished scenes of public mourning, in effect claiming the guise of representational realism for the violent spectacle. While Shin countered that he only intended to underscore the victims' misfortune, it appears as though Gil Film Company, the unit Shin established under his son's name, eventually settled with the victims out of court. Notably, in unrelated interviews, Shin pointed out that the highlight of the film for him was precisely the long midair explosion sequence, an admission that hinted not simply at his legal culpability but, more important perhaps, the primary cinematic focus of the project. Some sense of this may become clearer when the relative scale of the scene's financing is taken into consideration: nearly half of the film's total $2 million budget was invested with the U.S.-based special effects company Introvision to produce the 150-second sequence. In an uncanny echo of the abrupt train bombing in his North Korean *Record of an Escape* (*T'alch'ulgi*), Shin had invested disproportionately in the force of the plane's explosion and in rendering the effect of humans "flying away like pieces of paper." Sadly, the net outcome is both macabre and comical, a consequence of both the limitations of the special effects (which, oddly, fell below even the standards of the day) and the incongruity of the scene in what is essentially an espionage thriller. In its lurid dwelling on scorched and dismembered bodies, the scene corroborates the survivors' accusations of commercial exploitation. But it also, I want to argue, suggests the more essential politics at work within both the film's otherwise obvious propaganda purposes and the broader field of the era's filmmaking cultures.

Mayumi was among the last films produced within the state developmentalist model. In its promotional releases and in a variety of press reports, the film's production scale and economic profile were touted as its defining features. Not only was its budget the highest on record in Korean film history, it also won in advance the most lucrative-ever export deals (i.e., for a Korean film) in Japan (Cosmo Productions alone put up an unprecedented $1.5 million), West Germany, Hong Kong, and elsewhere. Further, *Mayumi* was filmed on location in no fewer than seventeen countries, though in many instances the scenes were less than two minutes long and the locale indicated in passing with shots of a street sign or identifying monument. The film also became the most prominent Korean film internationally, scoring entry at the Karlovy Vary and Venice film festivals and winning, perhaps inexplicably, consideration for the Academy Award for Best Foreign-Language Film. Had such incentives still been offered, *Mayumi* would have won film import rights and guaranteed financing on future productions for Shin's studio.[9] So, in spite of the film's rightfully adverse critical reception, *Mayumi* marked one of Shin's greatest commercial successes, notwithstanding that this success came not as box-office receipts but through "sale before harvest" speculation. It should come as no surprise then that Shin took advantage of the spotlight to offer a classic assessment of the state of the film industry and its governance. Arguing in one interview that Korean cinema circa 1990 was "alive on the outside, but dying on the inside," he identified two fundamental problems: the provincial vision of filmmakers and the laissez-faire approach of policymakers. For the former, he prescribed a broadened perspective fit for the contemporary "multinational age," one that would grow presumably from global experience and translate into films suited to the international market. For the latter, he had an uncannily familiar remedy:

> Finances, technology, skill, facilities are either lacking or backward. Democratization is fine, and so is money, but there are so many things that even money can't solve. . . . Film policy shouldn't be separated from politics but, like economic policy, needs to aim at modernization.[10]

Following on his experiences with the state developmentalist management of mass culture in the postwar South and, more closely, with the robust backing of the state for his film projects in the North, Shin could not help but blanch at the shortcomings of a Korean film industry just beginning to emerge from the doldrums of the 1980s. While it remains unclear whether Shin made *Mayumi* in response to government pressure or, conversely, to curry favor with it, the film—eminently Korean in content, driven by exports, and enormously ambitious in scope—embodied the ideals of postwar film policy. In this sense, Shin's intention to "confirm [his] identity" with the film may be read not only as an attempt to signal his true political affiliation but also to affirm his ability to make big pictures—that is, to make himself seen again. However, four years after the advent of direct foreign distribution and two years before the entry of corporate capital in film production, Shin's was an idiosyncratic and untimely filmmaking identity. Lucrative export deals, cosmopolitan exposure, and violent spectacle could neither save *Mayumi* from failure in the wilderness of the new film markets nor win for Shin's studio any lasting public support. The new idiom of the state's cultural policy was "promotion," and Shin Sang-ok's developmentalist grammar was virtually unintelligible within it.

Yi Hyŏng-p'yo, easily among Shin's most talented colleagues and perhaps his most astute critic, offered in his last years a severe assessment of Shin's politics. Contrasting him with author Hwang Sŏk-yŏng, who had similarly crossed over and back again from the North and written a series of volumes from the experience, most notably *Guest* (*Sonnim*, 2001), Yi laments the fact that Shin had not produced a work of comparable depth or insight. Instead, Shin had been too wrapped up in "play"—the horseplay of his

Manchurian pictures, the gunplay of his war pictures, and, finally, the aero-play of his hijacking picture.[11] In other words, Shin had misplaced his talents on spectacle and exploitation, forsaking the serious political treatments that had always been on hand with his material. And yet, as I have attempted to demonstrate throughout this book, the politics of Shin Sang-ok's work cannot be measured solely by the degree to which it projected clear ideological messages. Rather, the political signification of films like *Mayumi*, *Red Muffler*, or even *Pulgasari* rested on their capacity to disclose the conditions of their economic production and cultural visibility. The sort of cheap exploitation and cynicism for which Yi Hyŏng-p'yo and others criticize Shin is easily apparent in *Mayumi*, not only in its bombing or closing sequences but also, for instance, in a scene in which the camera leers at Kim Hyŏn-hui's nude body as she is scrubbed down by her female interrogators—a gratuitous image that recalls *Female Prisoner 407* (*Yŏsu 407-ho*) and a number of other films that took advantage of women's bodies. But, as in so many of Shin's films, the transparency of *Mayumi*'s political and commercial purposes is obscured by other moments and images within it. One instance of this is a scene that juxtaposes the tragic demise of the truck driver's father—who, traumatized, denies his son's death and waits for his return, only to be locked away in an insane asylum—and lively documentary footage of the opening ceremonies of the Olympic Games. This is a paralleling that ostensibly demonstrates the bittersweet triumph of South Korean development; at the same time, it implicitly suggests the trauma, silencing, and forgetting that sustains it. I do not mean to suggest that *Mayumi* or any other film in Shin's corpus harbors subversive flashes that destabilize their basic populist conservatism. In fact, by 1990 there was nothing implicitly subversive about critical reflection on the sacrifices of postwar developmentalism. And further, I do not think that the nominal ambivalence of Shin's films makes of any of them a masterwork like Hwang's brooding and philosophical *Guest*. Instead, it is in their very schizophrenic suspension of commercial exploitation and earnest instruction that they furnish a rich, irreducibly cinematic testament to the complexities of Korean modernity.

ACKNOWLEDGMENTS

THE DEBTS I have incurred writing this book will be impossible to enumerate fully, not least because I do not know where to mark a starting point for the learning that has informed its writing. Unequivocally, however, I owe heartiest thanks to Kyung Hyun Kim, whose sometimes jocular but always dependable intellectual and practical support over the past decade has been a vital foundation for my life and research. Utmost gratitude extends as well to colleagues I have had the good fortune to meet and from whom I have learned a great deal. Over the course of many winding conversations, Mitsuhiro Yoshimoto was always ready to dole out peerless advice and extract clearer ideas as only the best teachers can. Theodore Hughes's generosity and honesty were invaluable toward the later stages of this project, that is, when it needed the most encouragement and refinement. And Richard Okada, as irascible a mentor as there ever could be, showed me to the very end the inherent value of enthusiasm.

I have also been very lucky over the course of my graduate studies at the University of California, Irvine, and my early career at Princeton University to meet and to stay friends with a group of warm, supportive, and down-to-earth people who have helped this book in variously oblique and direct ways. I have known Baek Moonim, Jinsoo An, Michael Cronin, Su Yun Kim, and Kim Sunah the longest and look forward to continuing my scholarly life alongside theirs. I have also grown as a writer and thinker together with Michelle Cho, Youngmin Choe, Kelly Jeong, Phil Kaffen, Chika Kinoshita, Sangjoon Lee, and Travis Workman and owe them real thanks. I extend equal gratitude to my colleagues at Princeton who have welcomed me into the fold and given needed support, especially Amy Borovoy, Benjamin Elman, Sheldon Garon, Martin Kern, Joy Kim, David Leheny, Susan Naquin, and Atsuko Ueda.

The quality of this book was strengthened in vital ways through the guidance and example of scholars within the realms of Korean and cinema studies. These include writers whose work I read avidly as a student and who, in that magic way of academic transformation, began generously to engage my own work as that of a colleague's. Among them are Nancy Abelmann, Charles Armstrong, Chungmoo Choi, Rey Chow, Jim Fujii, David James, Kim Ch'ŏl, Kim So-yŏng, Kim So-yŏn, Jin Kyung Lee, Abé Markus Nornes, Janet Poole, Sonia Ryang, Andre Schmid, Sin Hyŏng-gi, and Yi Sun-jin.

The research for this book would have been inconceivable without the exposure to postwar Korean cinema afforded by the generous donation by Kim Hong-jun of some 140 videotapes to the University of California, Irvine library in 2003. Subsequent access not only to Shin Sang-ok's films but also to a remarkable variety of materials was made possible by the extraordinary research, collection, and acquisition work of the Korean Film Archive. I owe special thanks to Cho Chun-hyŏng, Chŏng Chong-hwa, and Kim Han Sang for their expertise and patient assistance during my many trips to the archive.

My experience with the University of Minnesota Press during the last stages of the manuscript's completion was seamless, and I wish to thank Jason Weidemann for his gracious and enthusiastic editorial supervision and Danielle Kasprzak for her impeccable support as I worked out the final details. The meticulous reports submitted by the manuscript's reviewers were invaluable and I hope that the book reflects their insight and enthusiasm.

Owing to my exceptional luck in landing my current position at Princeton, the only credit for the book's financial support goes to that most munificent of employers. A series of summer salary and University Committee on Research in the Humanities and Social Sciences grants, and a partially funded leave year assured that I did not go wanting over the years it took to finish this book.

Finally, I must thank my extended family for their love and unflagging support. First to my mother, Myung-ju, and my sister, Jeanie, for their unquestioning faith and bottomless good cheer through the past decade's ups and downs. Next, to my in-laws on Jeju, who twice afforded me a slice of writing paradise on their orchard in exchange for only a little bit of hard labor. And, of course, to Yang Hye Eun, with whom I have shared every adventure worth having, and who has held my hand through every stage of this work, my thanks forever.

NOTES

Introduction

1 I have elected to use the nonstandard romanization "Shin Sang-ok" because it is the most widely used rendering of the name in English-language publication. All remaining romanization of Korean in the book follows the McCune-Reischauer system, with the exception of a small number of names (e.g., Park Chung Hee) commonly rendered in nonstandard form.

2 Barthes, *Camera Lucida*, 27.

3 The body of this work, arguably preoccupying the mainstream of modern Korean studies for the past three decades, is too vast for even cursory citation here. References to and appropriations of aspects of this archive are made throughout the present volume. It must suffice to note here that the most publicly visible iteration of powerful campaigns to revise or "cleanse" history has been the Truth and Reconciliation Commission, established in 2005 to investigate state atrocities throughout the twentieth century.

4 Deleuze, *Cinema 2*, 280.

5 Yoshimoto, *Kurosawa*, 36.

6 North America–based English-language scholarship was an early and consistent critical force vis-à-vis Korean nationalist discourse. Particularly influential was the "colonial modernity" thesis advanced by Michael Robinson and Gi-Wook Shin, among others, as well as the work of Henry Em on colonial period ideologue Sin Ch'ae-ho, and Carter Eckert's research into the colonial roots of postwar Korean economic development. See Shin and Robinson, *Colonial Modernity*; Em, "Nationalism, Post-Nationalism, and Sin Ch'ae-ho"; Eckert, *Offspring of Empire*.

7 Chow, *Primitive Passions*, 49.

8 The finest example of this work is the two-volume collection, Yun Hae-dong et al., *Rereading Modernity*; a much more sprawling enterprise is the East Asian Research Institute's continually multiplying "everyday life" series, including the (to date) four-volume collection, Tonguk University, *Everyday Life and Modern Visual Media*.

9 Two engrossing volumes on this period's mass cultures are Sin Myŏng-jik, *Modern Boy, Strolling Kyŏngsŏng* and Kim Chin-sŏng, *Let There Be a Dancehall in Seoul*.

10 Naremore and Brantlinger, "Six Artistic Cultures," 3.

11 Hailing from an illustrious family of performers, the Kim Sisters rose to early fame on the U.S. military-base circuits doing dead-on rockabilly and big-band covers. They exploded on the U.S. scene in the late 1950s, appearing on *The Ed Sullivan Show* dozens of times throughout the 1960s, before returning to Korea with a more eclectic range of American and Korean numbers. Interestingly, one of their base-camp performances is captured (reportedly by a hidden camera) in Shin Sang-ok's 1958 *Hellflower*.

12 Adorno, "Letter to Walter Benjamin," 65.

13 For a rigorous examination of the position of ethnic Korean intellectuals in the colonial period, see Yun Hae-dong et al., *Coloniality's Gray Zones*.

14 For an incisive elaboration of this dichotomy in the 1950s, see Hughes, "Development as Devolution."

15 See, for instance, the historian Kim Su-nam's characterization of Shin as a "master of mise-en-scène" in his short essay, "Master of Mise-en-Scène," or, more recently, David Scott Diffrient's description of Shin's "political slipperiness" in "Military Enlightenment," 24.

16 This is the argument elaborated by Korean film critic Kim Ryŏ-sil in her examination of Na Un-gyu's work in *Projected Empire, Reflected Colony*. See also the commentary on *Arirang* in Kim Chong-wŏn and Chŏng Chung-hŏn, *One Hundred Years of Our Cinema*, 23.

17 While the concept of "nationalist realism" in Korean cinema ran through the mainstream of criticism throughout the postwar period, it was only elaborated as a relatively coherent theory in the 1980s alongside the ascendant "national literature" movements. Perhaps the most representative publication was the set of essays put out by the Seoul Film Collective in 1983, *For a New Cinema*, which featured polemics by ascendant filmmakers like Chang Sŏn-u ("New Life, New Cinema") and Hong Ki-sŏn ("On Korean Realism"). To that point, "nationalist realism" was constituted by critics, primarily, and filmmakers, secondarily, as presumptions about the tradition of politically engaged realist cinema from the colonial through the postwar and even contemporary periods. The concept's effect can be discerned as easily in the consistently high ranking given to films as diverse as Na's *Arirang* or Yu Hyŏn-mok's *Stray Bullet* on regular "best films" lists as it can in the founding of bodies like the Enlightenment Film Association (*Kyemong yŏnghwa hyŏphoe*). The most explicit formulations of the idea in the postwar period can be found in the historian Yi Yŏng-il's "A Genealogy of Korean Realism" and Yun Pong-ch'un's "Renaissance Man of the Silver Screen, Na Un-gyu."

18 Rancière, "The Paradoxes of Political Art," 140.

1. The Century's Illuminations

1 See Yi Yŏng-il's comments in *Korean Art Research*.

2 See especially his "Treatise on the Culture Industry."

3 See O Yŏng-suk's arguments on postenlightenment in her *Korean Film and Cultural Discourse in the 1950s*, 35–48.

4 The basic approach to identifying the inner and outer forms of literary genres is closely associated with René Wellek and Austin Warren and their influential *Theory of Literature* (1949). A number of critics have emphasized the delineation of syntax and semantics. The most important are Tzvetan Todorov in *The Fantastic: A Structural Approach to a Literary Genre* (1975) and Fredric Jameson in his early work. Citations for those approaches here are drawn, respectively, from Buscombe, "The Idea of Genre," and Altman, "A Semantic/Syntactic Approach to Film Genre."

5 In his meticulous study of Japanese documentary films, Abé Mark Nornes notes the pre- and para-histories of the form, listing, among others, "the *kiroku eiga* (record film), the *kagaku eiga* (science film), the *kogata eiga* (small-gauge film), the *kyōiku eiga* (education film), the *jiji eiga* (current events film), the *nyūse eiga* (news film)." All of these iterations were conjoined, Nornes argues, by claims to the representation of reality. The point here is that, similarly, the "enlightenment" marker arises as the dominant institutional shorthand for politically motivated and sponsored filmmaking. See Nornes, *Japanese Documentary Film*, 2.

6 Williams, "Melodrama Revised," 42.

7 Ibid., 58.

8 Ibid., 43.

9 Schmid, *Korea between Empires*, 32.

10 For an extended discussion of this body of texts and a consideration of their place in modern Korean literature, see Susie Kim, "The Ambivalence of Modernity."

11 For an incisive overview of the sharply politicized literatures of this period, see Jin kyung Lee, "Autonomous Aesthetics and Autonomous Subjectivity."

12 Yi Kwang-su, "Literati and Self-Cultivation."

13 See, as a most recent example, the dialogue between John Treat and Michael Shin in Treat, "Choosing to Collaborate," and Shin, "Yi Kwang-su."

14 See Hughes, "Development as Devolution."

15 For an illuminating discussion of the deployment of folk culture in *minjung*-movement literatures, see Choi Chungmoo, "The Minjung Culture Movement."

16 Namhee Lee astutely notes the "Kantian" impulse in *minjung*-movement discourse that figured student leaders and activists as forming a critical moral vanguard in the face of social and economic suppression. See Lee, *The Making of Minjung*, 14.

17 Kwŏn Yŏng-min, *Modern Korean Literary History*, 13.

18 Ch'ŏn Chŏng-hwan, "Enlightenment Literature and the Modernization of 'Entertainment.'"

19 See, for example, the emphasis on "bourgeois fantasy" in Chu, "The (Re)construction of Nation and Gender in the Postcolonial Nation-State."

20 Pak Wan-sik, "The Problem of Cinema and Education." All translations in this book are my own unless otherwise noted.

21 Yi Un-gok, "The Cultural Function of Film."

22 Kim Sŏng-gyun, "Japanese–Korean Cultural Exchange through Film."

23 This has been reprinted a number of times. My first encounter with it was in the excellent collection, Korean Film Archive, *The Koyrŏ Motion Picture Company and*

The New Film Order, 1936–1941. All quotations from the discussion presented here are drawn from this volume.

24 The watershed event was Yi Kyu-hwan's *The Wanderer* (*Nagŭne*, 1937), which, in 1938, enjoyed considerable box-office success across Japan. The film is mentioned throughout the roundtable discussion.

25 See Yi Sun-jin's entry for An Sŏk-ju in Kang et al., *Dictionary of Popular Artists in the Colonial Period.*

26 See Yim Chong-guk, *Pro-Japanese Literature*, and Kang Sŏng-ryul, *Pro-Japanese Cinema.*

27 In the preamble to his central arguments, Im writes: "Put succinctly, while the proponents of enlightenment-ism [*kaehwajuui*] or nationalism or proletarian or pure literature may have had different aims, they all shared the idealism of enlightenment [*kyemong*] or the advancement of culture itself out of the sphere of poverty. . . . Of course, the poverty and repression that was the station of the people [*minjung*] was the driving force of this idealism. . . . But for the past several years, it seems that the age of the cultural patriot and of the pioneer has been coming to a close." See Im, "Treatise on the Culture Industry," 57.

28 For an excellent discussion of this tension between art and ideology, as well as other aspects of Im's thoughts on cinema, see Paek, "An Ontology of Chosun Cinema."

29 Pak Song, "Pressing Problems in Chosŏn Cinema."

30 Ko Chong-ok, "Proletarian Cinema and Education."

31 From an unattributed *Kyŏnghyang Sinmun* article titled, "1958 Wrap-up—The Film Industry."

32 From an unattributed *Chosŏn Ilbo* article titled, "Quality Increasing: Big Industrialization Still Far Off."

33 Shin Sang-ok, "Twenty Regrettable Years of Korean Cinema."

34 Quoted in Pak Chi-yŏn, "Modernization and Film Policy," 177.

35 Both sources are cited in Yi Yŏng-il, *Complete History*, 74–75.

36 Ibid., 123.

37 See Yi Sun-jin's flat claim that anyone producing film in the early 1940s had de facto collaborated with colonial rule, in her informative paper, "Colonial Experience and Filmmaking in the Immediate Liberation Period."

38 Ostensibly, the most incommensurate political environment within the Korean cultural landscape is, of course, North Korea, and indeed the politics of North Korean cinema specifically and socialist filmmaking more broadly is a key inflection of the enlightenment modality in Korea. However, even a limited consideration of early postliberation and early postwar North Korean film and film criticism would both disproportionately bloat the scale of this chapter and take it off the tracks of one of its central tasks, which is to trace the manifestation of the enlightenment modality in the sort of mainstream, commercial filmmaking in which Shin Sang-ok's South Korean work is situated. However, some address of the enlightenment modality's life across the Korean peninsula's political division is taken up in subsequent chapters of this book, first in chapter 3 with its meditation on the suggestive cross-ideological overlaps of the "aesthetics of development," and later in chapter 5 with its rereading

of the formal principles of North Korean cinema. Suffice it to say here that I believe the enlightenment modality is a robust presence in North Korean cinema, that in fact its basic conjoining of mass education, national interests, and industrial expansion to scenes of conversion lies at the foundation of the North's cinematic theory and practice.

39 Yun Hae-dong, "Colonial Modernity and the Advent of Mass Society."

40 See Yi Yŏng-il, *Complete History*, 245, and Kim and Chŏng, *One Hundred Years of Our Cinema*, 255.

41 An, "Popular Reasoning of South Korean Melodrama Films," 140.

2. Regimes within Regimes

1 Silverman, "Fragments of a Fashionable Discourse," 181.

2 Barthes, *The Fashion System*, 273.

3 See the collection of essays, Kim So-yŏn et al., *An Age of Allures and Chaos*, and in particular the introduction, in which An Jinsoo distinguishes the filmmaking of the 1950s from the 1960s by marking the former's foreignness.

4 This idea is articulated throughout much of her work but receives its most explicit formulation in Hansen, "The Mass Production of the Senses."

5 Doane, *The Desire to Desire*, 31.

6 The use of actors and actresses in rallies and staged "public greetings" (*insa*) became standard practice in political campaigns and elections. See Kang Chun-man, *A Stroll through Modern Korean History*, 109.

7 For an informative overview of motion picture laws in the 1960s and 1970s, see Pak Chi-yŏn, "Film Policy." The article also touches on salient regulations of the 1950s.

8 The most compelling collection of analysis of the period's films remains the aforementioned Kim So-yŏn et al., *An Age of Allures of Chaos*.

9 Yi Yŏn-ho, "Shin Sang-ok: Who Are You?," 122.

10 Nine complete feature films from the colonial period have been uncovered and restored at the Korean Film Archive. One of these, *Sweet Dream* (*Mimong*, 1936), directed by Yang Chu-nam, is considered a wholly native production and was in fact recently featured among a number of films as a "national cultural asset." The others were produced in cooperation with private Japanese film studios or, later, under the auspices of the imperial film corporation. Ch'oe In-gyu directed *Homeless Angels* (*Chip ŏmnŭn ch'ŏnsa*, 1941) and codirected *A Statement of Love* (*Sarang ŭi maengse*, 1945), which in different ways lionized the act of sacrifice for the imperial cause. The point that needs to be made here is that there is an undeniable disparity between Ch'oe's pre- and postliberation films in terms of their technical quality. With the generous financial backing of the imperial propaganda machine and the professional support of filmmakers at Toho and other private studios, *Homeless Angels* and *Statement of Love* are sprawling, impeccably produced films. By contrast, Ch'oe's "liberation films," *Hurrah Freedom* (*Chayu manse*, 1946) and *The Night before Liberation* (*Tongnip chŏnya*, 1948), are undeniably crude, bereft of the fundamentals of visual storytelling language and continuity—a contrast for which the lack of proper

filmmaking equipment and the subsequent degradation of film prints can only partially account.

11 This is a well-documented history, the subject of many interviews and studies. See,
for instance, Yi Hyŏng-p'yo's reflections in Yi Sun-jin et al., *2005 Modern and Contemporary Korean Arts Oral History Series*, 33–37. See also, the recently completed,
seminal study of the relationship between U.S. and Korean filmmakers, Kim Han
Sang, "Uneven Screens, Contested Identities," especially chapter 6, which explores
the tensions within the "auteurist impulse."

12 The term was not new to the postwar period, having been used to describe cultural
texts and material objects at least as far back as the early colonial period, but its
usage by both critics and filmmakers in the 1950s is strikingly ubiquitous. As it does
today, *"seryŏn"* was used to describe films or performances that are assured, lack
artifice or pretension, and rise above the crudeness or awkwardness that appear to
have plagued contemporary work, particularly works that attempted to capture the
sophistication of American and European products. "The *seryŏn*," then, is not simply
a synonym for "the modern," but is rather an index of the degree to which the modern has been effectively assimilated.

13 The plagiarism phenomena has been noted in a number of publications but receives
its most intriguing treatment in An, "Popular Reasoning of South Korean Melodrama Films," 162–65.

14 See, for instance, Yi Hyŏng-p'yo's long interview in Cho Chun-hyŏng et al., *2008
Korean Film History*, 2:163–215. Notably, these interviews do not circulate from the
KOFA Library—a restriction levied at the request of the interviewees who were
apparently concerned about the sensitive nature of some of their comments.

15 See Kang Sŏng-ryul, *Pro-Japanese Cinema*, and Kim Ryŏ-sil, *Projected Empire,
Reflected Colony*, for their vigorous critique of the filmmakers of the colonial period
and the film historiography that has attempted to erase that past.

16 From an adapted interview with Shin Sang-ok: Kim So-hŭi and Yi Ki-rim, "Korean
Cinema in Retrospect, Shin Sang-ok."

17 Park, Warner, and Fitzgerald, "The Process of Westernization," 43.

18 Culture and Tourism Ministry of Korea, *Two Thousand Years of Korean Fashion*, 138.

19 Ibid., 144.

20 Ibid., 146.

21 Ibid., 142.

22 Ch'oe Tŏk-gyo, *One Hundred Years of Korean Magazines*, 549–61.

23 Strangely, while the authoritative *Korean Magazine Survey* lists *Yŏnghwa segye* as
having first been registered in 1956 and folding in 1964, the Korean Film Archive
holds issues dating back to January 1955. See Han'guk Chapji Hyŏphoe, *Korean Magazine Survey*, 367.

24 Private conversation with film historian Yi Sun-jin.

25 We may note here that an earlier, and, in tenor, more serious, film magazine,
Yŏnghwa Yŏn'gŭk (*Film and Theater*), had even more explicitly articulated the mar-
riage of the new medium to the old. See Ch'oe Tŏk-gyo, *One Hundred Years of Korean
Magazines*, 554.

26 Jinsoo An examines the role of the *pyŏnsa* in Korean film history and the interesting persistence of its function following the advent of the sound picture in the chapter, "Fallen Women on Trial: Configuration of Popular Justice in Courtroom Drama Films" from his PhD dissertation, "Popular Reasoning of South Korean Melodrama Films."

27 This statement clearly needs qualification that would stray far beyond the bounds of this study. It will have to suffice here to note that, following some foreshadowing and tacit action on the part of the governing authorities, the commercial film industry (which, of course, had never been free of strict government censorship) was shut down with the creation of the Chosŏn Film Production Company (*Chosŏn yŏnghwa chejak hoesa*) in 1940. Many films continued to be produced in colonial Korea, but these were wholly created under the auspices of the Governor-General and were explicitly produced in support of the war effort. The exuberant film-fan cultures of the preceding decade were effectively killed off with the closing of virtually all private publishing houses. Commercial film production started again immediately following national liberation in 1945. Over the next five years, fifteen to sixteen Korean films were screened in theaters, including Ch'oe In-gyu's *Hurrah Freedom*. Nevertheless, under the tremendous pressure of the intense ideological split between groups on the right and left such as the Chosŏn Film and Theater Writers Association (*Chosŏn yŏnghwa kŭkjakga hyŏphoe*) and the KAPF (*Korea Artista Proletaria Federacio*) successor, Chosŏn Proletarian Film Federation (*Chosŏn Proleta Film Federatio*), as well as the repressive force of the USAMGIK authorities, a commercial film industry was not viable. Finally, while feature films were indeed made during war, venues were in near total disarray. See Yi Yŏng-il, *Complete History*, chapters 5, 6, and 7.

28 Ch'oe Tŏk-gyo, *One Hundred Years of Korean Magazines*, 511.

29 For a full study of *Yŏwŏn*'s social and ideological dimensions, see Kim Hyŏn-ju, "The Women's Magazine," and the essays in the collection Han'guk Yŏsŏng Munhak Hakhoe, ed., *Yŏwŏn Studies.*

30 In this sense it is easy to draw a parallel between *Yŏwŏn* and the leading contemporary Japanese women's magazine, *Shufu no Tomo* (*Housewife's Friend*), a comprehensive publication whose format and layout were unmistakably similar to *Yŏwŏn*'s. Unfortunately, little serious research on postwar women's publishing in Japan has been published in English.

31 I should note here that because no print of *Ch'un-hŭi* survives, I have consulted the screenplay. Interestingly, Shin remade the film with a series of modifications in 1975, which the Korean Film Archive lists under the title *Ch'un-hŭi '75.*

32 Bazin, "De Sica: Metteur en Scène," 66.

33 According to Shin Films producer Ch'oe Kyŏng-ok, the house in fact belonged to the assistant secretary of transportation, apparently an acquaintance of Shin's who, as did many in administrative power, had an interest in the film industry. See Cho Chun-hyŏng et al., *2008 Korean Film History Oral History*, 1:60.

34 Dyer, *Heavenly Bodies*, 31.

35 For more information on these actresses, see the corresponding entries in Kang Ok-hŭi et al., *Dictionary of Popular Artists in the Colonial Period*, 97.

36 See Yi Yŏn-ho, "*Virgin Bride* Director," 164.

37 "The Misery of Adaptation," *Seoul Sinmun*.

38 "Refined *Sinp'a*," *Han'guk Sinmun*.

39 Yi Yŏng-il, *Complete History*, 266.

40 Yu Hyŏn-mok, *The Development of Korean Film*, 96.

41 Kim Su-yong, *Cinema, My Love*, 51.

42 Kim So-hŭi and Yi Ki-rim, "Korean Cinema in Retrospect, Shin Sang-ok."

43 Yu Chi-na, "Korean Melodrama," 16.

44 Chu Yu-sin, "Feminist Critique," 103.

45 See the excellent new study, Hughes, *Literature and Film in Cold War South Korea*.

46 "The Film [*Seven Brides for Seven Brothers*]."

3. Authorship and the Location of Cinema

 1 Yi Yŏn-ho, "Shin Sang-ok: Who Are You?," 122.

 2 Ibid., 126.

 3 Kim So-hŭi and Yi Ki-rim, "Korean Cinema in Retrospect, Shin Sang-ok."

 4 Yi Yŏn-ho, "Shin Sang-ok: Who Are You?," 125.

 5 Yi Yŏng-il, *Korean Film History Lectures*, 67.

 6 See the chapter, "The Lures of Tradition and Modernity: The World of Shin Sang-ok's Film," in Kim So-yŏng, *Cinema: Blue Flower in the Land of Technology*, 129–35.

 7 Cho Chun-hyŏng et al., *2008 Korean Film History*, 2:337.

 8 I am thinking, of course, of articles like Truffaut's 1954 "A Certain Tendency of the French Cinema" and any number of Bazin's treatments of filmmakers, ranging from Vittorio De Sica to John Ford.

 9 Andrew, *Concepts in Film Theory*, 115.

10 The true figure is unknown, largely due to Shin's habit of crediting junior studio directors with films of his own creation that were less than satisfying. Other filmmakers, such as Kim Su-yong who directed more than sixty films in the 1960s and Yi Man-hŭi who directed close to fifty, were actually more prolific over the same period, though of course they did not run their own studios.

11 For an informative but relatively succinct English-language treatment of this period, see Kim Hyung-A., *Korea's Development under Park Chung Hee*.

12 For this reference, and for the best treatment of postwar filmmaking policies, see Pak Chi-yŏn, "Film Policy."

13 This system, in which the right to import a small number of highly profitable foreign films was tied to the production of "quality" domestic films and success on the foreign and film festival markets, was central to the often byzantine workings of the postwar film industry. It was also crucial to the operations of Shin Films and will be duly treated below. For a compact summation of import film numbers, see the table tracing the productivity of studios over the period in Pak Chi-yŏn, "Modernization and Film Policy," 174. For a nuanced and often surprising account of the import and export activities of the postwar Korean film industry, see Sangjoon Lee, "The Transnational Asian Studio System," especially chapters 3, 4, and 5.

14 The full spectrum of these regulations was rather triumphantly announced in a July 1963 article, "A New Territory for Filmmaking," published in *Kyŏnghyang Sinmun*.

15 Though which among the sixteen registered companies actually met the new regulations is questionable. Those short of equipment apparently would borrow and loan pieces in anticipation of the infrequent inspections. See Shin Sang-ok's own comments in the adapted interview, Kim So-hŭi and Yi Ki-rim, "Korean Cinema in Retrospect, Shin Sang-ok."

16 Drawing on interviews with a number of producers, directors, and actresses active in the period, Pak Chi-yŏn asserts that, as of 1964, "most" of the films produced that year were made under this "borrowed name" (*taemyŏng chejak*) system. Pak underscores how the practice, while it made possible the production of otherwise unfeasible films, worked strongly to the benefit of the major studios, which could not only pocket the fees (paid in advance no less) but also more easily meet their annual production quota and further enjoy the refracted glory of any box-office or critical successes. For more details, see Pak Chi-yŏn, "Modernization and Film Policy." Clearly, as one of the few registered companies, Shin Films was well positioned to reap the benefits of the "borrowed name" practice. However, very little evidence indicates that it lent out its name with any regularity. In large part, this reticence would have stemmed from the bare fact that the studio's high output and financial success, at least in the first half of the 1960s, would have made any name-lending superfluous. And indeed, the varied directors under contract with Shin Films were already at work on a range of genre and program films that targeted the wider spectrum of film culture beyond the first-run theaters in central Seoul and downtown Pusan, Kwangju, Taegu, and so on, to the second- and third-run theaters on the periphery of those cities and into the rural reaches. Nevertheless, and while Shin seems not to have addressed the issue publicly, it is possible to speculate that Shin and his partners shied away from diluting the studio's nameplate with films that were not developed in-house. Instead, Shin Films opted to lock up, on short-term bases, reliable personnel such as the prominent director Kim Su-yong, whose 1965 film for the studio, *Sorrow Even in Heaven* (*Chŏ hanŭl edo sŭlp'ŭmi*), outperformed all other films at the Seoul box office that year.

17 Pak Chi-yŏn, "Modernization and Film Policy," 172.

18 Ibid., 173.

19 It is worth noting in passing here that while the success of *Romance Papa* owed substantially to its all-star casting and to the relative sophistication of its style, its script—or rather the means by which Shin obtained it—is indicative of Shin's business savvy and aesthetic sense. With its quick tempo and socially resonant plot (a breadwinner's ruin is gently counteracted by his industrious and loving family) *Romance Papa* was the most popular radio play of 1959. Shin consistently capitalized on the creativity of radio dramas and locked up many of the scripts during their broadcast. Other hits yielded through this practice include *Confessions of a College Girl* and *Until the End of This Life*.

20 "1958 Wrap-up."

21 "Quality Increasing: Big Industrialization Still Far Off."

22 Quoted in Pak Chi-yŏn, "Film Policy," 177.

23 These statistics were culled from chapter 2 of Pak A-na, "Research on Shin Sang-ok's Film Production and Genre."

24 Ibid., 19.

25 Kim So-hŭi and Yi Ki-rim, "Korean Cinema in Retrospect, Shin Sang-ok."

26 Yi Yŏn-ho, "*Virgin Bride* Director," 163.

27 Pak Chi-yŏn, "Film Policy," 176.

28 Significantly stricter controls over film content were instituted with the Second Revision to the Motion Picture Law in August 1966. While it reduced production quotas and introduced stringent measures against the "borrowed names" practice, the revision's most significant measure was its double and preemptive censorship policy. Responding to governmental pressures, the Korean Producer Association (*Yŏnghwa ŏpja hyŏphoe*) established a self-regulating Film Review Committee (*Yŏnghwa simŭi wiwŏnhoe*) on April 1, 1967. The Ministry of Culture and Public Information (MCPI) established another self-regulating six-member committee on December 1. These two bodies worked primarily to censor filmmaking in advance, reviewing production reports with the script before production (a task taken up primarily by the KPA) and again with the film before exhibition (overseen mostly by the MCPI's committee). Both regulatory bodies worked to encourage the production of ideologically acceptable "quality films," though with its authority to issue screening bans, the MCPI's committee played the most forceful policing role over content.

29 For a representative sampling of such commentary, see the long introduction to Kim Mi-hyŏn et al., *History of Korean Film Distribution* as well as comments scattered throughout the interviews in Cho Chun-hyŏng et al., *2008 Korean Film History*. Unfortunately, this latter two-volume set of raw interview transcriptions does not circulate outside of the Korean Film Archive library.

30 Kim Mi-hyŏn et al., *History of Korean Film Distribution*, 14.

31 Ibid., 41.

32 One of the principal means by which theater managers cut down on their payments to producers was ticket recycling (*p'yo tolli'gi*, or the Japanese "*mawashi*" as it was still called well into the postwar period). Quite simply, tickets issued to customers were collected upon their exiting and used as many times as the paper they were printed on could withstand. Since the tickets were used to calculate producer commissions, their deflated numbers obviously benefited the distributors and exhibitors at the expense of the producers. The well-known but seemingly incorrigible practice was a minor touchstone in the demands for a more developed direct distribution system. See Kim Mi-hyŏn et al., *History of Korean Film Distribution*, 86.

33 There were in fact three different subsystems within the larger scope of this indirect distribution system: the commission (*susuryo*) system in which producers received an often estimated percentage of returns, the linking (*yi'myŏn* or, in the commonplace Japanese, "*ura*") system in which producers tied smaller market returns to larger ones, and the single sales (*tanmae*) system in which the regional distribution agent set percentages for the very smallest theaters. See Kim Mi-hyŏn et al., *History of Korean Film Distribution*, 19.

34 For an excellent summation of the heyday of the block-booking system, see Balio, "A Mature Oligopoly."

35 Kim Mi-hyŏn et al., *History of Korean Film Distribution*, 18.

36 See Pak's description, part of a wide-ranging interview about Shin Films, in Cho Chun-hyŏng et al., *2008 Korean Film History*, 1:182–88.

37 See these comments in the interview with Kim Sŏng-gŭn, a theater and studio owner who specialized in the import of foreign films in the postwar period, in Kim Mi-hyŏn et al., *History of Korean Film Distribution*, 114.

38 See Sangjoon Lee's engrossing examination of Shin Films' "counterfeit co-production" in the chapter, "Enter the Shin Films: Rise and Demise of a Developmental State Studio," in Lee, "The Transnational Asian Studio System," 267–70.

39 From the late 1950s through 1966, Shin Films held an exclusive contract with one of the era's four largest theaters specializing in domestic films, the Myŏngbo in Myŏngdong, central Seoul. When the theater closed in 1966 (its bankruptcy rumored to have been precipitated by Shin Sang-ok's profligate borrowing against the ambitious export ventures detailed below), Shin Films and its newly formed subsidiaries relied on one-off sales in Seoul until it took over the Hollywood Theater from 1969 to 1973.

40 The only published evidence I have come across for the direct meddling of regional investors in the details of films and their production is from a bitter article that the director Kim Su-yong wrote reflecting on the radical changes to the industry in the 1970s. He describes the involvement in this way: "As a condition for sponsoring a part of the film, they would interfere with the actual film and intervene in the selection of staff. . . . They would try to demand extreme acting . . . without any thought for the director's vision. . . . So the actors had to eat mustard. . . . They would of course make demands in the casting of star actors and the use of certain directors, and even interfere with the plots of films." See Kim Su-yong, "Fifty Years of Korean Film History," 173.

41 Kim Mi-hyŏn et al., *History of Korean Film Distribution*, 134.

42 Quoted in ibid., 151.

43 Kim So-hŭi and Yi Ki-rim, "Korean Cinema in Retrospect, Shin Sang-ok."

44 See Kim So-yŏng, *Cinema: Blue Flower in the Land of Technology*, 129, for the "genre master" label, and Chŏng Nam-il, *The Film Worlds of Korean Film Directors*, 89, for the "mise-en-scène" designation.

45 This gap between the output of the studio as a whole and the films that Shin directed himself, which grew wider throughout the 1960s, is perhaps not at all a surprising symptom of the processes of industrialization that will be treated in some detail below. It should suffice here to note that, in response to the production quotas and, especially, the import licensing policies outlined above, Shin Films fell into the practice of grinding out "quota quickies" overseen by the second- and third-rate technicians in its employ. For a detailed examination of these operations and an analysis of the personnel problems that plagued Shin Films even in its heyday, see Lee, "The Transnational Asian Studio System," 223–87.

46 The contest was the subject of countless contemporary accounts and has been well documented across Korean film historiography. One index of the alternatively sincere

and absurd seriousness of the competition are the reports of espionage, sabotage, and outright criminal behavior waged between the two studios. Three days before the release of the Shin Films version, for instance, the studio's Yongsan office was pillaged and one of its staff members kidnapped in an apparent and failed attempt to delay the film's opening to beyond the holiday season. See "Trouble with the Two 'Ch'unhyangs?'"

47 It may be worth noting in passing here that the *p'ansori* form itself was the subject of multiple and often contested cultural, political, and social appropriations, from its beginnings as a commercial art form taken up by low-ranking or outcast *yangban* in the mid-nineteenth century to its resignification in the 1970s as both a radical *minjung* cultural practice and a state-sanctioned "intangible cultural asset." See Chungmoo Choi, "The Politics of Gender," which discusses *p'ansori* in the context of another major instance of its cinematization, Im Kwon-taek's 1993 smash *Sopyonje*. See also Paek Mun-im, *Ch'unhyang's Daughters*, for a cultural history of the tale and its adaptations to film.

48 Of course, this figure does not include the substantially greater box office numbers of the regional markets. Conservative estimates applying the standard 1: 4.35 Seoul to regional market ratio put the total figure at 1.65 million tickets nationwide. For this calculation, see, Kim Mi-hyŏn et al., *History of Korean Film Distribution*, 41. Similarly informal, though perhaps more telling, anecdotes describe the movement of overflowing bagfuls of cash into the Shin Films offices.

49 "*Sŏng Ch'unhyang*: Vibrant Color Design."

50 "The Careful Details of Shin Sang-ok's *Sŏng Ch'unhyang*."

51 Given its central place in Korean film historiography, Yi Yŏng-il's gloss over the films is striking. His *Complete History* simply concludes that *Song Ch'unhyang* was "an important test case for industrialization."

52 See Jinsoo An's chapter, "Fallen Women on Trial: Configuration of Popular Justice in Courtroom Drama Films" from his "Popular Reasoning of South Korean Melodrama Films," as well as Paek Mun-im, *Ch'unhyang's Daughters*.

53 Chŏng Chong-hwa, *Korean Film History Through Documents 2*, 47.

54 Kim So-hŭi, "Shin Sang-ok, Fifty Years."

55 For instance, the sprawling scene where Mongryong has an audience with the king is filmed, as were many period films of this vintage, at Ch'angdŏk'gung. See An, "Popular Reasoning of South Korean Melodrama Films," 92.

56 Kim So-hŭi, "Shin Sang-ok, Fifty Years."

57 Another important aspect of the photography was the meticulous attention paid to its color by the cinematographer, Yi Hyŏng-p'yo, a formidable filmmaker in his own right. Interviews with Shin Films producers allude to the tiring rigor with which Yi worked to get the color temperatures exactly right. Other studies have shown the advantage Shin enjoyed by using the more expensive Kodak-Eastman color film stocks and having them processed in the leading Eastern Film Development Labs in Tokyo. See Cho Chun-hyŏng et al., *2008 Korean Film History*, 1:57 and 157; and Chŏng Chong-hwa, "Korean Film Technology History," 244–45.

58 See, for example, Chu Yu-sin, "Feminist Critique."

59 See, for example, Kwak Hyŏn-ja, "War Widows and Western Princesses."

60 See, for example, Kim Ho-yŏng, "Shin Sang-ok's Historical Dramas."

61 Adapted from the nineteenth-century Guy de Maupassant novel (*Une Vie*), the film follows Nam-ju from her idyllic and sheltered childhood to a trying marriage to a philandering husband, to her struggles to rein in the profligacy of her son, and finally to resignation to the bitter promises of "a woman's life." Its psychic blockages and maudlin resolution hearken back to the heightened melodrama of Shin's late 1950s women's films, but the film holds back from the excesses of the notorious *I Still Love You* series (which would dominate box offices with five installments from 1968 to 1971) through the mature pragmatism of its protagonist, played most appropriately by a Ch'oe Un-hui just beginning to harden with age.

62 These were a set of films that were produced, though in somewhat tamer fashion, on the model of the Japanese "sun-tribe" films of the mid- to late 1950s. *Barefoot Youth* especially, in its winning combination of the year's hottest young faces (Sin Sŏng-il and Ŏm Aeng-ran), a soundtrack packed with hit songs (particularly the title track), and a mildly exploitative theme (a young thug sweeps an innocent college student into the pleasures of the city's nightlife), proved to be a lasting and iconic film. Interestingly, these youth films were also at the heart of the period's plagiarizing scandals alluded to in chapter 2. For a meticulous examination of the Japanese youth film, see Raine, "Youth, Body, and Subjectivity."

63 For a comprehensive overview of this body of films, see An, "Figuring Masculinity at Historical Juncture: Manchurian Action Films," chapter 3 of his "Popular Reasoning of South Korean Melodrama Films."

64 For a full exploration of the horror film in South Korean cinema, see Paek Mun-im, "The Korean Horror Film," or the more recent Hŏ Chi-ung, *Memories of Departed Souls*.

65 Kim Ho-yŏng, "Shin Sang-ok's Historical Dramas," 83.

66 An, "Popular Reasoning of South Korean Melodrama Films," 97.

67 Yi Yŏn-ho, "Shin Sang-ok: Who Are You?," 122.

68 Kim So-hŭi, "Shin Sang-ok, Fifty Years."

69 There was originally a fourth episode, but it was, inexplicably, lost. The film is a full-length feature nonetheless.

70 Both Pak Haeng-ch'ŏl, one of Shin's closest associates throughout his career, and Kim Kap-hŭi, who worked as a producer with Shin Films in its last years, recall Shin's as well as their own surprisingly laissez-faire attitude toward the injunctions of the censors. Kim, in particular, suggests that excised scenes from *Wild Dog* and other films were "taped" back into prints regularly to raise the notoriety of some more lackluster films. See Kim's comments in Cho Chun-hyŏng et al. *2008 Korean Film History*, 1:453, and for Pak's comments, 1:498.

71 Cho Hŭi-yŏn, *Park Chung Hee*, 49.

72 Kim Min-nam, *A Revised History of Korean Journalism*, 391.

73 For a detailed account of the often alarmingly large scale of the MPPC's productions as well as its other activities, see Pak Chi-yŏn, "Film Policy," 227–39.

74 Lee, "The Transnational Asian Studio System," 264.

75 Ibid., 267–70.

76 Yi Yŏn-ho, "Shin Sang-ok: Who Are You?," 122.

77 Shin was in fact prosecuted as early as 1966 on a number of charges, including conspiracy to improperly import Hong Kong films such as *Journey to the West* and *SOS Hong Kong*, though, as was widely reported in newspapers, he got off with a fine and was allowed to distribute both films.

78 Yu Chi-na, "Nation-Image Through the Representation of Films," 181.

79 For instance, in his *I Was a Movie*, he writes: "A lot of people seem to think of 'film author Shin Sang-ok' and 'film producer Shin Sang-ok' separately, but those are two sides of me that cannot be split. It seems that there are people who think that the film author was handicapped by the fact that I had to be a producer and manage a studio, but the reality is different. Of course, since the studio was under such pressure to make films I could not take the time to polish some of my films and I regret that. But on the other hand, I don't think that, had I had the time to devote simply to my own work, I'd have a better set of films. On the contrary, because I was a producer I could put my hand to the sort of films that I really wanted to try." Shin Sang-ok, *I Was a Movie*, 12.

80 Perhaps most notable among these was Yun Hyŏng-ju, a singer-songwriter who was immensely popular throughout the 1970s and 1980s.

81 Chŏng Chong-hwa, "1960s and 1970s Korean Film Technology," 265.

82 In fact, Yi is often credited for having directed the film in informal reflection. This is not entirely implausible, given both Yi's well-known technical prowess and Shin's equally known penchant for flexible crediting. Notably, Yi himself maintained that he simply "put his hand" to what was an irreducibly Shin Sang-ok film.

83 For an informative look at Sin Chung-hyŏn's career, as well as an overview of the history of Korean postwar rock, see Pil Ho Kim and Hyunjoon Shin, "The Birth of 'Rok.'"

4. Melodrama and the Scene of Development

1 Kim So-yŏng, "The Lures of Tradition and Modernity," in *Cinema: Blue Flower in the Land of Technology*, 129.

2 Korean film historian Kim Hak-su, in his popular *Offscreen Korean Film History*, writes that Shin's influence in the drafting of the First Motion Picture Law and its first amendment was an open secret among his contemporaries, many of whom, such as fellow director Kim Su-yong, resented him for it. For an excellent overview of the changes in film policy from the 1950s through the 1970s and the fate of Shin's production companies over that period, see Pak A-na, "Research on Shin Sang-ok's Film Production and Genre."

3 Yi Yŏng-il, *Complete History*, 254.

4 Pak A-na's "Research on Shin Sang-ok's Film Production and Genre" is carefully researched and valuable for its attempts to balance contextual and textual materials. Nevertheless, it firmly separates the history of Shin's film studios (which Pak argues were faithful children of the Park era's push for enterprization [*kiŏp'hwa*])

and readings of Shin's most-favored genre forms (the family melodramas and historical epics where, Pak finds, the ideological preoccupations of the Park regime are loyally reproduced). And Chu Ch'ang-gyu's erudite essay, "The (Re)construction of Nation and Gender in the Postcolonial Nation-State," invokes a broad range of postcolonial theories to argue that the dilemmas and contradictions of postwar nation building—including the pressing need to bury the colonial past and to create "new men"—are directly reflected in *Rice*. Through a straightforward reading (which he calls a "case study") of *Rice's* narrative, Chu concludes that the film clearly lays bare the "elite, bourgeois nationalist norms" internalized by Shin and the audiences with whom the film was such a success.

5 See the collection of essays in Kim So-yŏn et al., *An Age of Allures and Chaos*, for their diverse and important engagements with the film cultures of the period. Nancy Abelmann and Kathleen McHugh's edited volume, *South Korean Golden Age Melodrama*, remains the seminal collection of English-language scholarship.

6 The original novel, published serially in 1936 and as a monograph in 1946, quickly became an icon of colonial period literature. I treat its canonization in more detail below. I would like to note here though that its author, Sim Hun, identified almost exclusively with this narrative, was keenly interested in film and not only wrote a number of scenarios but also acted in a handful of films.

7 Administrative changes that took place sometime in the past decade positioned Muju in north Cholla province.

8 See Chŏng Chong-hwa, *Korean Film History*, for listings of box-office receipts as far back as the late 1930s.

9 The Grand Bells were inaugurated in 1961 under the auspices of the First Motion Picture Law and widely recognized as a state-controlled system of rewards for compliant filmmaking.

10 "*Evergreen* Goes to Cannes," *Cine21* (March 2003).

11 Some clarification is required here. As we saw in chapters 1 and 2, a fuller expression of mass culture in the colonial period was limited by the political and economic imbalances of public culture under Japanese authority. Cinema in South Korea arose in the 1960s as the most significant modern mass cultural formation, screening emergent subjects in the midst of astounding change and complexity. Concepts of national time and space and modern social and economic relations had already been established by the end of colonial rule. Cities had grown as sites of colonial extraction but had also become spheres of increased cultural exchange and consumption. And mass communications technologies had facilitated the broad circulation of not only imperial discourse but also the language, image, and idea of modern Korea. Modern culture, however, had remained dominantly the product of the metropole and of the colonial elite, and while this hegemony did not preclude the advent of national consciousness, it did inhibit the development of mass culture. The disassembly of formal colonial rule that began in 1945, almost wholly subsumed within the global conflict between neoliberal capitalism and authoritarian communism, engendered, especially in the South, little qualitative institutional or social change.

While popular entertainment media, in particular radio and film, thrived in wartime amid the proliferating import of American cultural products, the material ravages and extreme ideological polarization of the war yielded only a narrowly proscribed and radically polemicized cultural horizon. It was not until the latter half of the 1950s, with the burgeoning though radically uneven affluence attendant on South Korea's decisive inclusion into the global capitalist economy, that mass culture would fully materialize. Movie theaters, dance halls, and cafés became, in the absence of a viable civil sphere and before the domesticization of radio and television technologies, vital public spaces for the production and consumption of postcolonial/postwar modernity. The cinema, firmly ensconced in the life of expanding urban centers, emerged by the early 1960s at the forefront of the mass cultural formations that reconfigure the elite–folk or high–low dyad hitherto constitutive of the cultural field. Filmmaking is marked as a modern mass art form in its inherent links to industrialized modes of production and consumption as well as by its accessibility to a radically expanded spectrum of South Korea's population. Screening new social spaces, practices, and subjectivities, films address the social classes that emerge within the ideological tumult of national reconstruction and development.

12 For a general overview of the period's social and intellectual conflicts, see Kim Tong-ch'un and Kim T'ae-sun, *Social Movements of the 1960s*, and Choi Chungmoo, "The Minjung Culture Movement."

13 Kang Man-gil and Yi Yŏng-hŭi, *Korean Nationalist Movements*, 39.

14 See, for instance, the essay, Ham Sŏk-hŏn, "How Shall We See 5.16?"

15 These are Pak Chŏng-hŭi, *Our Nation's Forward Path* and *The State, the Revolution, and I*, both of which were quickly translated into English and other languages and distributed widely.

16 Williams, "Melodrama Revised," 59.

17 Ibid., 82.

18 See Abelmann, *The Melodrama of Mobility*, for a compelling discussion of the melodramatic modality of Korean women's accounts of their social status and mobility.

19 Though it can easily be argued, as indeed it has been by Chu Ch'ang-gyu, that Yong himself, accused of being a communist but rising to become a military (trained) hero, is a stand-in for Park Chung Hee. Interestingly, the coy anonymity was also the standard practice of North Korean films from after the war to approximately the late 1980s—that is, despite explicit references to the revolution and to a new national leadership, Kim Il Sung was rarely named, much less represented, in any of the films.

20 Yim Chi-hyŏn, "The Fascism within Us."

21 Cho Hŭi-yŏn, "Coercion and Control," 140.

22 Ibid., 149.

23 Yim Chi-hyŏn, "'Mass Dictatorship' and 'Post-Fascism,'" 311.

24 Ibid., 324.

25 Clearly, a number of highly complicit films were produced for the commercial market throughout the 1950s to the early 1960s, including anticommunist pictures like Han Hyŏng-mo's *Hand of Fate* (1956). Nevertheless, mandated or directly ordered

anticommunist films (including the quota-quickies that were mostly anticommunist) did not come into being until the mid- to late 1960s, when successive motion
picture laws became more stringent under the pressures of an increasingly repressive Park administration (culminating of course in the "*Yusin*" constitution). My
point here is that no commercial film company in the early 1960s, even the early
adopting and sometimes obsequious Shin Films, produced films that could be said
to be outright propaganda.

26 Kim Tong-ch'un, *Division and Korean Society*.

27 Both of these scenes have their own distinct and striking features. The letter that
Ok-pun reads is, of course, the only form of communication between the village
woman and her daughter who has left to work in a city. Literacy then is one among
the many modern nationalizing apparatuses of the colonial period. The other scene
is staged as a night class (which has its own political connotations) and is attended
mostly by women, an indicator of gendered effects of enlightenment.

28 Pyŏn Chae-ran, "The Constitution of Modern Female Identity through Labor."

29 The gender roles in *Evergreen*, notwithstanding some of Pyŏn's arguments, are quite
complex. While Ch'ae Yŏng-sin is ultimately subordinate to Pak Tong-hyŏk (who
as a leader of the rural enlightenment movement inspires both love and respect), she
is an unusually strong, self-motivated and resourceful character. Pak, meanwhile,
is pictured at times in the reverse gender role, sprucing up the domestic space for
Ch'ae's visit and acting as cheerleader at the school's opening. Further, *Evergreen*, as
many of Shin's films, is full of active female figures, such as the child Ok-pun who
herself instrumentalizes literacy and the women who attend Ch'ae's night classes.
Finally, the education and professionalization of women is made an explicit point in
the film, linked to the promises of modernization and civilization. Nevertheless,
within the melodramatic codes of the diegesis, Ch'ae is projected as a the archetypal
"suffering woman."

30 Among English-language publications, Kim U-Chang's essay "The Situation of
Korean Writers under Colonial Rule" remains one of the more poignant overviews of
the period's literary scene.

31 Social pretension and unproductive leisure were also subject to virulent attack. Perhaps one of the more striking passages in *The State, the Revolution, and I* is the quasi-
poetic plea for realism and sacrifice that closes the book: "You, a young girl sitting in
the second class compartment, your white hands holding a book of French poetry.
Your white hands I abhor./We must work. One cannot survive with clean hands.
Clean hands have been responsible for our present misery. Smooth hands are our
enemy" (Pak Chŏng-hŭi, *The State, the Revolution, and I*, 226).

32 There is, however, a precedent for the framing of a different sort of assembly: the
massified imperial troops and their admirers on the home front, a staple image of
the late colonial militarist films.

33 For a detailed history of North Korean cinema, see Sŏ Chŏng-nam, *An Investigation
of North Korean Cinema*; for a more concise analysis of thematic trends, see Kyung
Hyun Kim, "The Fractured Cinema of North Korea."

34 For a succinct summary of Soviet socialist realist codes and films, see Thompson and Bordwell, *Film History: An Introduction*.

35 See the introduction to Berry, *Postsocialist Cinema in Post-Mao China*.

5. "It's All Fake"

1 While many of the films were screened at film festivals and special events in parts of the old communist bloc, only a handful were screened anywhere after 1986. Since Shin and much of his work was disavowed in the North upon his departure, official distribution of prints became impossible. A number were shown at a 1988 film festival in Paris, apparently with prints that Shin managed to smuggle out of the country. *Salt* and *Record of an Escape* were slated for screening for a retrospective of Shin's films at the 2001 Pusan International Film Festival, but they were ultimately barred via a citation of the National Security Law. A commercial VHS copy of *Pulgasari* was produced in 2001. Virtually all other reproductions and screenings, including those at the pathbreaking 2008 North and South Korean Film Festival held at the University of California, San Diego, have relied on bootleg sources. Access to the films for the purposes of the present research was gained primarily through the Koryo General Trade Company in Gardena, California, a small firm dedicated to the dissemination of North Korean materials, though many of the films are now available for viewing at the Research Institute at the Ministry of Unification in Seoul, South Korea.

2 This is a broad characterization, of course, but the basic contours of a culturalist mode of analysis are traceable in a number of works, especially in English-language research. One striking example is in Bruce Cumings's recent revision to North Korean history, which characterizes the postwar regime as "the closest thing the modern world has to a neo-Confucian monarchy." See Cumings, *North Korea*, 43.

3 It may also be argued that, conversely, Shin's reputation as an apolitical filmmaker was formed within this very discourse of the politics of film.

4 While Adorno and Horkheimer wrote independently about mass culture throughout the 1920s and 1930s, the most coherent formulation of the concept of the culture industry can be found in their 1947 *Dialectic of Enlightenment*. I also draw here on some of Adorno's later essays on the subject, including "The Culture Industry Reconsidered" and "The Schema of Mass Culture."

5 Huyssen, *After the Great Divide*, 21.

6 Macdonald, "A Theory of Mass Culture," 60.

7 A great range of authors, including, of course, Adorno himself, have written with varying degrees of affirmation and critique of these tendencies in Adorno's cultural theory. One of the most recent and relevant engagements is Miriam Hansen's foregrounding of the aesthetic in Adorno's writing on film as a way of thinking around the technological determinism that seems to lie at its core. See Hansen, "The Question of Film Aesthetics."

8 I think this fairly characterizes Jameson's general approach. Among its most compelling articulations is his examination of *Jaws*, *The Godfather*, and other instances of American mass culture in "Reification and Utopia in Mass Culture."

9　In the years leading up to the publication of the present book, a veritable flood of books, films, and online material about North Korea has appeared in English-language media, the majority of which are nonacademic and aimed at the commercial market. These mark something of a departure from postwar and early post–Cold War-era writing and representation, clustered as that earlier coverage was around problems of Realpolitik and historical revision. With print titles ranging from a glossy collection of propaganda posters (*North Korean Posters: The David Heather Collection*) to prison memoirs (*The Aquariums of Pyongyang: Ten Years in the North Korean Gulag*), to films on mass games performers (*A State of Mind*), to farcical Web sites (*Kim Jong-Il Looking at Things*), the thematic range of attention has broadened dramatically. At the same, time the majority of these can be ordered into two rhetorical categories: urgent and earnest remonstration (of the gulag system, of the plight of refugees, etc.) on the one hand, and ironic and often comic observation (of propaganda and political spectacle, of antiquated public systems, of seeming self-delusion, etc.) on the other. Both of these, further, are conjoined by a common rhetorical structure, which is also a common logic: that North Korea is exceptional in its monstrosity or absurdity, and that its exposure within the given book, film, or imagery is unprecedented, exceptional, and authoritative. Indeed, and notwithstanding the simple pressures of marketing, it is striking how only the rare work on North Korea is not presented as "remarkable," "untold," or "seminal." But what is perhaps more striking is that this logic and rhetoric of exception is not simply one of representation, but rather of narrativization—that is, that the radical difference of North Korea is rendered precisely through a failure to reflect either on the historical conditions of its removal from "normal" interstate relations or on the similarly absurd injustices of "free" and "normal" nations that, in actuality, give the lie to the North's exception.

10　This mode of writing and reportage is ubiquitous and reached an apex in the early years of George W. Bush's administration. We only need to think of the rash of articles that accompanied the 2002 "axis of evil" speech, such as the *Economist* editorial titled "Is Kim Jong-il Insane?" and the *New Republic* cover that proclaimed him "The Most Dangerous Man in the World," which made repeated reference to Kim's "penchant for liquor, women, and film." Similar rhetoric and imagery surged again, though with amplified comic flair, following Kim's death in December amid reflection on his legacy and speculation about the succession to power of his son, Kim Chŏng-ŭn.

11　More careful studies include Selig Harrison's *Korean Endgame* and Michael O'Hanlon and Mike Mizoguchi's *Crisis on the Korean Peninsula*. On the opposite end of the spectrum we can find a host of books by self-proclaimed experts such as Michael Breen's *Kim Jong-il: North Korea's Dear Leader*, Helen-Louise Hunter's *Kim Il-song's North Korea*, or William C. Triplett's *Rogue State*.

12　The volume of writing on North Korea increased rapidly with the greater access to North Korean films and materials following the sudden thawing of the Kim Dae Jung presidency in the early 2000s. See Min Pyŏng-uk, ed., *A Historical Understanding of North Korean Cinema* and Chŏng Chae-hyŏng, ed., *Five Things You Wanted to Know about North Korean Film* for overviews of the historical development of North Korean film. Sŏ Chŏng-nam, *So Chŏng-nam's Look at North Korean Film* and Yi Myŏng-ja, *Modernity and North Korean Film* both offer analyses of filmmaking from the late 1980s onward. Interestingly, very little mention is made of Shin Sang-ok or the mid-1980s period in any of these studies.

13 Kim Jong Il, *Let Us Create More Revolutionary Films*, 1.

14 Park Myung-jin, "Motion Pictures in North Korea," 96–97.

15 This position is shared across the spectrum of research but is given most succinct and cogent expression in Chŏng T'ae-su, "Stalinism and the Formation of North Korean Cinema."

16 For a helpful summary of these developments, see Yi Myŏng-ja, *History of North Korean Film*, 23.

17 Prominent among these "southern faction" KAPF member were filmmakers such as O Yŏng-jin, who wrote the script for the popular 1941 *Maeng's Happy Day* (*Maengjinsa taek kyŏngsa*) and assumed leadership of the North's newly formed film division, and Kang Hong-sik, who starred in a number of colonial period films and who would direct *My Hometown* (*Nae kohyang*, 1949), the North's first feature. Im Hwa, one of the most prolific and influential left-wing intellectuals of the 1930s and 1940s, relocated to the North in 1947 and was instrumental in establishing a range of film-related initiatives there.

18 Not surprisingly, all of the purged southern faction figures are wiped from history, while those such as Mun Ye-bong, who also hailed from the South but continued to work in film through the rest of her life, remain, though in diminished form. See Yi Myŏng-ja, *History of North Korean Film*, 34.

19 Song Nak-wŏn, "The Formation of North Korean Cinema," 112.

20 *On the Art of the Cinema* was first published in 1973 and has been the sine qua non of film theory and criticism since. As with the rest of the massive volume of writing attributed to Kim Jong Il (and the even greater volume attributed to Kim Il Sung), the actual authorship is certainly in question but is largely irrelevant. These were clearly authorized texts and, as such, represent the official position. Nevertheless, it is tempting to see *On the Art of the Cinema* as Kim Jong Il's own work, given that he headed the Ministry of Information and Propaganda and considering his reputed cinephilia. The text was translated into English and published in 2001, and all references here are made to that edition.

21 Kim Jong Il, *On the Art of the Cinema*, 134.

22 Ibid., 132.

23 I should note here that I follow Andreas Huyssen in chiding Adorno for his curious affirmation of, "if only negatively, the power of language and words to represent reality." Huyssen, *After the Great Divide*, 23. I take this to mean that, for Huyssen, the political effect of the culture industry's advertising imperative is troubled by the unfaithfulness of duplication, and further want to suggest that, as in many other beleaguered and paranoid regimes, the North Korean state's incessant exhortation and management of the arts of the culture industry stem precisely from a recognition of this basic mimetic instability.

24 Kim So-hŭi and Yi Ki-rim, "Korean Cinema in Retrospect, Shin Sang-ok."

25 While this claim is often made in informal conversation, the only published mention of it found for the purposes of the present research is in John Gorenfeld's entertaining and surprisingly informative article, "The Producer From Hell."

26 Yi Yŏn-ho, "Shin Sang-ok: Who Are You?," 126.

27 Shin Sang-ok and Ch'oe Ŭn-hŭi, *We Haven't Escaped Yet*, 25.

28 See the full list on Korean Film Council, *Fifty Must-See North Korean Films*, 4.

29 "Shin Sang-ok Films We Saw in the North."

30 While allusions to and brief synopses of this film are scattered throughout Shin's memoirs and in North Korean cinema catalogs, *Breakwater* is the one film that was not available for the present study. Shin left North Korea before the postproduction process was completed, and it is not clear whether it, like other projects such as *Hong Kil-dong*, was taken up subsequently.

31 There seems to be a general consensus that the early "new tendency" writers such as Ch'oe Sŏ-hae staked out a political position that was closer to anarchism or vulgar communism than to theoretically informed Marxism. See Yi Chae-sŏn, *The Korean Novel*, and, recently in English, Kim Yoon-shik, "KAPF Literature in Modern Korean Literary History." It should also be noted here that while Kang Kyŏng-ae was not formally connected to KAPF or to the earlier "new tendency" school, she is broadly considered a sort of fellow traveller of the socialist writers of the late 1920s and early 1930s.

32 Yi Yŏn-ho, "Shin Sang-ok: Who Are You?," 125.

33 Though I might note that, in some rare instances, perhaps most strikingly in his 1963 *Romance Gray* (*Romaensŭ kŭrei*), Shin deployed zoom to incipiently modernist effect. The pseudodocumentary reportage of the film's central affair is lent self-consciously comic and ironic effect by the use of extreme zoom shots to isolate faces and objects. This is markedly different from use of the zoom lens in the majority of Shin's work, which serves, as it did for so many low-budget films throughout the 1960s and 1970s, especially in Hong Kong, to collapse space and evoke movement without the logistic and economic burden of actual camera movement.

34 For an illuminating elaboration of this distinction, see Suleiman, *Authoritarian Fictions*.

35 See "Gender and Cinematic Adaptations of *Ch'unhyangjŏn*" in Hyangjin Lee, *Contemporary Korean Cinema*, 67–101; and Wang Sun-nyŏ, "A Comparison of North and South Korean Ch'unhyangjŏn."

36 The literal translation of Shin's film, *Sarang sarang nae sarang* would be "Love, Love, My Love," but it is rendered here as it was in the catalog for the 2001 Pusan retrospective, not only because that translation is more wieldy but also because it captures the expressiveness of the original film and song title.

37 Lee, *Contemporary Korean Cinema*, 100.

38 Wang Sun-nyŏ, "A Comparison of North and South Korean," 167.

39 Ibid., 88.

40 The 1905 treaty, ratified under the coercion of an occupying force, granted Japanese authority over Korean foreign affairs and trade, officially signaling Korea's

"protectorate" status. While it was signed by five Korean ministers, the film suggests that the treaty also had Kojong's seal.

41 Shin Sang-ok and Ch'oe Ŭn-hŭi, *We Haven't Escaped Yet*, 331. Kim seems here to have been keenly interested in instigating the jealousy of South Korean observers.

42 See the entertaining interview with Satsuma in Schönherr, "Godzilla Goes to North Korea."

43 Another more complex but more easily accommodated approach would be to see the monster as a personification of capitalism itself (i.e., that which breaks the back of feudal hegemony and which must itself be broken for true freedom).

Conclusion

1 The three *3 Ninjas* films to which Shin put his hand—*3 Ninjas Kick Back* (1994), *3 Ninjas Knuckle Up* (1995), *3 Ninjas: High Noon at Mega Mountain* (1998)—were in fact preceded by the original *3 Ninjas* (1992), a Japan–United States coproduction.

2 See the sociologist Kim Hong-jung's poignant analysis of what he calls the "post-authenticity regime," an ethos of animalistic economic survival that in the 1990s displaced the earnest political identities of the 1970s and 1980s, in Kim Hong-jung, *Sociology of the Mind*. For Badiou's comments on the "real," see Badiou, *The Century*, 21.

3 For the best treatments of Korean new wave cinema in English and Korean, respectively, see Kim Kyung Hyun, *The Remasculinization of Korean Cinema*, and Kim So-yŏn, *The Death of the Real*.

4 Jameson, "Notes on Globalization as a Philosophical Issue," 60.

5 "Mayumi."

6 "Considering the Work's Crudity and Ill-formed Politics, MBC Cancels Its Contract to Air Mayumi."

7 Yi Yŏn-ho, "Shin Sang-ok: Who Are You?," 122.

8 "KAL Surviving Family Association Sues Shin Sang-ok and Others Involved with Mayumi."

9 Following tremendous pressure from the Motion Picture Association of America, the ROK government granted foreign direct distribution in 1985, putting an end to nearly three decades of the shifting but centrally important system of film import licensing.

10 "Interview: Back in the Spotlight with Blockbuster Mayumi."

11 Cho Chun-hyŏng et al., *2008 Korean Film History*, 2:310.

SHIN SANG-OK FILMOGRAPHY

Evil Night (*Akya*), Visual Arts Association, 1952.

Korea (*Koria*), Visual Arts Association, 1954.

Dream (*Kkum*), Sŏrabŏl Film Corporation, 1955.

The Young Ones (*Chŏlmŭn kŭdŭl*), Seoul Film Company, 1955.

Shadowless Pagoda (*Muyŏng tap*), Seoul Film Company/Shin Sang-ok Productions, 1957.

Hellflower (*Chiok'hwa*), Seoul Film Company/Shin Sang-ok Productions, 1958.

Confessions of a College Girl (*Ŏnŭ yŏdaesaeng ŭi kobaek*), Seoul Film Company/ Shin Sang-ok Productions, 1958.

It's Not Her Sin (*Kŭ yŏja ŭi choe'ga anida*), Seoul Film Company, 1959.

Ch'unhŭi, Hyŏndae Film Company, 1959.

Tongsimch'o, Korea Film Distribution Company, 1959.

Sisters' Garden (*Chamae ŭi hwawŏn*), Shin Sang-ok Productions, 1959.

The Independence Association and the Young Syngman Rhee (*Tongnip hyŏphoe wa ch'ŏngnyŏn Yi Sŭng-man*), Korea Entertainment Corporation, 1959.

Romance Papa (*Romaensŭ ppappa*), Shin Films, 1960.

**A History of Love* (*Sarang ŭi yŏksa*), dir. Yi Kang-ch'ŏn, Shin Sang-ok Productions, 1960.

Until the End of This Life (*I saengmyŏng tahadarok*), Shin Films, 1960.

**The Man Who Returned* (*To'raon sanai*), dir. Kim Su-yong, Shin Films, 1960.

Madame Whitesnake (*Paeksa puin*), Shin Films, 1960.

Sŏng Ch'unhyang, Shin Films, 1961.

**Iljimae the Chivalrous Bandit* (*Ŭijŏk Ilchimae*), dir. Chang Il-ho, Shin Sang-ok Productions, 1961.

**Ku Pong-sŏ's He Strikes It Rich* (*Ku Pong-sŏ ŭi pyŏrak puja*), dir. Kim Su-yong, Shin Films, 1961.

The Houseguest and My Mother (*Sarangbang sonnim kwa ŏmŏni*), Shin Sang-ok
   Productions, 1961.

Evergreen (*Sangnoksu*), Shin Films, 1961.

**Under the Seoul Sky* (*Sŏul ŭi chibung mit*), dir. Yi Hyŏng-p'yo, Shin Films, 1961.

Prince Yŏnsan (*Yŏnsan'gun*), Shin Films, 1961.

Yŏnsan the Tyrant (*P'okgun Yŏnsan*), Shin Films, 1962.

Chastity Gate (*Yŏllyŏmun*), Shin Films, 1962.

**Somewhere in this World* (*I sesang ŏdin'ga e*), dir. Chŏn Ŭng-ju, Shin Films,
   1962.

**Sword of Vengeance* (*Wŏnhan ŭi ilwŏldo*), dir. Ch'oe Kyŏng-ok, Shin Films, 1962.

**Teacher Waryong's Trip to the Capital* (*Waryong sŏnsaeng sanggyŏnggi*), dir. Kim
   Yong-dŏk, Shin Films, 1962.

**Beautiful Shroud* (*Arŭmdaun su'ŭi*), dir. Yi Hyŏng-p'yo, Shin Films, 1962.

**The Mountain Bride* (*San saeksi*), dir. Pak Sang-ho, Shin Films, 1962.

Torchlight (*Hwaetbul*), Shin Films, 1963.

Ch'ŏljong and Poknyŏ (*Ch'ŏljong kwa Poknyŏ*), Shin Films, 1963.

A Reluctant Prince (*Kanghwa toryŏng*), Shin Films, 1963.

Romance Gray (*Romaensŭ kŭrei*), Shin Films, 1963.

Rice (*Ssal*), Shin Films, 1963.

Red Muffler (*Ppalgan mahura*), Shin Films, 1964.

**Princess Talgi/The Last Woman of Shang* (*Talgi*), dir. Ch'oe In-hyŏn and Griffin
   Yueh Feng, Shin Films/Shaw Brothers (HK), 1964.

Samnyong the Mute (*Pŏngŏri Samnyong*), Shin Films, 1964.

**Queen Min and the Sino-Japanese War* (*Chung-il chŏnjaeng kwa Minbi*), dir. Yim
   Wŏn-sik and Na Pong-han, Shin Films, 1965.

**Sorrow Even in Heaven* (*Chŏ hanŭl edo sŭlp'ŭmi*), dir. Kim Su-yong, Shin Films,
   1965.

**Child Bride* (*Min myŏnŭri*), dir. Ch'oe Ŭn-hŭi, Shin Films, 1965.

**SOS Hong Kong/International Secret Agent*, dir. Ch'oe Kyŏng-ok, Shin Films/Lan
   Kwong Film Company (HK), 1966.

**Journey to the West* (*Sŏyugi*), dir. Yim Wŏn-sik, Shin Films, 1966.

The Remembered Shadow of the Yi Dynasty (*Yijo chanyong*), Shin Films, 1966.

**The Goddess of Mercy/The Great Tyrant* (*Taepokgun*), dir. Yim Wŏn-sik and Ho
   Meng-hua, Shin Films/Shaw Brothers, 1966.

Mountain (*San*), Shin Films, 1967.

Mounted Bandits (*Majŏk*), Anyang Films, 1967.

Dream (*Kkum*), Anyang Films, 1967.

Golden Bat (*Hwanggŭm pakjwi*), animated, Eastern Television, 1968.

Female Bandit (*Yŏmajŏk*), Shin Films, 1968.

The Wanderer (*Musukja*), Shin Films, 1968.

Taewŏn'gun, Shin Films, 1968.

A Woman's Life (*Yŏja ŭi ilsaeng*), Shin Films, 1968.

The Eunuch (*Naesi*), Shin Films, 1968.

Thousand Years Fox (*Ch'ŏnnyŏnho*), Shin Films/Shaw Brothers (HK), 1969.

Day Dream (*Chang han mong*), Shin Films, 1969.

Corporal Kim Il-byŏng (*Yukgun Kim Il-byŏng*), Shin Films, 1969.

When Women Rule (*Yŏsŏng sangwi sidae*), Shin Films, 1969.

Dead Woman (*Sa'nyŏ*), Shin Films, 1969.

The Eunuch Sequel (*Sok Naesi*), Shin Films, 1969.

Cruel Stories of Yi Dynasty Women (*Yijo yŏin chanhoksa*), Shin Films, 1969.

Yi Dynasty Ghost Tale (*Yijo koedam*), Shin-a Films, 1970.

Evening Bell (*Manjong*), Shin Films, 1970.

Pyongyang Strike Squad (*Pyongyang pokgyŏkdae*), Anyang Film Corporation, 1971.

War and Man (*Chŏnjaeng kwa in'gan*), Anyang Films, 1971.

Lover Thieves (*Yŏnae tojŏk*), co-dir. Ŏm Jun, Anyang Films, 1971.

**Seven Righteous Fighters/Six Assassins* (*Ch'il'in ŭi hyŏpgaek*), dir. Chŏn Ch'ang-hwa, Anyang Film Company/Shaw Brothers (HK), 1971.

Simch'ŏng the Filial Daughter (*Hyo'nyŏ Simch'ŏng*), Anyang Film Company, 1972.

**Ironman/Five Fingers of Death/King Boxer* (*Ch'ŏl'in*), dir. Chŏn Ch'ang-hwa, Anyang Film Company/Shaw Brothers (HK), 1972.

Lady of the Court (*Kungnyŏ*), Anyang Films, 1972.

**When Taekwondo Strikes* (*Hŭkgwŏn*), dir. Huang Feng, Anyang Film Corporation/Golden Harvest (HK), 1973.

Farewell (*I'byŏl*), Anyang Film Corporation, 1973.

Three Days' Reign (*Samil ch'ŏnha*), Anyang Films, 1973.

**The Half-Soul Woman/The Ghost Lovers* (*Panhonnyŏ*), Shin Productions/Shaw Brothers (HK), 1973.

The Han River (*Han'gang*), Shin Productions, 1974.

Boy, 13 (*13-se sonyŏn*), Shin Productions, 1974.

Ch'un-hŭi '75, Shin Productions, 1975.

Wild Dog and Rose (*Changmi wa tŭlgae*), Hapdong Film Corporation, 1975.

I Love Mama (*Ai rŏbŭ mama*), Shin Productions, 1975.

Female Prisoner 407 (*Yŏsu 407-ho*), Hapdong Film Corporation, 1976.

Female Prisoner 407, the Sequel (*Sok Yŏsu 407-ho*), Hapdong Film Corporation, 1976.

The Secret Emissary (*Toraoji anŭn milsa*), Shin Films Motion Picture Studio (DPRK), 1984.

Oh My Love (*Sarang sarang nae sarang*), Shin Films Motion Picture Studio (DRPK), 1984.

Record of an Escape (*T'alch'ulgi*), Shin Films Motion Picture Studio (DPRK), 1984.

**A Road* (*Kil*), Shin Films Motion Picture Studio (DPRK), 1984.

**Until We Meet Again* (*Hae'ŏjyŏ ŏnje kkaji*), Shin Films Motion Picture Studio (DPRK), 1984.

**A Million Li along the Rails* (*Ch'ŏl kil ttara ch'ŏnman li*), Shin Films Motion Picture Studio (DPRK), 1984.

**Run Chosŏn Run* (*Tallyŏra Chosŏna*), Shin Films Motion Picture Studio (DPRK), 1985.

Salt (*Sogŭm*), Shin Films Motion Picture Studio (DPRK), 1985.

Simch'ŏngjŏn, Shin Films Motion Picture Studio (DPRK), 1985.

Breakwater (*Pangp'aje*), Shin Films Motion Picture Studio (DPRK), 1985.

**Red Wings* (*Pulgŭn nalgae*), Shin Films Motion Picture Studio (DPRK), 1985.

Pulgasari, Shin Films Motion Picture Studio (DPRK), 1985.

**Hong Kil-dong*, co-dir. Kim Kil-in, Shin Films Motion Picture Studio (DPRK)/ Chosŏn Art Films Studio (DPRK), 1986.

**Im Kkŏk-jŏng*, Shin Films Motion Picture Studio (DPRK)/Chosŏn Art Films Studio (DPRK), 1987.

Mayumi, Gil Film Company, 1990.

Disappearance (*Chŭngbal*), Hapdong Film Corporation, 1994.

**3 Ninjas Kick Back*, dir. Charles T. Kanganis, Sheen Productions/Ben-Ami/ Leeds Productions/Three Ninjas Japan Inc., 1994.

3 Ninjas Knuckle Up, Sheen Productions/TriStar Pictures, 1995.

**3 Ninjas: High Noon at Mega Mountain*, dir. Sean McNamara, Sheen Productions/Leeds/Ben-Ami Productions/Tristar Pictures, 1998.

Galgameth, dir. Sean McNamara, Sheen Productions, 1997.

Winter Story (*Kyŏul iyagi*), Shin Productions, 2005.

*Denotes films referenced in the book, or otherwise notable, produced under the auspices of various Shin Sang-ok enterprises but not directed by Shin himself.

Abelmann, Nancy. *The Melodrama of Mobility: Women, Talk, and Class in Contemporary Korea*. Honolulu: University of Hawaii Press, 2003.

Adorno, Theodor. *The Culture Industry: Selected Essays on Mass Culture*. New York: Routledge, 2001.

———. "Letter to Walter Benjamin, 18 March 1936." In *Aesthetics and Politics*, 63–65. London: Verso, 2007.

———, and Max Horkheimer. *Dialectic of Enlightenment*. New York: Continuum, 1987.

Altman, Rick. "A Semantic/Syntactic Approach to Film Genre." *Cinema Journal* 23, no. 3 (Spring 1984): 6–18.

An, Jinsoo. "Popular Reasoning of South Korean Melodrama Films (1953–1972)." PhD diss., University of California, Los Angeles, 2005.

Andrew, Dudley. *Concepts in Film Theory*. New York: Oxford University Press, 1984.

Badiou, Alain. *The Century*. New York: Polity Press, 2007.

Balio, Tino. "A Mature Oligopoly: 1930–1948." In *The American Film Industry*, edited by Tino Balio, 130–59. Madison: University of Wisconsin Press, 1985.

Barthes, Roland. *Camera Lucida: Reflections on Photography*. Translated by Richard Howard. New York: Hill and Wang, 1981.

———. *The Fashion System*. Translated by Matthew Ward and Richard Howard. New York: Hill and Wang, 1983.

Bazin, André. "De Sica: Metteur en Scène." In *What Is Cinema?* Vol. 2. Translated by Hugh Gray, 61–78. Berkeley: University of California Press, 1972.

Berry, Chris. *Postsocialist Cinema in Post-Mao China: The Cultural Revolution after the Cultural Revolution*. New York: Routledge, 2004.

Breen, Michael. *Kim Jong-il: North Korea's Dear Leader*. Hoboken, N.J.: Wiley, 2004.

Buscombe, Edward. "The Idea of Genre." *Screen* 11, no. 2 (March–April 1970): 33–45.

"The Careful Details of Shin Sang-ok's *Sŏng Ch'unhyang*." *Han'guk Ilbo*, January 29, 1961.

Cho Chun-hyŏng, Kim Sŭng-gyŏng, Sin Sŏng-a, and Kwŏn Yong-suk. *2008 Korean Film History Oral History Records Series, Shin Films (2008-nyŏn Han'guk yŏnghwasa kusul ch'aerok sirijŭ Chujesa Sin p'illŭm)*. 2 vols. Seoul: Korean Film Archive, 2008.

Cho Hŭi-yŏn. "Coercion and Control in the Park Chung Hee Period: Rethinking the Relationships between Control, Tradition, Coercion, and Consensus" ("Pak Chŏng-hŭi sidae ŭi kangap kwa tongŭi: chibae, chŏnt'ong, kangap kwa tongŭi ŭi kwangye rŭl tasi saenggak handa"). *Historical Criticism* (*Yŏksa pip'yŏng*), no. 67 (Summer 2001): 135–90.

——. *Park Chung Hee and the Age of Developmentalist Dictatorship: From 5.16 to 10.25* (*Pak Chŏng-hŭi wa kaebal tokjae sidae: 5.16 esŏ 10.25 kkaji*). Seoul: Yŏksa Pip'yŏngsa, 2007.

Ch'oe Tŏk-gyo. *One Hundred Years of Korean Magazines* (*Han'guk chapji paeknyŏn*). Seoul: Hyŏnamsa, 2004.

Choi, Chungmoo. "The Minjung Culture Movement and Popular Culture." In *South Korea's Minjung Movement*, edited by Kenneth Wells, 105–18. Honolulu: University of Hawaii Press, 1995.

——. "The Politics of Gender, Aestheticism, and Cultural Nationalism in *Sopyonje* and *The Genealogy*." In *Im Kwon-taek: The Making of a Korean National Cinema*, edited by David E. James and Kyung Hyun Kim, 107–33. Detroit, Mich.: Wayne State University Press, 2002.

Ch'ŏn Chŏng-hwan. "Enlightenment Literature and the Modernization of 'Entertainment'" ("Kyemongjuŭi munhak kwa 'chaemi' ŭi kundaehwa"). *Historical Criticism* (*Yŏksa pip'yŏng*), no. 67 (2004): 343–64.

Chŏng Chae-hyŏng, ed. *Five Things You Wanted to Know about North Korean Film* (*Pukhan yŏnghwa e taehae algo sipŭn tasŏt kaji*). Kyŏnggi-do, South Korea: Chimmundang, 2004.

Chŏng Chong-hwa. *Korean Film History Through Documents 2: 1955–1997* (*Charyo ro pon Han'guk yŏnghwasa 2: 1955–1997*). Seoul: Yŏlhwadang, 1997.

——. "1960s and 1970s Korean Film Technology History" ("1960, 1970 nyŏndae Han'guk yŏnghwa kisulsa"). In *Korean Film History Studies, 1960–1979* (*Han'guk yŏnghwasa kongbu, 1960–1979*), edited by Yi Hyo-in, 244–45. Seoul: Korean Film Archive, 2004.

Chŏng Nam-il. *The Film Worlds of Korean Film Directors* (*Han'guk yŏnghwa kamdok ŭi chakp'um segye*). Seoul: Inmul kwa sasangsa, 2000.

Chŏng T'ae-su. "Stalinism and the Formation of North Korean Cinema" ("Sŭtallinjuŭi wa Pukhan yŏnghwa hyŏngsŏng kujo"). *Film Research* (*Yŏnghwa yŏn'gu*), no. 20 (February 2002): 7–30.

Chow, Rey. *Primitive Passions: Visuality, Sexuality, Ethnography, and Contemporary Chinese Cinema*. New York: Columbia University Press, 1995.

Chu Ch'ang-gyu. "The (Re)construction of Nation and Gender in the Postcolonial Nation-State: On Shin Sang-ok's *Rice*" ("T'al sikminji kukka ŭi minjok kwa chendŏ (tasi) mandŭlgi: Sin sang-ok ŭi *Ssal* chungsim'ŭro"). *Film Research* (*Yŏnghwa yŏn'gu*), no. 15 (2001): 52–81.

Chu Yu-sin. "Feminist Critique of the Melodrama Genre: On the Discourse of Female Spectatorship" ("Melodŭrama changnŭ e taehan yŏsŏngjuŭijŏk pip'yŏng: yŏsŏng kwan'gaek sŏng nonŭi rŭl chungsimŭro"). *Film Research* (*Yŏnghwa yŏn'gu*) 15 (2000): 91–114.

"Considering the Work's Crudity and Ill-formed Politics, MBC Cancels Its Contract to Air Mayumi" ("Chakpumsŏng ch'ijol pulgu chŏngch'ijŏk koryŏ, MBC pangyŏng kyeyak p'amun"). *Hangyŏre*, June 9, 1990.

Culture and Tourism Ministry of Korea. *Two Thousand Years of Korean Fashion* (*Uri ot ichŏn nyŏn*). Seoul: Misul Munhwa, 2001.

Cumings, Bruce. *North Korea: Another Country.* New York: New Press, 2004.

———. *Origins of the Korean War: Liberation and Emergence of Separate Regimes, 1945–1947.* Princeton, N.J.: Princeton University Press, 1981.

Deleuze, Gilles. *Cinema 2.* Minneapolis: University of Minnesota Press, 1989.

Diffrient, David Scott. "Military Enlightenment for the Masses: Genre and Cultural Intermixing in South Korea's Golden Age War Films." *Cinema Journal* 45, no. 1 (2005): 22–49.

Doane, Mary Ann. *The Desire to Desire: The Woman's Film of the 1940s.* Indianapolis: Indiana University Press, 1987.

Dyer, Richard. *Heavenly Bodies: Film Stars and Society.* New York: St. Martin's Press, 1986.

Eckert, Carter. *Offspring of Empire: The Koch'ang Kims and the Colonial Origins of Korean Capitalism, 1876–1945.* Seattle: University of Washington Press, 1991.

Em, Henry. "Nationalism, Post-Nationalism, and Sin Ch'ae-ho." *Korea Journal* 39, no. 2 (1999): 283–317.

"*Evergreen* Goes to Cannes" ("Kkannŭ ro kan *Sangnoksu*"). *Cine21* 394 (March 2003). www.cine21.com/new/view/mag_id/17850, accessed August 12, 2013.

"The Film [*Seven Brides for Seven Brothers*]" ("Yŏnghwa *7-in ŭi sinbu*"). *Tonga Ilbo*, October 23, 1955.

Gledhill, Christine, ed. *Stardom: Industry of Desire.* New York: Routledge, 1991.

Gorenfeld, John. "The Producer From Hell." *Guardian*, April 4, 2003.

Ham Sŏk-hŏn. "How Shall We See 5.16?" ("5.16 ŏ'ttŏk'he pwaya halkka?"). *Sasanggye*, March 1962.

Han'guk Chapji Hyŏphoe. *Korean Magazine Survey: Seventy Years of Korean Magazines* (*Han'guk chapji ch'ongnam: Han'guk chapji 70-yŏn sa*). Seoul, 1972.

Han'guk Yŏsŏng Munhak Hakhoe, ed. *Yŏwŏn Studies: Women, Education, Media* (*Yŏwŏn yŏn'gu: yŏsŏng, kyoyang, maech'e*). Seoul: Kukhak charyowŏn, 2008.

Hansen, Miriam. "The Mass Production of the Senses: Classical Cinema as Vernacular Modernism." In *Reinventing Film Studies*, edited by Linda Williams and Christine Gledhill, 45–71. London: Edward Arnold, 2000.

———. "The Question of Film Aesthetics." In *Cinema and Experience: Siegfried Kracauer, Walter Benjamin, and Theodor Adorno*, 207–50. Berkeley: University of California Press, 2010.

Harrison, Selig. *Korean Endgame: A Strategy for Reunification and U.S. Disengagement.* Princeton, N.J.: Princeton University Press, 2003.

Hŏ Chi-ung. *Memories of Departed Souls: Korean Horror Films of the 1960s Through the 1980s* (*Mangnyŏng ŭi kiŏk: 1960–1980 nyŏndae Han'guk kongp'o yŏnghwa*). Seoul: Korean Film Archive, 2011.

Hughes, Theodore. "Development as Devolution: Nam Chŏng-hyŏn and the 'Land of Excrement' Incident." *Journal of Korean Studies* 10, no. 1 (2005): 29–57.

———. *Literature and Film in Cold War South Korea: Freedom's Frontier.* New York: Columbia University Press, 2012.

Hunter, Helen-Louise. *Kim Il-song's North Korea.* New York: Praeger, 1999.

Huyssen, Andreas. *After the Great Divide: Modernism, Mass Culture and Postmodernism.* Bloomington: University of Indiana Press, 1984.

Im Hwa. "Treatise on the Culture Industry" ("Munhwa kiŏp ron"). In *Im Hwa: Collected Works on Literature and Art–Criticism 2* (*Im Hwa munhak yesul chŏnjip–p'yŏngnon 2*), edited by Ha Chŏng-il, 55–60. Seoul: Somyŏng, 2009.

"Interview: Back in the Spotlight with Blockbuster Mayumi, Director Shin Sang-ok Claims, 'The Progress of Korean Film Material Disappointing'" ("Int'ŏbyu taejak Mayumi ro tasi kakgwang Sin Sang-ok kamdok 'han'guk yŏnghwa sojae kaebang aswiwŏyo'"). *Kyŏnghyang sinmum*, June 13, 1990.

Jameson, Fredric. "Notes on Globalization as a Philosophical Issue." In *The Cultures of Globalization*, edited by Fredric Jameson and Masao Miyoshi, 54–77. Durham, N.C.: Duke University Press, 1998.

——. "Reification and Utopia in Mass Culture." *Social Text*, no. 1 (Winter 1979): 130–48.

"KAL Surviving Family Association Sues Shin Sang-ok and Others Involved with Mayumi" ("Mayumi kwallyŏn Sin Sang-ok ssi tŭng koso KAL yujokhoe"). *Tonga Ilbo*, August 11, 1990.

Kang Chun-man. *A Stroll through Modern Korean History: The 1950s* (*Han'guk hyŏndaesa sanch'aek: 1950 yŏndae p'yŏn*). Seoul: Inmul kwa sasang, 2004.

Kang Man-gil, and Yi Yŏng-hŭi. *Korean Nationalist Movements and the Masses* (*Han'guk ŭi minjokjuŭi undong kwa minjung*). Seoul: Ture, 1987.

Kang Ok-hŭi, Yi Sun-jin, Yi Sŭng-hŭi, and Yi Yŏng-mi. *Dictionary of Popular Artists in the Colonial Period* (*Sigmin sidae taejung yesulin sajŏn*). Seoul: Sodo, 2006.

Kang Sŏng-ryul. *Pro-Japanese Cinema* (*Ch'inil yŏnghwa*). Seoul: Rokŭ Media, 2006.

Kim Chin-sŏng. *Let There Be a Dancehall in Seoul* (*Sŏul e ttansŭhol ŭl hoha'ra*). Seoul: Hyŏnsil munhwa yŏn'gu, 1999.

Kim Chong-wŏn, and Chŏng Chung-hŏn. *One Hundred Years of Our Cinema* (*Uri yŏnghwa 100-nyŏn*). Seoul: Hyŏnamsa, 2001.

Kim Hak-su. *Offscreen Korean Film History* (*Sŭk'ŭrin pakk e Han'guk yŏnghwa yŏksa*). Seoul: Inmul kwa sasangsa, 2002.

Kim Han Sang. "Uneven Screens, Contested Identities: USIS, Cultural Films, and the National Imaginary in South Korea, 1945–1972." PhD diss., Seoul National University, 2013.

Kim Ho-yŏng. "Shin Sang-ok's Historical Dramas: On the Image-Text" ("Sin Sang-ok sagŭk yŏnghwa yŏn'gu: imiji teksŭt'ŭ rŭl chungsim ŭro"). In *Spiritual Culture Research* (*Chongsin munhwa yon'gu*) 4, no. 26 (2003): 79–110.

Kim Hong-jung. *Sociology of the Mind* (*Maŭm ŭi sahoehak*). Seoul: Munhak tongnae, 2009.

Kim Hyŏn-ju. "The Women's Magazine *Yŏwŏn* and the Birth of the 'Housewife as Institution" ("1950 nyŏn-dae yŏsŏng chabji *Yŏwŏn* kwa 'chedo rosŏ ŭi chubu ŭi t'ansaeng"). *Popular Narratives Research* (*Taejung Sŏsa Yŏn'gu*), no. 18 (December 2007): 387–416.

Kim Hyung-A. *Korea's Development under Park Chung Hee: Rapid Industrialization, 1961–1979.* New York: RoutledgeCurzon, 2004.

Kim Jong Il. *Let Us Create More Revolutionary Films Based on Socialist Life.* Pyongyang: Foreign Languages Publishing House, 1986.

———. *On the Art of the Cinema.* Honolulu, Hawaii: University Press of the Pacific, 2001.

Kim, Kyung Hyun. "The Fractured Cinema of North Korea: The Discourse of the Nation in *Sea of Blood.*" In *In Pursuit of Contemporary East Asian Culture,* edited by Xiaobing Tang and Stephen Snyder, 85–106. Boulder, Colo.: Westview Press, 1996.

———. *The Remasculinization of Korean Cinema.* Durham, N.C.: Duke University Press, 2004.

Kim Mi-hyŏn, Chŏng Chong-hwa, and Chang Sŏng-ho. *The History of Korean Film Distribution* (*Han'guk yŏnghwa paegŭpsa yŏn'gu*). Seoul: Korean Film Commission, 2003.

Kim Min-nam. *A Revised History of Korean Journalism* (*Saero ssŭnŭn Han'guk ŏllonsa*). Seoul: Ach'im, 2001.

Kim, Pil Ho, and Hyunjoon Shin. "The Birth of 'Rok': Cultural Imperialism, Nationalism, and the Globalization of Rock Music in South Korea, 1964–1975." *Positions: East Asia Cultures Critique* 18, no. 1 (2010): 199–230.

Kim Ryŏ-sil. *Projected Empire, Reflected Colony* (*T'usa hanŭn cheguk, t'uyŏng hanŭn sikminji*). Seoul: Samin, 2006.

Kim So-hŭi. "Shin Sang-ok, Fifty Years of Life in the Movies" ("Sin Sang-ok kamdok ŭi yŏnghwa insaeng"). *Cine21* 327 (November 2001). www.cine21.com/news/view /mag_id/5390, accessed August 12, 2013.

Kim So-hŭi, and Yi Ki-rim. "Korean Cinema in Retrospect, Shin Sang-ok" ("Han'guk yŏnghwa hoegorok Sin Sang-ok"). *Cine21* 402 (July and August 2003). www.cine21. com/news/view/mag_id/18947, accessed August 12, 2013.

Kim Sŏng-gyun, "Japanese–Korean Cultural Exchange through Film" ("Yŏnghwaro t'onghan naesŏn munhwa ŭi kyoryu"). *Samch'olli,* June 1941.

Kim So-yŏn. *The Death of the Real: The Displaced Introspection of the Korean New Wave* (*Siljae ŭi chugŭm: K'orian nyu weibŭ ŭi yihaengjŏk sŏngch'al*). Seoul: Pi dosŏ ch'ulpan, 2008.

Kim So-yŏn, Paek Mun-im, Yi Sun-jin, Yi Ho-gŏl, Cho Yŏng-jŏng, and An Chin-su. *An Age of Allures and Chaos: Korean Cinema of the 1950s* (*Maehok kwa hondon ŭi sidae: 1950 yŏndae ŭi Han'guk yŏnghwa*). Seoul: Sodo, 2003.

Kim So-yŏng. *Cinema: Blue Flower in the Land of Technology.* (*Sinema: tekŭno munhwa ŭi p'urŭn kkot*). Seoul: Yŏlhwadang, 1997.

Kim Su-nam. "Master of Mise-en-Scène Shin Sang-ok: The Massification and Globalization of Korean Cinema" ("Mijangsen ŭi taega Sin Sang-ok: Han'guk yŏnghwa ŭi taejunghwa kŭrigo segyehwa"). *Essays on the Arts* (*Yesul nonmunjip*) no. 34 (December 1995): 132–41.

Kim, Susie. "The Ambivalence of Modernity: Articulation of New Subjectivities in Turn of the Century Korea." PhD diss., University of California, Los Angeles, 2002.

Kim Su-yong. *Cinema, My Love* (*Na ŭi sarang ssinema*). Seoul: Cine 21 Books, 2005.

———. "Fifty Years of Korean Film History" ("Han'guk yŏnghwa 50-nyŏnsa"). *Film Magazine* (*Yŏnghwa Chapji*) 120, no. 9 (September 1973): 172–75.

Kim Tong-ch'un. *Division and Korean Society* (*Pundan kwa Han'guk sahoe*). Seoul: Yŏksa Pip'yongsa, 1997.

Kim Tong-ch'un, and Kim T'ae-sun. *Social Movements of the 1960s* (*1960-yŏndae ŭi sahoe undong*). Seoul: Kkach'i, 1991.

Kim U-Chang. "The Situation of Korean Writers under Colonial Rule." *Korea Journal* 16, no. 5 (May 1976): 4–15.

Kim Yoon-shik. "KAPF Literature in Modern Korean Literary History." *Positions: East Asia Cultures Critique* 14, no. 2 (2006): 405–25.

Ko Chong-ok. "Proletarian Cinema and Education" ("Pŭro yŏnghwa wa kyoyuk"). *Chosŏn Ilbo*, April 23–25, 1930.

Korean Film Archive. *The Koyrŏ Motion Picture Company and The New Film Order, 1936–1941* (*Koryŏ yŏnghwa hyŏphoe wa yŏnghwa sinch'eje 1936–1941*). Seoul, 2007.

Korean Film Council. *Fifty Must-See North Korean Films for Unified Koreans* (*T'ongil Han'guk'in i poaya hal Pukhan yŏnghwa 50-sŏn*). Seoul: KOFIC, 2002.

Kwak Hyŏn-ja. "War Widows and Western Princesses: The Dreams and Burdens of the Modern Korean Woman through Ch'oe Ŭn-hŭi" ("Mimang'in kwa yanggongju: Ch'oe Ŭn-hŭi rŭl t'onghae pon Han'guk kŭndae yŏsŏng ŭi kkum kwa chim"). In *Korean Cinema and Modernity* (*Han'guk yŏnghwa wa kŭndaesŏng*), edited by Pyŏn Chae-ran, Chu Yu-sin, Kwak Hyŏn-ja, Kim Sŏn-a, Pak Hyŏn-sŏn, and Pak Chi-yŏn, 115–44. Seoul: Sodo, 2000.

Kwŏn Yŏng-min. *Modern Korean Literary History 1945–1990* (*Han'guk hyŏndae munhaksa 1945–1990*). Seoul: Minŭmsa, 1994.

Lee, Hyangjin. *Contemporary Korean Cinema: Identity, Culture, Politics.* Manchester: Manchester University Press, 2000.

Lee, Jin-kyung. "Autonomous Aesthetics and Autonomous Subjectivity: Construction of Modern Literature as a Site of Social Reforms and Modern Nation Building in Colonial Korea, 1915–1925." PhD diss., University of California, Los Angeles, 2000.

Lee, Namhee. *The Making of Minjung: Democracy and the Politics of Representation.* Ithaca, NY: Cornell University Press, 2009.

Lee, Sangjoon. "The Transnational Asian Studio System: Cinema, Nation-State, and Globalization in Cold War Asia." PhD diss., New York University, 2011.

Macdonald, Dwight. "A Theory of Mass Culture." In *Mass Culture: The Popular Arts in America*, edited by Bernard Rosenberg and David White, 59–73. New York: Free Press, 1965.

"Mayumi" ("Yŏnghwa Mayumi"). *Tonga Ilbo*, May 26, 1990.

McHugh, Kathleen, and Nancy Abelmann, eds. *South Korean Golden Age Melodrama: Gender, Genre, and National Cinema.* Detroit, Mich.: Wayne State University Press, 2005.

Min Pyŏng-uk, ed. *A Historical Understanding of North Korean Cinema* (*Pukhan yŏnghwa ŭi yŏksajŏk ihae*). Seoul: Yŏknak, 2005.

"The Misery of Adaptation, *It's Not Her Sin*" ("Pŏn'an mul ŭi ko'ae, Kŭ yŏja ŭi choega anida"). *Seoul Sinmun*, January 18, 1959.

Naremore, James, and Patrick Brantlinger. "Six Artistic Cultures." In *Modernity and Mass Culture*, edited by James Naremore and Patrick Brantinger, 1–19. Bloomington: Indiana University Press, 1991.

"A New Territory for Filmmaking" ("Yŏnghwagye ŭi sae p'ando"). *Kyŏnghyang Sinmun*, July 3, 1963.

"1958 Wrap-up—The Film Industry" ("Chŏngni 1958-nyŏn/Yŏnghwagye"). *Kyŏnghyang Sinmun*, December 28, 1958.

Nornes, Abé Mark. *Japanese Documentary Film: The Meiji Era Through Hiroshima.* Minneapolis: University of Minnesota Press, 2003.

O'Hanlon, Michael, and Mike Mizoguchi. *Crisis on the Korean Peninsula: How to Deal with a Nuclear North Korea.* Washington, DC: Brookings Institution Press, 2003.

O Yŏng-suk. *Korean Film and Cultural Discourse in the 1950s* (*1950 nyŏndae, Han'guk yŏnghwa munhwa tamnon*). Seoul: Somyŏng, 2007.

Paek, Mun-im. *Ch'unhyang's Daughters: An Incomplete Genealogy of Korean Women* (*Ch'unhyang ŭi ttaldul: Han'guk yŏsong ŭi panchok tchari kyebohak*). Seoul: Ch'aek saesang, 2001.

———. "The Korean Horror Film: On the Grounds of Female Ghost Narratives" ("Han'guk kongp'o yŏnghwa yŏn'gu: yŏ'gwi ŭi sŏsa kiban ŭl chungsimŭro"). PhD diss., Yonsei University, 2002.

———. "An Ontology of Chosun Cinema: On Im Hwa's 'On Chosun Cinema (1941)'" ("Chosŏn yŏnghwa ŭi chonjae ron: Im Hwa ŭi 'Chosŏn yŏnghwa ron' [1941] ŭl chungsimŭro"). *Sanghŏ hakbo,* no. 33 (2011): 171–211.

Pak A-na. "Research on Shin Sang-ok's Film Production and Genre (Melodrama, Period Film) 1952–1975" ("1952 nyŏn esŏ 1975 nyŏn kkaji ŭi Sin sang-ok ŭi yŏnghwa chejak kwa changnŭ [mellodŭrama, sagŭk] yŏn'gu"). MA thesis, Chungang University, 2003.

Pak Chi-yŏn. "Film Policy from the Establishment of the First Motion Picture Law to Its Fourth Revision, 1961–1984" ("Yŏnghwa pŏp chejŏng esŏ che 4-ch'a kaejŏng kkaji ŭi yŏnghwa chŏngch'aek 1961–1984 nyŏn"). In *Korean Film Policy History* (*Han'guk yonghwa chongch'aeksa*), edited by Kim Tong-ho, 189–267. Seoul: Nanum, 2005. Available in English translation as Park Ji-Yeon. "Korean Motion Picture Policy and Industry in the 1960s and 1970s." In *A History of Korean Cinema: From Liberation through the 1960s.* Seoul: Korean Film Archive, 2005.

———. "Modernization and Film Policy Under Park Chung Hee: On the Legislation of Film Law and Corporatization" ("Pak Chŏng-hŭi kŭndaehwa ch'eje ŭi yŏnghwa chŏngch'aek: yŏnghwa pŏp kaechŏng kwa kiŏphwa chŏngch'aek chungsimŭro"). In *Korean Cinema and Modernity* (*Han'guk yŏnghwa wa kŭndaesŏng*), edited by Pyŏn Chae-ran, Chu Yu-sin, Kwak Hyŏn-ja, Kim Sŏn-a, Pak Hyŏn-sŏn, and Pak Chi-yŏn, 171–221. Seoul: Sodo, 2000.

Pak Chŏng-hŭi. *Our Nation's Forward Path* (*Uri nara ŭi naagal kil*). Seoul: Chiguch'on, 1997.

———. *The State, the Revolution, and I* (*Kukka wa hyŏngmyŏng kwa na*). Seoul: Chiguch'on, 1997.

Pak Song. "Pressing Problems in Chosŏn Cinema" ("Chosŏn yŏnghwa ŭi tangmyŏn han munje e taehan ilgoch'al"). *Chosŏn Ilbo,* September 15, 1929.

Pak Wan-sik. "The Problem of Cinema and Education" ("Yŏnghwa wa kyohwa munje"). *Chosŏn Ilbo,* February 15, 1930.

Park Myung-jin. "Motion Pictures in North Korea." *Korea Journal* 31, no. 3 (Autumn 1991): 95–103.

Park, Sunae, Patricia Campbell Warner, and Thomas K. Fitzgerald. "The Process of Westernization: Adoption of Western-Style Dress by Korean Women, 1945–1962." *Clothing and Textiles Research* 11, no. 3 (1993): 39–47.

Pyŏn Chae-ran. "The Constitution of Modern Female Identity through Labor: *Rice* and *Ttosuni*" ("Nodong ŭl t'onghan kŭndaejŏk yŏsŏng chuch'e ŭi kusŏng: 'Ssal' kwa 'Ttosuni' rŭl chungsimŭro"). In *Korean Cinema and Modernity (Han'guk yŏnghwa wa kŭndaesŏng)*, Pyŏn Chae-ran, Chu Yu-sin, Kwak Hyŏn-ja, Kim Sŏn-a, Pak Hyŏn-sŏn, and Pak Chi-yŏn, 85–114. Seoul: Sodo, 2000.

Pyŏn Chae-ran, Chu Yu-sin, Kwak Hyŏn-ja, Kim Sŏn-a, Pak Hyŏn-sŏn, and Pak Chi-yŏn. *Korean Cinema and Modernity (Han'guk yŏnghwa wa kŭndaesŏng)*. Seoul: Sodo, 2000.

"Quality Increasing: Big Industrialization Still Far Off" ("Chil ŭi hyangsang: taekiŏphwa nŭn ajikdo yowŏn"). *Chosŏn Ilbo*, July 2, 1959.

Raine, Michael. "Youth, Body, and Subjectivity in the Japanese Cinema, 1955–1960." PhD diss., University of Iowa, 2002.

Rancière, Jacques. "The Paradoxes of Political Art." In *Dissensus: On Politics and Aesthetics*, 134–51. New York: Continuum, 2010.

"Refined *Sinp'a*: Shin Sang-ok's Korean Adaptation of *Ch'un-hŭi*" ("Saeryŏn doen sinp'a: Sin Sang-ok ŭi Han'guk ponan *Ch'un-hŭi*"). *Han'guk sinmun*, May 22, 1959.

Schmid, Andre. *Korea Between Empires, 1895–1919*. New York: Columbia University Press, 2002.

Schönherr, Johannes. "Godzilla Goes to North Korea: An Interview with Kenpachiro Satsuma." In *Film Out of Bounds: Essays and Interviews on Non-Mainstream Cinema Worldwide*, edited by Matthew Edwards, 205–20. Jefferson, N.C.: McFarland, 2007.

Seoul Film Collective. *For a New Cinema (Saeroun yŏnghwa rŭl wihayŏ)*. Seoul: Hakminsa, 1983.

Shin, Gi-Wook, and Michael Robinson, eds. *Colonial Modernity in Korea*. Cambridge: Harvard University Press, 1999.

Shin, Michael D. "Yi Kwang-su: The Collaborator as Modernist against Modernity." *Journal of Asian Studies* 71, no. 1 (February 2012): 115–20.

Shin Sang-ok. *I Was a Movie (Nan, yŏnghwa yŏtda)*. Seoul: Random House, 2007.

———. *The Kingdom of Kim Jong-il (Kim Chŏng-il wangguk)*. Seoul: Tonga Ilbosa, 1988.

———. "Twenty Regrettable Years of Korean Cinema" ("Han'guk yŏnghwa isip nyŏn ŭi yugam"). *Chosŏn Ilbo*, August 31, 1965.

Shin Sang-ok, and Ch'oe Ŭn-hŭi. *My Name Is Kim Jong-il (Nae re Kim Chŏng-il imneda)*. Seoul: Haengnim Ch'ulp'an, 1994.

———. *We Haven't Escaped Yet (Uri ŭi t'alch'ul ŭn kkŭtnaji anattda)*. Seoul: Wŏlgan Chosŏnsa, 2001.

"Shin Sang-ok Films We Saw in the North" ("Uri ga puk esŏ pon Sin Sang-ok kamdok ŭi yŏnghwa"). *Daily NK*, April 13, 2006.

Silverman, Kaja. "Fragments of a Fashionable Discourse." In *On Fashion*, edited by Shari Benstock and Suzanne Ferriss, 183–96. New Brunswick, N.J.: Rutgers University Press, 1994.

Sin Myŏng-jik. *Modern Boy, Strolling Kyŏngsŏng (Modŏn ppoi, Kyŏngsŏng ŭl kŏnilda)*. Seoul: Hyŏnsil munhwa yŏn'gu, 2003.

Sŏ Chŏng-nam. *An Investigation of North Korean Cinema* (*Pukhan yŏnghwa t'amsa*). Seoul: Saengak ŭi namu, 2002.

———. *So Chŏng-nam's Look at North Korean Film* (*Sŏ Chŏng-nam ŭi Pukhan yŏnghwa t'amsa*). Seoul: Saenggak ŭi namu, 2002.

"*Sŏng Ch'unhyang:* Vibrant Color Design" ("*Sŏng Ch'unhyang:* Hwarŏhan saeksang"). *Han'guk Ilbo*, February 18, 1961.

Song Nak-wŏn. "The Formation of North Korean Cinema and the First Feature Film *My Hometown*" ("Pukhan yŏnghwa hyŏngsŏng kwajŏng kwa ch'oech'o ŭi kŭkyŏnghwa *Nae Kohyang* yŏn'gu"). *Literature and Image* (*Munhak kwa yŏngsang*) 8 (Spring 2009): 111–35.

Suleiman, Susan. *Authoritarian Fictions: The Ideological Novel as a Literary Genre*. Princeton, N.J.: Princeton University Press, 1992.

Thompson, Kristin, and David Bordwell. *Film History: An Introduction*. Boston: McGraw-Hill, 2003.

Tonguk University. *Everyday Life and Modern Visual Media: Cinema* (*Ilsang saenghwal kwa kŭndae yŏngsang maech'e*). Seoul: Minsokwŏn, 2007.

Treat, John Whittier. "Choosing to Collaborate: Yi Kwang-su and the Moral Subject in Colonial Korea." *Journal of Asian Studies* 71, no. 1 (February 2012): 81–102.

Triplett, William C. *Rogue State: How a Nuclear North Korea Threatens America*. Washington, DC: Regnery, 2004.

"Trouble with the Two 'Chunhyangs?' Mr. Shin's Office Ransacked, Employee Kidnapped" ("Tugae ŭi 'Ch'unhyangjŏn' i hwagŭn? Sin ssi samusil pusugo chŏng'ŏp'wŏn napji"). *Kyunghyang Sinmum*, January 22, 1961.

Truffaut, François. "A Certain Tendency of the French Cinema." In *Movies and Methods*, edited by Bill Nichols, 224–37. Berkeley: University of California Press, 1976.

Wang Sun-nyŏ. "A Comparison of North and South Korean Ch'unhyangjŏn" ("Nam-pukhan Ch'unhyangjŏn ŭi pigyo"). In *Five Things You Wanted to Know*, edited by Chŏng Chae-hyŏng, 154–72.

Williams, Linda. "Melodrama Revised." In *Refiguring American Film Genres*, edited by Nick Browne, 42–88. Berkeley: University of California Press, 1998.

Yi Chae-sŏn. *The Korean Novel, Modern and Contemporary Volume* (*Han'guk sosŏlsa: kŭn hyŏndae p'yŏn*). Seoul: Sol, 2000.

Yi Kwang-su. "Literati and Self-Cultivation" ("Munsawa suyang"). *Creation* (*Ch'angjo*), January 1921.

Yi Myŏng-ja. *History of North Korean Film* (*Pukhan yŏnghwa sa*). Seoul: Communication Books, 2007.

———. *Modernity and North Korean Film: Family Melodrama in the Kim Chŏng-il Era* (*Pukhan yŏnghwa wa kŭndaesŏng: Kim Chŏng-il sigi kajok mellodŭrama*). Seoul: Yŏknak, 2005.

Yi Sun-jin. "Colonial Experience and Filmmaking in the Immediate Liberation Period: The Case of Ch'oe In-gyu and Yun Pong-ch'un" ("Sigminji kyŏnghŏm kwa haebang chikhu ŭi yŏnghwa mandŭlgi: Ch'oe In-gyu wa Yun Pong-ch'un ŭi kyŏngu chungsim ŭro"). *Popular Narrative Studies* (*Taejung Sŏsa Yŏn'gu*), no. 14 (2005): 107–43.

——, ed. *2005 Modern and Contemporary Korean Arts Oral History Series: Yi Hyong-p'yo, 1922–* (*2005 Han'guk kŭnhyŏndae yesulsa kusul ch'aerok sirijŭ: Yi Hyŏng-p'yo, 1922–*). Seoul: Korean Film Archive, 2005.

Yi Un-gok. "The Cultural Function of Film" ("Yŏnghwa ŭi munhwajŏk yŏkhal"). *Tonga Ilbo*, January 5–6, 1937.

Yi Yŏng-il. *The Complete History of Korean Film* (*Han'guk yŏnghwa chŏnsa*). Seoul: Sodo, 2004.

——. "A Genealogy of Korean Realism" ("Han'guk riŏllijŭm ŭi kyebo") In *Scenario Literary Arts* (*Sinario munye*), 3. September 1959.

——. *Korean Art Research: Yi Yŏng-il's Depositions for Korean Film History—Yu Chang-san, Yi Ch'ang-gŭn, Yi P'il-u* (*Han'guk yesul yŏn'gu: Yi Yŏng-il ŭi Han'guk yŏnghwasa rŭl wihan chŭng'ŏnrok*). Seoul: Sodo, 2003.

——. *Korean Film History Lectures* (*Yi Yŏng-il ŭi Han'guk yŏnghwasa kangŭirok*). Seoul: Sodo, 2002.

Yi Yŏn-ho. "Shin Sang-ok: Who Are You?" ("Sin Sang-ok: Tangsinŭn nugusimnikka?"). *Kino*, no. 120 (October 1997): 120–27.

——. "*Virgin Bride* Director Ch'ŏe Ŭn-hŭi; From Yangban Mother to Virgin Bride" ("*Min myŏnuri* ŭi kamdok Ch'ŏe Ŭn-hŭi: yangban ŏmŏni esŏ min myŏnuri kkaji"). *Kino*, no. 162 (December 2000): 162–67.

Yim Chi-hyŏn. "The Fascism within Us" ("Uri an ŭi pasijŭm"). *Tangdae Pip'yŏng*, no. 8 (August 1999): 27–45.

——. "'Mass Dictatorship' and 'Post-Fascism': Advancing Professor Cho Hŭi-yŏn's Critique" ('Taejung tokchae' wa 'posŭtŭ pasijŭm': Cho Hŭi-yŏn kyosu ŭi pip'an e puchyŏ"). *Yoksa Pip'yŏng*, no. 68 (Fall 2001): 298–330.

Yim Chong-guk. *Pro-Japanese Literature* (*Ch'inil munhak ron*). Seoul: P'yŏnghwa ch'ulpansa, 1993.

Yoshimoto, Mitsuhiro. *Kurosawa: Film Studies and Japanese Cinema*. Durham, N.C.: Duke University Press, 2000.

Yu Chi-na. "Korean Melodrama: On Meaning Work and the Classical Form" ("Han'guk mellodŭrama, wŏnhyŏng kwa ŭimi chakyong yŏn'gu"). *Yŏnghwa ŏnŏ* 13 (1997): 1–23.

——. "Nation-Image Through the Representation of Films: From the 1970s Historical Films to Korean Film Renaissance Films" ("Yŏnghwa wa kukga, chungchŭngjŏk ŭimi chagyong ae kwanhan koch'al: 70 nyŏndae sagŭk kwa Han'guk yŏnghwa rŭnesangsŭ sidae taejung yŏnghwa tŭlŭl t'onggwa hamyŏ"). *Yŏnghwa yŏn'gu* 22 (2004): 177–96.

Yu Hyŏn-mok. *The Development of Korean Film* (*Han'guk yŏnghwa paldalsa*). Seoul: Ch'aeknuri, 1997.

Yun Hae-dong. "Colonial Modernity and the Advent of Mass Society" ("Sikminji kŭndae wa taejung sahoe ŭi tŭngjang"). In *The Paradox of Colonial Modernity* (*Sikminji kŭndae ŭi paeroŏdoksŭ*), 45–70. Seoul: Humanist, 2007.

Yun Hae-dong, Ch'ŏn Chŏng-hwan, Hwang Pyŏng-ju, Yun Tae-sŏk, and Hŏ Su, eds. *Coloniality's Gray Zones* (*Sikminji ŭi hoesaek chidae*). Seoul: Yŏksa Pip'yŏngsa, 2003.

———. *Rereading Modernity: Toward a New Paradigm for Korean Modern Consciousness* (*Kŭndae rŭl tasi ilknŭnda: Han'guk kŭndae ŭisik ŭi saeroun paradaim ŭl wihayo*). Seoul: Yŏksa pip'yŏngsa, 2006.

Yun Pong-ch'un. "Renaissance Man of the Silver Screen, Na Un-gyu" ("Ŭnmak ŭi mannŭngin Na Un-gyu"). *Yŏwŏn* 8 (June 1963): 74–75.

celebrities, 55, 63, 65, 67, 219n6; in Shin's films, 72–78, 88, 100, 109

censorship, 63, 76, 107, 140, 177, 221n27, 227n70. *See also* Motion Picture Law, Park regime

Chaplin, Charlie, 84, 86

Chastity Gate (film, Shin), 110, 112–14

Cheju 4.3 massacres, 11

China, filmmaking in, 154, 155–56, 170

Ch'oe In-gyu, 5, 59; *Homeless Angels*, 31, 33, 41, 219n10; *Hurrah Freedom*, 41, 219–20n10, 221n27; *The Night Before Liberation*, 219–20n10; *A Statement of Love*, 219–20n10

Ch'oe Sŏ-hae, 235n31; "Record of an Escape," 2, 181, 185

Ch'oe Ŭn-hŭi (wife of Shin): defection to North Korea, 5, 6, 18, 176–78; as fashion leader, 59, 69–70; in magazines, 65, 66; in Shin's films, 51, 54, 72–78, 88, 103–4, 109, 112, 115, 124, 135, 142, 186, 227n61

Ch'oe Wan-gyu, 102

Cho Hŭi-yŏn, 145–47

Ch'ŏljong and Poknyŏ (film, Shin), 111

Chŏn Ch'ang-gŭn, *My Liberated Hometown*, 40–41

Chŏng Ch'ang-hwa, 41, 102

Chŏng Chong-hwa, 29, 104

Chŏng-hyŏn, *Land of Excrement*, 28

Chosŏn cinema, 16, 31–46, 54, 56, 72, 168, 219–20n10

Chosŏn Film Production Company, 221n27; *The Chosŏn Straits*, 33; *Volunteer Soldier*, 32–33, 35

Chow, Rey, 9–10

Chu Ch'ang-gyu, 136, 150, 152, 228–29n4, 230n19

chuch'e socialist realism, 163, 166, 167, 168, 170–76, 204; Shin's films resembling, 18, 179, 181, 185, 199. *See also* socialist realist films

Chu Chŭng-nyŏ, 78, 115

Ch'ungmuro, 91, 102, 107, 146

Ch'un-hŭi (film, Shin), 53, 68, 221n31

Ch'unhyang, 43, 102, 103–6, 135, 191–95

Chu Yu-sin, 79

cinema. *See* film(s); filmmaking

Civilian Film Ethics Committee, 89

class conflict, in Shin's films, 2, 150, 154, 167, 169, 184–85, 187, 190, 192

Cold War, 3, 7, 11, 47, 53, 120, 152, 155, 161–62, 205–7

colonial period: culture, 13, 17, 229–30n11; enlightenment modality, 16, 23, 141, 150; filmmaking, 31, 167–68, 218n37; literature, 29, 32, 229n6; modernity, 7, 10, 36, 185, 215n6; modernization, 11, 150, 151, 231n27; monarchy, 111, 116. *See also* anticolonialism; Japan; postcolonialism

comedies, 55, 80, 102

commodification, 51–52, 56, 70–72, 160, 169

communism, 55, 185, 186, 204, 229–30n11

Confessions of a College Girl (film, Shin), 44, 53, 68, 70–73, 75, 78, 92, 135, 221n33, 223n19

Confucianism, 10, 131, 232n2; conflicts with, 73, 88, 126; repression of women, 44, 111–13, 116; in Shin's films, 101, 132, 149, 160

consciousness, 8, 23; class, 29, 185; mass, 42, 46; national, 29, 42, 229–30n11; social, 25, 27, 86

consumerism, 47, 53, 54, 67, 71, 229–30n11

Cruel Stories of Yi Dynasty Women (film, Shin), 6, 112, 114–16, 227n69

culture(s), 9, 42, 65, 119, 131, 146–48, 218n27; American, 11–12, 22, 42, 58, 80, 86–87, 141; colonial, 13, 17, 229–30n11; conflicts in, 111–13; developmentalist, 49, 207–8; enlightenment, 30–31; film, 17, 46, 64, 79, 221n27; Japanese, 12, 58; modern, 16, 229–30n11; nationalist, 31, 147–48; political, 87, 91, 162–63, 218–19n38; socialist, 168–69. *See also* mass culture

film industry, North Korea, 18, 154, 163,
    166; gaining international recognition,
    4, 196, 198, 199–200; history of, 164–71;
    Shin's impact on, *2*, 2–4, 6, 13, 18–19,
    132, 159–60, 176–87, 204, 211,
    218–19n38, 232n1
film industry, South Korea, 7, 122, 160,
    163, 167–68; Ch'ungmuro, 91, 102, 107,
    146; in 1950s', 16–17, 55, 78–81, 89–90,
    106–17, 121, 124, 229–30n11; in 1960s',
    106–17; in 1970s', 25, 106–17, 117–27,
    225n40
filmmaking: art of, 9–10, 31, 32, 35–36, 39,
    46, 229–30n11; authorship, 83–88;
    colonial period, 31, 167–68, 218n37;
    enlightenment in, 12, 21–25, 31–46,
    54, 64, 203, 217n5; financing, 96–97,
    99–100; ideology of, 40, 156–57, 160,
    172, 187; modernist, 29–30, 85, 100,
    113, 163; populist, 86, 102; pure, 13,
    25, 39, 187; state-sponsored, 37, 55;
    technical competence in, 56, 58;
    Western, 35, 87, 141–42. *See also*
    industrialization, of filmmaking;
    politics, of filmmaking
film noir, 52, 70
Flower Girl (film), 165, 173–76, 180,
    186–87
foreign films, 38, 90, 98–99, 100, 106, 122,
    125, 222n13, 236n9
Foucault, Michel, 131, 145

Galgameth (film, Shin), 205–6
gender, 72, 88, 111–13, 126, 130, 144, 149
    192. *See also* women
genre films, 25, 38, 40, 98, 100, 110, 124;
    Shin's production of, 6, 17, 85, 101,
    106–17, 125–26, 228–29n4
Gledhill, Christine, 79
globalization, 10, 180, 206, 207, 229–30n11
Grand Bells, 229n9

Half-Soul Woman/The Ghost Lovers, The
    (film, Shin), 118

Ham Sŏk-hŏn, 137
hanbok (Korean dress), 48, 62, 70
Han Hong-yŏl, 118; *Hŭksan Island*, 44
Han Hyŏng-mo, 53, 58, 80; *Female Boss*,
    55; *Hand of Fate*, 42, 43, 76, 230–31n25;
    Madame Freedom, 43–44, 52, 55, 62,
    73, 78, 79; *Pure Love Chronicle*, 56, *57*
Han River, The (film, Shin), 123
Hansen, Miriam, 54, 232n7
Han Sŏl-ya, 28, 181
Hellflower (film, Shin), 50–51, 53, 68, 69,
    72–78, 79, 216n11
historical films, 55, 130, 228–29n4. *See also*
    period films
Hŏ Chang-gang (actor), 104, 109, 135
Hollywood films, 18, 58, 80, 84; block-
    booking system, 94, 97; family
    melodramas, 24–25; leading ladies, 59,
    73; Shin's work, 6, 206, 207, 236n1;
    studio system, 37, 55, 108, 130, 131
Hong Kil-dong (film, Shin), 179, 181, 191,
    196, 199, 235n30
Hong Kong studios, 17, 38, 118, 122–23,
    125, 228n77
Hong Sŏng-gi, 58; competition with Shin,
    103–6, 135, 226n46
Horkheimer, Max, on mass culture, 18,
    161, 162, 163, 232n4
horror films, 102, 107–8, 110, 118, 123, 130.
    See also monster films
Houseguest and My Mother, The (film,
    Shin), 5, 73–74, 92, 107, 112–14, 135
Huyssen, Andreas, 161, 234n23
Hwang Nam, 58
Hwang Sŏk-yŏng, *Guest*, 211, 212

ideology, 36, 42, 149, 206–7; developmen-
    talist, 11, 154; discourses of, 145–47; of
    filmmaking, 40, 156–57, 160, 172, 187;
    of mass culture, 18, 161; North Korean,
    169, 176, 191, 196
I Love Mama (film, Shin), 17, 124–26
image(s), 4, 79, 81, 164; faces and bodies,
    65, 72, 75, 80; global, 18, 133; in 1950s,

Shin Sang-ok (Shin), 2; authorial
vision, 17, 56, 83–88, 101, 110–11, 124,
126–27, 131, 228n79; biographical
information, 5–6, 215n1; career, 1–3,
6–7, 8, 87, 123, 126, 131; defection to
North Korea, 159–60, 162, 164,
176–78, 204; legacy, 92, 113, 139;
memoirs, 6–7, 9, 178, 202, 228n79;
return to South Korea, 205–12;
scandals, 123, 177, 228n77. *See also*
politics, Shin's
Shin Sang-ok (Shin), as filmmaker, 10, 88,
118; counterrevolutionary elements,
162–63; directorial work, 83–84, 85, 86,
87, 97, 99–100, 109; as genre master, 85,
87–88, 102, 103, 107; heterogeneity, 88,
129–31, 145, 207; popularity, 98, 102,
103; as production work, 85, 99–100,
101, 228n79; technical achievements,
56, 58, 68–69, 105–6, 109, 125–26,
131–32, 135, 153–57, 180. *See also*
enlightenment modality, in Shin's
films; film industry, North Korea,
Shin's impact on; melodramas, Shin's
impact on; 1950s, Shin's work during;
1960s, Shin's work during; 1970s,
Shin's work during; Shin Films;
spectacle(s), Shin's production of;
and individual titles
Shin Yŏng-gyun, 88, 109, 135, 142
Silverman, Kaja, 50
Simch'ŏng-jŏn (film, Shin), 180, 191
Sin Kyŏng-kyun, *A New Vow*, 40–41
Sin Sŏng-il, 108, 227n62
Sin Tong-hyŏp, 28
Sisters' Garden (film, Shin), 51, 53, 59, *60*,
68–69, 71–73, 76
socialism, 31–32, 157, 161–62, 203
socialist-nationalist films, 31, 37, 197–98,
218–19n38
socialist-realist films, 3–4, 37, 156, 141,
168–71, 184–86, 196. See also *chuch'e*
socialist realism
Sŏ Kwang-je, 35, 168; *Military Train*, 34

Sŏng Ch'unhyang (film, Shin), 5, 17, 68, 74,
92, *106*, 109, 110, 112, 135; competition
with Hong's, 103–6, 226n46, 226n51;
North Korean version, 187, 191–95
Song Nak-wŏn, 168–69
South Korea: Americanization, 47–50;
capitalism, 180, 206; developmentalism, 152, 212; moral differences from
North, 206, 209; postwar subjectivities,
18, 120, 133, 145, 229–30n11; U.S.
military presence, 59, 61, 77–78. *See
also* film industry, South Korea; Park
Chung Hee regime
Soviet Union, filmmaking in, 37, 134, 155,
167–68, 169, 170
spaces, 70–71, 74, 190. *See also* time-space
spectacle(s), Shin's production of, 72–78,
186, 191–92, 194–96, 198–99, 203,
211–12
studios. *See* Hollywood films, studio
system; industrialization, of
filmmaking; Shin Films
studium (Barthes), 3, 4, 47–48
subjectivities, 39, 104, 161; modern, 22, 54,
107; South Korean, 18, 120, 133, 145,
229–30n11
sun tribe cycle of films, 27n62, 58
Supreme Council for National Reconstruction (SCNR), 88, 89, 92, 137–38,
138

Tale of Simch'ŏng (film, Shin), 198–99
television, 6, 17, 122, 166, 192
temporality, 10–11, 50, 172, 176, 180, 181,
196. *See also* time-space
tendency filmmaking, 31, 36, 168, 235n31
Thousand Years Fox (film, Shin), 110, 113,
114, 115
Three Days' Reign (film, Shin), 123
3 Ninjas (film series, Shin), 6, 206–7,
236n1
time-space, 7, 80, 140, 171, 172–73,
229–30n11. *See also* spaces; temporality
Todorov, Tzvetan, 217n4

STEVEN CHUNG is assistant professor in the Department of East Asian Studies at Princeton University.